DOOR TO GLORY

Dialogues with Apostle John

DOUGLAS GRADY

Copyright © 2020 by Douglas Grady.

ISBN-978-1-6485-8118-2

All rights reserved. No part of this book may be reproduced or transmitted in any form or by any means, electronic or mechanical, including photocopying, recording, or by any information storage and retrieval system, without permission in writing from the copyright owner.

The views expressed in this work are solely those of the author and do not necessarily reflect the views of the publisher, and the publisher hereby disclaims any responsibility for them.

Matchstick Literary
1-888-306-8885
orders@matchliterary.com

Contents

Foreword: About My Channeling ix

Introduction xix

Chapter 1: Heaven on Earth 1

Section 1.1: Fifth Dimension—Heaven on Earth 1

Section 1.2: Photon Energy 26

Section 1.3 Twelfth Dimension in Havona 55

Section 1.4: Hollow Earth 60

Section 1.5: States of Consciousness 76

Section 1.6: Chakras 87

Section 1.7: Illusion of Satan and Lucifer 95

Section 1.8: Energy 101

Section 1.9: Male and Female Energies..................................... 118

Section 1.10: Ego v. Spirit 137

Section 1.11: Relationships and Marriages during the
    Golden Age 177

Chapter 2: Dark Side 214

Section 2.1: John's Observation about Dark Side 214

Section 2.2: Origin of the Dark Side 217

Section 2.3: Harmful Effects on Health 233

Section 2.4: Nuclear Bomb 236

Section 2.5: New World Order 240

Section 2.6: End Times 242

Chapter 3:   Civilizations..246

Section 3.1: Super Universes...246

Section 3.2: Time Matrix 254

Section 3.3: Planet Nibiru..258

Section 3.4: Lost Civilizations, Atlantis, and Lemuria 260

Section 3.5 Myth of Great Flood 273

Section 3.6 Violet Race: Forefront of Present Civilization.............280

Section 3.7: Disappearance of the Lost Fifth Planet Maldek 289

Section 3.8: Red Planet..293

Chapter 4:   Reincarnation 302

Section 4.1: Reincarnation..302

Section 4.2: Origin of Souls.. 310

Section 4.3: Reference of Reincarnation in Scripture 318

Section 4.4 Jesus The Miracle Worker..321

Section 4.5: Rite of Sepulcher..338

Section 4.6: Life of Jesus after Crucifixion according to John 370

Section 4.7: Walk-in 378

Chapter 5:   Spiritual Realm..384

Section 5.1: Earthbound Souls...384

Section 5.2: Nirvana...401

Section 5.3: Spirit Guides..424

Section 5.4: Soul Journey..435

Chapter 6:   Channeling Notes with Apostle John 446

Section 6.1: May 18, 2014 446

Section 6.2: December 21, 2014 462

Section 6.3: January 27, 2015 469

Section 6.4: February 10, 2015 475

Section 6.5: February 18, 2015 483

Section 6.6: February 24, 2015 490

Section 6.7: March 3, 2015 496

Section 6.8: March 11, 2015 508

Section 6.9: March 31, 2015 516

Section 6.10: April 28, 2015 526

Section 6.11: May 19, 2015 539

Section 6.12: January 13, 2016 541

Section 6.13: January 26, 2016 545

Section 6.14: February 16, 2016 549

Section 6.15: March 16, 2016 551

Section 6.16: March 24, 2016 558

Section 6.17: April 14, 2016 560

Section 6.18: April 27, 2016 562

Section 6.19 October 11, 2016, Notes 564

Section 6.20 February 14, 2017, Notes 566

Section 6.21 February 23, 2017, Notes 570

Section 6.22 March 9, 2017, Notes 574

List of References 583

Foreword: About My Channeling

Marilyn Redmond

Channeling is a gift that gradually came into my awareness over many years. It evolved over time from inner voices talking to me. I first heard these messages as a child; however, my church did not recognize this information. In fact, at one time I was told it was the voice of the Devil. I, therefore, suppressed this information as I grew up. I was to listen to those around me—the minister, my parents (who were alcoholics and mentally ill), and authority figures. I know today that I was taught to listen to insanity.

Following the rules of society finally stopped working for me. The church told me to stay in an abusive marriage. The medical community told me I would have to take prescriptions the rest of my life to stay mentally ill. When my life got completely unbearable, I had to pay attention to my inner voice.

Instinctively, I first connected to the voice inside to pray for help. I knew that night my husband would kill me. I prayed from my heart and not from the hymnal. That was the turning point for my paying attention to the truth inside. I cried for help, and it did come. I am alive today because I began paying attention to my inner messages of guidance. These silent voices offer answers and information that actually help me as opposed to the old information and false beliefs that were bringing on more illness and difficulties.

Realizing that my life progressed when I applied my internal information, everything began to improve. Gradually, I listened to less outward facts, books, or experts. Following my new guidance was working. Over many years my health also improved until I was off all prescriptions and declared sane. Slowly, I was walking into a life of love and leaving my old fear-based life behind. I was feeling the best emotions I had ever experienced.

I found that during this change of focus, my childhood church of forty-five years no longer supported my newfound happiness and way of life. They told me, "Religion is not about feeling good." For several years I searched for alternative churches. Ultimately, I discovered that all churches have a dogma based on controlling their flocks.

During this time I began a PhD program in metaphysics for spiritual counseling. I received a phone call from a minister of a spiritual church asking me to speak at her church one Sunday as a guest. She had contacted my university and asked for a local student. I found that I matched the church well in my first invitation to speak. They were listening to their inner messages and offering communications of the spirit to others. I was not alone in hearing and having messages for people.

While in this church, I met a medium named David LeBaron. He did more than give messages. As a psychic, he could go into a trance during which Dr. Lang, a spirit doctor, would appear and heal people. David could bring in *apports*, do materializations, and contact people who had passed over. I talked in spirit with my parents; Edgar Cayce, the famous psychic of the twentieth century; and Sitting Bull on different occasions.

I went regularly for several years to his evening healings, classes, and séances. During these evenings with Dr. Lang, my energy was gradually renewing my well-being from a multitude of illnesses and addictions. In addition, my energy was changing with the help of my masters and guides into higher consciousness during his classes and healings. I was growing spiritually into a higher perception and understanding of the spiritual world.

My knowledge and application of spiritual ideas were growing through several spiritual support groups. I was ready to try going into a trance and to receive information. Before David died, he told me that I would be channeling Archangel Ariel.

Rev. John Lilek, another medium, arrived in my town, giving classes in trance work. He supported that I had the ability to do this. His confidence and assistance gave me the desire to pursue my further development. He suggested forming small groups to practice spiritual development. While in our development group, I did not have just an image or message for others, but my gatekeeper came to introduce John the Divine. John told me he was there to give messages through my voice.

The first time I was not courageous enough actually to permit it to happen. I talked with him and was too startled and hesitant to allow it. The next time I decided to go ahead, and I found myself channeling messages through my vocal cords. John usually provides spiritual information, answers people's questions, and tells about past lives.

My first gatekeeper was Long Feather, my father in this lifetime but now in spirit. Long Feather pronounced his own arrival, introduced John, and returned to close the sessions. His job was to keep me safe from harmful spirits that were not of the highest and best energy for my welfare. On my tour to the southwest Indian area, he appeared in a less dense material form as an Indian, and on a few other occasions since his passing, he has come to me in various forms.

I was surprised when John the Divine inhabited me to give his messages. I had expected Ariel. He was waiting beside me as I became brave enough to allow his voice to use my vocal cords. As I matured and my consciousness elevated more, Long Feather told me he needed to leave because I had outgrown his range of consciousness. Martha would become my new gatekeeper, he clarified.

Martha introduced herself as the sister of Lazarus in the Bible. Lately, she has added that she was a cousin of Jesus. She has also kept me safe from lower entities wanting to speak through me. About that time, Archangel Ariel arrived and started coming in to give blessings to those present. Over time I found Mother Mary, Archangel Michael, and Jesus can speak through me, all using different vocal cords for a different pitch.

Archangel Michael has magnificent energy and bellows out his messages when he feels his information is needed. He first came to me visually when I was in Spain. He appeared as an image on a veil of thin white material I could see through. Because he lowered his energy, I could see him. His massive energy was overwhelming and masculine as he stood next to me in the Catholic church in San Sebastian, Spain.

I began crying tears of joy as I heard his full message, which was so loving. He confirmed that I was teaching "the way, the truth, and the life." Then he continued with me on my trip through Europe, coming with Mother Mary. I was on a spiritual tour to visit the sites of Mother Mary's appearances in Portugal, Spain, and France.

I know today that Archangel Michael has been with me through many lifetimes. His protection has kept me alive several times in this lifetime and several past lives. Lately, I find he is with me daily as I move higher in consciousness.

Later, when I traveled to France, one of my spiritual sites to visit was the Baths at Lourdes. Archangel Michael's daily visits with Mother Mary prepared me to go through the rituals there. The water is not heated and is usually cold, around 12 degrees Celsius (54 degrees Fahrenheit). The immersion lasts around a minute, during which time prayers are recited and veneration of a statue of the Virgin is encouraged. At this time Mother Mary became my spiritual mother.

I was spiritually connected to Mother Mary from our past lifetime together as girls in the Essene community. We were friends as part of the twelve young girls preparing to be the mother of Jesus. During my experience at Lourdes, Mother Mary became my mother in an emotional way. My birth mother was not able to be emotionally available and nurture me while I was growing up. Immediately, I felt the love of a mother during the bath ritual.

I needed Mother Mary's mature feminine energy with the masculine power of Archangel Michael to restore my personal power into equilibrium from all my past traumas. Together, Archangel Michael and Mother Mary combined their energies for me to heal my post-traumatic stress disorder through the rite while immersed in the cold water. Their combined energies were necessary to balance my past episodes of profound shock.

I still find them both assisting me often in my life experiences. Archangel Michel continues to be with me almost daily as I keep growing through difficult spiritual tests. My rising in consciousness is necessary to channel higher information. Mother Mary often is comforting to me. She provides loving support and even material items that were missing when I grew up. Along with my guides, masters, and five more angels, they comprise my spiritual family.

At Christmas every year, Jesus spoke with the people attending David's séances. Jesus has continued to appear at Christmas when I channel, giving love and caring to those present. We join in a Christmas celebration, and each person in attendance then talks separately with Jesus. This is such a special gift, for Jesus to offer his help and comfort. His message is always one of love. I am deeply humbled by this work.

When there is major ascension information for growth, St. Germaine likes to give the message. His purpose is to assist in ascension, and he believes his information is vital for personal and spiritual growth. He told me at one channeling that his information was to become a book. Within the year *The Real Meaning of 2012: A New Paradigm for Bringing Heaven to Earth* was published in paperback and also as an e-book at Amazon. It explains diminishing the influence of the ego.

Before a channeling certain etiquette is explained and necessary to ensure the safety of the medium. During a channeling people are given instructions by her husband at the meeting to ensure that the energy attachment that connects everyone and is helping to provide energy for the channeler is not broken. There have been a few experiences in my sessions that could have been deadly.

During one healing, John the Divine was helping when a cell phone went off in the dark room. The sound of the phone ringing disrupted the energy abruptly. This is like waking with a jerk from sleeping when the telephone rings. I was out of my body and hastily went back into my body without being lined up to fit properly. For several days I could not tell why I did not feel quite right. I found another medium to take me out and put me back in with the proper placing. In addition, my spiritual partner tweaked some places to make the fit accurate.

Another time someone opened the door to the dark room where I was working out of my body, helping someone with a health problem. There I was in spirit with no physical hands to protect myself. My biggest fear was that I could not protect myself when out of body. I felt I had no way to be safe in spirit. This was extremely upsetting and scary. I had a medium friend near death in the hospital because of a similar experience.

My channeling is to provide information and caring tools for those moving into a higher consciousness of unconditional love. As you move into a higher vibrational energy, you move into more loving conditions that heal. The information brings healing when you are open to it. The Bible says, "Perfect love casts out all fear" (1 John 4:18). Love heals.

We are on earth to rise from the fearful duality of this third dimension, which is based in right, wrong, good, bad, criticism, and judgment, into a higher energy of compassion, forgiveness, gratitude, and unconditional love. I am here to assist in this process. This is called ascension. When you release all the fears and other negativity in your life, you create space for the love to fill the void left. This gradual process has been occurring for thousands of years. Rising consciousness into unconditional love is the goal of our souls.

Now with more energy beaming to earth, it is positive to release the selfishness, lack, and limitations of the past. Most people want love in their lives but have not understood that the obstacles are in their subconscious and need to be addressed consciously. They are like the tail wagging the dog until the denial is broken and the truth is revealed. Identifying these barriers brings them into awareness so they can move beyond diversion or *stuckness*.

Fear has been the force on the planet that stops progress into the higher consciousness of the fifth dimension, also known as "heaven on earth." The universe always supports you in all things, but this knowledge has been suppressed for centuries. Applying faith and trust will move you beyond fear onto your new path.

In prior years the masters raised their consciousness secretly in the mystery schools. The work of the masters is to share their understanding with those wanting to move into a place of peace on earth, often called the fifth dimension. Using their experience and methods to ascend into a loving environment will manifest as harmony, balance, and unity. Ascension was demonstrated on Easter when Jesus left the tomb in an *enlightened* eternal state.

The most famous of the masters is Jesus because he was the most visible. While in the desert for forty days, Jesus rebuked Satan, which represents our negative ego-driven emotions. The ego diminishes so we can live in eternity. Jesus ascended on the cross, as he had let go of the last of his ego-driven life of the third dimension. The crucifixion was his demonstration for releasing his ego's negative feelings—that is, guilt and fear. This allowed his moving into a consciousness of grace.

The ego tells us we are separated from God. This manifests as pain in our lives; however, his crucifixion on the cross was not painful as churches have preached. There is no pain or illness in the presence of God. He overcame the ego when he said, "Father, into your hands, I commit my spirit" (Luke 23:46). His words verified his return into the oneness of spirit. His atonement or his ability to be at one with God was successful.

Jesus is our example that we, too, can rise into God's presence. In doing this, Jesus rose into grace and returned to his original birthright—the presence of God—where there is no pain. He demonstrated that all can move into the grace that restored his Christ consciousness and healed his illusion of separation. There are many masters past and currently assisting people in this path of growth into ascending beyond the ego's influence.

Leaving the selfish self-centeredness behind to rise into the unconditional love of the spirit is ascension. The path is outgrowing irresponsibility into becoming mature. Taking responsibility is responding in loving ways to all events in our lives. When our consciousness moves beyond the material world into the spiritual realm of the fifth dimension, it is unconditional love. We create peace on earth.

Many masters, including Jesus, Sanat Kumara, Gautama Buddha, Maitreya, Confucius, Lord Lanto (Confucius's historical mentor), Mary (mother of Jesus), Lady Master Nada, Kwan Yin, Saint Germaine, and Kuthumi, are all familiar. However, many have stayed out of the limelight.

Now everyone who wishes to ascend into a higher consciousness into the thousand years of peace described in the Bible can. It takes releasing your lower negative energy from the fears, guilt, shame, and other negativity so that space is available for your heart to open and fill you with your inner love of your Creator.

My prayers were answered when I asked for a way to help people achieve this. I found myself flying to Virginia to take beginning and advanced classes by Henry Leo Bolduc. He was a pioneer in past-life regression since the days of Bridey Murphy, which was popular in the 1950s. I then became a member of the IBRT (International Board for Regression Therapy). In addition, I took classes in hypnotism and joined the American Board of Hypnotherapy. This combination came together with learning to include flower essences that shift energy and support higher consciousness.

I continued my training by graduating from a metaphysical school and also being ordained as a spiritual minister/counselor. Through meditation and development groups, I became psychic. Several years later I moved into a higher energy of mediumship where I channeled from the *higher realms*, which can be viewed on YouTube.

My counseling and speaking help people ascend. This is the meaning of Jacob's ladder in the Bible. My channelings and writings are about this shift in energy. My books, the articles on my blog, interviews, classes, and counseling all are based in progressing up the stairs of consciousness. My angels and masters assist in my methods, give me information, and provide guidance for the needs of my clients. It has become a wonderful combination.

The earth is coming into higher consciousness to support more awareness that is still to be revealed. We do not go to heaven, but we grow into heaven on the arms of those we help. Ascended masters and spiritual guides are helping people and assisting those ready to move into perfect, unconditional love. "Perfect love casts out all fear." This is the first time in history that civilization can experience this change in consciousness in a physical form. When you awaken, this process is the path.

Introduction

I graduated with a Bachelor of Science in Mechanical Engineering in 1980. The pursuit of engineering work has taken me around the country, from Newport News, Virginia, in 1980, through seven states, to West Lafayette, Indiana, in 2016.

My spiritual journey began when I discovered *The Book of Success* while working a closing shift at a bookstore in 1995. Finding that misplaced book was a crucial moment of my life, an awakening. It led me to learn the art of meditation, which resulted in receiving a spark within from God in 1999.

The response from God in the form of a Divine Spark in 1999 was remarkable. The magnitude of love from the flash was incredible. It was similar to what Paul experienced when he was struck by "lightning" in the Bible. That spark pervaded my whole being with love. Later, Apostle John explained to me that it came from within my soul.

I continued my journey to Seattle, Washington, through an employment opportunity with Boeing in 2010. I was still seeking the truth, and it took me on the road to meet Marilyn and Apostle John in 2011. I met Marilyn while attending her chakras cleansing class with Apostle John. This all-day seminar was in Edgewood, a suburb of Seattle, near Mount Rainier. During this course, Marilyn went into her trance, and her voice changed to a man's voice, that of Apostle John. He was leading the class for chakras cleansing. It was unbelievable to hear the transformation of a woman's voice into a man's voice in a matter of minutes.

After meeting with them, I was selected to write this book, and

Marilyn was to be my medium since she had access to Apostle John. This type of mediumship was not a new concept. All biblical writers of the Old Testament were mediums. King David had a team of notetakers for his Book of Psalms while he was in a trance, and the spirit of Melchizedek spoke through David.

I had attended an extensive Bible study at a Baptist church in 2006, which helped me prepare my questions for John. During my conversations with him, I revisited some of the biblical passages. He recommended books that would be useful for my research and developing questions for our channeling sessions. I have had 21 channeling sessions with Apostle John and asked over 500 questions since May 2014. The time has come to understand the truth.

I had a conversation with someone at a spiritual retreat in Connecticut during the fall of 2014, and we talked about only 5 percent of people having made it to heaven since the beginning of time. John had confirmed this figure during one of our channelings. The majority were left behind, earthbound because of fears of the unknown when confronting the tunnel. One of Jesus' primary undertakings was to free earthbound souls and release them to heaven over two thousand years ago. As I found out from Apostle John, a greater percentage of people are ascending to heaven today. The elite—the Sons of Belial (Baal) back in the days of Atlantis to the Illuminati today—that had perverted the truth of finding joy within our essences that was practiced by the Atlanteans for ages has lost its control. More people are discovering for themselves the hidden truths.

Apostle John wrote the Book of Revelation to reveal information to people, but they were not ready for it. The understanding of energy terms that we know today was too complex for them back at that time.

However, the time is right for my book to reveal the hidden truths. This book provides a better understanding of our existence, where we came from, and how we can overcome our fear that results from control by the forces behind the scenes. With the help from John, this book fills in the half-truths and mysteries that have kept us in the dark about the truth of joy and love that we are about to experience for the upcoming millennium. Dark forces have been at war with the throne of God for control of planet Earth. Exactly who are the dark forces? Where do they come from? They have been battling with the forces of God since the beginning of time.

Who are the forces of God? Who leads them, and what is their agenda of keeping us connected with the Heavenly Father? What is their endgame? Who will be part of the upcoming one thousand years of peace? When will it begin? Apostle John is among the ascended masters on the administration of the Throne, and he has revealed how Earth becomes a planet of peace by the next generation. Presently, there remain pockets of hatred in our civilizations due to the political and religious strife. Where will those people go after they die from this life? There has been misinformation about the future of our planet. It is here to stay, as God still retains the power, but He allows free will to take its course for the evil to get obliterated by the light. Evil is fast going away as people are experiencing more of God's light every day as the planet is aligning closer to the center of creation. We will experience an incredible joy of love for each other while more of us are getting connected to a vineyard, which is a metaphor for the oneness of God.

The book also touches on the disappearance of a planet in our solar system that could have had repercussions for our planet if forces of God had not stepped in to save us. Our earliest civilizations that had the right idea of living with love during our previous Golden Age thirteen thousand years ago have disappeared. However, the dark entities in control have suppressed this information.

John has talked about the media withholding information from the public, which was part of the control by the Dark Side. Also, we have spoken about the candidates of the 2016 U.S. presidential election. It was part of the overall scheme for the United States to establish peace for the world to help take down the troubles that are delaying the dispersion of the dark energies from the planet.

This book will help us prepare for the upcoming era of Love and Light and teach us how to overcome our limited DNA and prosper in the coming One Thousand Years of Peace. The flow of photon energy provides loving energy from the center of creation from God. The stage is set for mankind to experience incredible love in the fifth dimension. It will have a profound impact on how we relate to each other. Apostle John gives his views on marriage and divorce. The female energy will have a more significant influence for the New Age. Also, this book includes a conversation with my deceased father, who passed away last year. He shared his insights into heaven and his experience after death while he witnessed his family attending his funeral.

One of this book's most important messages is that we all have spiritual guides. We need to learn how to communicate with them internally through intuition and foresight to be able to benefit from their assistance and realize the true essence of love, joy, and light that the Creator has bestowed on us as His children.

This project was quite an undertaking, but my inner guide encouraged me. During a couple of my conversations with Apostle John, he called me Jacob. I asked him about it, and he confirmed that I had been among the 120 disciples during the time of Pentecost in one of my past lives. I was a quiet, conscientious individual at the time and worked at Apostle John's father's boating business in Capernaum, Israel. Marilyn was one of the twelve girls chosen to prepare to be Jesus' mother in her past life, and she was close to Mary and John. I have found a connection with them that gave me an impetus to write this book. It combines well with my analytical skills from my engineering career and Marilyn's wealth of experience from her spiritual ministry. This book brings you a much better perspective of how we remain in good hands with the loving care from our Heavenly Father for eternity.

Chapter 1

Heaven on Earth

Section 1.1: Fifth Dimension—Heaven on Earth

Since the beginning of mankind, man has wondered who he is, what he is doing here, and where he is going after death. He looked at the outer world and fell in awe before the forces of nature. He looked inside and discovered that he was more than a physical body. He experimented with plants and meditation and found that he and his environment also existed on other levels of consciousness.

At present, we live in a society where the emphases are on material gain and security, by which the other facets of life, namely the spiritual, have been well suppressed. Nevertheless, people continue to experience states of existence, and facets of life, other than the material.

The personality is the lower self, consisting of the physical body and the psychic soul. It has the genetics of its forefathers, the energy system to keep the physical body alive, and the psychological and psychic characteristics that define us as human. It has the abilities to express itself through thought, language, and other intellectual capacities. The personality is a unit of incarnation; it is all those bodies and all those characteristics you have taken on for this incarnation. As it belongs to the world of form, it is temporary. It was created to express ourselves in this world on a temporary basis. When we die, the personality dissolves. The experiences we have gained during our lifetime are then absorbed by our individuality.

The individuality is our higher self. It is the unit of evolution. It does not die but remains the same throughout the many incarnations. It learns from all the experiences in those incarnations. While the personality often does not know why it incarnated, as with every birth memory of the past has been wiped out, the individuality has an overview of all incarnations and of the meaning of everything that happens to the person. Eventually, the individuality will go back into the Divine.

The divine essence is what man always has been, at this moment is, and always will be. Each living being is a part of the Divine. It is often compared with a star or a light spark. Although it seems that each living being is a separate light spark in this universe of darkness, our divine essence links us all together, as in the Divine there is no distinction—only unity prevails. Our divine essence does not know duality, only unity. Our language is too limited to express the Divine, but we try it anyway, and thus we say that the Divine, and our divine essence, is perfect, immortal, eternal, unchangeable, formless, and so on. The individuality and personality are imperfect, mortal, temporal, subjected to change, have form, etc.

As man has different bodies, each body belongs to a sphere of existence, or world. All the bodies are functioning constantly, whether we are aware of them or not. In the daytime, consciousness is centered in the physical body and the physical world. At night, when the physical body rests, consciousness withdraws and shifts to the astral level. Then consciousness is centered in the astral body and can move around in the astral world. Usually it stays just "outside" the physical body and dreams. Occasionally it wanders around in the astral world, has a short visit to the mental world, or converses with other astral beings.

With traumas or accidents, consciousness can suddenly shift to the astral body. There are many reports of people who suddenly left their physical body and saw its condition from an eagle's point of view. In the last decades, we have given a lot of attention to the so-called near-death experiences. People died, went out of their body, and had certain experiences in the astral world, which they could recount when they were brought back to life. Some people can deliberately shift their consciousness to the astral level while remaining conscious. We usually call these out-of-body experiences.

In the world of duality, the elite of the world have held us prisoner by keeping us from our true consciousness. Paul described it as blinding our minds: "In whom the god of this world hath blinded the minds, that is, of the infidels, that the light of the glorious Gospel of Christ, which is the image of God, should not shine unto them." In other words, we are trapped in our body prison matrix of the third dimension. The body prison is our ego, consisting of the five senses: sight, hearing, taste, smell, and touch. These are parts of the body system that consist of a group of sensory cell types that respond to a physical phenomenon, and that sends signals to the brain.

Scripture has a couple of references to the term *body prison*:

- "Bring my soul out of prison, that I may praise thy Name: then shall the righteous come about me, when thou art beneficial unto me." (Psalm 142:7)
- "By which he also went, and preached unto the spirits that are in prison. (1 Peter 3:19)

We are a vast array of light beings that have already experienced living in a fifth dimension or higher elsewhere in God's creation. However, we reincarnated here in a third-dimensional body matrix designed by the Dark Side to keep us enslaved to the planet.

Imagine experiencing more than what exists today. To do this, we created a way of experiencing ourselves differently. This way was the creation of a holographic universe that operated on the pure light only. In this pure-light holographic universe, we have a playground to explore ourselves experiencing physicality.

Our pure consciousness can create all experiences in our lives and so much more beyond. However, because the elite had constructed a veil, we cannot see the part of the universe beyond earth. When we view existence in these terms, it will give us a new perspective on how we are enduring difficulties with the ruling elite on the planet. This life we experience now is not the real reality that we have seen before coming to this terrible prison planet. Outside this third-dimension holographic prison is a multi-dimensional holographic existence where we can nano-travel anywhere in the blink of an eye and build whatever environment we desire.

Spiritually, this dimension is the next stop down the ladder before we enter the realms of limitation. We incarnate here as celestial beings with light—luminous bodies seeded from space families, such as the Pleiadeans, also known as Nordic aliens, are humanoid aliens that come from the stellar systems surrounding the Pleiades star system as well as several other star systems. They are here helping us fight the evil space reptiles as part of the battle against the Illuminati. The actual Pleiades is a star system located about 400 light-years from Earth.

The Bible has talked about heaven being a better place and a more enduring substance. The question is this: Could it be here on earth, or is it somewhere else on the other side? Is this just a juxtaposition? Whether a physical location or our state of consciousness, it is indeed a better place to be. The other side is called *nirvana*, where our souls go for a permanent residence or a temporary rest from our previous incarnation. We consult with our spiritual guides and the ascended masters to determine our course for our next lives. Life-after-death stories have given a glimpse of this place but not beyond for those who have come back to life. All of them have wanted to stay there, whereas peace and love seem lacking here on the third-dimensional earth.

However, John had confirmed that Adam and Eve came to help humanity by providing better DNA for humankind. The serpent depicted in Genesis 3:1 represents man's ego, not a real being named

Satan. Therefore, Adam's fall represents the activation of the ego. Recognize how God cursed the snake so that it would crawl on its belly and eat dust all the days of its life? That scene—that the snake was originally upright and was cursed to eat dust—becomes necessary for Moses' actions later (Numbers 21:9). Symbolically, this representation teaches us that the ego is responsible for keeping us grounded in the realm of the physical via the five senses. The Bible states we are made from the dust of the field, and the snake is cursed to eat the dust of it. If our lives are under the ego's control, then we are eating this dust symbolically.

For example, let's return to Moses and the brass serpent. When the Israelites were complaining in the desert, they were not relying on faith. Instead, they depended on their egos. "And the people spake against God, and against Moses, saying, wherefore have ye brought us out of Egypt, to die in the wilderness, for here is neither bread nor water, and our soul loatheth this light bread." (Number 21:5) This entire scene illustrates the physical life condition of the soul in the desert. It is a bondage of the ego travailing through the wilderness conditions and making it to the Promised Land, which symbolizes a heavenly awakening from the bondage of the ego. In other words, the Israelites were on a spiritual journey to shed the ego and experience the Promised Land, the spiritual resurrection.

So, God gave Moses a symbolic representation of what would alleviate them. It is the brazen snake on the pole "lifted up" (Numbers 21:9). In the narrative of Adam and Eve, the snake was cast down, but it must be lifted up, which is a symbol of the ego's transformation. It restores the spiritual aspect of man's soul.

The Scriptures contains many metaphors to represent the holy temple of our human body and brain. If the snake is upright, then it resembles the spinal cord, and the head of the snake would be the third-eye chakra which features the pineal gland. The ancients understood it as a spiritual organ at the center of the brain.

In deep meditation practices, the Kundalini spiritual energy rises through the spinal column and opens the seven chakras, which symbolize the seven churches of Revelation, along the spine until it reaches the pineal gland, symbolizing a spiritually resurrected individual. This process can also be the serpent that transforms from the ego into the fully realized and awakened spiritual being. This experience raises the conscious awareness of an individual beyond the senses of the ego. It is one that ancient spiritual peoples—even the earliest Christians—were cognizant of.

Jesus made two statements to confirm the meaning of spiritual resurrection: "And as Moses lifted up the serpent in the wilderness, even so, must the Son of man be lifted up" (John 3:14) and "Remember, the kingdom of God is not outside of you, but it is 'within'" (Luke 17:21). Lifting up the Son of Man is another way of symbolizing the path to Christ consciousness, a state of being beyond the senses, emotions, and intellect.

Kundalini is a psycho-spiritual energy, the energy of the consciousness, which resides within the sleeping body. It is aroused through spiritual discipline to bring new states of consciousness, which include mystical illumination. Kundalini is a Sanskrit term for "serpent power" because it is believed to lie like a serpent in the root chakra at the base of the spine.

The power of kundalini is immense. Those were having experienced it claim to have unusual physical sensations and movements, pain, clairaudience, visions, brilliant lights, psychical powers, ecstasy, bliss, and transcendence of self. Kundalini is an energy that functions as liquid fire and liquid light. The Bible gave a description of how kundalini was a "flame" within, "And the house of Jacob shall be a fire, and the house of Joseph a flame, and the house of Esau as stubble, and they shall kindle in them and devour them: and there shall be no remnant of the house of Esau: for the Lord hath spoken it." (Obadiah 1:18)

Not all kundalini experiences are identical regarding awakenings. They may vary in intensity and duration. Typically, the yogi meditates to arouse the kundalini and then to raise it through his or her body. Initially, the yogi feels the sensation on heat at the base of the spine. It may be felt as intensely hot or pleasantly warm. The energy travels up a psychic pathway parallel to the spinal column, and the kundalini activates the chakras in succession along the way. Please refer to Figure 5 for information on the chakras. The body becomes cold and corpse-like as the Kundalini leaves the lower portions and begins to rise. The yogi is likely to shudder or tremble and feels the extreme sensation of heat and cold. The length of the kundalini may be sudden or last several minutes. The objective is to raise the kundalini to the third-eye chakra and get illumination. After receiving it, then the yogi attempts to lower the energy to another chakra, but not below the heart chakra because lowering it to lower chakras would produce ego inflation, excessive sexual desire, and a host of other ills. By repeatedly raising the kundalini to the third-eye, the yogi can succeed in having the energy permanently stay there.

The kundalini opens new pathways in the nervous system; the pain associated with this is due to the nervous system's inability to immediately cope with the energy. It is important to assert that the body is properly attuned for kundalini through yoga. Any early or explosive awakening can cause insanity or death.

The astral body matters are constantly moving as the particles are flowing through each of the force centers. Each of these centers evokes from the particles of the astral body the ability to respond to a certain set of vibrations that we call vibrations of light, sound, and heat.

We may in our consciousness not know anything of it. The only way to bring upon the consciousness of these astral experiences to the physical brain is by awakening the etheric centers. The method of awakening is precisely like that adopted in the astral body, by arousing Kundalini, which lies dormant in the etheric matter in the center near the base of the spine.

However, when arousing Kundalini prematurely, it rushes into the lower spiritual centers of the body (lower chakras) instead of upwards like the third-eye chakra, which resulting in the excitation of the most undesirable passions. As a result, the desires become intensified to such a degree that it is quite impossible for the man to resist them. The premature unfoldment of Kundalini also increases everything in nature, reaching, in fact, the lower evil qualities more readily than the good. Ambition in the mental body is very easily aroused and grows to an inordinate degree. Together with great intensifications of intellectual power there comes abnormal and satanic pride. The force of Kundalini is no normal force, but something resistless.

When we recourse ourselves to the spirit of love within, we are bypassing the urges of our ego senses. As a result, we feel are feeling the peace within with no worries and, it is likely we have arrived at the fifth dimension. Peace within is a feeling of joy with a sense of neutrality:

- "Deceit is in the heart of them that imagine evil: but to the counselors of peace shall be joy." (Proverbs 12:20)
- "These things have I spoken unto you, that in me ye might have peace: in the world, ye shall have affliction, but be of good comfort: I have overcome the world." (John 16:33)

The first practice of living in the fifth dimension is constantly thinking how the other people feel. If we see someone holding back because they are shy, make them feel part of the group. It is inappropriate to be a rescuer to help someone needy because it covers up their neediness by making them feel good, which is an aspect of the third dimension. At the fifth dimension, we are responding to the needs of others without any personal hidden agenda. As a result, the universe rewards us immensely. Act for our highest good. If something is not for the betterment of our highest good, then it is not for the highest good of others either. The reverse is also true. If it is not for someone else's gain, then it is not going to serve us. We cannot be busy while maintaining our vibration in the fifth dimension, so take time out to relax, meditate, and enjoy life. We need to surround ourselves with high-frequency people or people with a positive attitude. It raises the vibration for both parties. Take things lightly so that you enjoy the fun and laughter.

Keep your home in the vibration of the fifth dimension. Make it as harmonious as possible. It does not mean that we have to be a doormat just to keep people happy. Love raises the frequency of those in our household to maintain peaceful tranquility. At the same time, our home needs to be a safe refuge. Flowers, beautiful music, and colors help to emanate a vibration, which attracts work that satisfies us. In this higher dimension, we take mastery of our lives and our energy fields. So, we align our frequency to that of work which suits our temperament and deeply satisfies our soul.

Live with abundant consciousness and watch our thoughts and words. Make sure all our thoughts and statements align with the highest possibilities. We would not want to drag our vision down with doubts, fears, and poverty consciousness. Be generous.

Any activity where we are in contact with the earth is real. Walking, climbing, playing in a meadow as we picnic, standing barefoot in the grass, growing flowers and vegetables all help us connect to the fifth dimension planet. It is better to walk on the ground rather than a tarmac if we possibly can. Have a symbiotic relationship with the plants, trees, and all of nature. When we hug a tree, we can open up to the knowledge and wisdom it holds. Also at the same time, its roots help our roots move down deeply into our earth star chakra.

Being in nature keeps us in balance and harmony and helps us maintain a fifth-dimensional frequency. When we are fifth-dimensional beings with an opened third-eye, we are automatically aware of the spiritual dimensions around us. Take that step and walk hand in hand with angels daily. Be aware of the work the elementals are doing all around us and also be open to those spirit visitors from the astral world on the other side but still connect to earth.

Eat foods moderately that have a high vibration matching our own. Fifth-dimensional foods are organic. A nutritionally balanced diet must include plenty of green vegetables, fruits, and nuts.

These examples will come to our lives when new spiritual energies are entering the planet from the Photon Belt (see Figures 2&3), bringing shifts to economic, political, and climatic areas. Further predictions are offered for individual countries and include a time frame for this huge transition, anticipated to last until the earth moves entirely into the fifth-dimensional frequency in 2026. From what to expect to how to prepare, this exciting exploration serves as guidance for the next ten years, allowing readers to attune themselves to the upcoming spiritual forces.

Heaven on Earth has arrived, aided by a flow of photon energy emanating from space. Earth aligned to the fifth dimension, which is an era of Love and Light, on December 21, 2012. It is a high-level arrangement of love, peace, and harmony. This energy flow is a form of the Holy Spirit and is an energy arrangement that occurred on earth once before while Atlantis was in existence some twenty to forty thousand years ago.

Once the Dark Side took control of planet earth after the solar system had left the Photon Belt back around 8904 BC, the Atlanteans moved inside the earth to maintain their spiritual practices acquired from their Golden Age era.

* * * * *

DOUG: You're talking Atlantis or previous Golden Age, so they brought it back to the darkness.

JOHN: The planet was ready to ascend at the time of Atlantis and the Sons of Belial (Baal) sabotaged it with the great explosions where the continent submerged. And we have been spending the last 15,000 years bringing the planet back into consciousness for ascension. And there have been different people who have perpetuated leadership to stop this, which we call the dark side or the Cabal or the Illuminati. But they are just tools of the darkness to have that stopped from people being able to ascend.

*****

"Then the children of Israel did wickedly in the sight of the Lord, and served Baal." (Judges 2:11)

They left behind their writings of their Golden Age experiences of finding God in Christ consciousness that were the staple of their lives. The Books of Atlantis were placed in the library in Alexandria, Egypt, but were lost when the library burned. If we had access to those records, no doubt our religious experience would be different today. The Old Testament was written during the latter part of that era, but it in no way described the loving experience that the photon energy had provided for that civilization. God is love, but the Bible portrayed Him as an angry God. It brought fear to the people rather than uniting them, which is what we are going to experience in the coming years while our solar system returns to the Photon Belt. As John later revealed, our souls are a part of God, and the people surrounding us are a part of God as well. It was the mantra of Jesus' teaching of loving your God with all your heart and soul and loving your neighbor the same as yourself. It is the oneness of God that binds all of us together. Everything comes from the heart. People from inside the earth have been practicing love. However, we have been misguided by the Dark Side, because they have concealed the truth from us. We have never known about people's experiences during the previous Golden Age. All their writings were either burned or preserved but locked up in the catacombs of the Vatican.

In fact, the burning of the library at Alexandria in past centuries was to devastate and destroy real learning that had been accumulated at that time. Some books were rescued from that full fire of the library of Alexandria, and some of those books ended up in the Vatican library that is under lock and key, you might say, and hidden away.

So much literature was destroyed, and some of it was saved. But it was never exposed to the public because then people would know the truth. So it is not unusual for books to be destroyed. A very famous novel called *The Celestine Prophecy* is about people—the church—trying to devastate and destroy truthful information so the people would not have that available. So this kind of thing has been going on for centuries.

People from inside the earth are the ancestors of the people who lived during the Golden Age. They have not been able to come out while the world has been experiencing dangerous times. It is hard for them to make a transition from the love of the fifth dimension to the strife of the lower third dimension. They have remained inside for over thirteen thousand years, waiting for the moment that is about to arrive: Heaven on Earth.

The new era is coming in the foreseeable future. However, pockets of dark energies still exist on the planet. Life is going to get worse for those that remain in the third dimension mindset of control and fear. When we discover the power of love within us, which is Christ consciousness, we will survive the changes that take place before Earth become a planet of peace. There are many people today that aren't ready for it as there are hatreds among the populations, particularly the religious extremists that do not practice the basic Laws of loving God and loving thy neighbors. In addition, there are some remaining negative energies that need to go away before we achieve Heaven on Earth. Among them are finances. We may be facing some repercussions due to some governmental policies that have created unequal financial balances from the incredible growth of the financial markets during the past decades which have created greed and fear among investors that are not sustainable for the well-being of the citizens. These actions further polarize the egos, which impedes their spiritual growth.

With the incoming of new spiritual energies from the Photon Belt, the forces of love and light will prevail. People from inside the earth will come out to teach us how to grow spiritually. Also, people from other civilizations of other planets that have experienced love and light will help assist us. The barriers are being broken down. It is time to look forward to prosperity. The healthier we are, the more love we can share, because we will never feel alone. Christ consciousness is a state of mind where our actions are coming from our heart, such as doing a service for others rather than for ourselves.

However, the Ascended Masters remain transparent to society until the last remaining dark energies of the third dimension are eradicated. It does not stop there. They are looking at the bigger picture. They are eyeing the Isle of Paradise, which is at the center of creation. Then when our planet is populated with people with a higher state of mind, we will grow further into the love and light. John stated we will continue to grow to a higher dimension, as high as the twelfth and beyond.

As we grow spiritually to a higher dimension, more and more people of the third dimension are going to die off the planet and reincarnate elsewhere.

They will come back after a thousand years as they work out their dark energies to embrace more light. While they are away, people who remain here will learn how to live their lives with Christ consciousness. With the aid of photon energy beaming the energy of love and light toward us, we will learn the essence of Christ consciousness quite readily. As a result of experiencing this love, our ten missing strands of DNA will be restored. We will live optimum lives free of disabilities. While recapturing the missing strands, we will never feel lonesome. The love will always be in our hearts. When Jesus came down to earth for his ministry, he noticed people lacking love in their hearts. It created depression in their lives. As remarkable as it sounds, Christ consciousness keeps your focus on the love in your heart. God is there in your heart always.

The awareness of Heaven on Earth usually starts from the fifth dimension and continues to grow beyond. Our Ascended Masters, including John, are proactive with our spiritual growth. They know we reside in the youngest universe among the seven super universes encircling the Isle of Paradise. The other six universes have already ascended, and they are waiting for us to ascend. When that happens, then the entire ring of seven galaxies will be a part of the Isle of Paradise. It is how we continue to grow toward the twelfth dimension and beyond.

The third-dimensional existence is no longer in our vibration. We have crossed over into the next dimension upon our reentry in the Photon Belt. These people cannot begin to understand us or accept our new insights. We have a part of our reality at one stage, while the other part is ascending to the higher stage. We must straddle the dimensional border while still offering our services to humanity, the services that we know so well and have used for so long. At the same time, we must create the higher vibrating realities on our side of the dimensional border. Those closest to the dimensional border are ready and will ask permission to help others ascend. The ascended masters are presently living on the planet to offer their assistance. They primarily reside in the mountains, most notably in the Himalayas. There are some who live in Mount Shasta in California. They consider the inside the mountains as being inside the earth, where they are already in the fifth dimension. John stated Jesus took the twelve disciples through the tunnel to the inside of the earth beneath Jerusalem for initiation.

It is interesting to note that the two well-known mountains in Israel, Mount Hermon and Mount Tabor, have entrances to go inside the earth. The transfiguration took place at Mount Hermon, where Moses and Elijah came out from inside the mountain to greet Jesus.

* * * * *

DOUG: Is it true that the ring of the seven super universes could one day be engulfed into Havona (paradise of God)? Like right now, there are developing universes moving along a circle outside of our space path. Are the other six super universes are waiting for us to ascend so that we all can join God the Father in Havona?

JOHN: Yes, they are helping us and assisting us on planet Earth at this time so that everything can ascend.

DOUG: Okay, because you mentioned earlier that our dimension will continue to grow from the eighth to the ninth to the tenth to the eleventh. That is while we are in Havona, right?

JOHN: Yes.

* * * * *

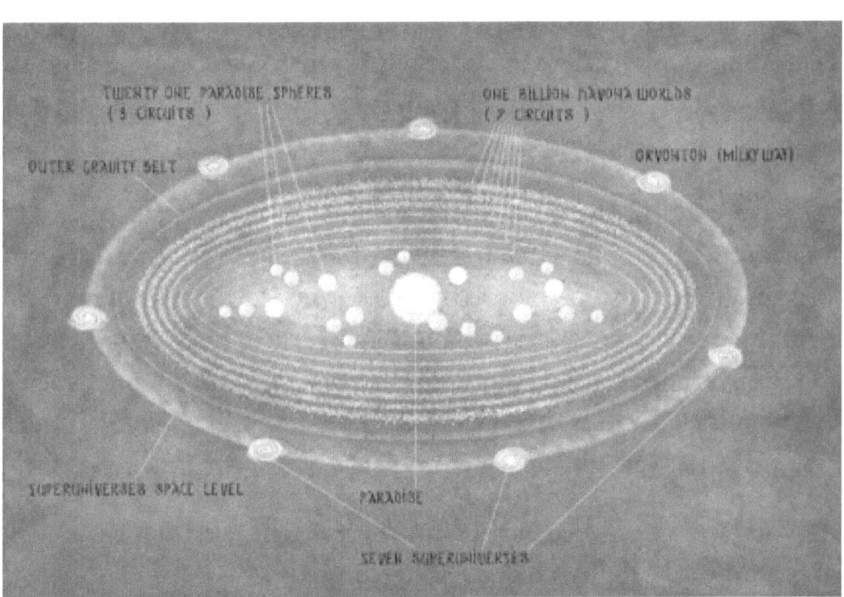

Figure 1—Isles of Paradise (Havona)

In the higher vibrations, it is not appropriate to offer services when you're not asked. There will be those who are not ready at all, who are not open to listening. As they cling to their old reality, these individuals will become wearier and more uncomfortable until they are willing to try something new. When something goes wrong, we tend to desire to open ourselves to the Spirit or perhaps angelic assistance. Our new beginnings on this path and the other side of the veil will involve new realities.

The source of love is pure from your heart. You base your actions entirely on love and never fear because fear is derived from your ego. You are unstoppable and living a miraculous life because love insulates you from your ego taking control of your mind. Immortality is within your reach. In a near-death experience (NDE), a person will travel through a long tunnel that traverses through the darkness of the lower dimensions through the fourth dimension with the help of a spiritual guide. It appears to be a dark tunnel because these dimensions are without light. At the end of the tunnel, you will enter into a bright opening of golden or white light (the fifth dimension). The tunnel is also where the energy of your soul travels through to your new body. Hence, it is considered both the birth canal of the soul and the doorway to heaven.

We have entered a new age, and we are not alone in the process. Angels are there for us. Archangel Michael has been overseeing God's mission on earth since before people populated the planet, and he lovingly oversees our divine missions in life. He guides your next step and helps you make important life changes. The following messages were channeled and transcribed by *The Golden Light Channel* dated May 18, 2016 (Ref. 20):

> "Greetings we are the Council of Angels, Archangel Michael and Archangel Metatron
>
> We wish to speak to you today of releasing all karmic debt that is tied to unhealthy patterns that have existed for you in your lifetime on earth. All beings have, to some extent or another, become entangled in a karmic web pattern during their earthen lives. Some have worked very hard to become free of this, others not as much.

This is a momentous time in the creation of your realities on earth to become free of all karmic debts, obligations, contracts, and entanglements that have existed for you before your lives on earth (as some of you have carried the karma from lifetime to lifetime), and during your current earth existence. All karma can now easily be cleared by you so that you have a clean slate as you progress on your spiritual ascension through the waves of higher dimensional frequencies now surrounding your earth, your bodies, and your spaces.

The channel had an enlightening awareness exercise today when she was able to clearly see the karmic patterns existing that she had been trapped in and through writing was able to clearly see these karmic patterns and easily release them. This is a heightened time of awareness and light that All can tune into now. Take some time for yourself to sit quietly with yourself and some notepaper and look at any karmic patterns that may be leading to anything that is not aligned with the divine qualities of the Creator – mostly feelings of separation and lack, but any kind of negative pattern where you feel stuck. This is also a time where the veils are lifting from the memories of your other lifetimes, pre-birth contracts with yourselves and others, and your life missions. If you take some time to sit quietly with yourself, you may draw upon these memories which will assist you in shedding light upon these karmic "entanglements" or "obstructions". For example, you may have a pre-birth contract with a family member or someone close to you in which you both agreed that each would act out certain parts of the paradigm of your life into which you were going to enter. A memory of this agreement will assist you in realizing why things are playing out now the way they are. Tune into your

Higher Self, master teachers and guides, and ask about what these pre-birth contracts with yourself and others are. Take a look at where your life is the most uncomfortable and you will see a pattern linking the contracts and agreements made in the spiritual realm with the current karmic situation. This then assists you in totally releasing this karmic pattern.

The veils are also lifting from memories of your pre-birth contracts for your own life, which ties into your life's mission. Ask your Higher Self, angels and guides to assist you in remembering these. The releasing of your karmic obligations opens up the pathway to your ability to practice fully your life's purpose and mission, and to live in full mastership and creatorship of your life and the realities you are creating.

It is most important at this time for All to begin to see these karmic patterns, bring them into your awareness, inquire of your higher self and guides as to your pre-birth contracts with yourself or others, and begin to see this overall karmic pattern for what it is. All happens for your growth on Earth.

Although you cannot all feel it at all times, you are inextricably linked to the Universe and this is an extremely auspicious time for All in the universe to begin clearing away the dross of that which separates All from Source. As the dross – including karmic debts and obligations– is removed, your clarity returns and you begin to realize that you are not in fact separate from Source or separate from the Creator indeed you are in fact an extension of the Creator and you are indeed creating your own reality as so many of you know. It goes a step further in that you are continually creating your own realities, and breathing into life the physical substance of the universe which is coalescing into the realities that you see before you. As you separate yourself from your karma, you begin to see that you are finally free to be the creator being that you are, manifesting your realities, and even more elaborate than this, you are all beginning to do this together for you see that since you are not separate from Creator and Source, you are indeed all of the same substance or same origin or, you are All the Same One Being seemingly split into little creator beings but in fact all functioning as independently moving parts of the whole.

As you sit quietly with yourself and look at any areas of your life that need to be transmuted and transformed and then released, you then become Free. Free to become a creator being who is free of the negative karma from the past or from any karmic obligations. As you look at these situations in your life and the light from creator source flows into your being and "sheds a light" and "enlightens" you to see the truth of why or how these were created, you can give yourself permission to Declare that you are free of the karma of this situation or situations, that you release these people or yourself from this karmic debt or obligation, across all space and time. You then become free to recreate your reality based on the higher qualities of joy, prosperity, abundance, nurturance, caring, well-being, and all higher dimensional qualities of the Creator.

The New Earth being created, or brought into being, by All of You and All of Us in the higher dimensional realms, is a place of such higher qualities – of beauty, joy, abundance, prosperity, fun, light, love and all of these lighter aspects of creation. As you begin to clear all karmic entanglements and debt from your life, by focusing within as you honor and love yourself, you then begin to project these higher qualities outward into your creationary manifestation. This is a beautiful vision indeed!

We honor you as you clear yourself from all that inhibits your upward journey towards the light of Source and All that Is, and we shine our soft light and love upon you always, ever near to assist you in your spiritual journey towards harmony, balance, and manifestation of love, joy, and light for all the world to share." (Releasing All Karmic Patterns, The Golden Light Channel.com May 18, 2016)

The following messages were channeled and transcribed by *The Golden Light Channel* dated February 8, 2017 (Ref. 21):

Greetings from the Council of Angels, Pleiadian Council, and Archangel Michael.

"We wish to speak to you today of finding your own inner truth and connecting to your higher self and Source of all love and light. There is much disinformation that you will come upon in your internet travels and we want to share with you a very simple way of the discerning your truth.

It is of great importance at this time that each person spend time practicing energy techniques of meditation, connecting with the Higher Self, and meditation, so that you may stay tuned into your own inner source of wisdom and guidance. There are many "channeled" messages on the internet, many websites relating to galactic information and so forth, and many discreditors and disclaimers of who is speaking which truth. It can all become extremely confusing, especially to those of you who are just beginning to delve into this field of information.

In the universe, multi-verse and beyond, there has always been Light and Dark. The light always pervades in the end because it emanates from the Source of all Source, the Light of all Light. There exists in the universe benevolent beings, and not so benevolent beings.

There also exists within your being, a larger part of you, that is connected to this Source and this Light, and this Love. This Source of Light is Love. You were created by this Source of Light in Love. You are a multifaceted spiritual being having a human experience. You come from the Light, and to the Light you shall eventually return after your many sojourns.

The part of you that is connected to this Source of Love, Light, and All, is your Higher Self. This Higher Self is a mirror image and emanation from the Source of all love and light. Your higher self encompasses your ENTIRE BEING and is the source of All of your good, your knowledge, information on your soul origins, your mission in life, your pre-birth agreements, and most of all your Truth. Through your connection with your higher self, you will be reconnected with Source, Love, and Light, and reconnected with the Higher Part of your Self that is a part of Source. Many, many people are unaware of this but the time is NOW for this awareness and for all to know of the importance of reconnecting with their higher selves. By reconnecting with this part of You, you will find all the truth you need, about many things; not only about yourself as a human being at this time on this planet, but about your origins as a soul, and about the Truths of some of the things that are occurring in your world at this time.

We encourage each of you to reconnect with your higher self . There are many techniques for doing this, many energy guides that will assist you. If you are strongly connected to your higher self, this also awakens your intuition, and you will automatically turn away from any information that is not true for you; you will automatically and easily be able to discern who is speaking truth and who is not. This will all be important in the coming days. As way of example only, this channel experienced the "Reconnection" technique which is now being taught all over the world. This began to awaken her dormant DNA and Chakras, and reconnected her strongly with her Higher Self and Council of Angels. Her Council of Angels is the council which was there for her soul in the most loving way before her birth into this life on earth; this loving council briefed her on many aspects of the life into which she was going, including her life mission, and in the arrangement of her pre-birth contracts, and more. When she had her "Reconnection" (1), it connected her with us, her higher self and council of angels, in a very strong way, and began to awaken her memory of her mission and pre-birth contracts. We are not endorsing this or any other method, we simply are saying this is the avenue she chose to reconnect with her higher sources. As you begin to explore this, you will find the right avenues for you.

She also began connecting with other loving energy guides who assisted her in some energy techniques to reconnect her with the lost knowledge of her soul and her mission. You too can reconnect with all of your lost knowledge and mission, and with your higher self. We encourage you to find energy practices that align you with your highest good. When something resonates with you and feels good, then it is for your highest good. The way to discern is through your instincts and feelings. If you have a "good" feeling about it, then you are on the right path. If something does not "feel right" (or "sound right"), then do not follow that path, simply continue your search. This is also the way to discern which information on the internet is for your benefit and which is not. Simply tune into whether it rings true for you and whether it feels good; or if it does not, then look elsewhere. The philosophy of "take what you like and leave the rest" is a good one to follow, and to "follow your heart" and "trust your instincts". These are always good practices to follow. Each of you have within you your connection to your own truth, your own Higher Self, and your connection to Source. You are connected to these whether you are aware of it or not. It is simply your AWARENESS, as with all else, that will bring it to your attention, or not.

All of you have a true mission here, a spiritual mission, a galactic mission, that is of the greatest importance. You are ALL important and all a part of this shift into the Golden Age upon the New Earth. As your awareness and spiritual abilities begin to increase during these times of the accelerating influx of energies, you will all begin to naturally tune into your higher self. Truth and awareness always has a way of manifesting, in one way or another. You are all beginning to find your truth, connect to your higher selves, and connect to Source and to the loving uplifting energies of the higher dimensions. As we ascend into the higher dimensions, duality slips away, along with negativity and its derivatives. All dimensions are pathways to source ~ the 1st, 2nd, 3rd, dimensions are those of duality, the 4th dimension begins to transcend that duality…….leading up to the 5th, 6th, 7th, 8th, and beyond, into the 9th, 10, 11th, 12th, and finally *all that is*, you see these dimensions are like energy vortex waves leading back to source, all are emanations from the Source, and the closer to source, the closer to *love and light*, and the less negativity can exist…so as we lift our consciousness ever higher, we return to the realms of love and light from whence we came and to which we shall eventually return. Soon we will all be vibrating and pulsing in synchronized harmony with the higher dimensional frequencies which are now locking into mother earth's crystalline grid and beginning to emanate from her celestial body. You too are being elevated and aligned and synchronized and harmonized with these higher dimensional frequency energies, within which negativity cannot exist.

Connect with your higher self and Source daily, find energy and meditation techniques that resonate with you for your highest good, meditate upon your connection with your Higher Self, which is bathed in the love and light of the creator Source, this source of light and love from whence you came and to which we shall all return one day. Bathe in the light of love emanating from the higher dimensions of the angels as we lovingly surround you in our unconditional love and light.

We are the Council of Angels, Pleiadian Council, and Archangel Michael. We send you many blessings of love and light to surround you at this time and we support you most lovingly in finding and connecting to your inner light and truth." (Connecting with your Higher Self, The Golden Light Channel.com February 18, 2017)

Start your day by meditating for ten minutes after getting up and ask God for guidance from the silent voice within. It connects you to the energy of God. You might want to just take a short time every morning, before getting out of bed even, and spend a few minutes in silence with God and asking Him. Say, "God, there's nothing You and I together can't handle today." And we'll probably find more peacefulness in our life because we are moving more in His Will rather than doing the will of our ego. As a result, we will feel His loving energy emanating within ourselves. Otherwise, we are getting our ego bruised and damaged and it humiliates us.

Based on an excerpt from John;

"And you might also include in your prayer or meditation in the morning to thank the Holy Spirit for being in charge of your next twenty-four hours because when you ask the Holy Spirit to come in, you are a whole spirit. And that puts you into a more mature way of handling your life, when you're whole. And most people have grown up as wounded little children with their souls splintered from abuse. And so, when you see yourself as a whole person, no longer splintered and wounded from your childhood and other situations in your past, you've brought your pieces together to become whole. You tend to handle your life in more mature and productive ways. It does tend to go better as you're handling things in a way that would be the next right thing to do."

Section 1.2: Photon Energy

The reference Photon Belt has been mentioned extensively in channelings by the ascended masters Jesus, Archangel Michael, and Archangel Metatron, just to name a few. It is an energy of love and light that the Holy Spirit emanates from paradise, the home of the Creator, God. It is one thousand years of peace as depicted in the Bible. Although the actual duration of passing through the belt lasts a little more than two thousand years, it is the same thing. We are entering the age of love and light. It affects the entire galaxy, not just the planet Earth. Our galaxy is approaching the closest distance to paradise when we are entering the belt, which is a time similar to the era of Atlantis. That was thirteen thousand years ago when our galaxy was on the other side of the Isles of Paradise (see figure 3 for details).

* * * * *

DOUG: I've got an illustration showing the Photon Belt back in 1996 because you mentioned we had entered the belt something like twenty years ago.

JOHN: Yes, approximately.

DOUG: Then I have another illustration that shows the position of our universe thirteen thousand years ago as well as six other super universes circling around the center of creation.

JOHN: Right.

DOUG: Then I have another graph that shows 11,104 BC, which was thirteen thousand years ago.

JOHN: Yes, that's approximately right.

DOUG: Now it's going to really establish historical dates of our ice age, which likely began around 21,000 to 22,000 BC.

JOHN: Well, there have been several ice ages, and it is all part of the evolution of energy moving into a higher consciousness, so there's not been just one ice age.

DOUG: Because basically, a complete movement of galaxies around the Isle of Paradise takes twenty-five or twenty-six thousand years?

JOHN: Exactly. That's the Mayan calendar.

DOUG: The reason the Ice Age began, when you mentioned about twenty years ago that this solar system has entered the Photon Belt already?

JOHN: Yes, it has.

DOUG: So which part of the solar system entered the Photon Belt before the planet Earth did?

JOHN: Well, it's hard to describe. You have a whole unit of planets in the universe and galaxies, and as they revolved around the central sun and moved closer and closer to the Photon Belt, it depended on where the planets and universes were at their time of entry. They were rotating and evolving and would move around, and they were not in a permanent place, so the whole unit moved into the Photon Belt. That is probably a better answer rather than each one individually because they all moved around and were independent of one another, and it's more of a unit of energy moving into the Photon Belt rather than individual planets or universes.

DOUG: Now we have talked about a particular group of aliens called Arcturus?

JOHN: Yes.

DOUG: Which super universe are they in? Are they in the sixth or the seventh super universe?

JOHN: You see, you're starting to split hairs. What happens when you move from the fourth dimension? You move into being multidimensional, so most of the dimensions are interlacing with one another, and there isn't a definitive separation between the other dimensions. That's linear thinking. When you move into Christ consciousness, you might call it a sup of energy, and so therefore, it is a mixture of all the different dimensions occurring at one time. (Think about man-made time.). You're looking at it from a third-dimensional point of view, but when you leave the fourth dimension and go into the fifth dimension, you actually become more of a circle of experience. There is not really a past or a future. It's all happening at once, so it's not about which dimension they are in. They are part of one total consciousness of God, and different awarenesses bring you into that dimension. It's not like a linear ladder, but it's where your awareness is. Then you will connect with that consciousness.

DOUG: So this is something that scientists have not been able to understand?

JOHN: Well, scientists are making great gains and understanding better that science and spirituality are the same with different terms, but there is not a device or a technique invented at this point that can actually measure something invisible. So this is on the forefront of science. There was some testing and experimenting going on in England. Researchers at an English college thought it could demonstrate some kind of a device to measure spiritual matter, but it hasn't been accomplished yet.

DOUG: And then there is a line of—what do you call it—new universes in the making?

JOHN: Yes, there are new universes in the making.

DOUG: So has Earth ascended to the fifth dimension?

JOHN: At this time, yes.

DOUG: Now if people do not align their energy with earth energy, they will go elsewhere, right?

JOHN: Exactly.

Door to Glory

DOUG: Would Mars enter the Photon Belt while Earth is entering it? Would Mars be in the third dimension?

JOHN: Very good question. Um, they will be entering the Photon Belt too, yes.

DOUG: Did the war between Atlantis and Lemuria occur before or after the golden age?

JOHN: Well, I don't know what your definition of the golden age is.

DOUG: That's the Photon Belt.

JOHN: They were created during the Photon Belt, and as Atlantis left the Photon Belt, then it lost its energy—high energy—and the people started lowering their energy, separating themselves from the God source within.

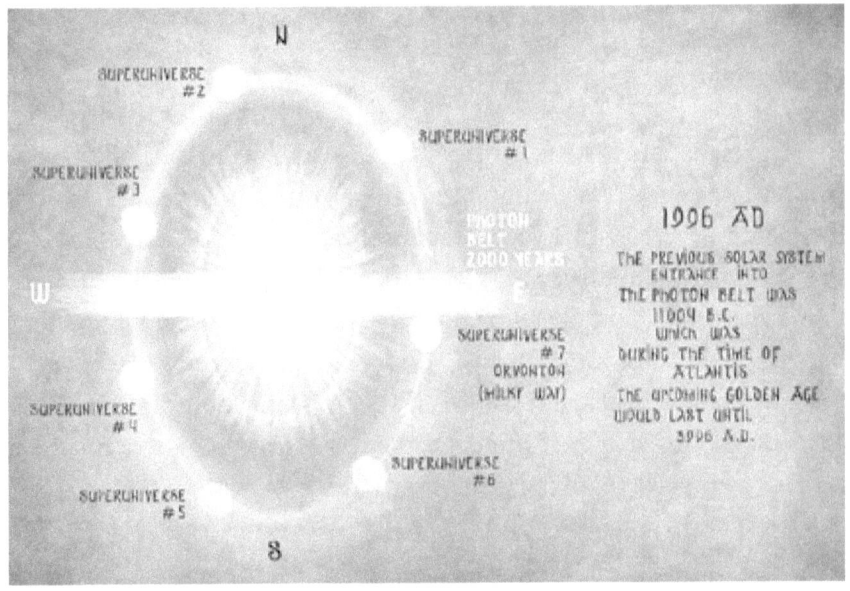

Figure 2—Location of Seven Super Universes Today

We reside in the Seventh Galaxy, or Seventh Super Universe, which is the youngest super universe of the latest line of galaxies in God's creation. We entered the Belt in 1996, according to John. The previous encounter was thirteen thousand years ago, when Atlantis was established, according to the Books of Atlantis. This book was taken to the library in Alexandria, Egypt before it was burned by the entities of the Dark Side.

The Books of Atlantis has provided a definitive time frame of its existence, giving credence to the Photon Belt theory and the Mayan calendar, as shown in Figures 2 & 3. Also, The Urantia Book (The Urantia Book 2015, paper 15) provided information about the existence of our galaxy and other galaxies before us. The books in the Old Testament of the Bible were likely developed during the time frame between 11,004 and 9,004 B.C.

* * * * *

DOUG: I have asked you about the Law of One (Ref. 1) and the Old Testaments of the Bible.

JOHN: Yes.

DOUG: Were the Old Testaments developed during the Golden Age?

JOHN: Yes, because the Law of One is the Law of Love or the Law of God, which is Love, and that's Lemuria, which was created in Love, and so that's the only law there is, and when people look at other places, they have left the Law of One and they've separated themselves from God and the only power that exists, and, therefore, they live in a fantasy or an illusion and have fear because as you leave love, you move into a fearful experience, so the Law of One is the truth and the reality of who we are, and any time a person chooses to focus differently, they have actually given away their power and moved out of the relationship they have with God the Father.

Door to Glory

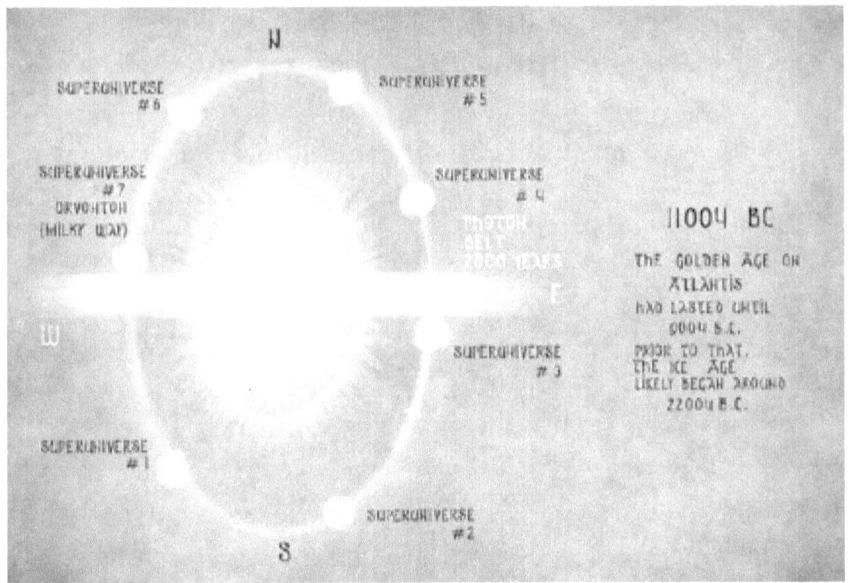

Figure 3—Location of Seven Super Universes in 11,004 BC

DOUG: Jesus taught that if you think anything negative, then you are following your ego. So too, if you were experiencing Christ consciousness, then you are only seeing the true reality, which is love.

JOHN: Exactly. That's exactly what it is all about. It's about seeing the love that's always been there, and that's the truth. So many distractions have obliterated or obscured that love and our journey on earth that it is hard to find those things that obscured the love so that we can move back into the Law of One.

* * * * *

There are great cycles in the cosmos that rule great events. One such is the cycle of the great zodiac age, which spans almost twenty-six thousand years around the Isle of Paradise. This span is the time it takes our planet's equatorial plane to completely regress one full cycle along the solar plane. The length of a zodiac age is from 1,986.37 to 2,291.28 years. The age of Pisces, which ended in 2012, was one of the shortest ages in the zodiac system. It began in AD 26, and it ended in 2012. In 1945, we entered the last degree of Pisces. Here are the ages and their durations.

Table 1: Astrological Breakdown of the Mayan Calendar

Zodiac System Based on Earth's Electromagnetic Composition	Years of Duration	Total Number of Years
Aries, Pisces, Libra, Virgo	1986.37 x 4	7545.48
Aquarius, Scorpio, Leo, Taurus	2129.04 x 4	8516.16
Capricorn, Sagittarius, Cancer, Gemini	2291.28 x 4	9165.12
	Total:	25226.76

The lengths are based on Earth's electromagnetic composition in astrological terms. The Mayan calendar consists of five stages of 5125.36 years. Mayan Great Year fell between the years 25,226.76 and 25,626.83 years. The Mayan Fourth World began in 3113 BC and ended in AD 2012. December 21, 2012, was heralded as a turning point, signaling the beginning of the end of the dark side's control.

* * * * *

DOUG: Now you mentioned before about the moving orbits of the planets. What do you mean by moving orbits?

JOHN: Well, Earth goes around the Sun, and the different planets go around the Sun at their particular velocity, so they have their own yearly calendar. And every so often you are going to have cycles where they make complete revolutions around the sun, and so it's a matter of where they are in the universe at that point in time. That's what astrology is about. It's about pinpointing those different times when the planet is in this particular place. You see, you have the signs of the zodiac, and as the planets move through those different signs, there's different messages and different understandings that go along with that. It's kind of like a map of what's going on in consciousness.

* * * * *

One major cycle is approximately twenty-five thousand years in the Mayan calendar. It is one trip around the Isles of Paradise, the center of creation. As we are entering the belt, we will see a transformation of how people relate with one another. The old third-dimensional strife will go away. The people who are contributing to existing conflicts and threats of war today are going to be removed from the planet and be displaced to another third-dimensional world elsewhere in a galaxy.

* * * * *

DOUG: Now that's not going to happen here on earth again because we have moved to the fifth dimension?

JOHN: The planet has moved into the fifth dimension, and we are raising our consciousness, not lowering it. Those who cannot move along, as you mentioned earlier, with that raising of consciousness will be transplanted to another consciousness that matches where they are. They will not even realize they have left the earth.

* * * * *

There are three cycles of this nature, during which those who have progressed may be harvested at the end of the three major cycles—that is, approximately between seventy-five and seventy-six thousand years. All are harvested regardless of their progress, for during that time the planet itself has moved through the useful part of that dimension and begun to cease being useful for the lower levels of vibration within that density. What this means is when we have attained higher consciousness spiritually above the consciousness of the planet, then we will likely either go elsewhere and help other civilizations or thrive in a higher state of love and light on another planet. More likely, people from higher civilizations will come here to assist us in growing higher in a new era of love and light.

* * * * *

DOUG: I got this time frame of twenty-five thousand year in a cycle from the Law of One (Ref. 1). Now do you recognize that major twenty-five-thousand-year cycle?

JOHN: That is a universal measurement of putting together a plan of energy changes, and the dark side has used that cycle to benefit their effort against humanity. Yes, that is the cycle.

* * * * *

Each astrology age has a theme, and the theme of the age of Pisces is Christianity. Both Pisces and Sagittarius are spiritual signs for higher meanings in life. The theme of the coming age of Aquarius is truth and brotherly union.

The most optimum age for this planet is Libra. The last such age had occurred approximately 11,004 BC. The age of Aquarius is an age when our solar system will be inside the Photon Belt. It occurs every thirteen thousand years. Our solar system receives the photonic energy for a period of more than 2,100 years. The last time this occurred was during the time of Atlantis, the previous golden age.

The golden age occurs when the solar system receives photon energy. It is a divine energy—what the Bible calls the Holy Spirit. It comes from the center of creation. This photon energy connects the planet and individuals to our divine source. It raises the vibratory level to the point where people transform into light beings. Or if they refuse to be transformed, then they will die and be moved to another planet.

Earth itself will be transformed and shine like a star as its inner central sun is finally fully turned on and becomes the new heaven on earth.

Our solar system began its entry into the belt around 1996. Earth's orbit has been fully affected since late 2012. This new energy powers everything on the planet. The old sources of energy, the dark energy of the third dimension, will no longer work.

During the upcoming millennium, everyone will work toward making this planet a paradise again. A great graduation is forthcoming for the souls who have achieved the status of light being. They will be given one hundred years to relive their lives and come to the truth. Another one thousand years of grace will come again when the Earth and the solar system enter the Photon Belt after a long night of 10,684 years. Nevertheless, the interior of the planet (inner earth) will remain a paradise.

Earth, including her inhabitants, will transform into a fifth-dimensional light body. Earth is a sentient being that is the physical manifestation of Gaia, shifting from a dense, material body to one of light (a star). However, the creation of this star is neither hot nor fiery. It is soft.

* * * * *

DOUG: Is there any more reincarnation after a person attains the fifth dimension?

JOHN: Well, that's an interesting question. It's not called reincarnation as you move into the fifth dimension. You still are growing spiritually, but you do not have to be part of the birth cycle when it comes to moving from the third into the fourth and fifth dimensions anymore. You have—so to speak—graduated out of that process of growing into higher and higher consciousness in the fifth dimension, so in that sense, there's no more reincarnation. However, the energy and the spiritual essence of who you are can come and go from the planet into other parts of the cosmos, and you are free to leave the planet Earth because you are no longer tethered to it through your fears. You've released all your connections, and so your spirit is free to move. So you do not have to reincarnate. You have moved out of the third dimension.

DOUG: So we have to attain the fifth dimension to be able to help others?

JOHN: Well, if you don't, you're still passing on your fear to them. See, what's inside of you is what you project out around you, so the more you open your heart and project love out to those around you, the more you create that loving fifth dimension. So it's a matter of releasing every obstacle and the fearful energy that you haven't yet released or transformed into love. The more you do that, the more you are in the fifth dimension. Then you're actually giving people the loving, caring support that they desire. Otherwise, you're just passing on your old—as you call them—demons.

* * * * *

Earth has made its transition to a new planetary alignment, securing itself in the fifth dimension. Most of us might not notice it, and we may continue with our third-dimensional lives as though nothing has happened.

For instance, every individual has a love of God which is best described by the Bible as the fruit of the Spirit, "But the fruit of the Spirit is love, joy, peace, longsuffering, gentleness, goodness, faith, meekness, temperance: against such, there is no law." On the other hand, the ego takes us away from our oneness from our divine nature. Overcoming our ego is what brings us to the fifth-dimension and experience Heaven on Earth. We will all eventually find love from God that provides the fruit of the spirit when we find Him. It just may take more time for some people. By providing love and forgiveness with one another, we can help foster the spiritual growth of our fellow man.

Maintaining third-dimensional habits will create trauma for us because the structures from this dimension will eventually disintegrate. The changing of the guard will leave us bewildered because people are slowly changing their old ways. You will notice more high-minded people as they become more loving and less controlling.

Money and finances no longer support your livelihood like before. Relationships no longer provide the security and support they once did. Our physical bodies are exhausted and feel like they have had enough. Yes, indeed, it is time to let go and embrace our new reality.

We might seem a little bewildered by the existence of the fifth dimension. Primarily, the most important difference between the third- and the fifth-dimensional realities is how we perceive them. Time and space are fixed facts in the third dimension. In the fifth dimension, they are fluid and are understood to be largely illusionary. It is the state of love in our consciousness (Christ consciousness) that takes away the uncertainties of life because we feel God within ourselves.

The *eternal now* is the fifth dimension. It is present, not past or future. It means that what we feel and experience in the present moment is the only intrinsically relevant experience. Maintaining the eternal now puts our state of mind in the present. Our present requirements are all that we need for the moment. The past and future have no relevance as such. What we create and experience for the now moment implies a huge philosophical shift from our past thinking. This movement attunes us with our guiding angels because they are our companions.

At last, many of us are here on the first level of the fifth dimension. We have released and purged so much over the last nine or ten years that we are holding considerably more light energy than ever before. We can manifest instantaneously with these new Fifth Dimension energies and may feel a bit uncomfortable until we absorb the complete transition. We slowly are becoming transparent. We are shifting into a new stage. Our intuition is our guiding force because it sees the coming change before we consciously embrace it. We will have strong desires to create small and higher-level communities and relationships, and when others are ready and willing, they will come on our own. These new sacred spaces will have higher connections with the stars as well as with spiritual beings as we ascend to their level.

We will establish stronger connections to the earth, to nature, and to animals. We will be able to communicate with them telepathically.

Once we understand these principles, we can move forward in the unfolding of the creative now moment. Understand that our reality will seem to move quicker because our vibration is now higher. Events will unfold rapidly. Things will change quickly. We will need to be fluid and flexible and open to rapid changes. We will have to absolutely trust that our higher selves in tandem with our spirits know what we need and where to take us, and then we can follow this unfolding with confidence and trust.

Finally, we will need to be in touch with our creative passion within our own energy. It is the only thing that will move us forward at this time. Otherwise, we will languish in the old dimension. In the fifth dimension, we will no longer moved forward in the career and work that once supported us. Now it is the energy and movement of our creative passion that will take us forward. Are we willing to let go of the old structures and move into the flow of new creations and new realities? The extent to which we hold onto old structures will exactly correlate to the extent of the anxiety and stress that we will feel. When we connect with the flow of creative passion, we will move forward in our own creative unfolding. This is the real essence of the multidimensional experience of who we are, and that is the gift of our new fifth-dimensional planet.

The third dimension's reality is dying. This death involves letting go of everything we know, including our money system, corporations, jobs, world powers, and daily living. This changeover creates fear and stress as well as an intense release. We are either leaving the planet, trapped in our fear in the third dimension, or continuing into the higher realms of the fifth dimension. When we choose to surrender and allow the new process to move through us, we immediately connect with those who give us comfort as we attempt to move toward a new reality in a unique place. At first, we may not know where we are and may begin to feel mystified. When a manifestation comes into our awareness, then it brings us clarity and comfort. After a while, we regain our bearings and are then able to progress in a new way with self-assurance, a divine connection, and a new lease of life. We are now fully residing in a higher dimension since many of us have completed our journey through the tunnel of death and are on the other side of this current energy phase. Many find themselves reconnecting with friends and loved ones and reestablishing other connections. We can find some anchor to hold on to while we seemingly exist in the emptiness. The new leaders and teachers, such as the ascended masters, embrace the entire planet in oneness. This transition is an important part of the process. If we have not yet had this experience in the physical, we may have it during our dreams. Reconnecting with the forgotten light of the divine and nurturing ourselves with energies make us feel good again, and this action includes the first stage of the reconnection process of our new existence in the higher realms of consciousness. Falling away from third-dimensional values will connect us to others with a higher energy of love and compassion, which always prevails. It brings all of us to our next evolutionary stage as well. We are in the dimension we wish, and love and feeling loved will indeed accelerate our spiritual aspirations.

* * * * *

DOUG: I guess when you get to a certain level, you can come back to earth to help out. At what spiritual vibration would you have to be at—like the eighth dimension? —to be able to come in through society and then come out?

JOHN: Well, the fifth dimension and above allows for that to happen in different ways. As people move into that higher dimension through what you call dying, they pass over into the spiritual realm (other side), and they can come back and be guides with their family and friends. If they are of a higher consciousness than fifth dimension, they can also appear in the dreams of the people they are intended to give information to. As they go into higher dimensions, they can come back and actually be spiritual teachers. Mahavatar Babaji has been on earth as a teacher, and for thousands of years, he has stayed a beacon of light for those trying to find their spiritual path. So there are different ways that those people—or I should say spirit entities—can come back and help the people on earth, and there are different degrees of their help.

* * * * *

While most are leaving the third and entering the fourth dimension, a selected few have found the second level of the fifth dimension. These are our new teachers. We are entering the stage where we will be connecting much more fully with our brothers and sisters, our children and neighbors, and new teachers as well as our loved ones. The unmanageable earth will change, and a change in living conditions is creating the need for unity. There has been a severe lack of unity on earth for thousands of years, and our planet is about to complete the process of a divine, necessary change. Going it alone, taking care of yourself only, and doing it all are now passé ideas. We need unity to exist in the higher realms. All is in divine and perfect order.

Because people are crying out for unity, which currently exists with the new fourth- and fifth-dimension energies, it can feel downright unbearable when it does not manifest in the desired form. Our intuition senses these new energies right now with the help of our spiritual guides. When the outside manifestations do not match the inside vibrations, you can feel sick inside. Then we are not in coherence with our environment. We are still connecting to the last stage of the third dimension, and we fear letting go. Not matching our outside reality with our inner processing always been one of the challenges of the ascension process. Our old life is dropping away as the vibration of society as a whole changes. Depression and frustration can result, but these are only temporary. The vibrations that we reconnect to will be different from the vibrations we have connected to before. Because we are vibrating higher, we will attract many more pleasant, healing, and incredible experiences. In addition, we are greatly encouraged to connect with one another. Open yourself up to infinite possibilities, and allow yourself to join others in learning, accessing, and using the new fifth-dimensional energies. Dare to step into the void, venture beyond traditional boundaries, and open the door to your greatest possibilities. As 2012 approaches, we are witnessing the spontaneous healing of disease, instant connections with everyone and everything, and time travel. We can now manifest our future the way we desire. Through the power of thought or conscious creation, we all are claiming and becoming one with our real heritage within the universe.

* * * * *

DOUG: So is that kind of like an out-of-body experience? Can you go anywhere in space?

JOHN: When you have released all of your attachments to the third dimension, you are free spiritually to move around the universe in any direction and way that is suitable for you. You are no longer attached with any tethers to the planet. This is what the masters have accomplished.

DOUG: What is the minimum vibrational level for either the fifth dimension or the eighth dimension, where you have the ability to change form, when you go to a different planet?

JOHN: Well, that is multidimensional, and that is when people ascend into the fifth dimension. That is the beginning of learning the necessary information to ascend into the multidimensional form. The lessons you learn in the fifth dimension are about how to organize your energy.

DOUG: So the first step is to find God within?

JOHN: Exactly. When you do that, the door is open.

* * * * *

When John the Baptist baptized Jesus in AD 29, Jesus ascended to the fifth dimension. He had the ability to disappear out into space with this newfound power. "As he was formulating this decision, Jesus was seated under the shade of a tree on an overhanging ledge of rock with a precipice right there before him. He fully realized that he could cast himself off the ledge and out into space, and that nothing could happen to harm him provided he would rescind his first great decision not to invoke the interposition of his celestial intelligences in the prosecution of his lifework on Urantia (Earth), and provided he would abrogate his second decision concerning his attitude toward self-preservation" (The Urantia Book 2015, Paper 136:7.1)

"Jesus knew his fellow countrymen were expecting a Messiah who would be above natural law. Well had he been taught that Scripture: "There shall no evil befall you, neither shall any plague come near your dwelling. For he shall give his angels charge over you, to keep you in all your ways. They shall bear you up in their hands lest you dash your foot against a stone." Would this sort of presumption, this defiance of his Father's laws of gravity, be justified in order to protect himself from possible harm or, perchance, to win the confidence of his mistaught and distracted people? But such a course, however gratifying to the sign-seeking Jews, would be, not a revelation of his Father, but a questionable trifling with the established laws of the universe of universes." (The Urantia Book 2015, Paper 136:7.2)

Jesus revealed the ascension to the fifth dimension. Prior to his baptism, his spiritual vibration was at the highest level of the fourth dimension, and he was going into the fifth dimension. Jesus could have gone on to the fifth dimension, but he chose instead to return to the third dimension for this particular mission. He was of the highest suboctave of the vibration of love (Ref. 1). Many people will become aware of the fifth-dimensional energies and the desire to begin their ascension to the higher vibrational levels (similar to what Jesus did more than two thousand years ago). His mission taught us the way to get there. "Follow me," he said. As we enter into the new dimension, we must remember that the key to survival is to rise above it, access the higher energies, and walk the planet, unaffected by the events occurring. We experience all of this while healing others and welcoming the unity of all during one thousand years of peace.

* * * * *

DOUG: Is it true that Jesus knew the dark side had too much control at the time for him to help people ascend to the fifth dimension two thousand years ago?

JOHN: Well, he knew that this was planned long before he was born. The Essenes was a sect of spiritual people who presented the pathway to allow his birth to happen. So there were many generations prior to him that had to occur for his mother (Mary) to be that pure soul—and therefore, his grandmother (Anna) a pure soul—so that he could come, and it was time to restore the love that's described in the Bible. He seemed to present and apply this love so people could see it. But it was distorted by people of different religions. However, he knew that his coming was necessary and that there were avatars that had some before him. But they weren't as well-known, and society wasn't ready for them. His particular advent on earth came during a time when people would be able to at least hear the Word even if they didn't understand it. The timing was everything. He was just the channel to bring the message of love.

DOUG: I'm going to get back to one question. When Jesus said, "Follow me," did he mean follow him to the fifth dimension?

JOHN: Yes, he wanted people to follow his example of living with unconditional love and forgiveness for those who were not able to handle situations, love, compassion, and forgiveness. As we are coming into an agreement in energy, so our energies come together as one.

DOUG: What is your advice for mortals to achieve heavenly status?

JOHN: What a wonderful question! To achieve heavenly status—how marvelous! That just tickles me to death. You must be as caring and kind to yourself and others, knowing that we are all God and we are all love. What we do for others, we are really doing for ourselves. We must extend love to those people. That makes the whole loving environment grow for all of us. It makes the world better for everyone not to hold anything back but to be as giving and caring as possible.

DOUG: We are heading in that direction?

JOHN: That's what Christ consciousness is all about. Many people will awaken more and more and find that our friends, neighbors, associates, or like-minded people will be coming from our circles.

DOUG: And that's the fifth dimension?

JOHN: That's the fifth dimension.

DOUG: And how long do you think it will be? Twenty years? Fifty years? Or a hundred years?

JOHN: Well, it's going to be around eighteen to twenty years before we are experiencing it on a regularly acknowledged basis. It's going to take time for us to adjust the laws and to take things away that are no longer necessary because we have moved into a new realm. So there will be a dismantling phase.

DOUG: So it's taking place right now?

JOHN: Oh, definitely. It's just not in the appearance. It's not in the news. The dark side still owns the news. Gradually, the news will offer more positive information and more truthful accounts of what's going on, acknowledging the fact that things are not what we've been told. So we are going to dismantle the old.

* * * * *

There is so much more to understand, engage with, and use for ourselves as we ascend to each new stage. All of us can unite and begin to break the limitations of whatever we imagined possible for humanity. Open yourself up, start a meditation practice, and pursue some new information. Walk away from fear, and readjust your belief system so that you remain open to the unknown and the reality of the fifth dimension.

* * * * *

DOUG: So what dimension would an entity be in if he or she has found God through meditation. Would that be the fifth dimension?

JOHN: Well, it's a little more complicated than that, Doug. Even though you have found God within, the consciousness still needs to change. A person can meditate but still harbor anger. Mediation just means you have removed the blocks from your connection to God. It doesn't mean they have disappeared and left. So if you still have leftover emotional baggage to remove, that would determine how much you can ascend into the purest forms of Christ consciousness.

DOUG: Could a self-realization fellowship be a good source to learn meditation?

JOHN: I would suggest someone like Edgar Cayce's study groups personally. From what I'm seeing Marilyn doing, you would like to have somebody with as clear and pure information as possible, and so a study group or *A Course in Miracles*, a study group with Abraham, who's channeled by Esther Hicks, or a study group through The Edgar Cayce Association called "Search for God" study groups. Those have a more pure basis to work from.

DOUG: Is it true that all of the planets will actually reach the eighth dimension?

JOHN: Yes, everything in the universe is growing emotionally and spiritually into higher dimensions. It's just a matter of time. In the right timing, it is going to evolve into higher dimensions.

DOUG: Is the eighth dimension the highest dimension?

JOHN: No, it is not the highest dimension. Because life is eternal, it is ever-expanding, and so the dimensions will increase as the consciousness increases.

* * * * *

The fifth dimension will bring us a new reality. However, it may not appear that way because those around us will live their lives with the old reality. Our exhaustion, anxiety, and lack of support may be the result of the constant shift of perspectives. Take solace that our inner being is our best friend, full of love and understanding. The process takes time. It is a battle between the energies of our ego (third dimension) and our soul (fifth dimension). This battle is either won or lost by the power of our choice. The Bible makes reference to the war in heaven.

* * * * *

DOUG: Like the Bible mentioned, there was war in heaven.

JOHN: Well, that's symbolic. Trying to put spiritual terms into earthly language can be difficult. Whenever there is dissension, it could be called a war, but there was not a war with bombs and bullets and armies. There's not that kind of a war in heaven. There could be a dissension. People may have different ideas. This was the case with the energy on earth. Instead of continuing to be in oneness as it was created at the time of Atlantis, some people decided, "Well, gosh, why don't we start taking charge and telling people what to think?" This was how they began pulling people away from listening to God and instead making others listen to their new leaders. So this dissension could be called a war in heaven, but it was a dissension. It was a decision to not join with God's forces.

* * * * *

Your heaven is your soul. It is your state of consciousness. Your state is either hellish or heavenly. In the hellish state, you will find it difficult to cope with life. Nothing seems to work anymore. You feel unsupported and abandoned in many cases. You are exhausted and anxious, and you feel as though you cannot go on anymore. You have the power to change that. It is up to you to start living the truth and the reality of the fifth dimension.

* * * * *

DOUG: The Holy Spirit is received to fulfill the Holy Trinity and the seven candles of the candlestick which are the seven chakras. Is that true? When you receive the Holy Spirit, then does it which means you have the Holy Trinity?

JOHN: Yes. I mentioned that earlier, that the Mother, the Father, and the Son are the Holy Trinity. All those parts are within you. You have a mature energy in you that is negative, a mature energy that is positive, and childlike innocence. And when they say to be like a child to enter the kingdom of heaven, they're talking about the releasing of all those fears and energies and worries that are negative. So you are cleansed. And so the Trinity is the spirit of God that is within you and is pure love. But it's the different parts. You know, there's only one spirit, but from the Third Dimension, people, to understand the different segments of that spirit, they give it a label. And Father, Mother, and Son are assigned to parts of the whole spirit.

* * * * *

"Verily I say unto you, except ye be converted, and become as little children, ye shall not enter into the kingdom of heaven. Whosoever, therefore, shall humble himself as this little child, the same is greatest in the kingdom of heaven" (Matthew 18:3-4). Male and female bodies are only symbols of male and female energies. The male energy corresponds to positive energy or the father aspect. The female energy corresponds to negative—negative polarity, not negative as in bad—or the mother aspect. All things that manifest are created by male and female energies, and the process of marriage or union unites all of these energies. All things in the universe are either positively or negatively charged, and they are influenced more by either the positive or negative energies that are either male or female. The positive or negative energies exist in everything from a subatomic particle to an atom, a human being, a planet, or a galaxy. Everything is either male or female. There is nothing that is 100 percent neutral except for the energy of purpose. All male and female energies in the universe are seeking stability or neutrality. In other words, they try to return to the power of purpose. The prodigal son is trying to return to his father. This stability (or performance) is always reached through marriage. Thus, marriage is a universal principle used to unite all male and female energies. To create balance, we must understand the purpose of the two energies. The male is radiant and action-oriented, sending energy. The female is magnetic and attractive, receiving energy.

The third component of the Holy Trinity, according to John, is a childlike innocence, the Son. You cannot enter the kingdom of God with fear. The emotional attachments of the third dimension are fears. The old third-dimension reality is dying, so we must let go of everything we know, including our money system, corporations, jobs, world powers, and daily living.

* * * * *

DOUG: So is the dark side the Devil?

JOHN: Well, what churches call the Devil is the dark side, but the Devil is only another term for your fear inside of you. You let fear be your guide instead of God. Remember Flip Wilson, the comedian who said the Devil made me do it? Well, you know that's what churches would make people believe, but you always have a choice. It is a choice between listening to your ego and listening to God. That's what you're on earth for, which is the premise of everybody being on earth. "Am

I going to choose God instead of choose my fearful energy, which is trying to tell me to run away because I'm afraid? I don't have any courage. I don't know how to stand up and be assertive. I don't know how to talk out and say my truths." So are you going to turn to God and be honest and truthful with yourself, or are you going to let your ego run your life?

DOUG: That's what keeps souls from getting to the other side?

JOHN: Yes.

DOUG: It's a lack of love.

JOHN: The lack of love, the lack of light, the lack of truth.

DOUG: But the key is love. Love conquers everything?

JOHN: Exactly. It even melts karma.

DOUG: How many levels are there? Are there twelve levels of spiritual growth?

JOHN: Well, even more than that. But most people, when they get up that high, basically, there are no levels. People use human terms to try to understand the gradual process. You might even call it a ladder. The progressive energies go higher and higher in vibrations. They go up to forty octaves before you come to the God source. So there are levels upon levels upon levels. And yes, people have identified them with third-dimensional terms.

DOUG: So what would the light in life be?

JOHN: Okay, those are terms for God. God is your life. That's the Spirit within you. Your life is the God within. That's the energy. The light is also another term for the Spirit. That's the energy within, but you have to be open to letting the light shine. Fears cover the light with darkness. Marilyn has written an article that explains all of this. The more you release the fear, anger, guilt, and shame, the more your light can shine. Then people will see you glowing so that light is inside of you. Are you going to be able to express it, share it, and give it away?

* * * * *

As worlds advance in the settled status of light and life, societies become peaceful. Human beings are still mortals, as they continue to breathe, eat, sleep, and drink. The physical evolution of man continues.

During this era schools will vastly improve and become devoted to the training of the mind and the expansion of the soul. In this time the art centers are beautiful, and the musical organizations are terrific. The temples of worship with their associated schools of philosophy and experiential religion are creations of beauty and magnificence. The necessities for competitive play, humor, and other phases of personal and group achievement are ample and fitting. The competitive activities of such a highly cultured world are rooted in efforts to help individuals excel in the sciences and philosophies of cosmology. Literature and oratory flourish, and languages are improved. Life is pleasingly straightforward. At last, man coordinates a high state of mechanical development with an inspiring achievement. The search for happiness is an experience of joy and satisfaction.

* * * * *

DOUG: Now Satan was supposed to be put away for a thousand years.

JOHN: Satan will be bound means—

DOUG: That means his door will be closed?

JOHN: Well, there is no Satan. It's your negative emotions, which people call the Devil or Satan. And those negative emotions, like when you are reacting from fear, they are another way of saying that's Satan or the devil. But it's your reaction to fear that's keeping you a victim. Because in reality, you're never a victim. God gives you all the courage you need to handle anything that you need to desire and treat in your life with confidence. So you have given away your power by reacting. So anytime that you're in anxiety or sick or whatever, those are times when, so to speak, you're letting the lower energies run your life. Instead of responding to God's love, you're reacting to lower, denser, fear-based energy. And so that's what Jesus said, "Satan, get thee behind me." He was releasing all the last of the fears, worries, and guilt and shames that as a human being happened in his life that needed to be detached and released. You see, they say, we're going to have longer than one thousand years of peace. That's a poetic term for Heaven on Earth. There will be no negative energy, and that's why it will be called heaven. No people will be hurt or harmed. Everybody will be working together for the good of all. All there is will be prosperity and abundance. Everything will fall together in harmony and balance and meet your needs. There will be no less, no loss, no lack, and no limitations.

DOUG: So the daily bread (God's blessing) makes that happen?

JOHN: You got it.

DOUG: At work I've been sharing these findings with people. There are two gentlemen who were more open, and there were two other gentlemen of the Bible. I saw that the two gentleman understood my findings, whereas the two other gentleman would only open up a little bit. It seemed to me they might have talked about my assertions with their church, and that probably limited their belief in spiritual values. Now how would those people change? I can see it is very difficult to get across the spiritual message?

JOHN: Well, this is one of the things not to proselytize. You see, Jesus didn't go around proselytizing. People followed him. He did not go out and sell tickets to a theater and say, "Come hear me speak Saturday night," and then worry about how much money he was going to make to cover all the bills. They gathered together in groups and homes and on mountaintops. It was never about preaching for people to change. It was about sharing the message. There's a different motivation. So when the apostles went out to start their churches, it was to share the message, and as the news grew, people were attracted to the message. That's your biggest concern. When you find like-minded people who are interested, say, "Well, let's start a spiritual study group and share what we're learning." I would suggest that for the two fellows, and if you want to include the other people, they could come and check it out. You might want to look into starting a spiritual study group called "Search for God." Edgar Cayce wrote two excellent books that come straight from the source. They go through all the necessary things that we are talking about as far as what is necessary to move into that heaven on earth. Regarding how you need to grow spiritually, each chapter takes you into a higher consciousness of growing yourself into this space you are trying to achieve in your life. You can go through the first and second volumes, and you can repeat going through these because each time you read them, you're at a new place in your growth. There's a little procedure you follow on a weekly basis. As you meet, you go through a little routine that starts with a prayer, and then you read a Bible verse and discuss it. You have an spiritual exercise that you practice that week, and then you share with your friends how it went. You read the *Search for God* book, and it explains more about changing your soul. It is an easier to read this book than the Urantia book, which also has practices for spiritual growth. It is a treasured study group, and you might find that this would be a way to grow with like-minded friends.

DOUG: Specifically, what is doing the will of God?

JOHN: The will of God is to send love to your vehicle, which you might call a conduit. Open your heart, and let the love flow through you and out to all those around you so that you can create heaven on earth. So the will of God is the first two commandments of Jesus. Love God with all your heart, mind, and soul. You have to love yourself to be able to open your heart to send out his love to others, and then you must love your neighbor as yourself. That is the will of God.

DOUG: Now how about knocking on God's door within? Is that doing the will of God?

JOHN: Seeking God within is the will of God because it's seeking the kingdom of God. The results will come to you. God is reality, so when you're seeking God, you're seeking truth. Everything else is an illusion.

DOUG: I found a passage from the Bible that perfectly addresses this. "There is no fear in love. A perfect love casteth out fear; for fear hath painfulness; and he that feareth is not perfect for love" (1 John 4:18).

JOHN: Well, that is a very excellent passage. It is one of my favorites because it does tell people about what I just explained. The fear is the darkness, and when you move into the light of God, it dispels the darkness. It fades away. It is not real. That illusionary aspect of the influence of the fear leaves. So yes, it is a choice to move into love, which is the reality of who you are, and to leave that fear behind. And there are many methods and various processes that are here to assist you. Marilyn's next book has step-by-step details about doing that. She helps others do this with hypnosis. Moving everybody into the love of who they truly are releases the fear. I think people should be more aware of this wise comment because it is a choice. And when they realize that they can move into the happier, healthy, loving environment of heaven on earth, there's no reason to stay in the discomfort of what they've been living.

DOUG: I might make this a slogan for my book.

JOHN: Well, I think that would be admirable. And when they realize that they can move into the happier, healthy, loving environment of heaven on earth, there's no reason to stay in the discomfort of what they've been living.

DOUG: Is it true that the application of the Law of One is in the Old Testament?

JOHN: Yes, it is. The Old Testament was written in code because the people of the times did not have precise information and knowledge and understanding about vibrations, energy, and how consciousness worked. These are all terms that they could not fathom and understand. So when they used the word Lord in the Old Testament, they're talking about the Law of One. "The Lord be with you" is referring to the law of love, the law of oneness. So the word *Lord* would be a good substitute for that.

DOUG: That's like Deuteronomy 4:29. That's like "loving God with all thy heart and all thy soul." So that is the oneness?

JOHN: Yes, that's when you return to being part of the energy force that is the creation.

* * * * *

The third dimension is a physical reality of the conscious being. It is where energy hardens into a dark, dense pool of matter. The densest level of this plane contains our own more worldly and material thoughts. This type of energy does not flow through your seven chakras. This action would inhibit love from emerging from your soul.

Because of our planetary coding, we can identify with matter, and therefore, we can become dense ourselves. The universe allows for the illusion of free will on the third and fourth Dimensions, which gives us the experience of acting like saints or demons or somewhere in between by choice.

Beings believe that the third is the only dimension agonizing over the illusion of separation from their Spirit. The physical senses (ego) cannot detect Spirit, which is beyond form. If we are not one with Spirit, then we cannot be at one with others. This dimension of thought can interpenetrate all of life. It's like a sort of etheric river of water. It does apply to the brain, which acts more as a kind of telephone switching station to all the thoughts that pass through it. Our ability to experience beauty while in such a dimension shows that we live in a loving universe.

Section 1.3 Twelfth Dimension in Havona

There is a Great Assembly or Angelic Presence that has watched over this world since the beginning of time. They are God in the Bible. It is the prerogative of the Angelic Presence to lead our world on the path to the fifth dimension and up to the twelfth dimension.

While the Universal Father rules His vast creation of trillions of planets, He entrusted the administrative affairs of our local world to His Creator Son, Jesus. "The plans, policies and administrative acts of the local universe are formed and executed by this Son, who, in conjunction with his Spirit associate, delegates executive power to Gabriel and jurisdictional authority to the Constellation Fathers, System Sovereigns, and Planetary Princes" (The Urantia Book 2015, Paper 33:0.1).

Jesus "fully represents and embodies the personality presence of the Universal Father to and in this local universe. He even represents the Father-Son. These relationships constitute a Creator Son the most powerful, versatile, and influential of all divine beings who are capable of direct administration of evolutionary universes and personality contact with immature creature beings" (The Urantia Book 2015, Paper 33:1.2).

Jesus and Michael are the same as depicted in the Bible. "And at that time shall Michael stand up, the great prince ..." (Daniel 12:1). Jesus had taken on many missions in physical presence to foster his teaching of love. Love is his answer to raising our spiritual vibration from the "shadow of death" to the upcoming era of Love and Light.

The administration has selected key individuals to play parts of their agendas to guide people on the right course toward the path of liberation. They choose certain prophets and mediums to write the Bibles. Both Marilyn and I were selected for this book, and John provides the information.

* * * * *

JOHN: I want to applaud your efforts. I want you to know that you are surrounded by your guides and masters that are helping you to write this, that you open up to their energy and …

DOUG: Thank you.

JOHN: Yes, just let it flow out, just let it … God's will is comfortable. It just flows, and it's in harmony, and it's just very peaceful, so just let it come out. You're doing a great job. You've got a lot of special help and a lot of spiritual help. Just be open and receptive, and it will be a real big success.

DOUG: Thank you so much again. I feel so blessed to be doing this work.

JOHN: You have been chosen, and you have followed through and listened to the messages, and you are to be commended. It takes great courage to step out and speak and do the things that you're promoting in your book. We all want you to know that on the spiritual side you are being applauded and cheered, and they're thrilled with you.

* * * * *

Jesus is our Creator Son, and he leads the administration: "And he showed me a pure river of water of life, clear as crystal, proceeding out of the throne of God, and of the Lamb" (Revelation 22:1).

Jesus and the ascended masters are on the other side of the physical world. The physical city of Jerusalem is a metaphor for heaven. The spiritual side of Jerusalem is Jerusem. It is invisible to the naked eye.

Only certain individuals can see their presences with the third-eye. They also have physical presences inside the earth, where many of them live in the Himalayas region. Many of the Atlanteans reside there as well as in many other areas.

The kingdom of God is on the other side. It is invisible. Our guardian angels and Ascended Masters are always with us, but we don't see them. Jesus proclaimed, "Teaching them to observe all things, whatsoever I have commanded you: and lo, I am with you always, until the end of the world, Amen" (Matthew 28:20).

* * * * *

DOUG: What dimension does the earth need to be before the ascended masters like you could dwell on it?

JOHN: Some are here in the land right now. Some are around people who are growing. They remain invisible for them as guides, helping them with their choices, and it's giving them information for their spiritual growth. Your masters are. They're invisible, and they're also with you on earth at this point. There are more teachers on the planet now than ever have been. We are at a new place where the earth is changing and transforming this new energy. More masters are helping more people than ever before to open up and find the answers within and become awake. So the masters can be in the Himalayas—some of them live in that area—and some of them are in South America. Some of them are right in your community.

DOUG: Now I read somewhere that like the twenty-four elders, they are located on the planet of Saturn at the eighth dimension.

JOHN: Are you talking about the ascended masters when you say elders?

DOUG: Right. But we can't see them?

JOHN: The masters are in a variety of different dimensions,

depending on, again, their spiritual ascension or growth into higher consciousness. So, some masters are on earth right now and have a physical form, but the teachers have moved on closer to the eighth and ninth dimensions because they have already assumed the Christ consciousness and are moving beyond that. Most of them have a very deep and practical understanding of the spiritual knowledge.

DOUG: What location in space would they be? Would they be nirvana, or would they be somewhere in space?

JOHN: Now that is a fascinating question because some of them live in Tibet in the mountains. Some of them live in other parts of the planet and come and go as they choose. They can come and go out of physical form and return to the spirit and then come back into physical form as they wish.

DOUG: Interesting.

JOHN: So, some are ... Well, we have Mahavatar Babaji living thousands of years on earth as a master and a spiritually high-evolved person who has come to save, keep the light on the planet for our growth, and come to save and agreed to be the anchor that keeps the light on the planet for our growth. So some come and go as they are needed.

St. Germaine was on the planet many, many times. At one point, for 400 years he looked like a young man. He was there at the beginning of the American United States as you know it today. He helped write the Constitution and the Bill of Rights, and he was there to make sure that those documents were signed and put into the public domain as the laws of the land. This country was supposed to be a land of freedom, and that is part of his focus—to develop America into this free country that is the leadership of the world for releasing the old and becoming the newer consciousness. So you see, sometimes they are living where you might not expect them. Some of them do not make themselves well known and stay more oblivious. We have

Marilyn being out of the limelight for a very good reason: she can do better work if she is not having what you might call paparazzi or a lot of people around so she can handle the necessary details of her work. You see that they can be in spirit, and many do stay spiritually around the students that they are mentoring, and many are physically alive on the planet. Many people go to their ashrams or wherever they are located to learn and be at their feet.

* * * * *

The upcoming Golden Age that is set to begin in 2026 AD will raise the spiritual vibration of the populace for the next 2,000 years. The Angelic Administration has set the target for the seventh dimension by the time it ends around approximately 4026 AD. By that time, we all will have returned to our original birthrights as light beings.

* * * * *

DOUG: So, it's a domino effect. When more people realize God consciousness, then we influence each other. Can reincarnation still be in play during that era?

JOHN: Yes, because you are spiritually continuing to grow. The levels of consciousness do not come to an end as Jacob's ladder does not come to an end, and we have eternal spiritual energy.

DOUG: So, the fifth dimension?

JOHN: Eventually you move into the sixth and seventh and eighth dimensions.

DOUG: Really?

JOHN: Yes, and they keep going up. It is just a plateau. Heaven on Earth right now, the earth is coming into a plateau of peace in the land, which was created so we can then move on to higher realms.

* * * * *

DOUG: Is it true that ring of seven super universes could one day engulf Havona (Paradise of God)? Like right now there are developing universes moving along a circle outside our space path. Could it be true that the other six super universes are waiting for us to ascend so that we all can join God the Father in Havona?

JOHN: Yes, they're helping us and assisting us on planet Earth at this time so everything can ascend, yes.

DOUG: OK, because you have mentioned earlier that our dimension will continue to grow from eight to nine to ten to eleven. That's while we are in Havona, right?

JOHN: Yes.

* * * * *

There are billions of planets in Paradise (Havona) as shown in Figure 1. It was said that our local universe had existed for over 13.5 billion years (www.space.com, Ref. 40) since the Big Bang, and it is one of the youngest universes in God's creation. It illustrates the fact that time is eternal with our universal Father.

It is the goal of our Throne of God to get us to Havona: "To him that overcometh, will I give to eat of the tree of life which is in the midst of the Paradise of God" (Revelation 2:7).

Section 1.4: Hollow Earth

We commonly conceive heaven to be in the skies and hell at the planet's center, and this would be plausible if the planet had a solid interior. However, our planet is a hollow shell with a luminous sun at its center. It is engineered so that both the outer convex surface and the inner concave surface can be inhabited when the planet's gravity is in the middle of its shell, not its center. Polar openings connect the two surfaces, and the inner sun illuminates and warms the planet's interior just as the sun in space does its exterior. Air and water flow from the interior to the exterior, and the ice caps act as a filtering system.

* * * * *

DOUG: Do people have physical forms inside the earth as well as in heaven on earth?

JOHN: Definitely, yes.

DOUG: Do people live inside the cores of planets with harsh surface weather conditions, such as Mercury, Uranus, and Pluto?

JOHN: Interesting question. Those planets are inhabited by spiritual forms other than humans or even animals. Their forms are suited to their planet's environment and spiritual growth. Many live under the surfaces of their planets, so you are not aware of them, and in some cases their energy is so high, you could not see them even if you wanted to. So you see, many planets in the solar system are inhabited by forms other than humans.

DOUG: They can be seen with spiritual eyes, right?

JOHN: Yes. Some people have journeyed to Saturn as large praying mantises. If they are spiritually attuned, people can actually experience different spiritual forms.

* * * * *

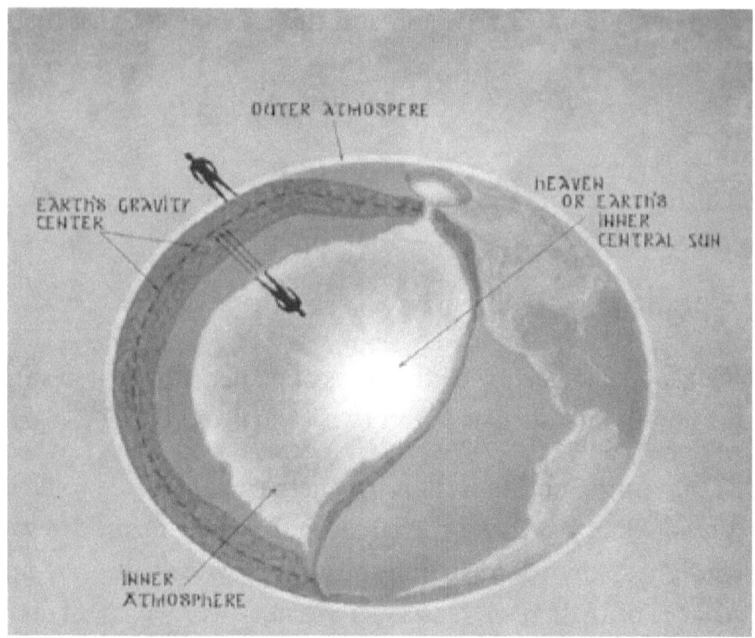

Figure 4 – Schematic of Hollow Earth

Not only are the inner and outer surfaces of our hollow planet inhabited, but the shell is as well. The planet Earth's shell, which varies from four hundred to eight hundred miles in thickness, is made up of several layers or strata, not unlike an apartment complex. Many civilizations and ecosystems exist on it. The shell is also honeycombed with tunnel and cavern systems, both natural and man-made. The caverns contain cities or communities, human and nonhuman alike. High-speed shuttles run through the tunnels, and these are similar to modern subway systems. Many of these transportation systems reach both the outer and inner Earth surfaces for trade and business functions. Only the privileged or high-level functionaries have access to these ports.

The Bible has made several references to the people living inside the Earth.

"There were giants in the earth in those days: yea, and after that the sons of God came unto the daughters of men, and they had borne them children, these were mighty men, which in old time were men of renown" (Genesis 6:4).

"Then God blessed them, saying, Bring forth fruit and multiply, and fill the waters in the seas, and let the fowl multiply in the earth" (Genesis 1:22).

"And I was with thee wheresoever thou hast walked, and have destroyed all thine enemies out of thy sight, and have made thee a great name, like unto the name of the great men that are in the earth" (2 Samuel 7:9).

"And I have been with thee whithersoever thou hast walked, and have destroyed all thine enemies out of thy sight, and have made thee a name, like the name of the great men that are in the earth" (1 Chronicles 17:8).

"But to the Saints that are in the earth, and to the excellent: all my delight is in them" (Psalm 16:3).

"And every plant of the field, before it was in the earth, and every herb of the field, before it grew, for the Lord God had not caused it to rain upon the earth, neither was there a man to till the ground, but a mist went up from the earth, and watered all the earth" (Genesis 2:5–6).

People were created from the dust of the earth's surface. Primarily, aliens who possessed greater knowledge about God's creation lived inside the earth. They had the technological means to travel between planets, and they were aware of the residences within the planets in our solar system.

* * * * *

DOUG: So there are other planets? I thought Earth was the only one.

JOHN: Well, the planets go around the sun. You've heard of Pluto, Mars, and Uranus.

Douglas Grady

DOUG: Oh.

JOHN: We all have lives on those planets. We call this a universe, but it's actually a multiverse. Our horizons will continue to expand as we move beyond the planet Earth.

* * * * *

All major outer-earth cities are connected to the inner or middle earth subcities by secret tunnels, ports, shafts, elevators, and other passageways that dignitaries and officials use to conduct commerce or exchange information. There is a tunnel to the inner earth below Jerusalem. Most of our technology comes from the inner earth. In the last few hundred years, inner-earth societies have groomed the outer earth into its present, modernized state. The goal is to fully integrate the inner and outer earths using one world government. Whether this will be a positive change remains to be seen. One of the great challenges confronting us is the safe integration of clean technologies in an otherwise organic world. Many believe that technology is a crutch the Devil introduced and that humans have the potential to surpass it.

Is the inner earth good or evil? It appears that the first two to three hundred miles both beneath and above sea level make up a region that's predominantly filled with negativity. For thousands of years now, this outer world of ours has been dominated by war and chaos, which has been instigated by forces that are against humans (dark side). There are two basic forces or spirits in our universe. They are embodiments of the mammalian and reptilian species, and they have always been at odds with each other. Both have claims to the earth. In the last great battle between these two forces, the reptilian (or satanic) forces were defeated and driven underground, where they now await judgment. These fallen angels who have lost their original human bodies and taken on reptilian ones continue to impede humanity despite their restraints. Humanity would have been destroyed instantly if such forces remained in their original human bodies. Instead they must use human leaders (Illuminati) and technology to continue their evil.

The true Christianity of the first few centuries AD was one of the greatest resistance movements against the satanic forces that sought to destroy humanity and make the earth their home. The Bible was modified by Roman Emperor Constantine and his advisors to formulate our present Christianity, which invented hellfire and eternal damnation. The Bible is a rehash of even more ancient manuscripts originating from India and the Orient. Over the centuries true Christianity has also gone underground, recruiting special individuals who have overcome sin and death and who will become part of the 144,000 leaders in the new heaven on earth. They are from all races and nations, and they are busy battling the dark forces in a struggle to reclaim this planet from the inside out.

World Wars I and II were the outer manifestations of the gigantic battle going on inside the planet for its repossession. They are part of the physical representation of the spiritual war resulting with the fallen angels. In preparation for heaven on earth's outer surface, God removed alien Grays from our solar system. In addition, the ruler of the Illuminati satanic force was deposed of his inner earth throne in 1948, taking his demons with him. Most of the inner earth is now under superhuman rule. The vanquished demons fled to the outer earth a few hundred miles beneath and above sea level. Pluto, discovered in 1930, represents the dark coming to light, and it is a heavenly sign that the planet Earth is undergoing an inner and eventual outer cleansing. Life on our planet is dying, but photon energy (Holy Spirit) will provide rebirth. This energy returned to earthly existence on December 21, 2012, although John did state that the planet Earth had entered the Photon Belt back in 1996.

The inner-earth leaders have increased their monitoring of the outer-earth surface since the 1945 nuclear detonations over Nagasaki and Hiroshima. They were regularly sending reconnaissance UFO ships and using satellite surveillance. The bridge between our technologies is closing. It is time for a reunification of both the inner and outer worlds. However, two opposing forces have contradictory agendas for this union. The negative inner earth denizens, located mostly in the middle of the earth (the planet Earth's cavernous shell) want human enslavement, whereas the positive inner-earth people, located mostly on the planet's inner concave surface, want human liberation and regeneration. Fortunately, the negatives are dwindling in number as more of the outer-earth people are choosing the path of peace and harmony. The vast majority of humankind will choose life over death and truth over lies. Eradicating the remaining negative forces, however, will be no easy matter, but it will and must be done if the prophesied millennium (or a new golden age) is to become a reality.

The end time is here for the negative forces. The photon energies of love and light are causing them to dissipate. Pockets of negative forces on the planet remain, but they will disappear in time. A new home or planet will be found for them somewhere else, more likely within another constellation. That way, they can get away from the influence of the Photon Belt. The negative forces have plagued and polluted our planet. Without them, earth will enjoy a much-needed golden age, a millennium of peace and fifth-dimension abundance.

Most of us grew up learning in science class that our planet is a round, solid ball of earth with a molten core at its center from which volcanic activity arises. While this may seem reasonable initially, the flaws soon become apparent. First of all, a solid Earth would have too much weight and mass to spin so quietly and perfectly on its axis. Secondly, whoever creates planets would be wise enough to both minimize weight and maximize space. A solid planet can only be inhabited on its outer surface, whereas a hollow one would have two livable surfaces. Also, a hollow planet would be easy to relocate should the need arise, whereas moving a solid one would cost energy. The interior of a hollow planet is more comfortable than its outer area, as it is protected from dangerous rays, winds, collisions, and invasions. A hollow, oblate Earth with polar openings also maximizes electrical or magnetic energy flow that provides greater room for multilevel existence and also simplifies travel.

The polar caps conceal the accesses to the inner planet. The north polar opening is the principle access to the interior and is some 1,200 to 1,400 miles wide. Snow and ice cover most of the South Pole. At about seventy-seven degrees north latitude, the planet starts flattening out, and at around eighty-two degrees north latitude, it starts curving inward. One can catch glimpses of the earth's inner central sun, which lights and warms the interior behind the aurora borealis. The temperature rises between these latitudes, and salt water becomes fresh. The compass needle goes wild, pointing south instead of the north. Admiral E. Byrd flew over and into the north polar opening in a secret 1947 American expedition and confirmed these facts before he was sworn to silence. All of the major powers have bases stationed in the Arctic. They are united in a hushed attempt to probe the secrets of the hole at the pole and the interior world. However, entry is restricted by the more powerful inner-earth governments, which they fear. Before every golden age, the ice and snow around the polar openings melt and evaporate, forming water or ice canopies around the planet and opening up access to the inner earth.

* * * * *

DOUG: I didn't realize that the planet Earth is hollow and that heaven is inside it. Is that true?

JOHN: Heaven is inside of you. Heaven is a state of consciousness in your thinking that provides you to be able to connect with your heart. So the hollow Earth, yes, there are people living inside the Earth at this point and have been for many thousands of years ever since Lemuria and Atlantis broke up. That's part of where some of the people went to be safe, so scientists and geology have not been completely accurate. They think it's a solid core to the center. And that's what they've taught and preached in science classes for years, but it's not accurate.

Douglas Grady

DOUG: I'm going to include something about hollow earth and people living inside.

JOHN: Admiral Byrd (of the U.S. Navy in 1947) communicated with these people when he discovered the pole opening.

* * * * *

Heaven is an inner, central, solar location, whereas heaven and hell are within you. It is your fears that make hell and your love residing in consciousness that makes heaven. The planet is like a wheel. Heaven is at the center, and earth is on the rim. The spokes of the wheel represent the gateways between the two. This scheme is universal and holds true for all heavenly abodes, whether they are lunar, planetary, solar, galactic, or universal. The exceptions are those abodes that have been corrupted by evil forces, but even then the basic structure holds.

Earth's outer surface, where we now live, was originally a paradise similar to its interior surface. A canopy of water vapor insulated the entire planet except near the poles. There may have been a series of these canopies, but they have been destroyed and rebuilt throughout history. Crystal bomb explosions were the most recent destruction occurring around 11,000 years ago.

The gravity center of Earth is seven hundred miles down from the outer surface to an area of zero gravity. The Earth's central gravity sphere is less than a mile thick, and it's around the planet's shell. As a sentient being, Earth is the spirit of peace and harmony. You are weightless and breathless here, and your mind dictates your body. And there is no physical decomposition, meaning that you can live forever. The true home of man is the inner earth. It is where he began and where he will return.

The interior surface of the planet can be called a paradise or Eden-like environment. The real Eden was in the Mediterranean. The interior surface is six-sevenths land and one-seventh water, and it is illuminated and warmed by the interior sun. Exodus 20:4 identifies this fact. "That are in heaven above, neither that are in the earth beneath, nor that are in the waters under the earth." The central sun ensures that it is never dark, and the temperature is always in the midseventies Fahrenheit but slightly cooler near the poles. There are no storms, and there's very little wind. Because of its ideal climate, crops reach significantly larger sizes than those of the outer surface. There are grapes the size of melons and trees the size of mountains. Even the animals and humans are huge. The average human is nine to fourteen feet tall, and a person will have a life span of six to nine hundred years. The people are mostly vegetarians or fruitarians, and some do not eat at all. Because of the natural abundance, there is little if any crime. There is no pollution, and there's no need for a government or an economy. Everyone is self-sufficient and spends time developing natural talents for the good of the community. Telepathy, clairvoyance, and all of the higher senses are natural. If people marry, they do so later in life, and sex is magnetic. People die willfully rather than the result of age or circumstance. They revere the deity who resides in the inner central sun, which they call heaven, and this is where their spirits go upon death. The inner earth is also the home of flying saucers, both of earthly and otherworldly origins. Middle and inner earth kingdoms, such as Shamballa and Agartha, keep in touch with groups from other parts of our universe. Our governments know about the inner earth, and they've even sent expeditions there, not all of which were successful.

The residents of inner-earth cities and all living conditions of higher vibratory levels are able to enter the earth's surface, and their bodies will remain viable upon entry. If inner-earth residents wish to come to the surface, they realign their vibratory attunement. Our bodies don't have that capability because we haven't reached that level of spiritual awareness (though there are a few exceptions).

The population seeding programs began on the surface long before Earth was named. Eden came later with the advent of the various extraterrestrial civilizations imparting their DNA and high degree of spirituality to the previous humans. However, it could be said that Eden does exist in inner earth because the highly evolved souls living there have created natural harmony. Adam and Eve are just names for the first soul beings on earth in physical forms. Before that, they came in spirit.

The reptoids and the evil leaders of the outer and middle earth wish to invade and conquer the inner earth. The reptoids are a race of reptilian alien beings originating from the Draco constellation, and they now live throughout the galaxy. Reptilians are also known as "lizard people." Reptilian aliens have been commonly associated with government conspiracies and the manipulation of our home planet. The reason many associate these reptilians with such actions is because of their inherently evil nature. Their attempt to take over the inner earth was thwarted. If it hadn't been, humanity and the planet would have ended. There will eventually be a war between the inner- and outer-earth leaders (dark side). These inner-earth leaders are the ten biblical tribes of Israel, which symbolize our lost ten DNA strands. The original human had twelve strands of DNA actively maintaining full spiritual function. Because of a preoccupation with left-brained thinking and closed hearts, these extra DNA strands have been lost, leading to a spiritually deficient society. Our intuitive and healing abilities have been reduced significantly, and we can only access a small portion of our brains.

The book of Enoch describes hell (or Tartarus) as a number of cavities in Earth's shell that imprison fallen spirits or angels and other monstrous entities. It is metaphorical because it was written before people understood the fear or negative emotional states that were most hellish. Once the divine plan for humanity is in place, the imprisoned entities will be judged after one thousand years of peace.

Nearby chasms contain the spirits of the victims of the fallen entities, many of which are crying for revenge continually. Apparently, provisions have been made within the shell and astral regions of the planet for the temporal or permanent housing of all manner of souls

Door to Glory

and earthbound spirits. While most of the hell regions are hundreds of miles within the earth, some are near the outer or inner surfaces, and one or more may even span the entire diameter of the shell. The Sinbad movies do a good job of portraying the distorted human shapes, animal men, apparitions, and eerie and invisible presences.

Admiral Byrd made two historic but unannounced trips to the Earth's hollow interior by airplane. Both were funded by the US government. In February 1947, he traveled 1,700 miles to the north polar opening in Alaska and described vast forests and what looked like running herds of animals. In 1956, he traveled 2,300 miles to the south polar opening in McMurdo Sound in the Antarctic and found vegetation and bodies of water before returning for fuel. While the purpose of these trips was to gather sensitive data concerning the earth's interior, leaked information about the events served to strengthen the notion that our planet is indeed hollow. However, further news was repressed, and Byrd was sworn to secrecy. Byrd, however, did leave some writings, some of which were leaked, and these described the admiral's ecstatic descriptions of "the Unknown Country" (Ref. 10).

There are a total of twelve continents or land masses on or in Earth—one for every planet in our solar system. Six are outer, and six are inner. The outer continents, all of which begin with the letter "A," include Asia (including Europe), Africa, Australia, America North, America South, and Antarctica. The Arctic is mostly ice, snow, and sea, and an enormous polar opening there leads directly to the hollow interior of the planet. Here, gravity reverses, and one reaches the shores of the seventh inner polar continent, which Admiral E. Byrd had the fortune of witnessing in his 1947 aerial trip. There, he saw vast forests and lakes and even animal life. Not much is revealed about the other five continents farther inward. Land on the outer surface may be ocean in the inner earth and vice versa. If this is so, then the inner earth's surface is three-fourths land and one-fourth water.

There are hundreds of large cities miles beneath the earth. Many are connected by tunnels with high-speed shuttles, and these use magnets for propulsion. Some of these are government or scientific installations while others are more alien or otherworldly. Some of these cities are located in and under mountains, while others are housed in large caverns. Nearly every major city on the planet has roots in an inner city beneath it. Secret elevators or shafts in some buildings lead to these duplicate cities, and only certain individuals have access to them. Most underground cities were built for protection in times of war or natural catastrophes, not to mention secret and often forbidden projects.

About a mile or so beneath Mount Shasta in Northern California, there's the domed city of Telos, where more than 1.5 million descendants of Atlantis and Lemuria live. The city was built more than fourteen thousand years ago as a haven from the crystal explosions. Telos is connected by transport tunnels to hundreds of other similar cities and the main Agarthean hub beneath the Gobi desert. The citizens of Telos use scientifically advanced teleportation and levitation devices. They grow their food hydroponically and have holodeck rooms. They use spaceships (noiseless and invisible) for interplanetary travel, and the city's main power source is a central crystal the size of a skyscraper.

According to the late theologian Theodore Fitch, ten times more people live inside the earth than on the outer surface. The total planet population, including inner-earth people, is more than sixty billion. The planet's eight-hundred-mile-thick shell is multilayered like an apartment complex, and it houses many strange civilizations. In his book *Inner Earth Peoples*, available at Health Research Books, Fitch also states that the earth was once much larger than it is today, with its boundaries stretching twice as far as the moon. There is a dark, negative, and almost impenetrable astral layer surrounding the planet some thirty to one hundred miles above where negative entities abide. In and beyond this are various belts of rock and ice invisible to the naked eye, separating the first (atmosphere), second (sub-lunar), and third (post-lunar) heavens, which is also populated. A planetary object in the third heaven is located the New Jerusalem. Outwardly and inwardly, this planet is more populated than we can imagine.

All inner-earth people walk upside down, their heads pointing toward the inner central sun. This stimulates their higher chakras more than their lower ones, resulting in higher brain and psychic functions. Here on the outer earth, our heads are pointing away from the inner central sun, with our lower chakras receiving most of the stimulation, resulting in more carnal pursuits. Lying down or standing on your head improves the situation somewhat, but the real solution is to live on the inner-earth concave surface. It is where your higher centers are always being stimulated by that life-giving orb overhead and where the lower centers are kept at bay.

Gravity decreases dramatically ten to twenty-five miles beneath the outer earth's ocean level, significantly improving physical health. Aging slows, and hunger and thirst begin to disappear. The air is richly revitalizing because of the solar light being filtered and dispersed as it penetrates the earth. Below twenty-five miles, people lose two-thirds of their weight and can float. They become younger, smarter, and stronger, and they need little rest. Light emanates from everywhere, so there are no shadows. All of these conditions intensify toward the planet's gravity center, seven hundred miles beneath the outer surface. Breath and heartbeat cease near the gravity center, and there is no weight. Telepathy becomes natural, and thoughts move and shape matter.

Contrary to scientific teaching and popular belief, Earth's true gravity center is not at its core but within its eight-hundred-mile-thick shell. Earth is hollow with polar openings and an interior sun. This sun is six hundred to seven hundred miles in diameter. Earth's shell varies between four hundred to eight hundred miles in diameter (thicker near the equator), and the polar openings are anywhere from eight hundred to 1,400 miles wide. Earth has two magnetic fields. One originates from the inner central sun. It travels slowly around the poles, and it is the source of our aurora borealis and Van Allen belt or magnetosphere. The other is from inside the Earth's shell. It provides gravity, and it is three hundred to seven hundred miles beneath the planet's outer surface. This gravity center within the earth's shell is the spirit of the earth itself and is the official dividing line between the inner and outer earth. Gravity is six times greater on the outer surface of the planet than on its inner surface, so more major effort is needed to sustain life here. At the equator seven hundred miles down, there is zero gravity (weightlessness). There, the body is at perfect rest and does not decay. Another one hundred miles into the inner surface, gravity reverses, and people and animals stand upside down. Their heads all point toward the inner central sun, which lights and warms the interior of the planet. With only one-sixth of the gravity of the outer earth, everything grows much faster and larger here, and the length and quality of life are also proportionately greater. Astrologically, the ascending sign of influence comes from this spiritual gravity center located deep within the planet's shell.

The heaving of our chests and the beating of our hearts are abnormal conditions brought on by an imperfect environment. Because of the outer earth's intense gravity, our bodies must work extra hard to distribute oxygen evenly. In zero gravity, however, no such pressure exists. Therefore, no breathing or blood flow is required. This perfect state of equilibrium is experienced in Earth's central gravity sphere some seven hundred miles below the outer surface. There, the mind becomes the ruler over matter, and there is no aging or degeneration. The inner-earth surface is also contains only one-sixth the gravity of the outer earth surface. This minimal gravity creates the cocooned state that makes the inner-earth so much like paradise. The outer surface can also become like paradise once the planet's water canopy is restored and its climate, light, and gravity are stabilized and equalized.

Many of the numerous earthquakes around the globe are being caused by titanic inner-earth struggles between the forces wishing to liberate this planet and those that want to continue enslaving it. The king of the world is targeting the Agarthean citadel beneath Tibet with the help of his evil serpentine magicians, all of whom were ousted from their stronghold in 1948 by a group of five hundred empowered lamas. The bulk of the most devastating earthquakes in recorded history tend to occur in and around China. The most recent one occurred in July of 1976 in Tangshan, and it killed a quarter of a million people. Nuclear and ray weapons are used in an outer/inner-earth joint effort to destroy the reptilian lairs that pocket the planet. Some of these lairs are embedded in the north and south polar ice caps, waiting to be reactivated when the ice melts. The great Alaska earthquake of 1964 could have indicated an attempted removal of such infestations.

At some point during the golden age, the polar ice and snow will evaporate to form a cloud, water, or ice canopy around the planet, equalizing the climate and opening up access to the inner earth. Ancient caves, tunnels, and portals will open, reestablishing a bridge between the planet's inner and outer surfaces. Magnetic grids, lea lines, and other power vortices will be reactivated to restore the world to its intended state. It will reconnect Earth to the rest of the solar system and beyond. When sixty billion people from all parts of the planet join with those of other worlds to pool their knowledge and resources, technology will progress astonishingly quickly. It will happen once the alien and hostile rulers of the world are removed.

The accelerated meltdown of the polar regions over the last forty years, particularly in the north, is leading to a merger between the hollow inner-earth world and the external one. In the last golden age of Atlantis, which was eleven to thirteen thousand years ago, a set of water or ice canopies covered the planet. It created a paradisiacal environment, connecting both the inner and outer earth via the polar openings, which were then ice-free. The Dark Side produced crystal bomb explosions that caused the eventual collapse of these canopies eleven thousand years ago, causing drastic climate changes, which in turn decimated the quality and length of our lives.

The floodwaters were created by the tropical climate throughout the world before the damage to the canopies took place that had caused the waters to gradually recede toward the polar regions and turned to ice and snow, forming a protective barrier over the pristine inner earth. Over the last three hundred years, the inner earth has been preparing the outer earth with its concepts and technologies for the eventual merging of the two societies. The melting of the regions and the reestablishment of the planet Earth's water or ice canopies is the next logical step to this merger.

Section 1.5: States of Consciousness

When outer-earth dwellers begin devoting our lives to discovering the consciousness that created and sustained us, we will begin a great adventure. On that day the quest will change. We will live no longer for ourselves but rather for something higher than us. We will be driven no longer by personal gratification but by lasting fulfillment and personal transformation.

Our adventure in higher consciousness will test, thrill, and satisfy us. We may fear standing before unknown dimensions of higher consciousness. Our minds will never guess at the future accurately. Presumptions are too limited and too predicated on previous experience in the outer world. Our emotions will be stretched beyond comfort, extending until they are capable of maintaining universal love and experiencing the ecstasy of pure being.

We will journey through the dark stages of the heart toward Christ consciousness. Christ consciousness provides us an experience of universal love. It creates a fundamental distinction between the real and the unreal. Wisdom is developed from the experience of the heart, and knowledge comes from the head of ego's limitations. Therefore, knowledge is limited. Wisdom goes beyond. This fact is unalterable and explicit. The law applies to everything that God has created, and only what He created is real. It is beyond learning because it is beyond time and process. It has no contradictions, as there is no beginning and no end. It merely is.

* * * * *

DOUG: Jesus taught that if we think anything negative, then we are following our egos. If we were experiencing Christ consciousness, then we would see only reality, which is love.

JOHN: That is what Christ consciousness is all about. It is seeing love. That is the truth, but many distractions have obliterated or obscured that love. Our goal on earth is to overcome the desires of our egos and the things that hide love so that we can return to the Law of One.

* * * * *

There has always been Christ consciousness, but it is hidden from us. It is eternal as God is eternal. It was revealed in a hidden Scripture message, and Jesus came down to reaffirm it. It has nothing to do with Judaism, Islam, or Christianity. It is all about our personal relationships with God the Father. We all have that oneness of God in our hearts. The dogmas of the churches did not teach this.

* * * * *

DOUG: Part of a verse from the book of Genesis reads, "[God] will make him fruitful and will multiply him exceedingly: twelve princes shall he beget, and I will make a great nation of him" (Genesis 17:20). Does this verse mean that Christ consciousness should be practiced? It mentions the twelve princes. Are they the twelve tribes of Israel?

JOHN: Yes.

DOUG: Now would the twelve tribes of Israel be a symbol for twelve strands of DNA?

JOHN: The strands of DNA are all the same. It was the twelve tribes that you are referring to. They are different characteristics of a person, but everybody has the same DNA. So it's a personality and characteristic differences, such as cultures. It is not about their inner essence. It is about their outer behavior.

DOUG: Okay. So it is not due to Christ consciousness?

JOHN: They all have Christ consciousness, but on the exterior there are different cultural values.

DOUG: "Seeing that Abraham shall be indeed a great and a mighty nation, and all the nations of the earth shall be blessed in him" (Genesis 18:18). Does this verse mean specifically that Christ consciousness should be practiced?

JOHN: Definitely. That is who you are.

DOUG: Interesting, okay. Can you elaborate more about that?

JOHN: That is exactly what Marilyn's next book is about. She is going to be teaching a class in March, showing everybody how to release all of the barriers and obstacles to their Christ consciousness so they can move into their Christhood. This Christmas is about revealing to everyone that the Christ in them, is born when they are babies. And what happened to Jesus happened to everybody. He is the example. And so that Christ consciousness has been smothered out by the culture, the Illuminati and the fears and all of the conditioning of the churches and the medicines and all the different parts of society that have stopped people from realizing their Christ consciousness. And people have been misdirected with their focus not to look inside. So they lost that connection. So when everybody can go back into being what is in their hearts and not their heads, which Christ consciousness can emerge again.

DOUG: Okay. Now is it possible that photon energy last appeared at the time of Atlantis?

JOHN: Yes.

DOUG: Could it be that the time it was living through Christ consciousness, but the dark side took that away or what?

JOHN: Well, it has to do with the energy in the universe. The Photon Belt is not—it's just one section of the universe that the planet moves through as it is rotating around the sun. And every thirteen thousand years, it goes through the Photon Belt. So when it left the belt, that's about the time when Atlantis fell. And we have been living in the darkness. Now that we are back into the Photon Belt section of the universe again, that is why your Christ consciousness can then be brought to the front and foreground again because the energy will be there, it is there to sustain it. So we moved away from that energy of the Christhood, and now you are moving back into that energy to reclaim.

DOUG: You mentioned that the book of Revelation states that photon energy allowed the golden age to last two thousand years, not one thousand.

JOHN: It was a little more than two thousand. However, the Bible demonstrates that people can move into peace, which was a profound announcement for its time. The Bible was written to help people who lived two thousand years ago understand messages from God. Furthermore, that was such a large time span for them to assimilate into their consciousness that to even expand on that was pushing the edge a little bit. So the Throne of God made a conservative estimate of one thousand years.

* * * * *

The world of perception is of time, change, beginnings, and endings. It is based on interpretation, not facts. It is the world of birth and death, and it was founded on beliefs in scarcity, loss, and separation. It is learned rather than given, selective in its perceptual emphases, unstable in its functioning, and inaccurate in its interpretations.

From wisdom and knowledge, two distinctly opposite thought systems arise. In the realm of wisdom, no thoughts exist apart from God because God and his creation share one will. The world of knowledge, however, is founded in separate wills that are conflicting with one another and with God perpetually. Most knowledge comes from the ego's teachings. People perceive only what conforms to their wishes. This leads to a world of illusions that requires relentless defense.

When caught in the world of perception, we are trapped in a dream. We cannot escape without help because our senses are merely witnesses to the dream. God has provided the way. It is the function of his voice and his Holy Spirit to mediate between perception and wisdom. He can do this because he knows the truth and recognizes our illusions without believing in them. It is the Holy Spirit's goal to help us escape from the dream world by teaching us how to reverse our thinking and abandon our mistakes.

The world we see merely reflects our internal frame of reference—the dominant ideas of our minds, our wishes, and our emotions. *Projection makes perception.* We look within to determine the kind of world we want to see, and then we project that world, making it the perceived truth. We make it true by our interpretations of what it is we are seeing. If we are using perception to justify our mistakes—anger, the impulse to attack, and lack of love—we will see a world of evil, destruction, malice, envy, and despair. All this we must learn to forgive, not because we are charitable but because what we are seeing is a lie. We have distorted the world with our twisted defenses. As we learn to recognize our perceptual errors, we will forgive them and ourselves, looking past our distorted self-concepts to what God created in us.

Sin is defined as a "lack of love." Since love is all there is, the Holy Spirit views sin as a mistake to be corrected rather than an evil to be punished. Our sense of inadequacy, weakness, and incompletion comes from the active investment in the scarcity principle that governs the world of illusions. From that point of view, we seek in others what we want in ourselves. We love another to get something ourselves. That is what passes for love in the dream world. There can be no greater mistake than that, for love is incapable of asking for anything.

Only minds can join, not bodies (egos). Those whom God has joined cannot be broken apart by men. However, true union is possible only at the Christ level, where it will never be lost. The "little I" (ego) seeks to enhance itself by external approval, external possessions, and external love. The self that God created needs nothing. It is forever complete, safe, loved, and loving. It seeks to share rather than to receive and to extend rather than to project. It has no needs and wants to join with others in mutual awareness of abundance.

Dream world relationships are illusionary. When given to the Holy Spirit, relationships can give rise to miracles that point toward heaven. The people on the outer-surface world use relationships as weapons of exclusion. The Holy Spirit transforms them into perfect lessons in forgiveness and awakening. They are opportunities for healing perceptions, correcting errors, and giving forgiveness. Each relationship is an invitation to the Holy Spirit and the remembrance of God.

Perception is a function of the body and represents limited awareness. Perception sees through the body's eyes and hears through the body's ears. The body appears to be largely self-motivated, yet it responds to the mind's intentions only. If the mind wants to use it for an attack, it becomes prey to sickness, age, and decay. If the mind accepts the Holy Spirit's purpose, the body instead becomes a communication tool that's useful when it is needed and gently laid aside when it is not. It is neutral just as everything in the world of perception is. The mind determines whether it is used to achieve the goals of the ego or the Holy Spirit.

The opposite of seeing through the body's eyes is the vision of Christ, which reflects strength rather than weakness, unity rather than separation, and love rather than fear. The opposite of hearing through the body's ears is communication through the voice of God, the Holy Spirit, which abides in each of us. His voice seems distant and difficult to hear because the ego, the little voice of the separated self, appears to be much louder. It is reversed. The Holy Spirit speaks with unmistakable clarity and overwhelming appeal. Anyone who does not choose to identify with the body will hear to God's messages of release and hope and gladly accept the joy of Christ in exchange for his or her own gloomy image.

Christ's vision is the Holy Spirit's gift, God's alternative to separation, sin, guilt, and death. It is the one correction for all errors of perception, the reconciliation of the opposites on which this world is seemingly based. Its kindly light illuminates another point of view, namely Christ consciousness, reflecting the thought system that arises from knowledge and guides us toward the inevitable return to God. With Christ's vision, injustices become a call for help and unity. Sin, sickness, and attack are viewed as incorrect perceptions that can be remedied through gentleness and love. Defenses are laid down because there is no need for them where there is no attack. Our brothers' needs become our own on our mutual journey to God. Without us, they would lose their way. Without them, we could never find our own.

Forgiveness is an action unknown in heaven, where the need for it is inconceivable. However, in this world forgiveness is a necessary correction for all mistakes. Forgiveness is accepting our own shortcomings and understanding that everyone has their own. We receive forgiveness only when we offer it, reflecting the law of heaven, which states that giving and receiving are the same. Heaven is the natural state of the sons of God as he created them. Only love and forgiveness exist in true reality.

Forgiveness will allow us to remember. Through forgiveness, our thinking of the world reverses. The forgiven world becomes the gateway to heaven because then we can forgive ourselves. Holding no one prisoner to guilt, we become free. We can acknowledge Christ in all our brothers since we all possess the Spirit of God within ourselves. Forgetting all our misperceptions, and with nothing from the past to hold us back, we can remember God. When we are ready, God will take the final step in our return to him.

However, those who appreciate the higher consciousness do not have difficulties. They merely seek the wisdom and guidance of their higher consciousness about their next steps. They know the power of the higher consciousness allows them to progress from one level to the next. They began walking down this path because of an inspired sense that they needed higher consciousness. It is only the grace of the higher consciousness and the Lord within that has enabled them in any way to stay on the path. For such devotees, it is quite simple. They submit themselves to the higher consciousness and seek its will. They do not want to abide by their individual wills. They know that when they do so, they hurt themselves or others. Through their gratitude to and appreciation of the higher consciousness, such aspirants attune their personal wills with the wisdom of the higher consciousness, which they have learned to love and trust.

Those who seek higher consciousness will overcome the many hurdles that others find difficult. They are blessed to be trained to synchronize more readily with the higher will. As they learn how to how to distinguish between the higher will and their own less adept wills, they find the higher will is more readily revealed to them. This alignment of one's being with the higher consciousness brings immense satisfaction and a sense of sharing in the ongoing creativity of this universe.

Through prayer and meditation, these wise people strive to further the act of creation and the expression of goodness in their daily lives. They feel closer to God in their hearts. Their personal wills do not conflict with the higher will because they have completely submitted their personal wills to the higher will. They seek to live in attunement. As some saints say, "I am the instrument. You, O Lord, are the operator of this instrument."

These are but the beginning levels of enlightenment. After these necessary tests and triumphs, there are new and more delightful experiences in store. There is no limit to the adventure and the reward of intimacy with our higher consciousness and our Creator.

* * * * *

DOUG: People like you and Gabriel are in the twelfth and thirteenth range?

JOHN: No, I am not in the twelfth and thirteenth range. I am at the tenth.

DOUG: So where would Gabriel be?

JOHN: The eleventh.

DOUG: I asked this question to Archangel Michael, and I thought I heard laughing. Can angels laugh?

JOHN: Yes, because there are a lot of angels in the higher realms not bogged down by the dimensions.

DOUG: I told him I'll put him down at one hundred. He said, "Fine, wherever you want."

JOHN: Michael is at a high level of vibration. These levels are not fixed and have an overlapping range.

DOUG: Am I in the third dimension or the fourth dimension because I have found God?

JOHN: I would say you have moved out of the third dimension and are now moving through the fourth dimension of the unconditional love that you were created in. You have some remaining barriers to the love of God that you need to release, but you are on the path through the Fourth Dimension.

Table 2 – States of Consciousness

Dimensional Level	State of Consciousness
1	Rocks, soil, minerals, plants, vegetation
2	Instinctual, emotional, animalistic
3	Intellectual, logical, rational mind, ego
4	Creative, imaginative, psychic, intuitive
5	Pure intelligence, insight, love
6	Casual level, soul level (last level of individually)
7	Oversoul level (group consciousness)
8	Avatar level (high level of mastery)
9	Christ level (unconditionally loving consciousness)
10	Cosmic level (cosmic consciousness)
11	God level (God consciousness)
12	Universal level (Universal consciousness)
13	The Void, the Great Mystery

Heaven on earth is a state of consciousness, not a physical location. "Neither shall men say, lo here or lo there: for behold, the kingdom of God is within you" (Luke 17:21). Only 5 percent of people have recognized the oneness of God within their beings. Egos prevent the rest from realizing who they truly are inside, and they are afraid to open their hearts to love. Public speaking and death are not the biggest fears on earth. Accepting the love of God is. There has been a significant flux of awakening. On December 21, 2012, the Earth realigned with the fifth dimension, a dimension of love and light. The dark energies that took hold of the planet for centuries are quickly dissipating away. The new consciousness of Earth is allowing people to open up to more and more love. It has an overwhelming impact on the growth of consciousness of the people. The new era of the fifth dimension is greatly renowned in the universe because it affects the whole solar system. It brings Earth's consciousness to a higher level, bringing it closer to the universes that have already reached the seventh and eighth Dimensions. We are coming of age on earth, and more people are growing into loving beings that reflect God.

Different souls have come to Earth at various levels in their spiritual development. As Earth transitions to a new dimension, these souls will return to help us grow to a higher dimension.

Not all souls here are ready for that transition into higher consciousness. After death they will reincarnate to other planets that are suitable for their vibrational levels. We have entered one thousand years of peace. By then, this planet will have a vibrational level at least as high as the seventh dimension. For those souls that have transitioned to another world, they will return to Earth and complete their ascension. There will still be more times to grow further into the oneness of God. We have a ways to go yet. After the golden age ends at approximately AD 3996, Earth will go through what is called the "post-millennium period." Eventually, there will be no governments. Instead the oneness of God will unite us. The negative energies that have held us hostage for thousands of years will move on to another solar system.

*****

DOUG: Jesus taught the kingdom of God, and that's a spiritual term because it is within myself.

JOHN: Exactly. You see, the article she wants to share with you talks about the light within you. The light is within you, and most people call that God because back in the Biblical days, they did not understand something invisible. And Jesus was talking about the Father within. The Father's the spirit. It's invisible. That energy force of wholeness, omniscience, omnipresence, and omnipotence is within you. You are powerful. You do not need to look to others. You have the power. It is within. As you open up your heart more and more -- and that's the counseling Marilyn does is to release the barriers that are stopping God's awareness into your presence and experience. Whatever you peel away like an onion, it exposes more and more of God. Anything dark energy, dense, fearful, guilty, shame, remorse, anger -- those things are barriers to God-consciousness. And as you release those in meditation, 12-step programs help people do it very well. You identify all those dark, dense energies from people that you have a grudge with that people have not forgiven, or people that have harmed you and you need to forgive them. All of those things need clear away so more of God's love can fill that space. And as you grow spiritually, it means that you are putting the light or the energy of a loving spirit onto the situation so that you are no longer emotionally connected to the negativity running your life. And people call that the Devil.

* * * * *

Section 1.6: Chakras

The human body is a receiver of cosmic energy, and with it, we can unite with spiritual realms in the afterlife. This receiver facet of the human body is made up of an arrangement of endocrine glands within our bodies that are points of contact with an associated system of spiritual energy centers or chakras. They are collectively called the astral body or soul. The spirit body is the vehicle by which people have near-death experiences, out-of-body experiences, and dreams.

Each spiritual center corresponds to one of the seven color in the light spectrum—red, orange, yellow, green, blue, indigo, and violet. With positive and negative vibes, a person can influence the inward working of the endocrine glands and their conforming spiritual center. The overriding vibration—positive or negative—within an individual's body reveals which spiritual center is dominant within an individual's life. It is the prevailing vibration of a person's life—body and spirit—that shows the level of the afterlife realm they have achieved. Certain yoga meditation methods (such as chanting mantras) have been used in the East to raise the value of the spiritual energy vibration to help heal the mind, body, and spirit.

The soul body is also the vibrant form of the physical body. The spiritual centers of the soul are points of connection where the physical, emotional, and spiritual attributes of the body come together. An endocrine gland connects with each spiritual center (chakra). The pituitary gland is the master gland of the body that is known as the third-eye chakra in the Eastern religions. The ancients considered it as a spiritual organ at the center of the brain.

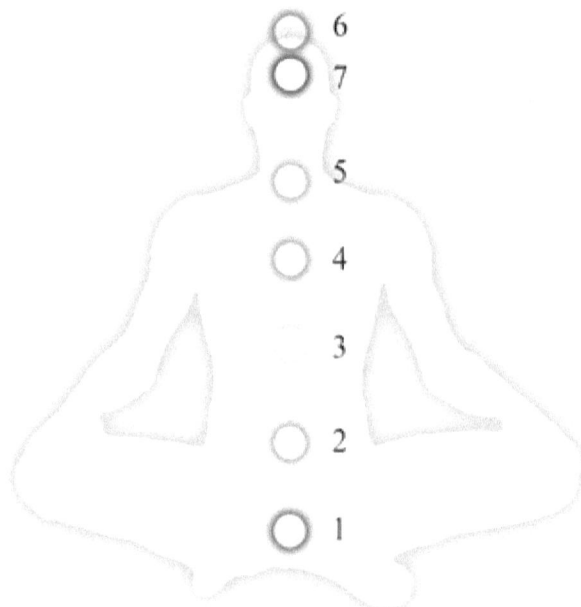

Figure 5 – Seven Chakras

The flowing of the energy of God through the chakras creates heaven on earth for our consciousness. The emotions affect individual chakras, and they can cause blockages that would inhibit the divine energy flow from the Creator.

The first chakra is the base chakra. The superstitions from our tribal or family dysfunctions as well as the genetics of the family can affect us, and these are part of the first chakra. The second chakra has to do with relationships and how well the families interact with one another, including what those relationships are in connection with the energy of God and how we want to define that. So as we go through the different chakras, we are open to the love of God and have the courage to act in the assertive way. Alternatively, are we fearful and act timidly as victims? So we can change that energy. Each chakra has an emotional impact that we need to clean out. Of course, the heart chakra (fourth chakra) is also the most important one because that is where we connect with the consciousness of God. We then move into the crown chakra, which is the sixth chakra. (The third dimension had it incorrectly numbered as the seventh chakra.) The crown chakra opens us up to the energy that surrounds us and fills us with the grace of God. So as we are in meditation, we are opening up to the fifth dimension. The crown chakra must be cleaned and cleared so that we are available to open up. Moreover, the seventh chakra is the third eye, which is located on the forehead between our eyebrows. So that is our spiritual site. So what happened when people came to Earth? Instead of using their spiritual side, they closed off the seventh chakra. So because of our physical nature, we started using our physical eyes to see. That is when the ego took over to give us information about feeling, touching, hearing, and seeing. So people are caught up in the third dimension of what they can see outside of themselves, and this took away their focus from the God within.

The colors of our chakras can reveal how well they are operating. Each chakra has a specific color that it vibrates and manifests in. If it is a bright and brilliant color, that means our chakras are open and receiving that spiritual energy. If they are like a dirty yellow, then it means that the spiritual health and energy of God are being blocked. We need to release all resistance or fear so that it can function as it was intended. The colors tend to show how our chakras are operating.

In addition to the seven major chakras, there are the soul star and the earth star chakras. The soul star chakra is six inches above our third-eye chakra. Typically, our third-eye is closed which prevents us from seeing the spiritual visions on the other side. However, the psychics and mediums can do that. What they do is to focus on the soul star chakra which is a white/gold star. It is the seat of our soul. Numerous out of body experiences originate from there. It can connect the soul to enlightenment by sending it divine light and love and spiritual awareness. Once this chakra awakens, the soul ascends beyond the human ego, which allows people to experience a more enlightened, spiritual, joyful and healthy physical existence.

The earth star chakra is 12-18 inches below our feet. It connects to our root chakra which aligns and connects our body and soul to the powerful energies within the magnetic core of planet earth. The earth star chakra is the grounding point for an individual's entire extended chakra system and their relationship to the planet and the universe. It is also believed to hold the keys to past lives, karmic patterns, and DNA origins. The earth star chakra is responsible for making us feel deeply connected to our energies and those of the planet and the universe.

* * * * *

DOUG: How does the Holy Spirit affect the green ray activation of the chakras?

JOHN: Well, the chakras between God's energy coming in, connecting into your life that you can utilize into your human body. So without the chakras functioning, you are just a zombie walking around the planet. When you finally open up to the awareness in your heart of the love, then the chakras can start to develop a connection that brings God's energy into your life. So you can move up that scale of consciousness into the light of God. So the chakras are necessary to be functioning and open for this transition to happen, and the different colors of the rays, as you call them, are to help balance out those energies that are necessary for it all work together. So different colors have different functions. Green tends to be a healing color, so if there has been a lot of trauma, drama, and chaos in a person's life, where they've been very distraught and depression and darkness, and the green light is a very healing light. And it is part of the chakras for the heart. The heart has green and pink colors. And the green, it means—if you're opening up your heart—that green can find the love and finally do the healing.

DOUG: What is the way to receive the Holy Spirit?

JOHN: To be totally open and receptive so that you move out of any chakras, you move out of your head and totally be. Your heart is open to receive all the loving messages of your soul. It just has to—all the knowledge that you need, and it's always been there. It's just that it's either been in their head. You have been not accessing that knowledge. You've been accessing human knowledge, not spiritual knowledge.

So the Holy Spirit is your connection to the chakras. There was a movie many years ago called *Contact*, where she was trying to make that connection, and it's just opening your heart entirely to the love that's already there and let that love start flowing out. And it manifests in your life, all around you, and things start to change. So the Holy Spirit is the feminine aspect of the total God energy.

DOUG: To receive it is the only way through meditation?

JOHN: That is the most used and visible way when people are out in certain nature environments. That's another way to be open to that consciousness that you see every tree and every grass and every shrub is filled with Spirit also. And if you're surrounding in a very primitive area of nature, out in the woods where there's no civilization, you might say, that has become a tourist trap, so to speak.

Then you are involved. You are engrossed with that Spirit around you, and as you are opening this up to, as you go to the ocean, the energy from the ocean is very profound and full of energy that would also be a meditative type of state. Every time you open up into an altered state, even hypnosis will put you into that meditative state. So there are options, and that's they when you're under hypnosis on people. It's so valuable. It brings them into that altered state of consciousness describing in time to become part of your situation, part of who you are. So it is possible meditation the most commonly used form of approaching that.

* * * * *

Table 3 – Details of Seven Chakras

Spiritual Center	Type of Chakra	Endocrine Gland	Color	Ideal Level of Functioning	Spiritual Church from Book of Revelation
1	Root Chakra	Gonads	Red	Physical health, abundance, security, sense of ease	Ephesus
2	Sacral Chakra	Cell of Leydig	Orange	Sexual/erotic health and fulfillment, ease with change, creativity, generativity, grace, feeling, fluidity, balanced	Smyrna
3	Solar Plexus Chakra	Adrenals	Yellow	Personal power, will, effectiveness, personal energy	Pergamos
4	Heart Chakra	Thymus	Green	Ability to feel compassion, love deeply, healthy intimate relationships	Thyatira
5	Throat Chakra	Thyroid	Light Blue	Ability to express self, manifest personal essence in the world, and communicate well, rich creative life	Sardis
6	Crown Chakra	Pituitary	Violet	Wisdom, spiritual connection, spiritual understanding, sense of connection	Laodicea

| 7 | Third-Eye | Pineal | Indigo | Clear thought, understanding, strong intuition | Philadelphia |

* * * * *

DOUG: "I am Alpha and Omega, the beginning and the ending, saith the Lord, which is, and which was, and which is to come, even the Almighty. I, John, either your brother or companion in tribulation, and in the kingdom and patience of Jesus Christ, was in the isle called Patmos, for the word of God, and for the witnessing of Jesus Christ." Is the reference "Alpha and Omega" another term for *infinite intelligence*?

JOHN: Yes, Alpha is the beginning, and Omega is the end. And there is no beginning or end to God. That is why he said, "I am the Alpha and the Omega," and those are terms out of the Bible.

DOUG: Now is the church of Philadelphia the seventh chakra (see Table 3)? That is like a spiritual church that was mentioned in the book of Revelation.

JOHN: Right.

DOUG: Now is this the "Door to Glory"?

JOHN: Well, the Door to Glory is in your heart, and so the book of Revelation is allegorical. It has terms, and it gives names and labels because people in those days did not understand energy. They did not understand consciousness, and they did not understand love was an energy. So all the things that were shared in the book of Revelations are told in a story form with words that the people could better handle because they did not have words like chakras. They did not understand the terms that we do today, so it was written for people two thousand years ago. They had a different vocabulary and a much lower consciousness, so the terms are not necessarily what they were talking about. It was about what was behind the words, what the words meant, what was the spirit was saying in a particular way.

DOUG: King Solomon described feeling colors and being able to perceive energies after leaving his body. I wonder how I recognized a fellow who had died. His name was Dwight. How did I understand his energy when he came to me in a spirit to say good-bye? I did not see him, but I felt him.

JOHN: Well, that is of the invisible spiritual world. You had eyes (physical) that could not see. If you used your spiritual eyes instead of your material eyes, you would be sensitive to that spiritual connection. So many people are closed off to the invisible; however, you are very sensitive to that, and you picked it up.

* * * * *

Opening our heart reflects the consciousness of God. When that love comes out and manifests itself in our lives, the aura shows the light. Our chakras are reflected in our auras. Our auras are combinations of how connected we are to our consciousness of God. Everybody is right in the place they are supposed to be, and not everybody will go into ascension. Not everybody has completed purging or clarifying their chakras and their energy, which is negative and dense, keeping them victimized in darkness.

* * * * *

(To use an analogy, I refer to the seven chakras as the seven candles of a candlestick. A candlestick is a symbol of light within our soul.)

DOUG: Does lighting a candlestick (within) indicate entry into the fourth dimension?

JOHN: It can bring spiritual energy, yes. No one has ever talked about this. This is a good question.

DOUG: The power of light.

JOHN: Yes, the candle is light, and in that light of energy, you will attract higher consciousness.

DOUG: Like the seven chakras.

JOHN: Well, the seven chakras are functioning as well as they can for the particular individual. What people want and need to do is to release any darkness in those chakras so that they can be more and more open to that light.

DOUG: So I guess the most important part is the initiation where it enables the energy to flow through the chakra centers, like seven candlesticks.

JOHN: Yes, it would be better to think of each candle with the color of the chakra. So you might want to get a red candle for the base chakra if you are connecting to and feeling that chakra. You may wish to get an orange candle, and then you may light that to work on the next chakra. I do not know if you know the colors that go with each chakra. Yellow would be the third. You would want a green candle for the heart, and you would want a blue candle for the throat. The actual organization of the chakras is not how Western civilization approaches it. The top chakra is your crown chakra. For that, you would want a violet candle. Then you go to the third eye, which is located on the center of your forehead, and that would be a very indigo blue. So you see, as you go up the chakras, you encounter different colors.

* * * * *

Section 1.7: Illusion of Satan and Lucifer

There is a perception that the Devil is a dragon or some spiritual leader of the dark world that created evils. Our lives are being defined by how we can overcome the ups and downs of life with no rationales about why things happen the way they do. As John pointed out, Satan and Lucifer are just illusions. Actually, the devils that carry negative emotions are among us.

* * * * *

DOUG: I'm going to read this passage from the Bible. It comes from Ephesians of the New Testament. It says, "Wherein in time past we walk according to the course of this world and after the prince that ruleth in the air, even the spirit, that now worketh in the children of disobedience." Was the prince in this passage the dragon, like the prince of this world, before Jesus took over?

JOHN: Yes, the prince of this world would be the - what churches would call the Devil or Satan but is just the lower, darker energy within you. See, the church - Marilyn just wrote about this. The churches didn't want people to know that it was their inner consciousness that was creating their problems.

They created an outside force called Devil or Satan and then said, "That's what is your enemy." And of course, our lower nature is not working with us in cooperating for a higher level of experience. So, it is an enemy within. So, when the Bible says the Devil, that's part of their dogma.

* * * * *

The Devil is an angel who has rebelled against God. The Bible called it Lucifer. "How art thou fallen from heaven, O Lucifer, son of the morning and cut down to the ground, which didst cast lots upon the nations?" (Isaiah 14:12).

DOUG: Was Lucifer removed from control in 2003?

JOHN: Lucifer only had the control people gave him. If they gave away their power, then they would be separated from God again. Lucifer doesn't have any power. He never had any power. So to think of Lucifer as a ruler of something is absolutely inaccurate. It's only people's misperception that he had power.

DOUG: So it's kind of like Satan. It's just a negative energy?

JOHN: Yes, it's just a negative energy, and it wasn't originally negative. The theological people used that as part of their doctrine to scare people. So the word Lucifer means light, so it was never intended to be darkness.

DOUG: Was he archangel though?

JOHN: Yes, but it was not [pauses]. He's been demonized by the church. Let's put it that way.

* * * * *

We all possess an angelic energy that exists in a physical form. We all have wings, and they are indications of our spiritual growth. When you have huge widespread wings, you are on your path and aware of who and what you are. Wings that are undeveloped and droopy signify that you still have much growth and learning. All angelic beings have fully grown, erect wings. As humanity has taken its toll, our wings have begun to sink and sag.

God is inside of us. He has been with us since birth, but the church doesn't teach that. All it takes is for us to knock on his door and ask him to be a part of our lives. "Ask, and it shall be given you: seek, and ye shall find: knock, and it shall be opened unto you. For whosoever asketh, receiveth, and he that seeketh, findeth, and to him that knocketh, it shall be opened" (Matthew 7:7–8).

* * * * *

DOUG: I wonder if one of my spiritual informants was communicating with my angel.

JOHN: Angels are vibrations, and she is communicating with your vibrations. That's what a psychic does. She reads your vibrations. You can call those your angels. You see, everybody has labels for these different terms. In the Bible, the writers oftentimes used terms that were relatable to energy because they didn't understand science at that time, and so Jesus was careful to word things using relatable terms. Even though people didn't understand feelings or consciousness, they called these concepts mansions. He tried to find words that would be suitable for the message. That way, the energy would be there for them, and they could get the message without understanding the more current, more sophisticated energy readings that we understand today.

DOUG: I was asking a psychic about Mary Madeleine whether she was an angel.

JOHN: Well, if you want to describe an angel, I would say that everyone on Earth is an angel. Inside all of us, there is angelic energy.

DOUG: So you are saying the Ten Commandments came directly from God?

JOHN: Right. If you are meditating or open completely to the spiritual energy that is within, that is God talking to you directly.

* * * * *

Someone could hold a grudge against you because of your newfound success. You have taken a different path, one that takes you to a different level of consciousness. There are many different circumstances that lead to success. You usually form friendships with people who share similar interests. You could develop a mutual admiration for one another because of similar values. Some friendships could last for a long time, and others could go for just a little while. Most of us renew our lives, and we find new friends with a new level of interest. We all have a new lease on life as we grow. It is a constant process. We have come to Earth to grow spiritually and to move away from our old habits. Some old habits might require several lives to overcome. This is perfectly okay. It is a process. The angels and masters are there to help us overcome our devils. The greatest lesson is to learn love. It is a powerful emotion that brings everybody together. We are being divided by a lack of love. Basically, it boils down to two things. Either we are guided by the love from our hearts, or we are guided by our egos. God is your heart, and Satan is your ego.

For instance, people with significant financial means are more comfortable being around people who have similar means. By the same token, people that are poor are more comfortable being with the poor. People choose friends and families that are comfortable to them. However, as we grow to a higher dimension, people will embrace one another without regard of these factors. Then this world becomes a much better place. As the society grows to a higher vibrational state, more and more people will value love from our hearts. The old third-dimensional materialistic values are going away. Some people may cling to their old ways of selfishness. This is going to change. When love comes to light, they will feel left out because people are seeking more love. Love brings acceptance of everyone regardless of their race or creed.

According to John, the Creator's master plan involves relocating souls to a different world to commensurate with their vibrational values. In the near future, some loving souls from other parts of the universe are coming here to help raise love and light on this planet. Those who resist the change will reincarnate elsewhere in the universe in a lower realm. People with evil intent, such as members of ISIS, terrorists, and murderers, will not be here on this planet in the future. They will be relocated somewhere else and dealt with by similar people.

Mother Earth has raised her vibration to love and light. We are in the early stages. We have taken on thousands of life journeys, and we are now coming to the point of raising our wings. Some people may not be ready to ascend, as they have not worked out their dark energies. They will reincarnate elsewhere to another third-dimensional planet.

The throne of God determines where we need to be for our next spiritual journey.

* * * * *

DOUG: If people were to die today and they remain in the third dimension, would they go to another planet?

JOHN: Well, that is a very good question. There's actually several answers. Everybody is in a different place spiritually. If they are new to the planet, they might have new souls and still have past lives or other lives to experience. So if they are new souls, they would definitely be transferred to another planet to continue their third-dimensional experience and change their energies. If they are an old soul, it is very likely that when they have passed over, they will move forward—you don't go backward—into the fifth dimension. In this lifetime, they will actual complete their struggles and the challenges that they needed to address. So you can't just make a blanket statement about where everybody is going. If people have ascended, they then have new choices to come back and help others or to move on to other planets and universes and go about the universe and do what is the right thing for them at that point. So souls will disburse in the right directions at the appropriate time.

* * * * *

When people have worked them out, then they will eventually grow in love and come back to the planet Earth. The book of Revelation has provided a time line of one thousand years. "But the rest of the dead men shall not live again, until the thousand years be finished. This is the first resurrection. Blessed and holy is he that hath part in the first resurrection: for on such the second death hath no power: but they shall be the Priests of God and of Christ, and shall reign with him a thousand years" (Revelation 20:5–6). We are heading into the realm of love and light. The "world to come" is the fifth dimension. "For it is impossible that they which were once lightened, and have tasted of the heavenly gift, and were made partakers of the Holy Ghost, and have tasted of the good word of God, and of the powers of the world to come" (Hebrews 6:4–5).

Section 1.8: Energy

The fundamental element of reality is consciousness manifested as energy. Physical energy consists of particles and waves. Throughout history metaphysicists have always believed that man and the cosmos were interconnected by an all-pervasive sea of energy that manifested in all phenomena. Physicists today know that matter is a form of energy vibrating at different frequencies. Energy comprises 98 percent of the universe, and matter is only 2 percent.

In subatomic physics an elemental reality is conceived as a focus of energy. Specific energy fields assume distinct forms when manifesting through individual frequencies. All articles in our empirical world are composed of energy frequencies, which, when arrested, manifest through forms. We reside in a universe of spiritual, psychic, and physical energies. All living things exist because of their ability to transmute this universal energy into something individual through thought. We create our own realities. It is how we perceive ourselves. Are we winners? Are we happy? Are we successful? We are who we think we are.

Through proper training, we can learn how to how use and preserve spiritual energy in self-transformation. We apply higher compositions of energy to maintain greater harmony and understanding or to transmute lower energy fields—either locally or at a distance. Higher thinking helps transmit our energy field, or individual unit of power. As energy transformers, we develop proportionately to the degree of universal energy we accept and how freely it flows through us. The more we transmit this energy or allow it to flow through us, the higher level of consciousness we can attain and the more alive, contented, and efficient we become. The spirit of truth at Pentecost is a good example of this occurrence. It occurred more than two thousand years ago, yet the energy force is still alive today.

Frederic W. H. Myers (ref. 37) was an early investigator of spiritual and psychic energy. He theorized that the subliminal self is in touch with a realm of spiritual forces from which it draws energy to infuse into the human mind. This energy ordinarily comes in limited quantities, but during altered states the amount of energy is considerable, elevating an individual's mental functions to exceptionally high levels. For example, while we are in a conscious state, the energy is typically received at a much lower level, according to Myers. Our thought forms are not nearly as effective because of the dark energy surrounding us that was created by our egos. Our prayers transmit energy to God, but they are more effective when done with a group. Collective prayer is much more powerful because it combines the energy of individuals. Halfhearted praying contains very little energy if any at all.

Myers argued that in terms of its evolution as an instrument, the brain is in its early stages. It is through the brain that the higher self (or soul) operates in the material world. In other words, the higher self is basically inactive. He believed that the subliminal self is part of the higher self, remaining unexpressed in our lives. The subliminal self surpasses the threshold of consciousness in its range of spiritual and psychic powers when attaining a higher state of consciousness.

During meditation we move our minds away from the conscious state to an unconscious or subconscious state, and thus, more energy flows to our minds. Our prayers are heard much more efficiently when we pray from an unconscious state like a trance.

The energy waves from God that sustain us are manifested in our separate frequency transmission. Our individual essence maintains itself by allowing Christ consciousness to flow through our chakras. The instant higher energy flows through us is the moment we are in absolute unity with divinity. The individual power with the flow of Christ consciousness is composed of the truth.

The universe is a web of energy that transmits life force. All entities receive and transmit energy through radiation. We create within ourselves an impelling force by combing spiritual, psychic, and physical energies. The best method to achieve the desired results is through meditation. Meditation is the door to the kingdom of God. It is joy in the Holy Ghost. When we have reached the kingdom of God, we have the energy of Christ consciousness.

Whatever the method we use to receive the spiritual, psychic, and physical energies from a higher dimension, it will increase our spiritual capability. We learn to attune ourselves to the universe's energy frequency, thus experiencing spiritual and psychic entrainment.

Chakras are the centers of energy that are physically and spiritually associated with various parts of our bodies. When kundalini energy moves through the chakras, our consciousness changes. Each chakra is said to correspond to a particular energy level. Please refer to section 1.6 for more details. By meditating on these chakras, we gain mastery over our bodies.

The original energy from creation is often called Akasha in Indian philosophy and modern occult circles. This elemental psychic energy influences spiritual, psychic, and psychological phenomena. One of the major functions of liberating energy of self-consciousness is to boost self-awareness. The ego has the lowest level of self-awareness. The higher self has the highest.

In the vast majority of humanity, this self-awareness lies passively at the base of the spine, coiled like a serpent. After learning to contact the various focal points of energy, an individual can move his or her locus of consciousness into the different areas of the chakras. If and when the higher self is reached, spiritual awakening can occur. Attaining our higher selves allows a descent and another ascent of this energy, which awakens the psychic centers.

Boosting self-awareness is linked to sexual and creative forces in humans. Sexual desire is a fundamental evolutionary impulse along with higher intellectual forces. The need for positive orgasmic experiences is biologically and psychically rooted. Sexual experiences within the context of genuine love involve spiritual transcendence.

Theorists such as Sigmund Freud and researchers such as Wilhelm Reich have studied psychic energy from a psychological perspective, viewing it as a complex mental, sexual, or libidinous energy in our unconsciousness. Psychological sufferings are the result of blockage of psychic energy.

According to Freud, all conduct is motivated by the desire to feel pleasure. That motivation is organized and directed by two instincts—sexuality and aggression. Freud theorized that both of these instincts were powered by a form of internal psychic energy, which he called the libido—an underlying psychic energy.

This sexual drive can be used positively within a mature love relationship as Freud described in his psychoanalysis. In contemporary society, however, libidinous drives are generally corrupted, resulting in psychological disorders.

Spiritual energy can be directed by meditation, which is how prayer and spiritual healing work. Since external and internal energy affect our states of consciousness so directly, we must attentively select the inputs we allow into our experiences. These inputs might be the people, activities, and environments we encounter. Every time we interact with another person, there is a transfer of energy, either positive or negative. Continuous interaction with people who have negative energy fields may harm us and leave us with a tremendous amount of harmful energy debris. To preserve our energy, we need to learn to recognize negative energy and remove it. If we don't, then we can suffer physical, emotional, mental, and spiritual problems. Fortunately, the opposite is equally true. Spending time with positively charged persons and cultural phenomena, such as enlightening music, art, and literature, can have positive transformative effects.

Our spiritual and psychic energy can be misused or wasted in some ways. Negative mental and emotional states rapidly leak energy, particularly in the third dimension, where the ego dictates behavior. This leakage can retard our spiritual progress. Self-importance is one of our greatest enemies, especially when we allow ourselves to be weakened by the misdeeds of other people. Our self-importance requires that we spend most of our lives being offended by someone.

* * * * *

DOUG: Does personality survival have to do with not making it to the fifth dimension?

JOHN: For the personality to survive, we need a flexible awareness that we are among peers who may be sucking our energy reserves dry for their own survival while we are in the third dimension. As you move into higher consciousness, such as into the fifth dimension, you are no longer a victim but an empowered individual. So your personality will move into who you are as an empowered child full of light with all the peace of Christ consciousness. Thus, personality changes as consciousness changes.

DOUG: You mentioned personality survival or my energy being depleted by other energies. Am I protected when I reach the fifth dimension?

JOHN: In the fifth dimension, you have graduated beyond the ego-based life completely and moved into a heart-based or a love-based life. Your energy has changed completely, so there is no negative energy remaining.

DOUG: You know, I was with a group of people over the weekend. Because of work, I had not been in a social situation in three or four months. I did not want to interact with people whose negative energies would bog me down. I was right. After interacting with these people, I felt completely drained, and when I got home, I felt all kinds of negative energy. I avoided going out until I finished this book.

JOHN: Well, I think it is good to protect yourself from that negative energy. It keeps your energy high so that you are coming from the place that you want to come from. And you can pray for like-minded people to come into your life and for opportunities to acquire new friends who have states of higher consciousness. It is not uncommon for people who are growing spiritually to gain new friends, leave some of the old friends behind, and move into a happier place. And yes, you may no longer fit in with many of the people from the past.

* * * * *

Appropriate self-regard is certainly an important factor in any healthy conception of oneself, but what we are referring to is called malodorous self-importance or pomposity.

It is first necessary to identify with our higher selves and develop a moment-to-moment awareness of what's happening in our personal energy fields and the energy networks affecting us. We learn to notice how we feel around certain people and in certain situations, whether energized or enervated. Power struggles are about stealing one another's energy. If you feel drained after having been with a particular person, you are probably losing power to that person.

We develop the ability to observe our emotions and thoughts as they occur. If we come in contact with an individual or idea—either meeting face-to-face or while watching movies or television—something that regularly pushes our buttons, we must learn to control our energy field so unconscious reactions do not wreak havoc on our emotional lives. Jesus demonstrated love when someone was accusing him of *playing* God. Jesus responded calmly to the man, and the Devil (the negative emotion of jealousy) went out of him because he felt love (respect) coming from Jesus. It was possible that Luke had an opened third eye so that he could see the spirit of negative emotion (the Devil) leaving the man. He says, "And in the Synagogue there was a man who had a spirit of an unclean devil, which cried with a loud voice, Saying, Oh, what have we to do with thee, thou Jesus of

Nazareth? Art thou come to destroy us? I know who thou art, even the Holy one of God. And Jesus rebuked him, saying, Hold thy peace, and come out of him. Then the devil throwing him in the midst of them, came out of him, and hurt him nothing at all" (Luke 4:33–35).

With this love, Jesus protected himself by not challenging the man, thereby preserving his energy. He demonstrated love and forgiveness. Self-important persons transmit spiritual and psychic energies to people, events, and objects in the external world. This phenomenon is usually seen by us as the person being *uncomfortable* or *self-important* to a greater or lesser degree. We sometimes say of such people that they are "full of themselves," "always on camera," or trying to "charm" other people. What we mean is that their energy is flowing outward through their eyes to *see* what others are thinking and feeling about them, attempting to pull another person's energy toward them.

The "outer-directional energy flow" syndrome is not always present in mere show-offs. Such "constantly on stage" performers may or may not have an outer-directed optical energy flow. The "outer-directional energy flow" is most easily seen in a person's eyes. However, the same uncontrolled energy discharge can transpire in other dysfunctional behavioral phenomena, such as loud talking, ungoverned negative thinking, and foolhardy destructive actions.

Spiritual energy is an invisible realm to a naked eye, but not to an opened third eye. Select individuals have that capability today. These people can communicate with the angels from the spiritual realm. The angels could manifest themselves into physical bodies at will. We can attain a spiritual growth to the eighth dimension, and then we would be able to change forms among the physical and spiritual worlds. We are just entering the fifth dimension, so we are a long way off from achieving this.

The third eye is the seventh chakra. Western philosophy listed it as the sixth chakra. The third eye is the spiritual eye. It is a gift.

* * * * *

DOUG: Ghosts are visible with a third-eye, so at what spiritual dimension would a person have to be able to see with his third-eye?

JOHN: Well, that is what a psychic does. Psychics see through a third eye into the invisible or spiritual world. Moreover, psychics deal with what they see in the fourth, third, and lower dimensions. A medium can look into the fifth dimension and beyond.

DOUG: Obviously, my third eye is closed because I do not see spirits. However, is there a technique I can learn to be able to do that?

JOHN: Yes, you can have your chakras cleared. Marilyn could help you with that, or somebody else, but when you clear your chakras and open them up you will begin to see in a more visual way. You do not have to actually experience the visual; it becomes a knowing and a feeling. There are different ways of seeing spiritually. Clairvoyants see visually, while clairaudiences see auditorily, while still others see through feelings.

DOUG: Is the spiritual eye the sixth chakra?

JOHN: Technically, it is the seventh chakra, and the sixth chakra is the crown. Most people have done a revision of the Eastern version of the chakras. In Psalm 23, which says, "Was brought in the staff, they comfort me," the staff refers to the chakras, and the chakras come up in the shape of staff. So as you are coming up through the chakras, you get to the third-eye.

DOUG: This woman checked to see if energy was flowing through my chakras. However, she said that she could see much vibration somewhere around my hair but that my spiritual eye was closed. So what you're describing would probably fix the chakras and the energy flowing through me but not the seventh chakra.

JOHN: Well, part of opening up your last chakra, which God asks you to open, is requesting to be open and receptive in a meditative state. At some point after you have asked, you will feel an energy change. For Marilyn, when her third chakra opened, it opened partially, and she had a spiritual vision. Then at a later date, a cork, not unlike a cork in a wine bottle, popped out, and she experience an even a higher vision. So there are various levels of that spirituality, and it doesn't necessarily happen all at once.

* * * * *

"The light of the body is the eye: therefore, when thine eye is single, then is thy whole body light: but if thine eye be evil, then thy body is dark" (Luke 11:34). Our ability to see from our third eye is contingent on our chakras level. If the energy does not flow through the chakras, then likely there is still some dark energy residing in our soul and blocking us from attaining Christ consciousness. As we move into the new age, more and more people will discover this power and attain it. The free flowing energy from God is the "fountain of the living water."

The living water heals our bodies from various ailments. We can maintain the vitality of our health, and then our ten missing strands of DNA are activated as well. Attaining Christ consciousness helps restore our energy balance. "O Lord, the hope of Israel, that forsakes thee, shall be confounded: they that depart from thee, shall be written in the earth because they have forsaken the Lord, the fountain of living waters. Heal me, O Lord, and I shall be whole: save me, and I shall be saved: for thou art my praise" (Jeremiah 17:13–14).

Our health during the New Age will improve dramatically. Eventually, all forms of disabilities will go away after they are healed by God. Hearing impairment, vision impairment, physical impairment, mental retardation, and emotional impairment are a result of the missing strands in our DNA, which was orchestrated by the dark side.

As John revealed, up to this point in existence, we have been given just two strands of our DNA. For the upcoming ascension, we all will attain higher spiritual vibration. In the past, Christ consciousness was difficult to maintain in a third-dimensional world, as negative emotions dominated our lives. It is difficult to love one another as neighbors while we are missing a key component of love. When we feel unbalanced, we tend to rely on our egos to feel better about ourselves. We tend to look to others for approval. We lack appreciation of ourselves. These feelings have caused many conflicts, much racial strife, and many differing belief systems to emerge. When our DNA is restored, we will return to the oneness of God. The oneness of God in Christ consciousness binds every human being together. Love conquers all fears.

As the new age is imminent, more and more people with a higher dimension will be able to help others overcome the remnants of the third dimension. We are about to ascend to the fifth dimension. Jesus attained this level more than two thousand years ago. The spirit of truth began the process of an energy change on the planet. It was an invisible phenomenon, and people were largely unaware of its significance. God the Father is an energy—an energy of love. He does not judge you. His essence makes you feel whole. The messengers of God were the ones who have expressed the wrath of God, not God the Father. It did not come from him. He is the only loving energy among us. It was their emotional response through their individual vehicles that expressed their feelings. God is light and love energy.

Our souls carry a piece of God, so they are also energy. Our guardian angels are energy. They are among us. People and churches back then had no clue what energy did since scientific understanding was still primitive. Even today with numerous technological advances, spiritual energy cannot be quantified or identified by scientists. Science has come to a better understanding about energy over the past seventy years. Einstein declared that energy cannot be destroyed but only transferred. The soul journey transfers energy from one place in time to another. We are all light beings. Reincarnation is about transferring the dark energies of our souls to another place. We never die. Our souls are eternal. We are being transformed after each passing incarnation. Nirvana is the place where our souls go for spiritual cleansing. I had a conversation through a channel with my deceased father who had passed away last summer, and he said was going through a surgical procedure on his soul in Nirvana. Our souls contain seven chakras, and they remain with us for eternity. Our bodies are just overcoats for our soul journeys, and they are built for just one lifetime. Our souls enter new infant bodies when we are born to our parents, which we selected before leaving Nirvana. Our energies go from there to the mother's womb, and only God the Father can make that possible. "And shall put my Spirit in you, and ye shall live, and I shall place you in your own land: then ye shall know that I the Lord have spoken it, and performed it, saith the Lord" (Ezekiel 37:14).

* * * * *

DOUG: I want to understand how this works. Suppose I come back in another life. I am looking at the verse in the Bible that says, "And shall put my spirit in you and ye shall live, and I shall place it in your own land." Does this mean God the Father places the soul in the mother's womb based on a consultation with the spiritual guides in Nirvana?

JOHN: Well, we are talking about birth, and you are talking about Nirvana. I am not sure what your point is.

DOUG: I am just wondering how this works. If I am in Nirvana and I met with the committee and they have given me choices of where I want to go, do I then make the choice?

JOHN: Right.

DOUG: So how does my energy leave Nirvana and get to the mother's womb? Does God the Father make that transfer from Nirvana to the mother's womb?

JOHN: Yes.

* * * * *

Your own land is your body. It is made from "dust of the ground." "The Lord God also made the man of the dust of the ground, and breathed in his face breath of life, and the man was a living soul" (Genesis 2:7).

Every incarnation builds up energy charge to our chakras. This cannot be done in one lifetime because the energy of God is so powerful that it can burn up your chakras. The energy charge has to be gradual in your chakras. I would liken this buildup to a capacitor. We can only build up the charge incrementally. Apostle John revealed in our channelings that our chakras are being expanded from seven to twelve for the upcoming ascension that is the golden age. It is the thousand-year reign as described in the Bible (Revelation 20:4–6).

Satan, as depicted in the Scripture, represents negative energy. Satan does not exist as a real entity. This is simply a label for people who did not understand the term energy. During the thousand-year reign, people who turn to their hearts rather than their egos will continue their soul journeys here on the planet Earth. For others, they will reincarnate on another third-dimensional planet. There is no death, and there is no lake of fire. During the golden age, societies will transform into loving environments. Eventually, the spiritual vibration will continue to grow in the era of love and light beyond the eighth dimension. We are presently in the fourth dimension. There are still pockets of hatred and wars on the planet today. The current warmongers like ISIS will likely disappear as they are reincarnated to other planets and work out their karmas in an environment where they reap what they have sown. They will be confronted with like-minded states of consciousness. When you allow for the Spirit of God to shine within you, you will feel loved, and you can pass on that love to others. You love others as neighbors. "Master, which is the great commandment in the Law? Jesus said to him, Thou shalt love the Lord thy God with all thine heart, with all thy soul, and with all thy mind. This is the first and the great commandment. Moreover, the second is like, unto this, thou shalt love thy neighbor as thyself. On these two commandments hangeth the whole Law and the Prophets" (Matthew 22:36–40).

Earth is a sentient being. She moved to the fifth dimension on December 21, 2012. People can choose to go along with the new age of the fifth dimension, or they will die off the planet. We need to live our lives from our hearts, not from our egos. The energy of God is in your heart, and it allows us to forgive people and love them readily. Forgiveness is what transforms societies here on Earth. We are here together, and we can help one another grow spiritually into light beings. The angels of God are always there monitoring our progress.

Heaven on earth is a physical manifestation of the "world to come," as depicted in the Scripture. "For it is impossible that they which were once lightened, and have tasted of the heavenly gift, and were made partakers of the Holy Ghost, and have tasted of the good word of God, and of the powers of the world to come" (Hebrews 6:4–5).

The omnipresence, omnipotence, and omniscience is already within us. The cookie batter was already stirred together, and we are part of that wholeness of God. This idea is not one perpetuated by the church. If we are sinners, then we are easily controlled. However, if they told us that we were already whole spirits, then there would be no reason for authority, and the world would be in a different place. Finally, we are coming to an understanding that we are in a higher consciousness, which was not what we were originally led to believe. Our doors and hearts have opened to the love within, so fears are dissipating.

Many people do not realize this, but our thoughts are considered energy. When we are angry at people about something, they will feel it. All of our thoughts are real. If we have a disagreement with our boss at work or if we are upset with our family members or friends, it is wise to send love and forgiveness to that person. It will help ease the situation to a manageable level. As we are entering into a new age, more people find a way to forgive others so that it will be easier to relate to them. We will become more interconnected during the age of love and light during the golden age. We encounter a daily grind of choosing between the wishes of the ego and the righteousness of our hearts. Faith comes from our hearts. The energy of God is in our hearts. When we are envious of someone or not forgiving someone, it creates guilt later on and puts a tremendous burden on our hearts. We all are eternal beings. Some may be more fortunate than others. This is because these individuals have gone through situations before, and they've overcome them. I am not talking about just this lifetime but also previous lives. They've fought their battles. We may be dealing with those battles today. Keep in mind that we will eventually become victors. So we keep living our dreams and moving on to better things. It is all about life's lessons. The end game is joy for every one of us. We all are dealing with a battle similar to the one that Jesus had with the ego. His ego was trying to lead him astray, yet he stuck with his heart. His faith was in his heart. Jesus was showing us the right use of energy. He told his disciples to follow him. Listening to our hearts is a choice we make. Feeling that we are not leading a perfect life is totally acceptable. There are no rights or wrongs. We are just experiencing the rights or wrongs so that down the road of our soul journeys, we become closer to the reality of eternal joy. We are humans. We are imperfect creatures. God is patient. He waits for every one of us to achieve the ultimate goal—eternal joy. We have guiding angels with us. They are there all the time to help us. If we make a mistake, they understand. They are aware we are growing spiritually, and they are there to help us grow.

Before Jesus was born, he was assured angels would watch over him, guide him to the right people, protect him from any dangers, and help him fulfill his mission. His mission was to show us the right use of energy.

* * * * *

DOUG: I realized that Jesus, and possibly you as his disciple, had an opened spiritual eye so you could see and help earthbound spirits.

JOHN: Well, that is what Jesus came to explain was the right use of energy. So many people have taken his information and made a religion out of it. He came to show people the right use of energy, and of course, many looked at this method from different angles. Evidently, his information was used against individuals rather than to benefit them.

* * * * *

To elaborate further on John's comment regarding what Jesus was trying to convey about the right use of energy, let's remember that Jesus was trying to emphasize the power of love from within and for us to enjoy living on earth with that love. Instead people have incorrectly emphasized fear rather than love. Forgiveness is a perfect recipe for living coping with imperfect lives. We are imperfect because we are here to learn the truth of love and forgiveness. Once we have mastered it, then we will spiritually grow to a higher dimension of love and forgiveness and pass it on to others who are learning to grow. The right use of energy is when we follow our hearts. As we enter the next golden age, more and more people will become intuitive and follow their hearts. The dark energies were created by our ego. The ego of Jesus wanted him to be a king. However, he listened to his heart. He overcame it. He was crucified, but he did not feel the pain during the process because the love of God was in his heart. The battle Jesus had to face was similar to what we are dealing with today. It is a fight between the ego and the essence of God in our souls. We are living souls. Scripture gives a description of a war in heaven. It is not a war in space but a war within us. Our egos always want more. The ego does not know when to stop wanting. It leads us astray. The ego of Jesus was trying to manipulate his desires. Who would not want the riches of the world? Jesus could have had riches and people worshipping him for the rest of his life. However, the ego is not everlasting. The essence of God within us is everlasting.

The spiritual reality is an individualized part of us. We are all one with God. The oneness of God is an ocean of love. Our spirit merges with other spirits. However, we still retain our unique individual characteristics. We will grow spiritually to the eighth dimension and beyond in the age of love and light. We will all get there. If we do not feel that way, the process of reincarnation will get us there. We are never alone. When we leave the world and pass over to the other side, we will come back in other bodies, and people will never know us. For some, it might be imminent; for others, it may take a hundred years later. If we need to experience our next soul journey with a certain soul or soul mate, then we have to wait until that individual is ready to move to the next life. For instance, my mother was my sister in one of my past lives.

I had an interesting channeled conversation with my father. The transcription of the conversation is shown in chapter 5 of this book. During his last days, he was suffering from pain. His health was deteriorating because of his multiple sclerosis. He admitted he did not have God in his life. He was a devout Catholic. However, it did not insulate him from pain in the end. He was not cognizant of the power of God within him. He was not taught that way. We all possess a living God. The energy of God is within us.

> Then Jesus answered, and said unto them, ye are deceived, not knowing the Scriptures, nor the power of God. For in the resurrection they neither marry wives nor wives are bestowed in marriage but are as the Angels of God in heaven. And concerning the resurrection of the dead, have ye not read what is spoken unto you of God, saying, I am the God of Abraham, and the God of Isaac, and the God of Jacob? God is not the God of the dead, but of the living. (Matthew 22:29–32)

Following our hearts steadies our focus on today, not tomorrow. We were given a life contract before we entered the world. Some people die sooner than others. We and our spiritual guides in heaven (Nirvana) already agreed upon the contract. Our journeys have already been predestined by our spiritual guides. My best friend's sister passed away unexpectedly of a heart attack last month. She is gone, but she had lived up to her contract.

It is always devastating to lose our loved ones. However, it is not the end of their existence. Their souls are still alive and are in heaven. They will come back for another soul journey. In Jesus's case, he did not need to learn a lesson. He descended to fulfill a mission. He was doing a service for the sake of mankind. Jesus played different roles as a teacher.

An ego is forgetful after one life journey. Any material riches we have accumulated do not go beyond our graves. Our bodies are not a part of that energy. Only the soul is. It is eternal. Our egos cease to exist after death. However, our souls live on for the next journey. Living for today and not tomorrow is important. If we are thinking of salvation, then we are not thinking of the matters at hand today. We are ignoring our life's lessons that are needed to grow spiritually. Our consciousness is a part of our energies. Passing our fears to others can retard our spiritual growth. We need to work these fears out before we move to the next level of consciousness. Love is a powerful force that always yields positive results. We are learning to go away from service to self and toward service to others. The universe is always expanding. As we attain divine consciousness, we will function as angels or spiritual guides to help lower the consciousness of people in other parts of the universe. There is always room for growth when it comes to helping others. The aliens, specifically the Arcturus, are helping us, though they live in an advanced civilization and reside in another galaxy. They live beyond the fifth dimension. Eons ago they were in the third dimension, what we are growing out of today. It is an evolving process. Spiritual life goes on forever.

Section 1.9: Male and Female Energies

Male and female energies are two aspects of the one. Therefore, they are two faces of one energy. The male energy is the characteristic that is outwardly focused. It is that part of God or the Spirit that drives outward manifestation and makes the Spirit materialize and take form. Therefore, the male energy knows an active, creative force. It is ordinary to the male energy to be highly focused and goal-oriented, traits that create individuality. The male energy allows us to separate ourselves from the one and from the whole and to stand alone and live as specific individuals. However, the female energy is the energy of home. It is the energy of the flowing light. It is the inner aspect of things not yet established. The female energy is all-encompassing. It does not differentiate or individualize. The female energy is becoming aware of a particular movement inside of her, a desire for reaching outside of her boundaries to attain experience. There is a longing for something adventurous. It is the male energy that desires to be of service. The male energy shapes the female energy, and with their support, the total sum of energies can take a whole new direction. A new reality can be experienced in ever-changing forms of manifestation.

The dance of the male and the female brings forth the fluctuating spectacle of the reality we've created. It is a scene of great beauty where the male and female energy worship each other and celebrate their cooperation and playful joining. The male and female energy belong together since they are two aspects of the one. Together, they celebrate the joyful manifestation that creation is supposed to be.

The final realization of who we are, the only truth that matters is "I Am." So in this mystical mantra, precisely those two aspects merge. The "I" is the male energy, and the "Am" is the female energy. Male and female bodies are only symbols of male and female energies. The male energy is a correspondence between positive energy or the father aspect. The female energy corresponds to negative polarity or the mother aspect. The "I" or the self is constricting and differentiating.

It gives focus. It gives direction, and it individuates. The "Am" is all encompassing of the female energy, the inexhaustible source that knows no bounds and differentiation. The flowing and joining attribute is the core of the female energy. In the "I Am," the male and female come together and joyfully join their energies or during the process of marriage.

Every creation in the universe contains either the positive and negative energy, or they are either male or female. This includes everything from a subatomic particle to an atom, a human being, a planet, or a galaxy. Only the energy of purpose is 100 percent neutral. All forms are polarizing in either male or female energy. Each form is composed of wavelengths with active interplay between both energies. Within the genetic makeup of a human male, there are many female energies at work, and the female deals with numerous male energies within her. Marriage, too, is much more than the joining of two physical persons. Marriage is a universal order, a bonding relationship as it unites the male and female energies into a united whole. All male and female energies seek this union.

It is interesting to study the marriage of atoms. In perceiving them we must realize that every form, whether an atom or a planet, possesses consciousness and is either positively or negatively charged. In other terms, it is either male or female. The chemist identifies the male atom as a positive particle and the female atom as a negative one. Within the atom, we have the positive or male nucleus, and the negative or female electron shells. These are married to produce something better than each in isolation, namely a whole atom. In the case of the union of the female electrons to the male protons in the nucleus, the ratio is constantly one to one. For example, with nitrogen, if there are seven protons, they are balanced off with the energies of seven orbiting female electrons. These subatomic particles never diverge from this one-to-one ratio.

An interesting principle to consider is that all male and female energies in the universe are seeking stability or neutrality. In other words, they try to return to the energy of purpose. The prodigal son of this form is attempting to go back to his father. A marriage achieves this stability.

With one moon, Earth is like an enormous hydrogen atom, but the sun is also similar to an atom with the planets circling it. On an even bigger scale, the galaxies, which are composed of billions of stars, relate to electrons and positrons. The universe is like a giant proton.

The sexual center is the only center that has one polarity in a body. The male body and the female body counterparts both have one polarity, even though they are opposite. When they unite sexually, they both sense completeness. They are no longer two but "one flesh." However, for other parts of the human body, they do not have such a need to connect with the opposite sex to feel complete. Nevertheless, when the other centers of the male and female share a similar vibration, there is a nonpossessive transfer of energy that generates high states of joy in both of them. To create balance, we must understand these two energies. The male energy is a radiant or sending energy. The female or negative energy is magnetic, attractive, and receiving. Keep in mind that all physical creations are symbolic of spiritual energies, not to mention their outward manifestation in the physical bodies of the two sexes.

During sex the male body is the sender of the seed. The male genitals are undeniably the sending unit. The female body is the receiver of the seed, and the female genitals receive the male. The growth of the baby is an automatic process. By the power of magnetism, the materials for the growth of the body are drawn to the woman who is an aspect of female energy.

There are two apparent energies in the universe that are male and female. For instance, the two energies that sustain the universe are radiance and magnetism. The sun and the stars give off the light, heat, and radiation that give life and support to all things. Magnetism gives form to all things and holds all creation together. Magnetic energy is invisible, but its effect is just as powerful as radiance. Gravity is an example of magnetic energy. However, radiance energy is visible. There would be no form to impart radiation without magnetism, which produces the form.

Because the female energy (or magnetism) is not visible, its importance has gone unnoticed. Male energy has dominated in recent times because it is a more visible energy. The radiant energy is more attractive than the magnetic because the use of this energy is easier to perceive. The feminine energy is a mystery because its effects are seen, but the operation of the energy is not.

* * * * *

DOUG: Why were women dominant back in the time of Jesus?

JOHN: Women's intuition and their spiritual connection are assessable to Mother Mary. Mary is the feminine aspect of God, which is the loving character that can manifest in human form. So this was considered a charming talent, and women were said to have that ability to connect with the feminine side of God. However, there was an uprising when the masculine energy decided from an egotistical point of view that they did not want that feminine energy in control anymore. So that has been part of the enormous problems with Earth coming into a higher consciousness. We must overcome the masculine, which is trying to overtake the feminine energy.

* * * * *

In history we see male and female energies drifting apart, making them appear as opposite forces. The yin and yang symbols demonstrate this situation well. In the masculine there is always a core of the feminine. In the feminine there is a core of the masculine. However, in the course of history, this mystical unity of the masculine and feminine energies has been neglected. Right now we are in the last phase of this history of conflict. The male energy has played the part of the perpetrator for many centuries. The male energy has long been oppressing and destroying the female energy. There were times when the female energy had the upper hand and ruled the male energy. However, the conflict took a different turn at a certain point and reversed the roles of perpetrator and victim. The male energy has been in power for some time. This has led those with the female energy to not realize the integrity of their beings anymore. Whenever the masculine and feminine are in discord, the disintegration of both is inevitable. Where the feminine gets victimized more and more and gets lost in self-denial, the male energy loses itself in hard-hearted violence.

The masculine and the feminine hinge on each other. When they battle each other, the consequences are disastrous. However, times are shifting. Since the nineteenth and twentieth centuries, the female energy is reclaiming its strength, climbing above the role of victim. This renaissance comes from deep within the feminine energy. Women have conclusively reached the outer limit of their self-denial. They have examined themselves and have said, "This is as far as it goes."

There is a common dynamic between victim and perpetrator. Change starts when the victim refuses to accept more, and this change is evidenced by the women's liberation movement starting the late 1960s and persisting throughout the 1970s. The perpetrator could well hang on to his role longer, as he has less reason to stop. Revolution begins when the victim refuses to accept the perpetuation anymore and finally takes back her power. In all situations of repression, the real moment of change is when the woman (or the feminine energy within a person) decides for herself, "I will not take this any longer." It is when change starts to take place. External measures are impractical until this moment presents itself.

The female energy has arisen, and its star is rising. The most crucial matter in this time and age is the transformation of the male energy. It is now time for a new characterization of male energy. It is a rebirth of the male energy. A reunion with a mature and balanced male energy will enable the female energy to flourish again. The female energy has in the past century (even before that) regained power and strength. It has begun to thrive in a new and more balanced way. Despite the inequality of the sexes, which is still present in our society, the rise of the female energy is inescapable. However, without any cooperation with the male energy, the female energy cannot gain full strength and vitality. It goes on the collective level as well as the individual. The female energy cannot make its final breakthrough without the support of and connection with the male energy. It is not because of an inherent weakness in the female energy but because of the essential nature of male and female energies. The fact is that they are intertwined and can only fulfill their brightest potential in cooperation. It is vital now that the male energy reshapes itself for the coming fifth dimension. When we look at the interplay between male and female energies on a cooperative level, the female energy is now waiting. At present, there is a battle going on within the collective male energy between the old and the new. A new wave of energy is emerging within the collective male energy that honors and compliments the female energy. This new trend of male energy wants to bond with the female and together enter the new age. However, at the same time, an older wave of male energy is still resistive.

The male energy in its old role of a heartless aggressor is showing its nasty side. In the ones who commit these horrific attacks, there are dark emotions, the common threads of the dark side—aggression, anger, powerlessness, and helplessness. From this total failure, they appeal to the most brute and damaging displays of power. This male energy is dying. It senses that there are significant changes going on collectively and that humanity is on the threshold of a new era. We will see the control by the churches lessen as we move forward to a new age.

For a balanced collaboration between male and female, we need to understand how to deal with this kind of heartless energy. What are we going to do about this old male energy that is attempting to create as much havoc and destruction as imaginable in its downfall? The former male energy has lost the power struggle. However, it will not give up easily, and it will resist to the end with aggression and merciless attempts at domination. Changes have already started to take place in preparation for the Fifth Dimension. The churches are crumbling, and people are speaking out for their personal rights as seen in the Irish referendum on gay rights. More and more people recognize their loving energy within themselves. In simplistic term, we are following our hearts is doing the will of God. The more we allow our hearts to manifest in ourselves, the more balanced our lives become. It brings balance for the male and female energies and enables them to coexist. Much will depend on how the inner collective attitude will be toward these aggressors. Will we allow anger and powerlessness into our energy field as a reaction to acts of violence? Then we open up to the energy field of the aggressors. When we feel overpowered by our anger and resentment toward them, they have reached their target. We become integrated into their energetic vibration, and we are then willing to kill as well—kill the murderers of the innocent. It is all very understandable, but it is vital that we realize what is happening. As soon as we sense intense emotions, it is best to take our focus away from them and pause in silence. Go back to the quiet, knowing part of yourself and ask, "What is going on here?" It is all about our wisdom and discernment now, our ability to see through things and to feel what is at stake. Terrorist powers will not capture the world. The old male energy has served its time, and its dying hour is at hand. The most important message about terrorism, which is a manifestation of old male aggression, is to stay conscious. Do not let yourself become imbalanced by emotions of powerlessness or victimization. Know that this aggressive energy does not affect us that that we need not allow it into our energy field. If we do not react with anger or hatred, we will not draw it to ourselves. We will be safe and protected from our light. Everything that happens together mirrors processes at the individual level.

To illustrate the importance of balance between the feminine and

Door to Glory

the masculine energies on the individual level for the energy chakras centers and they are either male or female.

The root chakra is the energy center that connects us to Earth. The energy in this chakra reaches out to Earth and allows us to manifest our soul energy in physical form on the dense, material level of reality. Given the fact that the energy reaches out and manifests, not to mention how the root chakra is a red color, we may call it a predominantly male chakra. A chakra is never entirely male or female, but one may say that the male energy has the advantage.

The second chakra is the navel or belly button chakra, and it is the center of emotions. This center allows us to live through the highs and lows of an emotional life. It is a receptive center or a female center. It is a chakra that the female flow of energy dominates.

The third chakra or the solar plexus is a center of action and creation. It is a center that reaches out and allows energy to manifest in physical reality. We may compare it to the sun, the outpouring of rays and the power of the yellow sunlight. In the solar plexus, our thoughts, ideas, and desires are transformed into outer manifestation. This is the chakra of action and notable expression. It is also the center of the ego, meaning the earthly personality, though without any negative inferences. The predominant energy is male.

The heart chakra has the unique ability to connect different flows of energy of the lower three chakras and the upper three chakras. The upper three chakras are considered the connection to cosmic reality. The heart is the bridge between mind (head) and emotion (belly). From the heart we are also able to connect with others and transcend ourselves. The heart transcends the boundaries of the ego and enables us to feel at one with the source. It is a center of connection and is therefore predominantly feminine (See Figure 5 in Section 1.6)

* * * * *

DOUG: If a person can keep his chakras clean, then the energy of

God will continue to flow through. That person pretty much will experience heaven on earth.

JOHN: Exactly. That is what you are cleansing out. The emotions affect the chakras. Your different emotional parts of your lives affect different chakras. The first chakra is the root chakra or the base chakra. The superstitions you were raised with, the family lies or tribal dysfunctions that you were raised with, the way the genetics of your family affect you—those are part of the first chakra. The second chakra has to do with relationships and how well your family members interact with one another (or don't). So as you go through the different chakras, including the third one, are you open to the love of God, and do you have the courage to act in your assertive way? Alternatively, are you fearful and act timid and as a victim? Also, you can change that energy. So each chakra has its emotional impact that you need to clean out. So of course, the heart chakra is the most important one because that is where you connect with the consciousness of God.

DOUG: The fourth chakra?

JOHN: The heart chakra. That is where you connect with God. Consider the throat chakra. People who have thyroid problems are also afraid to speak their truth. I am giving you very simplified explanations here. As you move into your crown chakra, which is the sixth chakra, you open up to the energy that surrounds you and fills you with the grace of God. So as you meditate, you are opening yourself up to the fifth dimension, but your crown chakra must be cleaned and cleared so that you are available to do that. The seventh chakra is your third eye, which is on the forehead between your eyebrows. Also, that is your spiritual site. So what happened when people came to Earth. Instead of using their spiritual side, they closed off the seventh chakra. So because of our physical nature, we started to see with physical eyes. Moreover, that is when the ego took over and gave you information about feeling, touching, hearing, and seeing. So people were very caught up in the third dimension with what they could see outside of themselves, and they took their focus off God.

DOUG: Now when people reincarnate, would the chakras stay with the soul?

JOHN: Yes. Those chakras stay with your soul as they come into to clean a little bit more. So cleansing of your soul is a gradual process with each reincarnation.

* * * * *

The throat chakra is male. From this center, ideas and emotions are given physical shape through speaking, crying, laughing, singing, yelling, and so forth. Here, the spiritual life is expressed outwardly by communication through the voice and language. This center enables us to make our inner life known to others by using physical signals, such as words, sounds, and concepts. It is a center of manifestation that allows us to focus our energy outwardly into the physical plane. It is also a center of creativity.

The seventh chakra is the third eye, and it is feminine. It receives extrasensory, intuitive impressions and transcends the boundaries of the five physical senses. It is the seat of clairvoyance and clairsentience, and we can feel the energy of someone else. Through the emotions, the pains, the joys as our own. With this ability of empathy, we transcend the boundaries of the ego, and we connect with "that which is not us."

Finally, the crown chakra is an interesting combination of both energies that is neither male nor female. Alternatively, we might say it is both. In this chakra we rise above the duality of male and female. The crown chakra is an interesting combination of both energies. While this chakra is balanced, the consciousness within is in a state of receiving as much as reaching out. It seeks spiritual meaning or deeper layers of the self. At the same time, there is a quiet and tranquil alertness, a knowingness that the answers will come in the right time. It is a form of consciousness that is highly focused and highly receptive. In this way of thinking, we come close to the unity that inspires male and female energies, the energy of God.

The lowest three chakras are the most enmeshed in the earthly realm. The lowest three chakras are of importance in our inner road to healing, for the deepest traumas and emotional scars occur there. We often feel we are earthly beings opening up to the spiritual. However, the angels see it the other way around. They see us as spiritual beings opening up to Earth. Earth is a brilliant destination, a hidden diamond that has yet to reveal its true beauty. Earth is the Promised Land.

Heaven is our birthplace. The adventure of creation brings us to new destinations. We are always expanding and progressing toward a wholly new type of consciousness. Earth is a foremost part of this journey. We must transform our energies from a lower vibrational state to a higher blissful state.

* * * * *

DOUG: Would every single soul eventually find a home with God?

JOHN: Yes, this is the ultimate agenda, and those spirits that have left—some spirits have not come to earth in physical form—those spirits that have left God to have a human experience, to experience love out beyond the oneness of God will eventually find their way home because all there is, is God. So, there is no reason for them not to return; it is just a matter of when. Because we are all one in spirit, it is just that when will that happen is an individual choice.

* * * * *

However, in our manifestations on Earth and our attempts to express ourselves there, we have suffered much pain. Almost all of us have severe emotional wounds in the lowest three chakras caused by experiences of rejection, violence, and abandonment. It may have happened in past lives or in this lifetime. Almost all energy blocks in the upper chakras come from emotional hurt in the lowest three chakras.

Our connection to Earth has become emotionally burdened, especially for the light workers. Because we have met with grave resistance over many lifetimes, there is much fear and reserve in us when it comes to truly grounding ourselves. Grounding ourselves means being fully present in our earthly bodies and expressing our innermost inspiration in material reality.

In the second chakra, the emotional center, we have also been affected deeply by experiences of being threatened or deserted and by being severely restricted in our self-expression. The dominance of male energy would have contributed to this. The solar plexus or the third chakra is heavily affected by the burdens of the lowest two chakras. It has to do with a life force of creative energy and power. There are few examples of what true power means. In the solar plexus chakra, we often see that a person manifests him or herself either in a controlling way or in an overly modest way. Both ways are the result of basic feelings of helplessness because of a wounded first and second chakra. For the fhird chakra, it is all about finding a sensible way of handling power and control. It is about a balanced ego.

The ego is okay when it has a proper function. It lends focus to our consciousness, which enables us to manifest our individuality. Yes, we are a part of a better whole; however, we are also composed of individuals who are separate and different. The ego is a necessary counterpart to the spiritual part of us that transcends the individual. The energy of the ego is completely honorable and justified within the active reality in which we live. True power is in the joyful alignment with the ego and the Spirit.

The lowest three chakras contain the most important area for self-healing and inner spiritual growth. We need to take care of this wounded area in ourselves. Meditating to transcend physical reality or connect to elusive cosmic levels is not our primary goal now. Our goal is to give our gentlest understanding and loving support to those hurt inner children within us and to restore their beauty and playfulness. We all have spiritual guides within us. We just need to be cognizant of their presence by meditating and asking for guidance. We must also stay attuned with our Creator through unceasing prayers. These are the recipes for spiritual success. It is our spiritual journey. Here lies the greatest treasure. Cherishing and respecting the human side of us leads down our road to divine compassion and enlightenment.

Two out of the three lower chakras are male. It shows that especially concerning the male energies within each of us, much healing work is necessary. Therefore, heal the male energy. The feminine energy is getting better and fostering the strength needed to express itself fully and beautifully. The female qualities are being appreciated more and more individually as well as collectively. However, it is not so clear what a balanced male energy truly looks like, as the male energy got lost in false images of what it means "to be a man." The stereotypes always boil down to power through aggression. It is vital to recognize and express the true nature of male energy. The female side needs the balanced male energy to be able to fulfill her role. The female energy is regaining its self-respect, and it now wants to manifest itself forcefully and joyfully in the course of reunion with the male.

So what then is the power of balanced male energy? It holds true for the male energy in both men and women. A healed first chakra and balanced male energy lead to self-consciousness. The male energy does not have to fight and struggle. It is present through self-consciousness. Presence in the *now* means collaborating with our inner angels and spiritual guides, both of which are fully present within our soul. Essentially, we must remain centered on our true form. Being present self-consciously means staying aware of ourselves, remaining centered, and not getting lost in someone else's opinions, expectations, or needs. The balance is in connecting with others and being true to ourselves. A balanced male energy in the root chakra allows us to remain centered and aware of ourselves while we interact with others and the outside world.

It is essential to develop this quality of self-consciousness, for it will protect and guide our female energy. The female energy is logically inclined to connect with others and to be present with the other in a caring, nurturing way. The male energy makes for restrictions and help us find a balance between giving and receiving. The male energy in the lowest chakra actualizes the role of anchor and backbone.

The solar plexus achieves the same role in another way. This chakra is the energy center of the ego. We still have trouble with this concept of the ego. We live in the world in which two energies cooperate and form the building blocks of creation. One inclines to connect and seek for unity; the other creates separation and individuality. Also, the latter energy is just as viable and valuable as the former one.

It is essential to make peace with the male energy to embrace our individuality and our uniqueness. In life, there is a basic *aloneness* that has nothing to do with loneliness but has everything to do with us being a unique individual. Embracing this aloneness does not stand in the way of experiencing deep connections to others. If we truly embrace our individuality, then we become empowered, independent, and creative individuals. We can share our energy deeply with anyone or anything because we are not afraid to lose ourselves in it or give up our individuality.

The male energy of the solar plexus helps us become truly creative and empowered. The female energy in us is waiting for such empowerment. Our heartfelt inspiration wants to make itself known on the material level. It wishes to come out in an earthly manner and to bring tidings of love and harmony to Earth. The female energy is the mover of the new age, but it needs a balanced male energy to manifest and grow roots in material reality. Thus, the healing energies of the first and third chakras are important for the balance of male energy.

The energy of a vigorous ego, the healed solar plexus, is self-assurance. In the first chakra, it is self-consciousness. In the third chakra, it is self-confidence. It is not the kind of arrogance we see in an inflated ego. It's about simply trusting ourselves and saying, "I feel that I can do it!" It is being aware of our deepest inspiration, our creative abilities, and then acting accordingly. We must let our energies flow out of us, trust our natural talents and gifts, trust who we are, and show ourselves to the world! It is time. It is our destination, and in this, we will find our greatest fulfillment.

Make peace with the male energy within ourselves. Do not hesitate to stand up to receive abundance and to take good care of ourselves. Be content in the pure and neutral sense of the word. We are egos. We are individuals. We cannot and need not be forgiving and understanding all the time. It is not spiritual to tolerate everything and anything. Clearly, there are moments when we have to say no or even farewell and not compromise who we are. Do this without remorse or fear, and feel how the male energies of self-consciousness and self-confidence empower us to let the delicate flower of your female energy flourish and shine.

It is all about the teamwork between the energies. Male and female energies have shared a long and painful struggle together. They will also rise together, for one cannot be stable without the other. Now that the female energy is eager to ascend above the remnants of humiliation and repression, there is a persistent need for a rebirth of the male energy. This rebirth of the male will become visible on a collective scale eventually, and it will first manifest in each of us separately, man and woman. We all are the keepers of these ancient energies within us, and it is our birthright to make their partnership equal and joyful.

Another characteristic of male-female energy is involution and evolution. Involution is the force that pulls the Spirit into matter or the world of experience. Evolution is the force that pushes the matter back up to the spiritual realm. Involution is female energy, and evolution is male. In the early days of man, when his prime goal was the experience, the female energy prevailed. Desire, emotion, and feeling are female energies, continually pushing us toward the experience. The biblical Eve influenced Adam with her desire for the forbidden experience. The obedient of Adam to Eve was symbolic of the time of involution or the dominance of female energy.

The mind is a male energy that is meant to command the female emotions in us all in the cycle of evolution, wisely direct us to avoid heartbreaking experiences, and guide us from matter to spirit. In ancient times there was a change in the polarization of humankind from involution to evolution. Men no longer worshipped the goddesses but rather turned to male gods. Because the mind is beginning to manage the world and is leading us toward the Spirit, the male energy has been genuinely dominant. The heavy male dominance is being equalized, however, by the opening of the next faculty in the man of intuition, which is also feminine. However, even when the intuition rules over mind, the male energy will still be slightly dominant because we are heading toward the ascension of the fifth dimension, which is led by the mind. The mind is the overall dominating energy for spiritual progression.

In all male-female relationships, the male unit is mostly radiant and sending, and the female is polarized as magnetic and receiving. If this combination does not occur, then the energy of the relationship will be out of balance. It is especially true in the human kingdom, for humanity is the only kingdom where it is even plausible for the sexes to not apply their proper roles. In the animal and plant kingdoms, the males and females assume their appropriate semblances without rebellion.

Both sexes are equal in value as one cannot exist without the other. Just like there is no such thing as one hand clapping, there is no creation with just one sex. They must work together. We must keep in mind that the female is magnetic and receiving. The male is radiant and sending. Even though we are all contrasted with one or the other sex in our lives, which are dependent on the body, we realize that there are various male and female cycles in us.

* * * * *

DOUG: Now this is interesting about masculine and feminine energy. Could a priest seek the kingdom of God without union with feminine energy?

JOHN: Well, the feminine energy is not the same as a woman. The energy inside may ask, "Are you a caring person? Are you kind to others? Are you tolerant?" That would be a feminine energy.

DOUG: Oh, really?

JOHN: A masculine energy would be strong, capable, and able to handle difficult situations that need strength and wisdom. This is a stronger wisdom than a feminine energy, so we are not talking about a man and a woman. We are talking about blending the left brain with the right brain of the person. When we come into being balanced, then we have achieved what we are all trying to achieve, and it doesn't matter if we are priests or regular people. We are all attempting to achieve that masculine and feminine energy in a balance that brings us into a higher way of handling our lives.

* * * * *

There are two parts of our being. The first part is our physical manifestation as a man and a woman. The parents' X and Y chromosomes determine the sex of the baby. However, our spiritual energy, which comes from our DNA, determines our character expressing male energy or female energy. It is possible for a feminine energy to enter a physically male body or a male energy going into a female body. It's not a question of morality and whether we are right

Door to Glory

or wrong about heterosexuality or homosexuality. It's a matter of what we needed to experience for continuing our spiritual growth. A person with a right-sided mind tends to focus more on educating themselves in the field of art and music. These areas bend toward the expressions of love and understanding. They are the glue that keeps families and friends together. Jesus had some women disciples in his ministry. However, the church did not agree with this practice and removed them from the Bible.

* * * * *

DOUG: Why wasn't Mary Magdalene considered a disciple?

JOHN: That is a church thing. She was very much a disciple in the eyes of Jesus. There were just as many women disciples of Jesus as there were men. However, that is where this masculine energy tries to control all the feminine parts of spirituality. So the masculine energy was trying to overcome and dominate over the feminine. The church wrote out the women who were disciples. Mary Magdalene was one of them, and so was his wife. They were all disciples that hung around Jesus. For the most part, he had some friends he visited, but the Bible distorted that particular perspective. And yes, women were disciples. They just were eliminated from the Bible.

* * * * *

However, a union between two women or two men should not be discouraged or construed as evil by churches. It is not. God already knows that the spiritual energy of a female might reside in a male body or vice versa. It is our free will in what we choose for our lives. The union is simply representative of a left-sided mind being with someone with a right-sided mind. A union is a lesson in learning the traits of the other. One might teach the value of love, while the other may teach the importance of making difficult decisions. A marriage or union brings balance into their lives. Some people say that homosexuality is a result of a domineering mother or father. That is not so.

* * * * *

John mentioned that we are approaching the ages of love and light. The dark side is losing control. The Catholic church has been a part of the dark side.

DOUG: So the dark side is still in control today?

JOHN: No, they lost their control. Their bricks are crumbling as we speak. There are changes going on, and government regulations are making changes that are not necessarily observable to the public because the news is still controlled by the dark side. However, all these changes are happening. If you follow some of the news, you'll start seeing better things happening here and there. So they have lost their stronghold.

* * * * *

In speaking about churches losing control, the Vatican was quite moved by the gay referendum in Ireland. They have proclaimed a "defeat for humanity."

For the churches it was all about controlling people's lives. They are operating under the auspices of the Illuminati. Their purpose is to keep people enslaved and feeling unworthy. We are coming to the end time of the dark side. The dark side has been operating and building its agenda since the beginning of time, so it will put up resistance to the forces of light for the next thirty years. They have control of all financial infrastructures in the world today, so there will be some financial repercussions in the years ahead.

Section 1.10: Ego v. Spirit

One of the greatest events in the history of the world was the Pentecost. Humanity was on a verge of a self-destruction brought upon by the ego. A similar fate had befallen another planet in our solar system named Maldek. The entities in power had misused its advanced technology by destroying the population of the planet with nuclear weapons. The population was comprised primarily of a mixture of human and reptilian species. Eventually, the planet skewed off course and was destroyed by a collision with one of the Nibiru moons. The remains of this collision created the asteroid belt located between Mars and Jupiter. More details are provided in Section 3.7.

Here on the planet Earth, we have been besieged by a constant war between powerful nations and individuals. The ego played a significant role in these skirmishes. As table 5 in section 2.4 shows, the United States and Russia possess 94 percent of the total nuclear weapons that are capable of destroying the population on Earth. According to John, the Creator God laid out an edict that there would be no more nuclear detonations. Some nuclear missiles were launched at Pennsylvania and Florida in the United States, but both were thwarted by our alien protectors, according to my spiritual informants.

The ego dominated the third dimension. During the upcoming new age, we will move away from that darkness and enter the loving environment of the fifth dimension, the same place to which Jesus ascended more than two thousand years ago, saving mankind in the process. Jesus saved us from suffering the same consequences as those who inhabited Maldek.

The spirit of truth is energy. It is the power of the loving spirit to defeat the forces of the ego. The ego considers itself distinct from others and God because of its identification with the physical body and impressions in various centers of the subtle body. In short, the ego makes us believe that our existence is limited to our five senses, our mind, and our intellect. When the person has an inflated ego, this individual does not identify with the soul, resulting in a collection of dark energy surrounding the body. When one's ego is inflated, the flow of grace from God is blocked, and the person's life is impacted negatively. As Mark says, "Thefts, covetousness, wickedness, deceit, uncleanness, a wicked eye, backbiting, pride, foolishness. All these evil things come from within, and defile a man" (Mark 7:22–23). This Scripture passage demonstrates that pride keeps you away from God. The more loving we are, the more we are doing the will of God.

Our human body was created from the dust of the earth. As it says in Genesis 2:7, "The Lord God also made the man of the dust of the ground, and breathed in his face breath of life, and the man was a living soul." God created the body to cover the soul. It is an overcoat that protects our soul as we journey through the necessary lessons that remove the ego's dark energy. When we die, we take this overcoat off before passing over to the other side in heaven.

The ego lacks wisdom. It doesn't know its limits, and it always wants more. According to Sigmund Freud, the ego is the representation of the outer world to the id. In other words, the ego represents and enforces the reality of the ego, whereas the id is concerned only with the pleasure of the ego. While the ego is oriented toward perceptions in the physical world, the id is oriented toward internal instincts. While the ego is associated with reason and sanity, the id belongs to passions. The ego, however, is never able to fully distinguish itself from the id. In fact, the ego is a part of the id, which is why Freud does not provide a hard separation between the two.

Jesus overcame his ego. Many people have theorized that he had no ego. However, everybody who was made from the dust of the earth has an ego. He had a human body, yet he was able overcome it. While Jesus was up in the mountain for forty days, the Bible tells us that Satan tempted him there. However, it was actually Jesus's ego that was tempting him. It was his negative emotions. Our negative emotions are considered the Devil. Satan isn't real, according to John.

The terms Satan, Lucifer, and other devils are all third-dimensional terms. They represented evil in the eyes of the third-dimensional world when energy terms were often beyond comprehension for most people. They were simply symbols and metaphors. When Jesus said, "Get thee behind me Satan," he was referring to his negative emotions. Those negative emotions were created by his ego. He wanted to show us that we can overcome these emotions by focusing on the love of God within. He did not eat for forty days. He was hungry. He also knew his days were numbered. His emotion was probably telling him that he could discontinue his teaching and reign on Earth like a king. "Then the devil took him up into a high mountain, and showed him all the kingdoms of the world, in the twinkling of an eye. And the devil said unto him, all this power will I give thee, and the glory of those kingdoms: for that is delivered to me: and to whomsoever I will, I give it" (Luke 4:6). Jesus, a teacher, wanted to convey a message that he could overcome the adversaries of life by channeling his thoughts toward God, who was already within him. The love from God was all he ever needed, and it helped him overcome the desires of his ego.

Overcoming your ego elevates your consciousness to Christ consciousness. When doing that, your ten missing strands of DNA are restored by God. Presently, our DNA only carries two of the twelve strands. When we ascend to the fifth dimension, the ten missing strands are reactivated. When this happens, there will be no more disabilities. Deafness, blindness, and physical disabilities will be eradicated in the fifth dimension. The ten strands represent the ten tribes of Israel in the Scripture. However, we need to do our work here on Earth to receive these missing strands.

Keep in mind that chakras are from the soul, not from the body. The chakras are energy, and to requote this famous saying from Albert Einstein, "Everything is energy, and that's all there is to it. Match the frequency of the reality you want and you cannot help but get that reality. This is not philosophy. This is physics." What he means is we can create our own reality based on what we want. Our thought is energy. If we want something that might seem far-fetched, then we have to have a deep conviction for it, or else that reality will slip away. It starts with a goal. When we expound on it and follow the plan step by step, then we will likely achieve it. The power of positive thinking is a powerful energy force that motivates us to believe in ourselves and turn a possibility into a reality.

God the Father is both an energy and a real existence. He is a Creator God that resides in the center of creation. He is also an energy of love that resides in every life-form. He doesn't judge us. He provided us with free will. The godheads judge people. Moses, Isaac, Jacob, and Aaron are all godheads named in Scripture. They have expressed negative emotions in their biblical writings. God does not express emotions. He is only spirit. He is an energy of love. If you have sinned, he does not leave you. He is always with us. We just need to invite him to be our companion. His love will help us overcome the lures of our ego.

Jesus came down to demonstrate the right use of our energy. The Spirit of Jesus was God. We all are God in the Spirit. However, we have to overcome the senses of our egos to realize it. As it is recorded in the book of Psalms, "I have said, ye are gods, and ye all are children of the most High" (Psalm 82.6). Also recorded by John, "Jesus answered them, is it not written in your Law, I said, ye are gods? If he called them gods, unto whom the word of God was given, and the Scripture cannot be broken" (John 10:34–35).

I have always been bewildered by the response from my Sunday school teacher several years ago. I asked, "What is the difference between saved and salvation?" He responded that we were saved from eternal separation from God if we accept Jesus Christ as our Savior. If a nuclear war had broken out today, it is very plausible that the nuclear reaction would have a devastating effect on our soul energy matrices. This circumstance would have separated us from God because our matrix energies would have been all tangled up, causing the loss of our identities. To this day, the angels in the spiritual realm are still trying to find the souls of the Japanese victims from the WWII nuclear explosion.

* * * * *

DOUG: What is the difference between saved and salvation?

JOHN: Well, they are basically the same thing. When you go inside and reduce and release the ego, you have saved yourself from the ego. And that is your salvation. You have saved yourself. And that is where churches get into dogma that says you have to look outside yourself to be saved. And there is nothing outside yourself that can save you. Nothing outside of yourself can give you peace as it says in the *Course in Miracles* (ref. 11). It is a matter of looking within.

* * * * *

Our soul is a form of energy. It can be transformed but never destroyed. The energy of God is among us. It is what gave us life. The goal of fulfilling the teaching of Jesus is achieving Christ consciousness. We have overcome the ego, the power of the Devil. "To open their eyes, that they may turn from darkness to light, and from the power of Satan unto God, that they may receive forgiveness of sins, and inheritance among them, which are sanctified by faith in me" (Acts 26:18).

During the upcoming millennial reign of Christ, more people will be transformed because they have found the love of God in their hearts. They have overcome the negative influence of the dark energy that surrounds them. They have been made whole with twelve strands of fully functioning DNA. The grace of God is given to you to meet your needs. "And in their prayer for you, to long after you greatly, for the abundant grace of God in you. Thanks therefore be unto God for his unspeakable gift" (2 Corinthians 9:14–15).

The grace of God is blocked because of the ego as shown on figure 6. For a long time, churches have not understood this concept. Jesus cannot alone remove the dark energy from every soul of some seven billion people. Hence, we reincarnate when the dark energy has not been fully eradicated. Jesus was quoted by John as saying "Ye think to have eternal life, and they are they which testify of me. But ye will not come to me, that ye might have life. I receive not the praise of men. But I know you that ye have not the love of God in you" (John 5:42). He was alluding to his Christ consciousness. He was fully aware that his teaching of Christ consciousness was not well received. Even John revealed that he and other disciples did not ascend to the fifth dimension until later in other lifetimes. When you receive it, then the black energy surrounding you goes away. You have manifested your spirit in your physical world, and your soul glows with light. You glow like a saint, and only people with an opened spiritual eye can perceive the light.

"I am come in my Father's Name, and ye receive me not (Christ Consciousness): if another shall come in his own name, him will ye receive. How can ye believe, which receive honor one of another, and seek not the honor that cometh of God alone?" (John 5:39–44).

When we commune with God alone, the dark energy dissipates. It opens up our aura to the grace of God. Our prayers are heard by God, and he'll respond. Our soul's energy is brighter when the energy of the ego disappears. As a result, we attract more positive energy. Jesus was referring to Christ consciousness when he said, "Receive me not." The energy of Christ consciousness was derived from the spirit of truth. Although it was introduced more than two thousand years ago at the Pentecost, the energy is still viable today.

* * * * *

DOUG: I mentioned to you that I felt the baptism of the Spirit, the energy I felt within my soul, but I wasn't sure what that was. Was that the spirit of truth?

JOHN: Well, the spirit of truth is another way of saying the Spirit of God. So as you talk about truth, you are talking about God, and baptism in truth is the baptism of spiritual love. It is overwhelming your spiritual being, and you are moving into that higher consciousness. So baptism in the Spirit means that you are open and receptive.

DOUG: Now what is the difference between the adjustor fusion and baptism of spirit?

JOHN: Well, yes, your adjustor is yours, and some people would call it the Holy Spirit. It's the part of God that comes to you and gives you guidance. It is that silent voice inside. It was called the adjustor when Jesus said, "I need to leave so that the adjustor can come." He was talking about you trusting the God within. The message is that the Father and you are one, so if you're listening to the voice of the silent voice inside, which is God, you are listening to the adjustor that adjusts your life to the truth.

DOUG: The spirit of truth comes from the baptism of Spirit?

JOHN: Right, you're open to hearing truth. You see, so many are in denial, which means they are closed off to hearing what's real. They live in their own world of denial and illusion, so they do not live in reality with truth.

DOUG: Now you just mentioned in the Bible that you need to be born again to enter the kingdom of God. Is that the baptism of Spirit?

JOHN: No, that's what Jesus was talking about yesterday. It's the death of the ego.

DOUG: Okay.

JOHN: You die to the ego and to that illusion of your existence so that you can move into the truth and reality within God. You and the Father are one, so you die to the ego that says you are separated from God. You have always been one with God. The ego has deceived you.

DOUG: I understand that all it takes to accept God is to invite him in my inner life?

JOHN: It is an invitation to become totally loving, which is the presence of God. You open your heart to unconditional love. So many people in the world are afraid of this love because of the ills they've experiences, whether abuse, punishment, or conditioning that has led them to believe they aren't good enough or smart enough. When you realize we are not separated from God, your thinking changes, and you accept that you are God's love.

DOUG: Now for my next question. In his second epistle letter, Peter says, "For the prophecy came not in old time by the will of man: but holy men of God spake as they were moved by the Holy Ghost" (Peter 1:21). And my question is this: Is the Holy Ghost mentioned by Peter the thought adjuster?

JOHN: Yes, yes. You see, that's a very important verse in the Bible that many people disregard. You see, men wrote the Bible. God did not write the Bible. The men who were channeling the Word of God wrote the Bible. And because it came through human references, that's why it was not totally accurate. And so many people get caught up in saying, "Well, it's in the Bible, so we have to say it is a positive, loving statement and thus truth." But anything negative is not of God. So as you're going through the Bible, you have to understand that people have distorted what God said according to their own understanding. It might not necessarily be from God. All people have frailties and shortcomings. Their egos are in control of their lives, so they are not always reporting the truth, even if they intend to do so.

* * * * *

Door to Glory

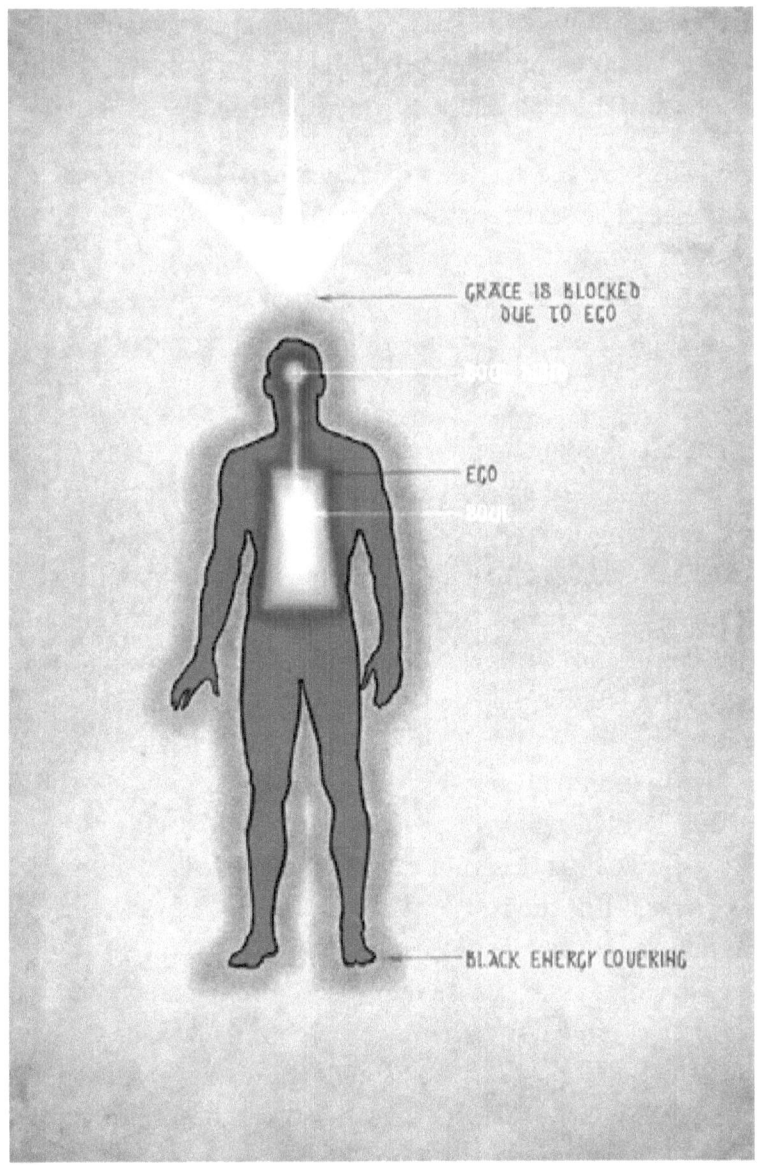

Figure 6 – Dark Energy from Ego

A thought adjuster is a direct gift from God. It is a Holy Spirit that helps you lead a very fulfilling life. Although the universal Father is a resident in paradise at the very center of the universe, he is also present in the minds of his countless children. It is an energy form of the highest and most divine order. It lovingly guides us along the path of life. At the same time, the eternal Father is the furthest removed from and most intimately associated with his planetary mortal sons.

The adjusters are the actuality of the Father's love incarnate in the souls of men. They are the veritable promise of man's eternal career imprisoned within the mortal mind. This is something man can foretaste in time as he progressively masters the divine technique of living God's will step by step, ascending through the universe. At the end he will meet the divine Father.

God, having commanded man to be perfect, even as he is perfect, has descended as the Adjuster to become man's experiential partner in the achievement of this preordained destiny. The fragment of God that dwells the mind of man is the absolute and unqualified assurance that man can find the Universal Father, even in the days of the flesh. Apostle Paul was a recipient of the divine Adjustor. He described his experience in the Bible as being struck by a lightning: "Now as he journeyed, it came to pass that as he was come near to Damascus, suddenly there shined round about him a light from heaven" (Acts 9:3). Paul defined what a true church was. It is within ourselves where we find Christ Consciousness: "Now rejoice I in my sufferings for you, and fulfill the rest of the afflictions of Christ in my flesh, for his body's sake, which is the Church" (Colossians 1:24). It was a mystery to Christians because they did not understand science term of energy in those days: "Whereof I am a minister, according to the dispensation of God, which is given me unto youward, to fulfill the word of God, which is the mystery hid since the world began, and from all ages, but now is made manifest to his Saints" (Colossians 1:25-26).

Any mortal who has seen a Creator Son has seen the Universal Father, and he who is indwelt by a divine Adjuster is indwelt by the Paradise Father. Every mortal who is consciously or unconsciously following the leading of his indwelling Adjuster is living in accordance with the will of God. Consciousness of the Adjuster's presence is consciousness of God's presence. Eternal fusion of the Adjuster with the evolutionary soul of man is the factual experience of the eternal union with God.

Any mortal who has seen a Creator Son has seen the universal Father, and he who is indwelt by a divine adjuster is indwelt by the paradise Father. Every mortal who is consciously or unconsciously following the leading of his indwelling adjuster is living in accordance with the will of God. Consciousness of the adjuster's presence is consciousness of God's presence. Eternal fusion of the adjuster with the evolutionary soul of man is the factual experience of the eternal union with God.

It is the adjuster who creates within man that unquenchable yearning and incessant longing to be like God, attain paradise, and worship the infinite source of the divine gift before the actual deity. The adjuster is the living presence that links the mortal son with his paradise Father and draws him nearer to the Father. The adjuster is our compensatory equalizer, who addressed the enormous universal tension created by the distance of man from God.

The adjuster is an absolute essence of an infinite being imprisoned within the mind of a finite creature, which can eventually consummate this temporary union of God and man and veritably actualize a new order of being for unending universal service. The adjuster actualizes the truth that God is man's Father. The adjuster is man's infallible cosmic compass, always and unerringly pointing the soul toward God.

In the evolutionary worlds, creatures traverse three general developmental stages from the arrival of the adjuster to comparative full growth. At about twenty years of age, the monitors are sometimes designated as thought changers. From this time to the attainment of the age of discretion at about forty years, the mystery monitors are called thought adjusters. From the attainment of discretion to deliverance from the flesh, they are often referred to as thought controllers. These three phases of mortal life have no connection with the three stages of the adjuster's progress in mind duplication and soul evolution.

The origin of the thought adjusters is one of the unrevealed functions of the universal Father. We have every reason to believe that none of the other absolute associates of the first source and center have to do with the production of Father fragments. Adjusters are simply and eternally the divine gifts. They are of God and from God, and they are like God.

* * * * *

DOUG: I was baptized by *fire* in 1999. That's based on the verse in the Bible that says, "A man can receive nothing except if to be given him from heaven."

JOHN: Well, you have choice. And the choice is to accept God's love or to move through your intellect and your ego, which keeps God out of your life. Say that verse again.

DOUG: Actually, it came from John 3:27.

JOHN: Okay.

DOUG: "A man can receive nothing except what is given him from heaven." That's like baptism by fire.

JOHN: Oh, well, no. Actually, what he's talking about is something different.

DOUG: There's another verse.

JOHN: Well, let's just finish this one. What he's talking about is if it is truly yours in spirit, you will have it. You don't have to go buy something to acquire something. It will come to you. "Seek ye first the kingdom of God and all things will be added." That's what he's talking about. If your focus is on God's consciousness and the love of God only, then the Spirit will physically manifest in your life.

DOUG: Is that the Holy Spirit?

JOHN: You are a Holy Spirit. The Spirit of God is whole, and you are part of God, which is whole. And that's another church idea that they changed. They thought if they told you weren't whole, then they would need to save you. So in reality, you never left God. God has always been in your heart. He's been a part of you. That is your inheritance. You are part of the sugar cookie dough or whatever kind of cookie dough you want to make of it. That is who you are—a whole spirit. Indoctrinating people to believe otherwise is how the church has maintained its control.

* * * * *

When you seek the kingdom of God, then the Spirit will manifest in our lives. Christ consciousness takes control away from our ego. In their relationship to people who have received baptism by fire, they reveal a supernal love and spiritual ministry that is profoundly confirmative of the declaration that God is spirit. "The fruit of the Spirit is love, joy, peace, longsuffering, gentleness, goodness, and faith" (Galatians 5:22). The Father fragments must be the gift of the absolute God to those creatures whose destiny encompasses the possibility of attaining God as absolute. As the universal Father fragments his personal deity, so the infinite Spirit individuates portions of his mindful Spirit to indwell and actually fuse with the evolutionary souls of the surviving mortals of the spirit-fusion series. But the nature of the eternal Son is not fragmented. The spirit of the original Son is either diffuse or discretely personal. Son-fused creatures are united with individualized bestowals of the Spirit of the Creator's sons of the eternal Son.

There were moments when I had to stop and think before taking my next action. I have been tempted by my own ego to go ahead and follow through with lures from some women. The thought adjuster would lovingly provide me with a message like "Don't do it." The whole place would come to a standstill while I processed my internal information. This one particular instance took place in Seattle at a restaurant. I was visiting with my old college friend. While my friend was in the restroom, the waitress asked me what my plans were for the weekend. She was a very lovely girl, and she gave me her phone number. Naturally, I was tempted. However, it was my ego that was tempting me. At that moment it was a battle between my thought adjuster and my ego. There were two choices for me. God does not impose your will. It has to come from your own willpower. So at that moment I slowly walked away from the restaurant, feeling a little bit dazed. My ego wanted it badly, while my heart was waiting for my verdict. So I processed the information, and my heart won. I decided to move on with my friend, and I discarded the phone number and moved away from the restaurant. I have had these moments at other times. My thought adjuster has guided me out of potential troubles. I am not against sexuality, but doing it with the wrong person and not knowing the person might lead me to some unwanted circumstances for my life. I was already given a script to live this life before my birth. My guardian angels are there to guide me through the process. Receiving the thought adjuster might have been a wildcard play for me. It might not have been part of the script. However, I have proven to God that I need him in my life, and he is all I ever need. The Spirit is forever, while our body fades away after completing life's journey.

Meditation is a key to finding God within ourselves. I took a home study course on meditation from "Self-Realization Fellowship" (ref. 16) and learned how to meditate. I would go through various spiritual practices every day for almost a year before receiving a divine response from God. These techniques were handed down through the ages from the Indian masters. During his missing years from the Bible (ages twelve through thirty), Jesus went to India and learned from the religion there.

Self-Realization Fellowship was founded by Parmahansa Yogananda from India. He is a disciple of Mahavatar Babaji. In our conversation John said, "Mahavatar Babaji right now has been on Earth as a teacher ... for thousands of years, and [he] has just stayed as a beacon of light for those trying to find the spiritual path." So there are different ways that those spirit entities can come back and help people on Earth. There are different degrees of their doing just that. Jesus along with Mary Magdalene went back to India after his crucifixion, That's where she was buried, according to John.

* * * * *

DOUG: Where was Mary Magdalene buried? In France or Israel?

JOHN: I believe she was buried in India. Jesus lived in India for some time after the crucifixion, and I believe she was there.

* * * * *

Self-Realization Fellowship teaches people how to meditate to find God within. "Ask, and it shall be given you: seek, and ye shall find: knock, and it shall be opened unto you. For whosoever asketh, receiveth: and he that seeketh, findeth: and to him that knocketh, it shall be opened" (Matthew 7:7–8). I knocked on God's door, and I received this incredible loving spark from God. I felt a pulsating vibration throughout my chest and mind that lasted for a split second. It amazes me that this vibration would come from the sky and find me! However, John said it came from within me.

* * * * *

DOUG: I was wondering about a time back in 1999. I felt the spark of love from God, and you mentioned that it came from within.

JOHN: Right.

DOUG: I felt it within, so it must be coming from within.

JOHN: Right, yes, it comes from within. But it emanates around you, and there are people who can read your auras.

DOUG: A former work colleague passed away on Monday morning

of March 2, and I hadn't seen him since December 11, my last day at work. Then in the wee hours on Wednesday morning while I was still asleep, I felt his energy. He came and said good-bye to me in the spirits. He saw my aura, and I immediately told him to go to the light. He saw his loved ones at the tunnel, and he followed. (I will talk about this experience in my book.) Now my question is this: Did my aura come from God's love through meditation?

JOHN: Your aura is another term for soul, and it emanates from you. As you're meditating, it opens up and is more accessible, so when you're in a meditative state, your soul is open to many influences.

* * * * *

The word *saint* comes from the Greek word *hagios*, which means "consecrated to God, holy, sacred, pious." *Saints* make up a group of people who are set apart for God and his kingdom. The Christian churches believe all Christians are considered saints because they were baptized in the name of Jesus Christ. However, there is a missing piece to that theology.

Paul was referring to Jesus Christ as Christ consciousness. People in those days did not understand the phenomena of energy, so Paul had to use physical terms for people to comprehend his message. It is true that we are saved from our ego only if we attain Christ consciousness. It is a habitation of God by the Spirit. Christ consciousness is represented by the ten tribes of Israel, the ten missing DNA strands. We currently possess only two strands. During the upcoming one thousand years of peace, the ten missing strands will be activated by God. The ten strands will heal our bodily imperfections. Deaf people will hear. Blind people will see. Intellectually challenged people will experience love, and physically challenged people will walk. However, the world wasn't ready in the past because the concept of Christ consciousness was not well understood.

Jesus comes to Marilyn's channeling every Christmas. Here is his 2015 message for the group's participants;

> Heavenly greetings! To everyone in this room, I am so pleased that you are here today to hear my message. I have been looking forward to this. Marilyn and I are so pleased for you to just sit back and enjoy yourself. I have some interesting information that I hope will give you more pleasure in your life and more relaxation so that you really can be on the path in a way that you have not been before.
>
> I would like to start out by saying ascension is about raising your energy into a higher consciousness. It is not about physical ascension. We are talking about moving into what some people call heaven or peace on earth. This is what we are going to be describing in ways that you have not heard before. I hope that you will gain some new insight and new information. Fear is just the lack of information. I hope today will bring some new knowledge you are unaware of or maybe had misunderstood. Sadly, there is a lot of misunderstanding out there, and we hope to bring some truth to that today. So as we are talking about rising into the higher energy you are coming into, and you are now, raising your energy into this higher consciousness.
>
> That is what 2012 was about, to bring that energy shift. You are going through the Photon Belt. Some of this was described in the last channeling, but I will just briefly give a little understanding for those who are new today. We have entered the Photon Belt, which is Christ Consciousness. The earth is aligned at this point. The energies of the planet have been brought back to Christ Consciousness

from which it was created. It is your opportunity to align with that Christ Consciousness and to join in the celebration of moving forward into ascension into a new consciousness a higher consciousness, a consciousness of unconditional love. This has been going on for thousands of years to be ready for this time in history. The original seed was planted fifty thousand years ago, so you see time moves slowly in the past through the darkness.

It has been a slow evolution to move into this space. Many of you know that BC on our calendars of the past was describing the darkness before the planet was ready for this evolution to occur. That is what is depicted in the Old Testament. With the advent of AD, the calendar changed to a new energy of love, the Dispensation of Love with the old and dark energy of the past releasing the Dispensation of Law.

This is the message I came to bring. There is a way out of the darkness; the light will dispel the darkness and the light is within you. It is not just a little bit within you—it is your soul. You have gone through the darkness of obstacles and fear, obliterated your access to the total light of who you are. That's what we are going to talk about so you can ascend out of the darkness into the light into the spirit of the sunlight of God.

With the 2012 changes in history and energy, we are now able to move into the Dispensation of Compassion. You will be able to apply this love in your life. Not just talk about it, not just preach about it, but actually have compassion in action in all the parts of your coming and going. All the events and all of your thinking and consciousness can be in higher consciousness for all those on the path.

This is such a glorious thing to know, and so many people have trouble understanding that the God within is the God that made you. You remain in the spirit and consciousness of God, but sometimes people like visuals. So I would like to use the example of the Christmas cookies you likely made this year. You put in all the ingredients in the bowl and stirred it up thoroughly. So all ingredients were mixed in and you could not tell one from the other. It was blended completely. You took your spoon to scoop out a ball of cookie dough and place it on the cookie sheet. It did not change; the cookie dough is the same dough as was in the cookie bowl, just like the love of God that soul of God is within you completely. It is not just a little part; it is not a spark at this point. You are born in Christ Consciousness, just as I was. I am the example that you too can remove all those obstacles and barriers that prevented the Christ Consciousness from coming full bloom into your awareness and circumstances. We are at a time in history, the first time in history, when this is possible to ascend out of the darkness of Third Dimension completely.

You see, we are talking about unconditional love, the kind of love you would find from a dog. If you have ever been a dog owner you understand that whatever you did to that dog, it always came back loving you no matter what. It was loyal, trustworthy and you could depend on that dog when you were down or when you were having a good time. That dog was just as loving and accepting of you as possible. That is the same kind of love that God has for you. He is loyal, dependable, responsible, and always there for you. That is called unconditional love, the love that you accept within yourself, knowing it is the love in your heart, and it has always has been. It has just been covered up by the traumas and dramas of the Earths consequences of Third Dimension. There have been many fearful ways to keep people in stress, trauma, drama, and a great deal of fear. However, with the light of God, this can all be dispelled.

I have another story to illustrate. You will laugh because you have probably experienced this with your children. They call out from the dark bedroom at night that there is a boogeyman man under the bed, and you go into their room, pull back the covers, and turn on the light. There is no boogeyman. That is what has happened to you. It is time to grow up, leave the boogeyman man out of your story, and realize that there is no negative energy, fear, Devil, or Satan to cause you any difficulty or harm. The light of God is the most powerful energy ever and always. Love is your power and has always been in you. It is now time to employ it and apply it in your life today and always. You can march forward in courage and compassion to help those around you and as you allow that light to fill you and be there for you. You can move beyond the fears that have stopped you; stop the fears. They will dissipate and are not an issue any longer.

We welcome you on this wonderful journey of faith. This faith is your connection to God, and consciously be aware of being in that connection to God. You see, in the Bible, Jesus used parables. That is because they did not understand energy. Their vocabulary was totally without an understanding of physics. The universe is all about physics. Therefore, they did not understand that it was an energy that was hidden inside by obstacles and barriers they could not access. Today moving out of Third Dimension through the Fourth Dimension of awareness becoming more conscious and aware through the years of your growing spiritually, you are coming into a higher consciousness.

You are the toaster on the counter, and for years you did not get any toast. The bread was in the toaster, but it never toasted. When you came into awareness, you plugged your toaster into the electrical outlet and low and behold, the electricity flowed. When you pushed down the lever, the bread toasted and it popped back up because you were connected. Your faith is your connection, and keeping your focus on that connection is absolutely essential if you want your bread to be toasted.

In the Bible they shed light by saying to pray unceasingly; this prevents your ego mind from influencing you; you are free of that distraction. There are so many distractions in the physical world, the material world. The duality has been extreme, you are right or you are wrong, you are good or your bad and you should be punished. Or maybe there's been a lot of criticism, judgment, and condemnation in your life and therefore you didn't have the self-worth with which you were born. You saw yourself through the eyes of those around you and you believed it, because that is what that they were experiencing in their lives. They were not doing any better, and they were not allowing you to do any better, so therefore it was a difficult time.

When you feel like a victim you, you feel used and abused and you have no resources to move out of that situation. Well, you are lucky people because you are on a path that is moving out of Third Dimension, out of that darkness and fear and untruth. The Fourth Dimension has been your ladder, you have been climbing out on Jacobs Ladder. You have been moving more and more into the light. You now have one foot in Third Dimension and one foot in Fifth Dimension. It is time to boost you out of the Fourth Dimension, all the way up. Your growth has come to the point where it is possible to get that last few steps into the Fifth Dimension. Where there is peace and the peace inside of you will create peace on earth. You have come to do that; this is your job. You have come to create this energy and as you accomplish removing any obstacles to that Peace. You have come to discover that from Third Dimension that there is nothing outside of you that can save you. In addition, there is nothing outside of you that can give you peace. It always comes from within. That cookie dough within you is the power of love and all the ingredients are there and more powerful than anything of Third Dimension.

God is more powerful than anything that is reality. If it was not made in love, it's not real as are all the institutions and organizations, groups, and clubs that having tried to tell you how to live your life. I include medicine, religious dogmas, and politicians who think they can lead you out of despair and provide for you. Wherever you have looked for your help outside of yourself, it is fruitless, as you have probably come to understand.

Door to Glory

The real power is within. Accessing that power puts you into Fifth Dimension. When you apply it to all parts of your life, you start to get well and be healed. It is time to give yourself permission to heal. Say, "I am in the Fifth Dimension." It is time to pick up that foot that is in the Third Dimension and put it into the Fifth Dimensions so you are standing on solid ground. You see, a house that has been built on sand has shifting sand. That is what has happened in your past. There has been a lot of shifting and your foundation has been very wobbly. As you move into Fifth Dimension, you are building your house on the rock of God. You are grounded on the rock of love, truth, peace, abundance, faith, and unconditional love. Your feet are on the ground, finally.

I would like to give you another little story. Mack and Marilyn were visiting Mesa Verde and they had gone down the Indian ladders into the cliff dwelling. They were enjoying the tour in the national park. Then she had to go up the ladder to reach the area where the buses were to pick them up. She was able to take the first few steps easily, but closer to the top it became a big concern if she was going to make it. Mack came and pulled, helping her to get up. My message is that if you do the work necessary to go up your ladder, I will pull you up to the solid ground of Fifth Dimension. I will be that power that will get you up there. I will get you onto the solid rock of God. You see, it has always been there and it has always been ready for you. Your awareness today is there and you can now say, "I see beyond the physical into the invisible. I see that spirit beyond the words; I hear the message beyond the spoken. That silent voice inside has become my direction and my guidance. I will pay attention; I will follow that. It will lead me where I need to go because doing the right thing is never wrong. It will guide me into a light of unconditional love."

One of the things I said in the Bible is "to go and I will condemn thee not." I have never condemned anyone. Your Third Dimension has been very focused on punishing people and who is wrong; who is the bad person. There are no bad guys. No one did anything wrong, you have been going through the lessons necessary for your emotional growth. There is no right or wrong to it. There is no reason to condemn anybody, you see, as you go through your lessons, you grow into maturity. As a child to emotionally react in fear was appropriate and the boogeyman really seemed to be there. Now you have grown into the light of God. You see, that there is nothing to fear, all is good. It's "All systems go" and there is nothing to stop you from moving forward at this point. You see, there never was. Now the Earth's energies support you, you are not just doing it on your own.

When I went through the initiations to get to this point, it was much more difficult. The energy of the planet was very dark. So as the Masters and I went through our initiations. It was all very secretive, because those who did not understand love could not handle the love that we were acquiring through our initiations and our growth threatened them. Now it is very accepted in society because your planet has come to the point where many more are waking up.

Today people are less threatened. Tell yourself, "This is who I am. I am a child of God; I am proud of it. I am happy to claim it and I want to live in that life that God prepared for me. I was born as a Christ child and now I can actually live that life which is a life of unconditional love taking compassionate action for those around me. I always wanted that life. That's peace on earth." In the Fifth Dimension, we work together in communities supporting each other in unity and cooperation. We are there to support each other in need and we do not see what is wrong with people, but we see them through the "eyes of God." We see beyond their shortcomings, and we see beyond the miserable situations they have had to endure to balance their energy. They had difficult times to endure; we love them in spite of it. We love them because they are God's children and they are our brothers and sisters.

That is when you learn to love yourself, love completely as much as God loves you. Then you have completed the first commandment I gave to you: "Love God with all your heart, mind, and soul." Then the second commandment just falls into place: "Love your neighbor as yourself." You love yourself so much you cannot contain it. You pass it around. Christmas is a beautiful time to pass that love around letting others know how wonderful they are and how much they have accomplished in their life to get to this point. They are wonderful children who have grown into a new place that is so much better than where they were. Look at the how much progress they have made. You see, your beliefs have held you back.

So many beliefs have come from dogma, which were intended to hold you back. Now you can see beyond the box; you can see out of the box. You can open the box, put the light of God into it, and see that there is more to it. Your beliefs can become unlimited because

God is unlimited. It is time to see that everything is perfect as it was designed to be; the lessons have been learned, and the growing has been accomplished. You do not even have to believe but you can just know in your heart, how loved you are. That you have survived many past lives to come into this awareness today. It has been a long struggle, through many lives to get to this point of awareness. I would like to say that the Bible has wonderful metaphors and so many people take the written word as gospel rather than the energy behind the messages and the stories. The parables are all about vibration, energy, and physics.

I would like to explain that what I have been talking about is actually described in the Bible with Moses and the story of the Red Sea and the Israelites. They did not know about physics. They did not know about love in those days. They did not understand how vibrations, energy, and higher consciousness worked. Therefore, they had to be told the messages in a language they could understand.

Moses going to the mountain is another word for meditation. That is the highest consciousness you can have. To have a high conscious connection with God is meditation. In his meditation, he was told to lead the children of Israel out of Egypt. He was connecting with God, following directions. He had so much power from that information and connection that he was able to perform some of the necessary things so that the children of Israel could come out of bondage. That is where you have been. You have been in bondage to the ego to the fear and all the negative information that has been perpetrated on purpose to keep you there.

Nothing comes from God but love. Everything, all the harms, have been manmade. There is nothing to fear. In this case, he led the children to the Red Sea with the armies following. His higher conscious was so powerfully strong and connected he was able to clear a path, a path through the ego. He separated the ego into two walls of water that could not come into the consciousness of God. Therefore, his higher consciousness allowed the Israelites to cross the Red Sea on dry land. Safely, easily, to the other side, they were walking in the higher consciousness of God. They were in a real place where they were safe, protected, and unharmed. When they arrived at the high cliff on the other side of the Red Sea, the soldiers in their chariots were coming behind them trying to stop them, trying to make sure that they did not get away. What happened? The ego came back in and the Red Sea was together again. They drowned in their ego consciousness of trying to punish, capture, and control people. So, you see, God led them out through consciousness of his awareness and their faith.

As you know, they wandered for 40 years in the desert. That is because when you come into a new consciousness, it takes a couple generations for the new energy to become part of the culture. So their wandering was like coming into a new world, being reborn and having to learn how to handle their life from a new perspective, a higher perspective. They could do that because they were out of bondage, their connection and faith to God brought them out of the fears of the past that had them in bondage for thousands of years. God brought them out by their trust and belief that it could happen. You see, when you part the Red Sea, you have allowed God's energy to come in, and that is the most powerful energy of all. The Red Sea cannot harm them; the ego is not available to do them any harm and take them out by drowning. When the soldiers came, and they were not in the consciousness of God, things went back to their traditional way.

I (Jesus) had to go through the same lesson, but in a different way in the New Testament. I was in the desert for 40 days being tempted by what some of you would call Satan, which is your lower energy of fear. Each time I said, "Satan get thee behind me," I was telling my ego and my fear to move behind me because I wanted to move forward into Gods higher consciousness. I did not want to go back into the bondage of fear. I wanted to be free of that bondage of self. I wanted to be free to be in Christ Consciousness. I had to make choices each time there were temptations to make that choice for God, again. I cannot serve two masters, so I serve God. I chose to replace that fearful ego message with the light and realize that the boogeyman is not there; you can do that too.

Each time you renounce the lower messages of darkness, temptation, jealously, envy, greed, fear, lust, shame, guilt, all lifetime experiences, you can replace each one as you release it. However, you have to name each one, you cannot do it a as blanket release. As they pop up in your life, identify each one and say "Satan get thee behind me" or "I release this into the hands of God." However, do remember as you do the releasing and letting go to, replace it immediately with God's love and grace so you move forward into "what you do want."

Your intention is most powerful because it tells the body where you are going. If your intention is to move out of Third Dimension and Fourth Dimension, and get your foot up there on Fifth Dimension with the rest of your consciousness, now you can finally be on solid land. You can finally build your life and move forward, no concern for the past, no worries, and no harms. You can give up all your concerns and doubts because you are on solid ground, the rock of God. The past is over, if you choose to take that route.

You are on a planet of choice; it is all about energy shifting, not physical shifting, but your consciousness. It can open up to a multi-Dimensional world where you see what others do not see and you hear what others do not hear. You move into the spiritual realm where there is heaven on earth. There is no condemnation, no criticism, or judgment. You have moved into compassion and you help the planet move into compassion. That is what you came to do. This is peace; it is a peace inside that is very powerful. Today I am so pleased that people are ready to get their foot out of the Third Dimension so it is up where it belongs. You have moved up that ladder and it is time to say, 'I'm doing my best to move in that direction." Your intention is most important. The Universe will bring the rest together so it can happen. Do not be impatient; it will happen at the right time for you and in the right situation.

All things are in divine and perfect order. If you accept that right now is right where you are supposed to be. You are loved no matter what has happened in your surroundings. It is not necessary to know everything or have control over circumstances. It is not about someone else's story. Their story may have been very important to them and was carried out in a way that was very devastating to you. Nevertheless, remember fond memories of the good times, focusing on the love that was there, knowing that it was their time to move on in a different way than you planned. It is most important to say, "I choose to be in a life of love, I choose to move on and make life better for others and myself, and that someone does not have to bring us all down. That we can move on and help those who are in wounded ways, needing our love and compassion."

Leave your ego behind and move in to the sunlight of God. I welcome you with full arms, embrace you, and say welcome home. You really never left, you might say; however, you have been through a nightmare, and it can end anytime you choose.

I give my love to all of you. I care for you. This love comes from the central sun and it is in everyone. See that love in everybody, share it, and let it heal you. There will be no more disease, things will happen differently as in the past. You will notice little children walking sooner than they used to, talking sooner than they used to. They will even know things you know as adults because they do not have to start from scratch. You will say how they know that, it took me 3 years of college to figure that one out. They are starting at a much higher level of consciousness.

Know that disease is gone in this higher consciousness and give yourself permission to move into that help. To move into the new places that will be unfamiliar and unusual but so much better, because when ye "Seek ye first the kingdom of God, all things will be added."

Welcome to the kingdom of God, a very Merry Christmas, and a Happy New Year that will bring you many blessings. This coming year, I assure that you will have some big wonderful surprises. Be wide awake. See the changes that are going on around you, but stay on the rock of God. You will be in the world at this point but not of it. It cannot affect you because you have faith and keep that faith. That is the most powerful place to be. Blessings! Know that you are loved, always have been loved, and God knows every one of your names and every hair on your head. You are very special people today. Bless you, and I bid you fond adieu.

This message came from Jesus in heaven, and it was channeled by Marilyn Redmond.

Rev. Marilyn Redmond, BA, CHT, IBRT, is an internationally known, award-winning writer, speaker, therapist, and consultant. Her lectures, interviews, and channelings appear on YouTube. Her website is www.angelicasgifts.com. Marilyn is a spiritual counselor who is internationally board certified to do regression. She is also a past-life therapist. She offers tarot/psychic readings and private channelings. Her blog is marilynredmondbooks.blogspot.com, and her books and writings are available on Amazon.com and her website.

Channeling is not a new concept. King David used channeling to receive messages for his book of Psalms. He had a group of people taking notes while he was in a trance.

* * * * *

DOUG: The Bible was written by the prophets based on messages from God. Were the messages delivered by the silent voice within or by the angels of God through meditation?

JOHN: Primarily, it was the inner silent voice: *Be still (trance) and know that I am a God.* Yes, it was written down by man through what you might call channeling, but many people in the churches take offense to that. But God did not write the Bible. People did through inspiration. And the churches took that information and of course changed it greatly to serve their needs.

DOUG: Did all biblical writers function as mediums?

JOHN: No, they were learning and growing in spiritual ways, but none of them achieved mediumship as such. There were mediums in the Old Testament, they were the priests that went into the holy of holies and would listen to the Word of God and come out and tell the people what they heard, and those were, the priests of Old were mediums. But no the disciples were not mediums. But they were very spiritual and that they could, some of them could do healing, some of them could do various things that were spiritually based, because of their higher consciousness that they were growing into. But as far as being a medium, they were not. They were still on the path of spiritual growth.

DOUG: Was Paul a medium?

JOHN: Paul was not a medium, no.

DOUG: He was not, okay. But the Bible made it appear that he was a medium based on the book, Psychic Streams because Paul wrote many Epistle Letters.

JOHN: You don't have to be a medium to realize some of these things because physically and intuitively, people do get information constantly. It's the type and level of consciousness that makes you a medium. And so, Paul would have had to be a master to be a medium, a master, and he did not achieve that in that lifetime.

DOUG: Oh, interesting. Okay.

JOHN: He did at a later time. Mediumship is higher that a psychic. A psychic can be aware of what's going on with other people intuitively.

A medium is in connection with archangels and masters and Jesus in the higher realms. And so, Peter - Paul, rather. Paul was not a connection with the highest of realms. He very likely was psychic, however. Is that maybe where you're coming from?

DOUG: I called a psychic, and she wants to know if she is doing a good job translating information for me?

JOHN: You see she is questioning herself, and I would say if she is questioning herself she is probably doing a good job. You see everybody is a little different, and her answers are going to come through her frame of reference and so on where she is at she is doing a good job. Now the difference between a psychic and Marilyn is both a psychic and a medium. Psychic deals with the third and fourth-dimensional vibrations, but medium deals with the fifth dimension and higher. So, when psychic talks to those that have died on the other side, which Marilyn does that kind of thing, you know psychic gives information about your life, how it's going, etc., which Marilyn can do. But a medium also can talk to archangels and masters and your guides and Jesus as yesterday can come through, so the higher energies are medium.

* * * * *

The energy of Christ consciousness transformed energy on the planet on the day of Pentecost. Peter led this service among the group of 120 newly minted disciples. The spirit of truth is Christ consciousness. "And when the day of Pentecost was come, they were all with one accord in one place. And suddenly there came a sound from heaven, as of a rushing and mighty wind, and it filled all the house where they sat. And there appeared unto them cloven tongues, like fire, and it sat upon each of them. And they were all filled with the Holy Ghost, and began to speak with other tongues, as the Spirit gave them utterance" (Acts 2:1–4). The energy of spirit of truth is still alive today;

* * * * *

DOUG: Jesus poured out the spirit of truth, so how could that affect the future generations when we weren't there? How do you receive the spirit of truth?

JOHN: Well, God's words are truth and have survived the test of time. They have survived wars, floods, and sin on earth. Truth will always survive because it has power. If you read Joel Goldsmith, you will realize how anything in the dark does not have power. If you put a plant in a closet in the darkness, it's going to die. If you think of that plant going out to the sunshine, it's going to blossom with fragrance and beauty, and you are going to enjoy the lovely benefits of that flower.

* * * * *

Attaining Christ consciousness is what makes you a saint. From the passage to the Colossians, Paul gave the definition of a true church. It is within the temple of your body. "Now rejoice I in my sufferings for you, and fulfill the rest of the afflictions of Christ in my flesh, for his body's sake, which is the Church. Whereof I am a minister, according to the dispensation of God, which is given me unto youward, to fulfill the word of God. Which is the mystery hid since the world began, and from all ages, but now is made manifest to his Saints" (Colossians 1:24–26).

Paul acknowledged the mystery of the Bible. At the time of his writing, the energy of the spirit of truth was made available through the church, and this occurred after the Pentecost. However, only the saints were able to grasp the concept of this energy. It is the kingdom of God as well. It is where you receive Christ consciousness. It is the spirit of God that makes us feel whole because we reactivate our missing ten strands of DNA. Our DNA becomes twelve fully functioning strands with the power to heal ourselves. "But when the people knew it, they followed him: and he received them, and spake unto them of the kingdom of God, and healed them that had need to be healed" (Luke 9:11). Jesus's disciples did not ascend to the fifth dimension until later on in their lifetimes.

* * * * *

DOUG: I wondered about the twelve disciples. Were they in the fourth dimension or the fifth dimension after they were blessed by Jesus?

JOHN: Well, most of them were in the fourth dimension. But all of the dimensions have different levels and different stages, and every dimension has seven levels within and then seven more levels within those. So it's kind of like climbing stairs, you might say, but everybody is moving forward through a higher consciousness through those dimensions of evolution. And so some are in lower levels of the fourth dimension. Some are in higher levels of the fourth dimension, but none of them actually achieved what Jesus achieved until later in other lifetimes. So it was a matter of being in the fourth dimension and having a different perception of what they were able to accomplish in their spiritual growth at that time. And you know, some of them picked up on what Jesus said more easily than others. So no one was just perfectly in tune with Jesus. They were all in different spaces, but very much growing and progressing toward what he was teaching.

* * * * *

We have to do our side of the work to climb the ladder of higher consciousness. Some of Jesus's disciples progressed up the ladder faster than others. We have to do the same thing. There is no time table to achieve Christ consciousness, as God is patient and willing to wait for us to achieve it.

* * * * *

DOUG: *The Book of Urantia* says that God grieves over our failures.

JOHN: God does not have feelings, so it's not true that he could grieve. Feelings are only of a human planet, so this is the planet with feelings, but God just waits patiently. God has a spirit; God has no human attributes, and feelings are a human attribute.

* * * * *

The majority of the books in the New Testament were written by Paul. He had an ascension experience with his consciousness. "I know a man in Christ above fourteen years ago, (whether he were in the body, I cannot tell, or out of the body, I cannot tell: God knoweth) which was taken up into the Third heaven. And I know such a man (whether in the body, or out of the body, I cannot tell: God knoweth.) How that he was taken up into Paradise, and heard words which cannot be spoken, which are not possible for man to utter" (2 Corinthians 12:2-4). The man in Christ was Christ consciousness. He never had ascended physically, but his state of consciousness had ascended. He was meditating from within. "For I delight in the Law of God, concerning the inner man" (Romans 7:22).

Paul wrote eleven books for the New Testament, including the book of Hebrews. There were disagreements among biblical scholars about the writer of the epistle to the Hebrews. John confirmed it was Paul.

* * * * *

JOHN: Well, I'm doing very well. Thank you. And I do have some information for you this morning that you asked me for earlier, and I do want to tell you that yes, Paul wrote the book of Hebrews.

DOUG: Oh, great. Okay.

JOHN: I thought you might want that information since I had to postpone telling you.

* * * * *

The words *sanctified* and *holy* come from the same Greek root as the word that is commonly translated *saints*. Christians are saints by virtue of their connection with Christ consciousness. It applies to any religious denomination—Judaism, Hinduism, Buddhism, and Islam. The basic tenet for all of these religions is finding the kingdom of God within. When we attain Christ consciousness, we are in God's kingdom. During one thousand years of Christ's reign, the planet will experience heaven on earth. People who have attained Christ consciousness or who are about to attain that level will remain on the planet. For those who are resisting higher consciousness of love or brotherly love, they will reincarnate on another planet that resembles Earth, one that has not been discovered by scientists in the universe. They won't return until one thousand years later.

How does the Roman Catholic understanding of saints compare with the biblical teachings of saints? Not very well. In Roman Catholic theology, the saints are in heaven. In the Bible, the saints are on earth. In Roman Catholic teachings, a person does not become a saint unless he or she is canonized by the pope. In biblical teachings, everyone who has received Jesus Christ by faith is a saint. Also, the saints are called to revere, worship, and pray to God alone. These two varying theologies do not involve spiritual realities, just physical realities. However, we are saints only if we attain Christ consciousness.

"The light of the body is the eye: if then thine eye be single, thy whole body shall be light. But if thine eye be wicked, then all thy body shall be dark. Wherefore if the light that is in thee, be darkness, how great is that darkness?" (Matthew 6:22).

Our eyes are the entrance to our hearts and minds, and as such, they provide a doorway to our very souls. When we attain a higher state of consciousness, our auras are lighted. Saints are considered lighted souls. Symbolically, the seven eyes of God are like the seven chakras. "John to the seven Churches which are in Asia, Grace be with you, and peace from him, which is, and which was, and which is to come, and from the seven Spirits which are before his Throne" (Revelation 1:4). The seven spirits of God are the chakras, a conduit between our bodies and our souls through the seven glands of our bodies.

* * * * *

DOUG: I wonder if the Bible was written by third-dimensional people of the third dimension. Were those who were baptized with fire similar to the lit candles of my candlestick?

JOHN: Well, you can call it your candlestick. You can call it fire. But however you describe the spirit inside, it is a very powerful energy. And yes, it lights up your life. So a candle is a wonderful description of lighting up your inner light. So that light inside is finally coming up so that you can dispel the darkness. Yes, fire could signal the flame of the candle if you want to think of it that way. You see, the terms in the Bible were actually very well picked for what the people of the time could understand. And flames, candles, and candlesticks were very hands-on, tangible examples of the third dimension. And that's what you're trying to explain. You are trying to describe fifth-dimensional, invisible energy with third-dimensional terms. Therefore, you look beyond the words for the spirit behind what is being said.

* * * * *

The following sets of Scripture passages from Paul's writings demonstrate the difference between third-dimensional terminology and fifth-dimensional terminology regarding Jesus Christ and Christ consciousness:

Third Dimension (Philippians 4:7)

"And the peace of God which passeth all understanding, shall preserve your hearts and minds in Christ Jesus".

Fifth Dimension (Philippians 4:7)

"And the peace of God which passeth all understanding, shall preserve your hearts and minds in Christ *Consciousness*".

Third Dimension (Philippians 4:21)

"Salute all the Saints in Christ Jesus. The brethren, which are with me, greet you".

Fifth Dimension (Philippians 4:21)

"Salute all the Saints in Christ *Consciousness*. The brethren, which are with me, greet you".

Third Dimension (Ephesians 3:8-9)

"Even unto me the least of all Saints is this grace given, that I should preach among the Gentiles, the unsearchable riches of Christ. And to make clear unto all men what the fellowship of the mystery is, which from the beginning of the world hath been hid in God, who hath created all things by Jesus Christ".

Fifth Dimension (Ephesians 3:8-9)

"Even unto me the least of all Saints is this grace given, that I should preach among the Gentiles, the unsearchable riches of Christ *Consciousness*. And to make clear unto all men what the fellowship of the mystery is, which from the beginning of the world hath been hid in God, who hath created all things by Jesus Christ".

Third Dimension (Ephesians 3:16-21)

"That he might grant you according to the riches of his glory, that ye may be strengthened by his Spirit in the inner man. That Christ may dwell in your hearts by faith: That ye, being rooted and grounded in love, may be able to comprehend with all Saints. What is the breadth, and length, and depth, and height: And to know the love of Christ, which passeth knowledge, that ye may be filled with all fullness of God. Unto him therefore that is able to do exceeding abundantly above all that we ask or think, according to the power that worketh in us. Be praise in the Church by Christ Jesus, throughout all generations forever, Amen".

Fifth Dimension (Ephesians 3:16-21)

"That he might grant you according to the riches of his glory, that ye may be strengthened by his Spirit in the inner man. That Christ

Consciousness may dwell in your hearts by faith: That ye, being rooted and grounded in love, may be able to comprehend with all Saints. What is the breadth, and length, and depth, and height: And to know the love of Christ, which passeth knowledge, that ye may be filled with all fullness of God. Unto him therefore that is able to do exceeding abundantly above all that we ask or think, according to the power that worketh in us. Be praise in the Church by Christ Jesus, throughout all generations forever, Amen".

Third Dimension (Ephesians 2:13-18)

"But now in Christ Jesus, ye which once were far off, are made near by the blood of Christ. For he is our peace, which hath made of both one, and hath broken the stop of the partition wall, in abrogating through his flesh the hatred, that is, the Law of commandments which standeth in ordinances, for to make of twain one new man in himself, so making peace. And that he might reconcile both unto God in one body by his cross, and slay hatred thereby. And came, and preached peace to you which were afar off, and to them that were near. For through him we both have an entrance unto the Father by one Spirit".

Fifth Dimension (Ephesians 2:13-18)

"But now in Christ *Consciousness*, ye which once were far off, are made near by the blood of Christ. For he is our peace, which hath made of both one, and hath broken the stop of the partition wall, in abrogating through his flesh the hatred, that is, the Law of commandments which standeth in ordinances, for to make of twain one new man in himself, so making peace. And that he might reconcile both unto God in one body by his cross, and slay hatred thereby. And came, and preached peace to you which were afar off, and to them that were near. For through him we both have an entrance unto the Father by one Spirit".

Third Dimension (Ephesians 2:4-7)

"But God which is rich in mercy, through his great love wherewith he loved us, even when we were dead by sins, hath quickened us together in Christ, by whose grace ye are saved. And hath raised us up together, and made us sit together in the heavenly places in Christ Jesus. That he might show in the ages to come the exceeding riches of his grace through his kindness toward us in Christ Jesus".

Fifth Dimension (Ephesians 2:4-7)

"But God which is rich in mercy, through his great love wherewith he loved us, even when we were dead by sins, hath quickened us together in Christ *Consciousness*, by whose grace ye are saved. And hath raised us up together, and made us sit together in the heavenly places in Christ *Consciousness*. That he might show in the ages to come the exceeding riches of his grace through his kindness toward us in Christ *Consciousness*".

Section 1.11: Relationships and Marriages during the Golden Age

Relationships are undergoing a major transformation in the new era. Relationships are the connection of the deepest emotions within us, reaching from great joy to deep agony. In relationships, we may become aware of an inner pain that is essentially much older than the relationship itself, even older than our human existence. Today we share our energies and join the cosmic energy (photon energy) that arrived on Earth in 2012. The new era is no longer a perception of the future. It is already manifesting itself in the daily life of innumerable individuals.

If we read the paper or watch the news, it may seem that the time is not right yet. However, the awakening brought forward by the new era or the golden age starts at the level of the individual. The standard of awakening comes later for governments, institutions, and organizations. It is in our everyday existence that a new flow of energy presents itself. It is the flow of our heart that invites us to live and to act according to its lightness and wisdom.

It is how the birthing of the new era takes place with everyday individuals being attentive to the whispers of their hearts. Spiritually, the groundwork for any real change or transformation is on the individual level. The energy awakens in our hearts, and it will gradually find its way through institutions and organizations that hold on to the old paradigm of ego-based consciousness. Old strongholds of power will break down, not by force but by the compassionate energy of the heart. If the heart takes control, the old will collapse, not under the pressure of power but under the pressure of love.

We are invited and often challenged to achieve a profound self-healing in the field of relationships. Because of the new energy now offered, it is possible to change the destructive factors of relationships into a positive flow of energy. However, healing and personal transformation mean that we let go of relationships in which we cannot accurately express ourselves. It frequently means that even if we love someone dearly, we may have to say good-bye because our inner path takes us to a different place. Whether it leads to renewal or to departing in a relationship, we must face the issues in this area of personal bonding. The call of the heart and the heart-based energy that marks the new era has entered our daily lives, and we cannot ignore it anymore.

We can explain why relationships can hurt us so much and turn our lives completely upside down. These hurts have carried over through our lifetimes since our original birthing pain as souls. It is a pain that is much older than this life, older even than all our former lives on Earth.

Allow our imagination to travel freely for a moment. We are not in bodies. We are pure consciousness, and we are part of a vast energy field that surrounds us in a comfortable way. We feel that we are part of this unity, being cherished without conditions. This area of energy encloses us as an immensely comfortable blanket. It's an abundantly loving energy that allows us to explore and develop freely without ever doubting ourselves or our intrinsic right to be who we are. This feeling of comfort and security constituted the prebirthing conditions from which we emerged as individual souls. It was a cosmic womb. Even far removed from our present state, our hearts still ache for this sense of completeness and wholeness, the feeling of absolute safety we experienced in that blanket of love and benevolence. That feeling of oneness we remember was God. Together in this blanket of love, we embodied God.

Within this divine consciousness, it was decided to create a new situation. We can imagine that in God, which is a unity of awareness, there was a longing for something different, something other than unity. There was a longing for the experience. When we are assimilated into a wholeness of pure being, we do not experience things. We simply are. Despite the ecstasy and the total safety of this state of being, there was a part of God that wanted to explore and to evolve. This being "departed from itself."

We are this part of God. At a certain point, our consciousness agreed to this experiment of leaving from unity and becoming an entity in itself, defined individual awareness. It was a huge step. From the bottom of our being, we felt that this was a real thing. We felt that the longing for creativity and renewal was an active and valuable aspiration. However, the moment that we departed from the field of oneness, there was a pain. For the first time in our recollection, there was a deep pain. We were torn loose from a realm of love and safety that had been entirely self-evident to us. It is the birthing pain. Our innermost being tells us everything was going to be okay even during this first intense experience of desolation. However, the pain was so deep that it created confusion on the outside. It became trying to keep in touch with the most profound knowledge inside, the inner level at which we are God and where we know that all is well.

The inner child is the tormented part. Our soul or our unique individuality carries within itself the extremes of pure divine knowledge on the one hand and a distressed cosmic child on the contrary. This unity of God and child, knowledge and experience, started the long journey of an individual soul. We began to investigate and experience what it was like to be a defined person.

God had transformed a part of himself into the soul. The soul needs the experience to find its divine origins again. The soul needs to be alive, to encounter, to discover, to self-destruct, to recreate, and to feel who the soul is, namely God. The manifestation of being one and whole had crumbled, and we needed to regain that by experience. The birthing of the I-consciousness was a miracle. It had never existed before.

Often we try to transcend the boundaries of our individuality to experience oneness and profound unity again. We might say that is the aim of our spiritual quest. However, consider this. From God's point of view, it is the individuality and the separateness that constitutes the miracle. The state of being one was how it had always been. Within the miracle of being an individual soul, there's an immense beauty, joy, and creative power. The reason that we do not experience it like that is that we are still struggling with our birthing pain as a soul. Somewhere deep inside us, the primal scream of anguish and betrayal still resounds. It is the recollection of being torn apart from our mother/father and their omnipresent blanket of love and safety.

We have gone through journeys of time and experience. We have tried all different kinds of forms. There were many incarnations, and we did not have the shape of the human body in some. What matters to us in this context is that throughout this long history, we were led by two different motives. On the one hand, there was the eagerness for exploration, creation, and renewal, and on the contrary, there was the sense of being cast out of paradise and an overpowering loneliness.

Through the adventurous, progressive part of ourselves—the energy that pushed us out of the cosmic womb—we have experienced and created a lot. However, because of the birthing pain and homesickness we carried within, we also had to deal with much trauma and disillusion. Therefore, our creations were not always benevolent. During our journeys through time and space, we have done things we have regretted later on, things we might call "evil." These actions were merely the result of the determination to plunge into experience and venture into the unknown. As soon as we decide to become individuals and to break away from the self-evident oneness, we cannot experience light only. We have to find out everything new. So we will also experience the dark. We will experience all there is, including all of the extremes.

It is about truly embracing our divinity, and from that self-awareness, we can experience joy and abundance. In the moment of our cosmic birth, the time that desolation and pain enveloped us, we started to feel tiny and insignificant. From that moment on, we began to look for something that could save us—whether a power or force outside of us, a God, a leader, a partner, or a child. In the awakening process, we realized that the essential safety we are longing for is not there in anything outside of us, whether a parent, a lover, or a god. However strongly this yearning or homesickness may be in a particular relationship, we will not find this necessary safety there, not even in a relationship with God.

The God we believe in, specifically the God who has been handed down to us by tradition and who still profoundly influences our perception, is a God outside of us. It is a God who outlines things for us, who lays out the way for us. However, that God does not exist. We are God. We are that innovative part of God who decided to go its way and to encounter things in a different way. We had the confidence that we would be able to heal ourselves from the primal wound of birth. We could say that the expansive energy of exploration and renewal is a male energy, whereas the energy of unification and joining, the energy of the home, is a female energy. Both these energies belong to the essence of who we are. From one of the gospels, Jesus was quoted as saying, "Jesus answered them, and is it not written in your law, I said; ye are gods? If he called them gods, unto whom the word of God was given, and the Scripture cannot be broken." As souls, we are neither male nor female. Essentially, we are both male and female. We started our journey with both these ingredients. It is now the time to let them work together in harmony, which means to experience actually wholeness in ourselves. After others have denied our greatness for so long, we will start to long for the God within our being.

It is the ultimate breakthrough to enlightenment to realize that we are the God we are craving. There is nothing outside us that can bring us into the heart of our power, our wholeness. We are it. We are "the one," and we have always been the one. Lighting this flame of self-awareness within brings such joy and such a deep sense of homecoming that it puts all of our relationships into a new perspective. For example, we feel less concerned about the things that other people tell us. If someone criticizes or distrusts us, we do not automatically take it personally. We seem less affected or eager to react. We let it go more quickly, and the need to defend ourselves drops away. When we are easily affected emotionally by what another person thinks, this indicates that we give too much power to the adverse opinions of others. This self-contempt is not solved by instigating others but only by going inward and getting in touch with the emotional scars within ourselves. These scars are much older than this particular moment of rejection.

In fact, the pain of rejection and relationships goes back to the original unhealed birthing pain. It may have seemed as if our pain was coming from our partner. It may seem as if something outside of us causes the pain. It may also seem that the solution to our problem lies in the behavior of the other. However, we are dealing with an ancient pain that had long existed within ourselves. We may easily get entangled in relationship issues that can be painful if we are not aware of this.

In a love relationship, we try to forge a kind of unity and safety among us that parallels the primeval state of oneness that we vaguely remember. Subconsciously, we are attempting to recreate the feeling of being comfortably wrapped in a blanket of unconditional love and acceptance. There is a child within us who is crying out for that unconditional acceptance. However, if this child in us puts his or her arms around the child part in our partners, too often it results in a suffocating grasp that blocks both partners from genuine self-expression. We become emotionally dependent, and then we will start to want the love or approval of the other person to maintain our well-being. Dependence always creates power and control issues because to need someone is equal to wanting to control his or her behavior. It is the beginning of a destructive relationship. To give up our individuality in a relationship, guided by a subconscious longing for absolute unity, is destructive toward ourselves as well as the other person.

True love between two individuals manifests two energy fields that can work completely apart from each other. Each area of energy is a unity unto itself and attaches to the other by that union. Where partners are dependent upon each other, there is a tendency of not wanting or not being able to function without the other. It leads to an entanglement of energies as demonstrated in the auric fields. The partners feed each other with the addictive energies of dependence and control. This kind of energy entanglement indicates that we have not taken responsibility for ourselves and that we have not come to grips with the old wounds that only we can heal. If only we would address this deepest pain and take responsibility for it without having to depend on someone else and liberating ourselves from the destructive aspect of the relationship.

Karmic Relations

Karmic relationships are relationships between people who have known each other in other lifetimes and who have experienced intense emotions concerning each other. The sure sign of a karmic relationship is that the partners carry unresolved emotions within, including guilt, fear, dependency, jealousy, and anger. They are drawn to each other in another incarnation because of this unresolved emotional charge. The goal of the renewed encounter is to provide an opportunity to resolve the issue at hand. It happens by recreating the same question in a short period.

When they first meet, the karmic players feel a compelling urge to get nearer to each other. Eventually, they find their old emotional patterns resurfacing. It sets the stage for them to deal with the old issue again. In a new era of love and light, it is more likely they will handle things in a more enlightened manner and resolve them. The spiritual purpose of the renewed encounter is for both partners to make choices other than the ones they made during that former lifetime.

For instance, a woman had a husband who was possessive and bossy in her previous life. For a while she accepted this kind of behavior, and at a certain point, she thought she had had enough. She broke up her relationship. Afterward, she felt remorse because the husband committed suicide. She carried this sense of guilt with her for the rest of her life because she did not give him another chance. They met again in another lifetime, and there was an odd attraction between them. At first, the man was exceptionally charming, and she was the center of his attention. He adored her. They entered into a relationship. However, he became increasingly jealous and possessive because he suspected her of adultery. She found herself in an inner struggle and got angry that he wrongly accused her. However, she also felt a strange obligation to forgive and to give him another chance. *He is a helpless man*, she thought. *He cannot help it that he has this fear of being abandoned.* She justified her behavior in this way by saying, "Maybe I can help him get over this." However, she allowed her personal boundaries to be violated, and the relationship negatively affected her self-esteem.

The most liberating choice for the woman would be to break off the relationship and go her way without feelings of guilt. The pain and despair of the husband are not her obligations. His pain and her sense of guilt have led to a destructive relationship. Their relationship was already inherently charged because of the past lives. The essence of the renewed engagement is that the woman must learn to let things go without any feelings of guilt. It is also the man's opportunity to stand on his own feet. So the only real fix is to break off the relationship. As part of her life's lessons, the woman's karma is to let go of her sense of guilt about her husband's suicide in her former life. The departure of his wife in this life would confront the man again with his pain and fear for his next life. It offers him a new opportunity to face these emotions rather than living again to learn this lesson.

We may recognize a karmic encounter by the fact that the other person appears strangely familiar to us. More often than not, there is a mutual attraction, something compelling in the air that urges us to come together and to discover each other. If the opportunity is available, this strong attraction may grow into a loving relationship or a massive infatuation. The emotions we experience may be so overwhelming that we think we have met our twin soul. However, things are not as they appear. In such a relationship, often the partners become involved in a psychological conflict with ingredients of power, control, and dependence. By this, they repeat a tragedy that they subconsciously recognize from former lives. In a past life, one could have been a lover, a parent, a child, a boss, a subordinate, or something else altogether. However, they always seemed to touch a profound inner pain in each other through acts of unfaithfulness and abuses of power, or by contrast, there may have been an intense engagement between them, one that caused a deep wound and emotional trauma. That is why the forces of attraction—as well as repulsion—can be so violent when they meet again in a new incarnation.

The spiritual invitation to all entangled souls is to let each other go and become free and independent. Karmic relationships are almost never stable, loving relationships. They are destructive rather than healing. Often the underlying purpose of the encounter is to succeed in letting each other go. It is something that could not go away in one or more past lifetimes because of the strong emotional bonds. However, now there is another opportunity to release each other in love.

Intense emotions refer to deep pain rather than mutual love. The energy of love is characteristically calm, peaceful, and inspiring. It is not exhausting and tragic. If a relationship exhibits these traits, it is time to let it go.

Sometimes we convince ourselves that we have to stay together because we "share karma" and we have "to work things out together." We call upon the nature of karma as an argument for prolonging a negative relationship while we are both suffering immensely. In fact, we are distorting the concept of karma here. We do not work out karma together. Karma is an individual challenge. Again, resolving karma is something we do on our own. Another person may touch or trigger something inside us that creates much drama between us. However, it remains our sole task and challenge to deal with our inner hurt, not with the other person's issues. We only have responsibility for ourselves.

It is important to realize that we are not responsible for our spouses or partners. That is one of the main pitfalls of relationships. Sometimes we are so connected to the inner children of our partners and the emotionally hurt part inside of them that we feel we should be the ones to *rescue* them. Alternatively, our partners may be trying the same with us. However, this is not going to work. We will be reinforcing emotions of powerlessness and victimhood in the other person. It would be more helpful if we drew the line and stood up for ourselves. We desire to feel whole and complete, which is the most important condition for a genuinely fulfilling relationship.

Healing Relationships

In healing relationships, partners respect each other for what they are without trying to change each other. They take pleasure in each other's company without the feeling of unease or loneliness. In this kind of relationship, we offer understanding, support, and encouragement to our loved one without trying to solve their problems. Peace and freedom pervade in the healing relationships. Now and then there may be some misunderstandings here and there, but the emotions they bring up are temporary. Both partners are inclined to forgive. There is a connection between them, and they have indicated that they will not take the other person's emotions or mistakes personally. They are independent, and they don't draw their security and well-being from the approval of their mates. They do not fill a void but add something new and vital.

In a healing relationship, partners may have known each other for one or more past lifetimes. However, in these cases, there is hardly ever an emotional, karmic burden. The two souls may have associated with each other in a past life in a supportive way. As a parent and child, friends, or partners, they have perceived each other as soul mates. It creates an indissoluble bond throughout several lives.

For example, a young man comes from a low-income family during the Middle Ages. He is gentle and sensitive by nature and does not fit in well with his surroundings. His family was rather hard working, rough people who think little of his dreamy, idealistic nature. When he entered a monastery, he finds himself unhappy with a restricted life there. Also, there is little human compassion or togetherness among the people living there. However, there is one man who is a bit different. It is a priest who has a higher rank but with no authority and someone who is genuinely sympathetic to him. There is a recognition between their similar minds. There is a silent connection from the heart. Even though they seldom meet or speak much, the priest is an inspiration for him.

In the following lifetime, this man was now a woman. Again, she had a gentle and dreamy nature. She struggled with standing up for herself. When she was an adult, she was involved in a marriage to an authoritarian man. At first, she fell for his powerful charisma. However, later on, she realized how his dominance affected her. She finds it problematic to break free from him. At her work she mentioned the subject to a colleague who's an older man. He inspired her to stand up for herself and to stay true to her needs. Each time she spoke with him, she intuitively knew that he was right. Then after a lot of inner conflicts, she divorced her husband. The influence of her colleague changed now. She felt a strong attraction for him. He turned out to be single. She felt so much more comfortable with him. It felt as if they had known each other for ages. They started a relationship, one that was affectionate, relaxed, and encouraging for both of them. The sympathy that flowed between them in a former life now became a fulfilling relationship as husband and wife.

It is a healing relationship. The woman made an essential decision in leaving her husband and choosing for herself. With this, she affirmed her emotional independence. That created the basis for a loving, well-balanced relationship with a congenial soul.

Twin Souls

The idea of twin souls exerts a profound attraction for us. However, it is potentially quite dangerous because it may reinforce the birthing pain and emotional dependence in each one of us. It happens when you start to believe that there is another person who perfectly suits you and makes you whole. This notion of the twin soul is often thought of as one's other half. We then assume that the oneness and safety we are missing so deeply is us missing out on our perfect matches.

According to this immature notion of twin souls, the souls are two halves that together make up a single unity. Commonly, the two halves are respectively male and female. So this notion not only suggests that we are incomplete unto ourselves but also that we are inherently male or female. We can probably see that this concept of twin souls is not healthy or healing from a spiritual point of view. It makes us reliant on something outside of us. It denies the fact that we are everything, male and female, and that we are whole and complete unto ourselves. It creates all kinds of illusions that lead us far away from home and the divinity of our individuality. No soul is supposed to be someone else's other half.

Twin souls do exist, and they are what the word implies. They are twins. They are souls with the same *feeling tone* or vibration, not unlike with biological twins. The particular time and place of birth makes for a uniquely charged feeling tone inside the souls. They are not dependent upon each other in any way. They are neither male nor female. However, they are certainly tuned into each other as kindred spirits.

What is the reason for twin souls? Why do they exist? We often think that the raison d'être for something is the learning process it affects. The aim is simply joy and creativity. Twin souls have no function within duality. We will meet our twin souls when we transcend duality and we identify ourselves again with the God inside ourselves, which is whole and undivided and which can take any form. Twin souls meet again on their journey back home.

* * * * *

DOUG: It's kind of like my special friend and myself. I guess we're twin souls?

JOHN: When people have that same energy so that you match together, twin souls become androgynous, is masculine and a feminine of that particular soul. And that can be very true, yes.

DOUG: We get along so well every single day.

JOHN: Well, that's beautiful. That means that you're very much in tune with harmony, and that's what it's about.

* * * * *

Returning to the moment at the beginning of the voyage for the soul, the moment we leave the state of oneness with God and become individuals, we enter duality. Suddenly, there is dark and light, great and small, sickness and health. The reality is split. We have no frame of reference anymore for who we are. At first, we took our identity from "being part of a whole." Now we are a single piece torn loose from the whole. However, without consciously knowing, someone accompanies us, someone who is equal to us and resembles us as closely as anything could. We took up *the same space* in the blanket of oneness, so near to each other that we did not know that we were two until we were born. What connects the two of us is something beyond duality, something that antedates the history of duality. It is hard to put into words correctly because it defies our usual definitions of identity in which we are either one or two but cannot be both at the same time.

Now we were both setting out on a journey, a long journey throughout many experiences. Both of us have experienced the extremes of duality, and we have discovered gradually that our essence does not lie in duality but outside of it in something that underlies it. As soon as we become intensely aware of this underlying oneness, our journey back begins. Little by little we feel less attached to external things, such as power, fame, money, or prestige. We understand more and more that the key is not what we experience but how we experience it. We create our happiness or misery by our state of awareness. We are discovering the power of our consciousness.

Once we have gone through all the highs and lows of duality, there will be a moment when we meet our twin soul. In the energy and appearance of the twin soul, we will recognize a dark part of our essence beyond duality. With this recognition, we will start to understand ourselves better and become aware of who we are. Our twin is a frame of reference that carries us outside of the limited beliefs about ourselves that we took in during our lives and lifetimes before. We liberate ourselves by seeing these reflections in our twins. These are reminders of who we are, and they have nothing to do with emotional dependency. The reunion helps each of us become stronger and more self-aware individuals, expressing our creativity and love. It accelerates our return journey as it helps us step up to a higher level of oneness while fully retaining and expressing our individuality.

Ultimately, we are all one. We are supported by an energy that is universal in all of us. However, there is individuality in all of us. The twin soul is the link between individuality and oneness. It is like a path to oneness. If we connect with our twin souls consciously and materially, we will bring about the creation of something different—a third energy that is born out of their combined action. That energy enhances unity recognition to a larger extent than just the two of them. Since they are on their way home, twin souls feel inspired to anchor the energies of love and oneness. They do so in a way that deals with their particular talents and skills. In this retrospect, the love between twin soul forms a stepping stone for "being One."

* * * * *

DOUG: Were Jesus and Mary Magdalene considered twin souls?

JOHN: Yes.

* * * * *

There is a profound inner bond between twin souls. Their joining brings love and joy, and their meeting augments creativity and self-realization. They support each other without descending into the dangers of emotional dependence. The love between twin souls is not meant to make each other whole but to create something new. Instead of the two becoming one, the two shall become three.

* * * * *

DOUG: Is it true that our soul mates help to purify our hearts?

JOHN: Well, it can if you see it from that point of view, so many people think that a soul mate is someone you marry and with whom you live happily ever after. However, that is not the real meaning of a soul mate. A soul mate is someone who reflects a part of your personality that needs to be changed. Soul mates are near to you and help you in parts of your life. So when you first get together with the person and you see all the wonderful characteristics he or she has, you also see you and your little features. However, people tend to deny those issues that they do not wish to look at in themselves, so divorce is often imminent because they do not want to accept their shortcomings.

DOUG: Could living in the fifth dimension and higher make it easier for people to find their soul mates because they look at the heart rather than physical attraction or money?

JOHN: Exactly, in that dimension there is no negative energy, so you see the soul of Christ in everybody. Everyone becomes a soul in the fifth dimension.

* * * * *

Healing the Cosmic Birthing Pain

We will meet our twin soul at some point. Please let this knowledge be enough to us. Try not to dwell on hopes and expectations that take us out of the here and now. What matters at this moment is that we fully realize that the love and safety we deeply desire are present within ourselves.

It applies not only to loving relationships but also in parent-child relationships because there is the temptation to find absolute oneness or security in the other. For instance, think of a father who secretly wants his or her child to realize all the dreams that he did not fulfill.

Also, consider a child who as a grown up and still clings to his or her parents and considers them to be his or her absolute haven.

It is important to become cognizant of the underlying dynamics and motives in our relationships and to heal them in the light of our consciousness. Our cosmic homesickness is not going to be healed by or in a relationship. It will be done by us alone and by the full realization of whom we are, by realizing our light, beauty, and divinity. It is the destination of our journey. We will not return to the state of oneness from whence we came. The blanket of love from which you were born constituted your embryo stage. Now we are becoming mature gods. We will create a field of absolute safety and love from our own hearts. Also, it allows others to share in this without any conditions. That is the aspect of God—unconditional love that radiates, creates, and cherishes without any agenda. The unconditional love is within us. Let's be silent for a few moments to feel true to our individuality, our unique being unto ourselves. When people surround us, we for a time feel our "I" strongly. Unconditionally, we are this part of God. No one can take this away from us because it is an undeniable presence.

Furthermore, now feel how this undeniable fact of our "I" presence can be a source of joy and strength to us. Say yes to the miracle of our being and embrace it. "Yes, I am me. I am separate and unique in my being." One may connect deeply with others but also ever remain an "I." We may think that behind this fact lies solitude and desolation, but go beyond these thoughts and feel the power and vitality within us. If we say yes to our individuality, we experience self-confidence and trust. On that basis, we will create loving relationships, and the solitude and desolation will dissolve.

When feelings of loneliness and desolation overwhelm us, we must give affection to our inner children. Our inner child is longing for the total security it once knew as an embryo. It wants to see that security reflected in the face of a partner, in the face of our child, in front of your mother or father, and in the face of a therapist. Then show the child your face. You have the face of an angel for this child. You are meant to heal this child in any way you can imagine. Neither "I" nor any "master" can do it for you. We can only show the direction. We are the saviors of ourselves.

* * * * *

DOUG: I see. That is interesting. Now we are entering a new era of love and light.

JOHN: Yes.

DOUG: Sexual energy has been suppressed by the churches for many years.

JOHN: Well, the energy they suppressed was the love of God being shared in a spiritual energy way with another living person so that it can expand. What happened because of this is people still had sex, but the motivation was from lust. It wasn't from sharing love because if you're a fearful person having sex with another fearful person, it doesn't grow. It doesn't manifest and provides a loving, blissful experience. It's using one person for the good of another to feel better, but not in a healthy way, so when people have sex for the wrong reason, it's like a vampire sucking blood from one person to another for their survival. They are sucking the spiritual energy from one person to survive at the expense of another person. So the church obliterated unconditional love between people. Catholic church said sex was just for procreation, and otherwise, it was not to be encountered. But pure sex, true love being shared sensually is the highest energy you can accomplish. You can move into a higher state of being, and they didn't want people to move into this higher state. That's why the priests were there telling them what to do. They didn't want people to access that loving of unconditional energy that would expand and make their lives so wonderful. Because then they wouldn't need the church to tell them what to do, so they were suppressing real true love. The energy of the sexual love that is a blissful experience and climaxes are in that bliss of ecstasy, and you can experience that 24-7 if you move into the fifth dimension. So they were suppressing people from growing spiritually.

DOUG: Okay. I came up with a phrase. It's not a phrase but a statement about it. Love is the heart, and lust is the ego.

JOHN: Exactly. Lust is using another person to make you feel good. When you're using somebody, you're being selfish, but if you're coming from the heart, you're sharing of abundance and wanting the other person to be part of that sharing. Then the energy expands because God is energy and expansion and so coming from the heart. If your heart is open and you don't have any barriers to block that love from flowing out through you to the other person, your love will grow, and you actually will see your relationship grow. This is what Marilyn and Mack have. Their relationship keeps growing and growing as they share their love, and this is something that neither of them had before because their hearts were closed.

DOUG: Interesting. Like my particular friend. We've been together for two years; I've mentioned her to you before.

JOHN: Yes.

DOUG: With no emphasis on sex, we just emphasize respect and love for each other. We've traveled together for companionship sake and enjoyed each other's company because we just felt it from the heart.

JOHN: And that is a pure, true love. That's what the musical *Man from La Mancha* is about. He loved from his heart, and there was no sexual involvement in that musical show. And the story of Don Quixote, it about loves from his heart without manifesting it into physical ways, and so that is a beautiful true kind of love, which more people are growing into.

DOUG: Now next question—is the real marriage between a man and a woman?

JOHN: Well, marriage is a contract, and it can be between any two individuals. Sex, you see, is something that was also third dimensional because in spirit we're all one. We all have male and female and masculine energy within us. We need to balance, and so when the sexes are marrying their sex, it's part of their script to balance their energy. So marriage is between two people bringing together the love that needs to be balanced in their lives. So often the society judges people in their spiritual growth. And so often the people who are coming together in a marriage today, which is what they call same-sex, are people further down the spiritual path than those that are staying in heterosexual marriages. The ones in heterosexual marriages are very judgmental. They are afraid to move on and beyond, and so they condemn those who have.

DOUG: Now I wrote a section (section 1.9) in the book about male and female energies.

JOHN: Yes.

DOUG: Could conflict of, for instance, a gay relationship involving male/male energies or female/female energies prevent them from attaining the kingdom of God?

JOHN: That's a man-made church rule. There are no gates to heaven if people open their hearts and move into a higher consciousness of love, so that is man-made and not real. You see, we have many people today going through the last stages of what is necessary for their energy to go through every experience, to move into the oneness of God. One of the best experiences right now is Bruce Jenner becoming Caitlyn. His energy has to experience both of those situations for him to continue spiritually growing. People do not understand that. You will go through every vibration to return to the God consciousness. So sometimes what we have to go through looks unconventional to the public. It is scary to them because they do not understand that everybody goes through that. The people in the news are not the only ones who are experiencing that. They just happen to be the more visual objects of the media, but everyone goes through every vibration. You have all been robbers, thieves, rapists. You've all been philanthropist, rich, and wonderfully caring, sharing people with others. You go through every stage to heal the past energy so that you are clean in your energy. When all that old energy has been experienced, and you can move through it as gracefully as possible. Then you move on into these higher realms. And you would have completed your human experience, so people, when they are judgmental of others going through their changes, it's all part of their spiritual growth. And they will be doing it if they haven't already, they will be doing it themselves, but it's their fear that causes the problem.

DOUG: Since marriage is just a paper agreement, a divorce does not prevent an individual from achieving ascension to the fifth dimension?

JOHN: The paperwork is part of the church, a way of controlling people. People in your hearts can be married. In a way, you're married to this woman that you talk about because your concern and love which is a very natural love and that is marriage. So marriage does not have to be on a piece of paper. But what happened was in the years earlier women were bringing dowries to the marriage, and so the marriage was a contract on paper of what she brought to the marriage. And so the churches turned that into a sacrament and made that piece of paper the way of saying, "You are now legitimately a couple," but that has nothing to do with it. The legitimacy of a couple is more of what is in your heart, so you can have a marriage without being on paper.

DOUG: The Ten Commandments were a warning for the third dimensional world because people lacked forgiveness and tend to want revenge for the misdeed. Jesus declaration of loving God with all thy heart and they neighbor was really for the fifth dimension, where people are more forgiving of the mistakes.

JOHN: Well, that's one way to put it, but the Ten Commandments were to discipline people who did not understand that their actions were creating their environment and their reality. So if you start with the first commandment, you need no others. Have no other God's before you, and you will not act in betraying your neighbor. You would not take things from your neighbor. You would not glorify other things other than God. So the Ten Commandments are all part of the first commandment of ways that you would live a disciplined life and love. But the people in the Old Testament did not understand what love and light were about, so they were written in terms that they did understand. The New Testament brought Jesus message of love God with all your heart, mind, and soul and love your neighbor as yourself. The Old Testament spoke to the people in their language of what they could understand. Jesus brought to the New Testament a new interpretation rather than what you don't do, and he brought what you need to do. And now the fifth dimension is—we will apply what he brought as the message into our lives, not just talk about it from our heads and not just read it in the Bible but live it in our lives every day so that who we are is loving our neighbors. Who we are is that God is first in our life so that we are coming through a spiritual evolution of moving into that dimension that Jesus wanted first to proclaim the people were still not really understanding because when you read in the New Testament, there was still a lot of problems with people trying to learn how to love their neighbor but now we have accomplished enough of that energy change that he brought the first messages of love, more and more people are moving into that loving experience and realizing that is a beautiful place to be.

DOUG: During the upcoming new age, people will find their soul mates more readily because everything was planned out by the conference committee in Nirvana? It helps further our spiritual growth?

JOHN: That is very true. People are finding others who have similar energy, and those people wrote the scripts that at some point they would come back together. It is happening in and occurred in

Marilyn's situation. It is going on in her daughter's case. It is going on with many people today that they are returning to the love of those people who came to help them during this time. And to experience the healthiness of love that they had to go through, the different experiences of trauma and drama, but now that life is improving, it is time to reunite with those who are truly their companions.

DOUG: Yes, this woman must be my soul mate. I think it was meant to be for us to be together.

JOHN: Well, I believe we do have those reunions with the right people at the right time.

DOUG: Yeah, because she seems perfect for me. I appear perfect to her.

JOHN: Well, I think that is beautiful.

DOUG: Yes. Is it true that multiple marriages mentioned in the Bible existed from the previous era of love and light (time of Atlantis) when people had a higher state of consciousness?

JOHN: It is possible to have relationships with more than one person. However, your culture and the man-made laws have come in and exempted that as appropriate and acceptable. So it is possible to have multiple relationships as one particular religion seems to accept. However, they do it not from a loving point of view. It is more of ownership and possessiveness rather than actual relationship and evolving with that situation. However, it is not wrong. It is just that the society has adopted the philosophy. Mostly from the church because they can control people better if you are in a family setting, and so it has been curtailed. So you have one man and one woman in a relationship. It is possible, but culture does not condone it.

JOHN: I do want to say one more thing about relationships.

DOUG: Okay, sure.

JOHN: You wrote Marilyn that you were concerned about relationships, and this particular piece of information is very vital because it will bring harmony to all those relationships that are in trouble. If the people involved with the relationships are willing and ready to release any part of their egos, which some people call edging God out, if they release their ego, what is left is God's love. So a relationship that is without ego will be in harmony, will be in peace, and will grow and expand in beautiful ways. It's the ego that causes the trouble in relationships. So people are willing to outgrow the fear in their lives and outgrow the unknown, which is the fear of the unknown that often brings problems. If you are willing to be less selfish and come from being selfless and give to the others what they want for themselves, you will not have the ego involved, and relationships will come into a new harmony that you have not experienced before, so being without an ego creates the perfect relationship.

DOUG: I certainly agree with that. My first marriage was a conflict of egos, and it was a miserable marriage. With this one, the person I'm with now, there is no ego because we are thankful for each other.

JOHN: Exactly. So as you are experiencing that, it will be easy for you to write about that because you write from your experience, and it comes through the pages of your book. You are doing a marvelous job, Doug. I want to congratulate you on your perseverance and hard work, and I know that the Spirit is coming through you as you do this work. And the book will be precious to many people.

DOUG: Thank you. I wonder—was it helpful to receive a spark from God that perhaps broke the shell of my ego so that I could receive spiritual messages better?

JOHN: Well, you were willing to let that divine energy within come out of its protected shell of your heart and open your heart up to be open-hearted and open-minded, and your willingness to follow through with that has brought you a new life, yes.

DOUG: Was the Catholic church aware that Jesus married?

JOHN: Yes, that is part of why they have made people so ... taught them so much that you can. That is why the Catholic church did not even want the divorce. They did not want what they called loose cannons. If people were in a marriage, it was easier to control them, and the Catholic church was all about control. So they set up their laws and rules instead of what was spiritually the way of a loving and spiritual experience, forcing people to follow their rules, and it was because of control.

DOUG: Was Mary Magdalene a wanderer?

JOHN: She was married to Jesus.

DOUG: Right. Was she a wanderer?

JOHN: In the Jewish faith, you marry. Jesus was a rabbi, and she was his wife. It was a marriage, and their families knew each other before. They were young children, and they were raised together in the Essenes. I would not think of her as a wanderer.

DOUG: I mean like suppose, you know, I am talking about if a couple is having sex, and they love each other. If they do this just for fun, then that means they will not have children. If the couple is really in love and they want to have a child, then usually that will happen because they love each other so much.

JOHN: Well, the reason children come into a marriage can be out of just lust, or it can be out of love. It is a matter of that person's soul. The child's soul picks the parents who will best give the information and nurture or experience necessary for that soul's growth. So the soul chooses the parents of those people who are willing to join and have that soul enter the child when it is born. So the soul hangs around until it is the right time to come into the body of the baby. Usually, the soul comes in within twenty-four hours after birth, sometimes before birth but generally after birth, and so the soul has picked those people to learn the lessons that are in that family's dynamics. See, sex is important. It can bring you spiritually together and enhance and increase your spiritual connection. However, sex is not the same as love, and you are talking about real love, so I applaud you for finding the difference and seeing what that difference is like. I think that is admirable. More people should have that kind of influence rather than lust.

* * * * *

The fourth dimension is a transitional period from the third dimension, which ended in 2012, to the era of love and light of the fifth dimension. Our lives will transform during this transition. For two thousand years, ego-centric behavior made the free expression of love impossible. People with dark energy lacked mercy. Heaven on earth is a state of conscious love and forgiveness. With loving thoughts, we will become heavenly.

* * * * *

DOUG: Now talking about relationships for the fifth dimension, is there going to be a transition for people to go from the fourth dimension to the fifth dimension about understanding the difference between love and lust? That's why there is going to be a transition for people to learn real love, how to grow into the fifth dimension.

JOHN: Yes, there is going to be a new understanding of relationships. You are there to help, assist, encourage, and expand the other person's spiritual experience. Lust is about decreasing actually and taking away using and abusing that person for your gratification, and that will not be acceptable in the fifth dimension. Unconditional love will be the acceptable behavior and motivation. Moving out of the fear-based, using of other people, being selfish in relationships which all comes from the ego, edging God out, relationships will move into merging God into their relationship. *How can I be helpful to that person? ow can I support that person: I need to be honest in this relationship. I need to speak up and share what I'm thinking or feeling. Also, I need to express myself in honest ways rather than lie and be deceitful.* So there will be a transparency of relationships in the fifth dimension.

* * * * *

As we progress to the fifth dimension, we will marry less and engage in more relationships. This will bring more love to more people and increase tolerance and understanding. We have lived thousands of lives in which we have shared experiences with unique people, and these experiences will come together during the new age. We will find ourselves associating with acquaintances, lovers, and spouses from past lives, and we will be able to choose partners who inspire our hearts the most. We are entering a new age in which we will be led by the Holy Spirit beaming from the center of creation through the Photon Belt. It will guide our hearts during the upcoming one thousand years of peace. It will bring inspiring peace and love. Ego is lust, which is chaotic and temporary. It awakens the ego and causes guilt. The ego's purpose is to incite fear because only the fearful can be egotistical. In heaven there is no guilt because the kingdom is attained through atonement, which allows creation. The word *create* is appropriate because the Holy Spirit undoes what we make, and the blessed residue is then restored and continues in creation. Blessed actions are incapable of giving rise to guilt, only to joy. Once we experience heaven on earth through love, we will recognize it more readily and overcome the ego.

Table 6 – Difference between 3rd Dimension and 4th Dimension Relationships

3rd Dimensional Relationships	4th Dimensional Relationships
The way relationships normally work with us here in our 3rd dimension.	The way relationships normally work with us here in our 4th dimension.
Separation Separation from the God source, each other, and aspects of ourselves are illusions only.	**Integration + Reintegration** Everything and everyone is connected.
Secrecy Withholding information from our partners and ourselves. With secrecy, partners never understand each other fully. This keeps individuals separated from an aspect of themselves.	Partners are completely honest with each other, allowing them to be 100 percent authentic. They do not withhold comments or information to avoid hurting each other or to control the relationship. Partners understand that they can never know what will hurt others or how they will react to honesty. Therefore, they do not assume responsibility for the others' emotions and reactions to honest, nonmanipulative communications

Fear-Based Monogamy	Relationships by Choice
Monogamous relationships separate partners from the vulnerability of additional relationships, allowing them to feel safe but also separate.	Monogamy by choice, Polygamy by choice, or Polyfidelity by choice. There is no inherent right or wrong in any type of relationship; all are inherently neutral and acceptable. If one partner chooses monogamy, this does not entail that the other do the same.
Conditional Love	**Unconditional Love**
We love each other as long as needs and expectations are fulfilled. We withdraw love in the case of dissatisfaction.	Even if needs and expectations are not fulfilled, we love each other for who we are, without trying to change each other.
Commitment	**Being in the Present**
Commitment allows us to avoid fear of multiple relationships. Commitment is a third-dimensional illusion that does not ensure security.	Commitment takes us out of the present. We do not need commitments because we trust that the future will take care of itself.
Expectation	**No Expectations**
I want, expect, and try to get my partner to fulfill my expectations and needs. I use my partner to satisfy my needs.	I trust and have no expectations from my partner. I enjoy my partner, but without expectations.

Manipulation We use both obvious and hidden manipulation to meet needs and remain protected from fear. We only see partners as who we need them to be, not who they really are.	**Allowingness** We allow partners to be who they need to be. Only then can we see who they truly are.
The Need to Control We do not trust that everything that occurs is for the highest good. Therefore, we attempt to control relationships so that they take the forms we wish. We feel like we *own* our partners.	**Absolute Trust** We trust that everything that occurs is for the highest good. Therefore, we have no desire or need to control our partners.
Relationship takes precedence to *personal growth*.	*Personal growth* takes precedence to *relationship*.
Dependency We depend on others in order to be happy.	**Self-Sufficiency** We recognize that only the self is the creator of our individual realities. Therefore, only the self can generate happiness.
A Person Cannot Fully Love More than One Person. The third dimension emphasizes duality, the illusion that if our partners begin to love another, they will have less love for us.	**A Person Can Fully Love More than One Person.** The fourth dimension emphasizes multiplicity. No matter how many other people our partners love, their love for us does not diminish. No matter how many other people we love, our love for our partners does not diminish.

Our partners spending *less time* with us is worrisome.	Our partners spending *less time* with us is fine because if we love ourselves unconditionally, the time spent with ourselves is equal in value to the time spent with our partners. We love ourselves as much as we love our partners. Therefore, the time we spend alone is just as enjoyable as the time spent with our partners.
Ending a relationship creates *pain* and *loss*.	*Ending a relationship* does not create *pain* and *loss*. In realizing that a relationship is no longer serving us, we choose to harmoniously end it. We recognize that the relationship is going in different directions, so we allow it to end without negativity, only with love.
Fear or Pain of Loneliness Loneliness, like separation, is a third-dimensional illusion.	**Feeling Connected to Significant Others** Even if our partners are not around us, we feel connected to them, whereas separation is an illusion, being connected is reality.

Anger at Another	Anger at Myself
(Externalized anger)	(Internalized anger)
We are angry at our partners for not meeting our needs.	We are angry at ourselves for creating realities that we do not desire.
Victimhood *Hurters* and *Victims* We sometimes hurt and are hurt by the comments or actions of others. The dichotomy of *hurters* and *victims* is an illusion. There is no victimhood since everyone creates an individual reality.	**I Create My Own Reality.** Self-Responsibility Self-Empowerment We create our own realities, and this includes others' reactions to our actions. We can never hurt or be hurt by other people. Only the self is responsible for personal reactions to other people's comments or actions.
Feeling Responsible for the Needs of My Partners Our partners seek to have their needs met externally by us, but people's needs can never be met by anyone but themselves, meaning partners are bound to become angry with each other for not fulfilling needs.	**Being Responsible for What I Would Like to Give to My Partner and Our Relationship** We are pure in our intentions for our relationships. We are 100 percent authentic with our partners. We are responsible for what, in our integrity, we would like to give to our relationships.

* * * * *

DOUG: During the upcoming fifth dimension, will there be marriages, or will people be sharing love with people?

JOHN: There will be more sharing love with others, fewer marriages. There will be more sharing love with others, fewer marriages. The climate change for the New Age will be a controversial issue. The planet is changing into a Mediterranean climate like at the time of Jesus. So there will not be the extreme climates that we have, like where you are right now. You would be finding yourself in a lovely warm, comfortable Mediterranean afternoon or morning with the sun out, and it would be very pleasant and a very friendly atmosphere to be enjoying. Moreover, so the whole planet is moving into that kind of environment, and the scientists, of course, do not have the prophecy to understand that the Earth is changing into a new higher consciousness. There still will be mountains to go skiing, and there still will be areas that will be similar to what you have today. But primarily, it is moving into a hot and moderate tropical climate.

DOUG: Right. And that's why we'll see less marriages and more relationships because people will be living from their hearts.

JOHN: Exactly.

DOUG: Oh, okay. Okay. So that kind of fits the pattern where people will be more loving toward one another.

JOHN: Well, Jesus brought new commandments in the New Testament to love God with all your heart, mind, and soul and to love your neighbor as yourself, and that's this dimension. When you are so in tune and only God is your focus, that's the first commandment. "Thou shall have no other gods before me." When you are so totally in focus with God, you see we are all one spirit, and that's all energy of love. We are all one and together, and that is when we are cooperating with one another. We're taking care of one another. We're kind and respectful of one another. That's heaven on earth. When we have judgment, criticism, condemnation, wars, and fights and frustrations, all those things are not seeing that oneness of the love of God that's already here. We have blinders on. We have earplugs in our ears to see the love. And so your book and Marilyn's book and all those that are on the path hopefully will remove the blinders and the earplugs so people can start to receive the true message we are already in the fifth dimension.

DOUG: Now there's just one issue I had with the Self-Realization Fellowship, where I learned meditation.

JOHN: Yes.

DOUG: Don't get me wrong. Their method worked. It got me close to God. I got the spark from God, but I did not feel spiritual growth because they suppress sexual energy.

JOHN: Well, there's two kinds of sexual energy. There is positive, and there is negative. So if you are having sex through lust, that is of your lower nature. Then you are damaging the other person and yourself. It is like a vampire sucking blood from somebody. However, if you are having sexual relations where you are open and spiritually available and merging your energy with another, you are expanding energy. Moreover, in that case, you are glorifying and enjoying and being part of a genuine energy of love. So it is your motivation that has a lot to determine how healthy the person is that you are cooperating with. If they are people who are not happy, joyful, loving, and caring, you would not want to facilitate or be part of those relationships. So it is picking the right partner and having both of you in the right spiritual places for it to grow and enhance your life.

DOUG: Basically for that purpose, that is a real purpose.

JOHN: It is always done for the glory of God and to grow spiritually. Then you have the right motivation.

DOUG: Is green, yellow, red, blue races come from white race through marriage?

JOHN: No, they were all independent of—their origins were all clear and unique, different origins. And it's only in the current culture that the integration of those cultures and races has been more prominent.

And originally, they were very definitely defined in various areas of the planet.

DOUG: Now when God said in the Bible that "Get ye to multiply," did he mean multiply with people from inside Earth because they were higher spiritually? They have higher consciousness?

JOHN: He was basically referring to spreading the word of love, and the people who are inside the Earth were not considered as part of that. However, you could look at it in that way. It was primarily trying to say spread the Word of God, and with all incoming people, newcomers in the planet, to share the message of love. It was what he was trying to promote, the message of love.

DOUG: So if we learn from a spirit of love, that's how we grow spiritually.

JOHN: Exactly. We—it's learning to love yourself, love God. The first two commandments in the Bible are in the New Testament, our wonderful commandments, because it says to love God with all your heart, mind, and soul and to love your neighbor as yourself. So if you have God as your soul and your neighbor is also part of your soul, you're all one. And that was really the message—we're to love everybody.

DOUG: Something is wrong about marriages today as there are too many divorces. So basically, and I am going to talk a little bit about marriage.

JOHN: The information is becoming more open to the public that marriage was actually a way for the church to control people, and it's not a spiritual sacrament. It's a cultural one. It was imposed on culture for control and manipulation. So the original marriage was a contract because the man received a dowry, and it was a contract. It was not a religious marry, as said. It was a financial contract, and then the church enlarged upon it and adopted it to—for people to feel that they needed to have a marriage as such in the eyes of church to be accepted.

It was a matter of shaming people if they didn't get married. And if you're in shame, you're better ... or at least more easily controlled. So more people are beginning to understand that this was not really part of the original plan. However you want to word it is fine. I just think ... I think people are becoming, from my seeing of what goes on in Marilyn's life, people are better understanding that marriage is really an agreement between the two people to love each other, and the piece of paper is not really what provides love. It's God that provides the love.

DOUG: However, people will want to know this about marriage.

JOHN: Well, it's time for them to realize a piece of paper does not mean you have the marriage that people are looking for. The paper is just a piece of paper. And what does it mean? And what's behind it, and where is the heart of the person that is in the marriage? Where is the heart? That's what makes a marriage.

DOUG: Now this question. I might have asked this before. However, is it true that when a spiritual energy is rising, we will feel a more sexual energy like uncoiling the serpent from the base of the spine?

JOHN: That is exactly what happens. You have been suppressed with your spiritual energy, and as you wake up, as you grow spiritually, as you raise your consciousness—they call it the serpent—and the spine raises up into awareness and openness and being available to the energy around you and in you. So yes, it does feel like you might say a climax, a sexual climax that's going on in your life.

DOUG: So when we are heading to the new age, we will have more loving relationships and people will be more spiritual?

JOHN: Exactly. That is what love is—to expand. Moreover, as you expand and share your love with others, as you are of service, as you are helpful, as you are contributing to the welfare of the society that you live in, the love grows and grows. Also, you feel better and better, and you are more excited within as that energy rises.

DOUG: So, for instance, you making a marriage is a marriage of the heart?

JOHN: Yeah. There are very few marriages of the heart. In your society, through television and movies and your books and romance novels, most of the people think of love as sexual and being sexy. So that is not what love is at all. So what that organization was trying to do was remove people from that concept that sex was love because sex and love are not the same things.

* * * * *

Chapter 2

Dark Side

Section 2.1: John's Observation about Dark Side

You (author-Douglas) are looking for the truth and separating it from the false. What I (Apostle John) hope to bring you today is more truthful information because you have been looking for third-dimensional answers for fifth- and higher dimensional questions. Also, the answers you have been looking at have been in the realm of the material physical world that you've been living in, where fears have been perpetuated in society for numerous years. Many, many people have collected together under the umbrella some people call the Illuminati, some people call the Cabal, and some people call the Elite or the 300 Families. Together, they have formed a coalition to dominate the planet and bring it into their best interests for the people to be under their dominion.

This was a long, slow process that did not happen recently. They have been patient for thousands of years, bringing people's thinking into a closed-minded place, one that is closed to God, the God of reality. They have done their best to keep people in their heads, in their egos. Some people call egos "edging God out." For thousands of years, the group has been trying to keep others focused not on the truth of who God is and who they are but on what the group wants them to believe through their fearful ways of keeping people under their control and manipulation.

Written documents on planet earth are infiltrated and dominated by their controlling the strings from behind the scenes. If the truth were known, the Bible was not written by God. Most of it is memories of what people heard. Jesus did not write any of his words down. He did not want people to pass them on and attribute them to him. He did not wish to create a church. He was a Jewish rabbi. He was trying to promote a new understanding of what people were about. People in the government did not like this because Jesus said, "I have come from a different world, a different kingdom." This was threatening to them. They did not understand it was a spiritual, invisible world that he was opening up the doors to.

He was not even talking their language because their culture did not have an open mind. It was closed mostly because the government was in control, not only of the norms of the state but also of the rules of the church. These people's control from behind the scenes has extended into the church through the order of the Jesuits.

As content was put together, there was much of what might be called cherry-picking of what would go into the Bible. Yes, some honorable books are in the Bible; however, it is not totally truthful in many ways. There are half-truths. Many truths were left out of the Bible because for one reason, the people would not have understood what Jesus was talking about, such as the third dimension and moving into the fifth dimension, which is ascension. They would not have understood energy or physics to measure light as we do in the scientific world.

There have been many influences beyond the church. Education seeks to keep children in their intellect, in their left brain. It does not open up to intuition, inspiration, and the silent voice of guidance that comes from the soul. This is also true of popular technological advances, such as television, computers, cell phones, video games, and movies. Even books influence people. All these areas are being infiltrated to keep people out of the spirit.

The omnipresence, omnipotence, and omniscience is already within individuals. The cookie batter was already stirred together, and each person is part of that wholeness of God. That is not what they have wanted to perpetuate in the church. If people are sinners, then they can be easily controlled. However, if the church had been saying, "You already are a whole spirit," there would have been no reason for its authority, and the world would be in a different place than it is now as it moves into the fifth dimension, finally coming to the understanding that we are a higher consciousness than what we have been led to believe. Our hearts have opened to the love within, and the fears are dissipating.

When planet Earth was first brought into being, it was created for the glory of God. Earth is a living form just like people have form, and the planet is a spiritual form as are the people who came to the world. It took eons and eons of evolution for plants and so forth to come about. It did not happen in seven days. That is just a condensation of how it came together as people began to arrive on planet Earth from space because humans are all seeded from a space family. They came in their Christendom and their Christ consciousness. The first continent was Lemuria. It was spiritual. People had only spiritual bodies, not physically touchable bodies. Jesus first came in a spiritual, nonphysical body to that continent, as some people call it, "the first Adam." Then another continent called Atlantis appeared, and they, too, were spiritually oriented. However, as their civilization progressed, they become highly technically evolved. The Lemurians were peaceful, agricultural people who were happy with living on the land and sea and having unsophisticated lives. The Atlanteans were much more aggressive and technologically oriented, and their technology progressed even beyond what is on planet Earth today. They relied heavily on crystals for their energy and power supply. Some of them were enormous and enabled the Atlanteans to create many of their technical advances and abilities.

There was a faction called the Sons of Baal, and there was another group that wanted to stay one with God, the Law of One, the people who were following the oneness of Christ's consciousness. They began to have disagreements with the Sons of Baal, those without light, the dark side. When the Sons of Baal wanted to be in charge of the planet, they blew up the primary power source of the crystals. Those were the explosions that were heard in Atlantis. The blasts devastated it. Lemuria was damaged through explosions and volcanic eruptions too, and the continent sank. Many people but not all from those continents left as best they could. Throughout the many centuries since this devastation, it was strictly out of wanting to control by the dark side. They have gradually taken over control of the planet, and we are coming to the end times of that control.

Today the dark side is a group that observes a form of belief known as enlightenment. It is Luciferian, and they educate their followers that their origins go back to the ancient mystical religions of Babylon, Egypt, and Celtic druidism. They claim they considered the best of each practice and joined them together into an occult discipline. They worship ancient deities, such as El and Baal. They also teach traveling astral planes, time travel, and other metaphysical phenomena. It is a combination of cult mind control, drug inductions, hypnosis, and some actual demonic activity. These people teach and practice evil such as black magic.

The authorities behind science, education, and the media endeavor persistently to convince us that the human has advanced from the Neanderthal. The paradox is that although we did not evolve from this primitive form, one might say that the dark side running our planet did.

Section 2.2: Origin of the Dark Side

The Leviathans, with their family lines, formed the dark side, extending from the Atlantis period to the present day. By around 9104 BC, after the solar system had left the Photon Belt, the Leviathans were on a mission for planetary realignment and rebuilding their

DNA. The Leviathans, both the resistance group and the bio-regenesis group, were quickly directed by their puppet masters, the fallen ones, from their extraterrestrial vantage point.

Neanderthal man had a genome comprised of Anunnaki and ape genes as well as a few other minimal species. The guardian ETs had a hybridization research program for the reintegration of DNAs, and some of the fallen ETs, who had defected to their side, were requesting this bio-regenesis program. The guardians decided to utilize Neanderthal man since it already possessed compatible genes. They upgraded the Neanderthal to Cro-Magnon and then to Homo sapiens that contained many human genes and a body form indistinguishable from humans. Bio-regenesis involved permitting these fallen ETs to incarnate into these bodies, combining DNA strands, and through experience and constructive living, they rehabilitate their mutated and reverse-coded DNA. These nonhuman souls in human-type bodies were called the Anu-Melchizedek Leviathans.

Unfortunately, the rebellious invader ETs seized this opportunity to further their world-domination program. They realized that these bodies/DNAs contained compatible genes and could be used for incarnations to operate physically on Earth and control world affairs more directly. As a result, Anunnaki, Drakonians, and hybrids were compatible to be born into these human bodies, however, with a far different consciousness from humans. They have a deficient emotional structure with the absence of compassion, but they possess great mental abilities.

Thus, the entities of the dark side do not necessarily know who they are or that they are given information only on a need-to-know basis. Just as there are competing factions of ET races, there are corresponding factions of the dark side. However, the important point here is the nature of the souls that enter the bodies, and in this case, they would be nonhuman, fallen ET souls.

The term *lizard people* refers to those with the reptilian soul, and they

Door to Glory

are essentially part of the dark side. They represent the minority of the population, but they essentially have controlled the world's affairs since the beginning of time.

* * * * *

DOUG: Now I'm going to ask you—approximately what percentage of the population today comprises lizard people?

JOHN: Well, basically, less than half a percent.

DOUG: Half a percent, okay.

JOHN: But they have expanded their range through other people, so even though there are few of them on earth, their power has exceeded their numbers.

DOUG: Now for the lizard people, do they worship Satan?

JOHN: Some. There needs to be a definition that some lizard people are of what you might call a spiritual energy that is of a higher range. And there are those that are not of the light, and yes, they do serve Satan.

DOUG: Now do some of them run churches?

JOHN: Yes, they do.

* * * * *

Currently, many Anu-Melchizedek Leviathans under invader ET control are running governments, science, religion, and education. There are also good people in general who are unsuspecting victims of astral tagging (implants) or targeted with psychotronic mind control and compromised by consciousness/DNA infiltration. Wherever possible, their pet control dogmas are exploited to push the human into some obsessive religious doctrine or ideas of God or belief systems. These motivations related to science and politics. In other words, humans were tricked into playing unholy roles. Human evolution began 1.2 million years ago with the Neanderthals. As mentioned earlier, they were the ancestors of alien Anunnaki who wanted to dominate humans for their benefit.

The Anunnaki from the twelfth planet Nibiru created Neanderthal man as a slave race for mining gold. They intended to use humans but realized they were too intelligent. The Anunnaki discovered that gold, in its white powder form, has positive, regenerative effects on their deteriorating DNA. They even put it in their atmosphere. However, they ultimately discovered it distorts the DNA and the consciousness. Today, individuals are realizing this white powder and are convinced of its regenerative powers (Ref. 12).

* * * * *

DOUG: Could white powder gold help regenerate DNA?

JOHN: It could assist it and support it, yes, because gold has a high energy.

* * * * *

The dark side is a loosely knit organization that interconnects different smaller sections of that network that are involved with projecting dark energy onto people through various sources. The dark side also applies to individuals as well that lacked light. For this book, I'll refer to them in general as the *dark side*.

Today's economic colonial Europe is yesterday's administrative colonial Europe, the Holy Roman Empire of the day before yesterday, and the Roman and Byzantine Empires of last week. It is the same power ruled by the same spiritual authority, and it has merely changed its clothes to look different. This final form of Euro-Roman power is depicted in the thirteenth chapter of the book of Revelation in the Bible as the beast that has the patchy appearance of a leopard for many peoples and nations, the feet of a bear (Russia), the mouth of a lion (Britain), and seven heads for seven kingdoms (1. Britain,

2. Belgium, 3. Holland, 4. Denmark, 5. Norway, 6. Sweden, and 7. Spain). One of the heads is cut as unto death and yet healed (that of Spain, which was abolished for forty years), and on its seven heads, it has ten horns that are crowned with ten diadems. (The authority is exercised by temporarily elected governments and not by kings.) This Euro-Christian power has an expiry date early in the twenty-first century.

The councils have administrators who handle finances. They comprise bankers, businessmen, and local civic leaders. They are well educated and involved in their churches. These are the regional councils that help form the policies and agendas for each region, and they interact with the local leadership councils. Members of the umbrellas of the dark side heavily occupy or control the higher-level political positions in all Western countries. They use their excessive wealth to finance their goals and interact with the leaders of other countries. They teach secrecy by all means to maintain their transparency and push effectively through their agendas. They are not nonsensical people running around, fiddling with witchcraft.

Certain groups of the dark side exist in every major city in the United States. They believe in controlling an area through its banks and financial institutions as well as local government and media. They encourage their children to go to law, medical, and journalism schools. Some of these children are trained for the military or politics, while others are ready to take important business positions. All through their lives, most family members in these bloodlines have no awareness of their dual lives. They appear to be regular, upstanding citizens to their neighbors and others.

One of their major territories is Hollywood. They believe that to influence the media is to manipulate the public. It is one of their agendas. They target finances, media, law, government, and education to dominate society. They form small investment corporations to fund movies with ideas that they like. They select scripts and hire actors and producers and directors, but they never mention their affiliation publicly or why they are doing this. Money talks in Hollywood. Money can get anything accomplished. They also channel money into advertising campaigns for their films. For instance, how many Christian films have had major ad campaigns in the past twenty years? Only a few. It has been a slow, subtle process because they are patient. They have been working behind the scenes for centuries, and they know that the public is reluctant to accept new ideas.

An example of its symbology is the pyramid on the back of the US one-dollar note with the capstone containing the "eye of Horus" detached and hovering above the rest of the pyramid. The pyramid is an age-old form based on the holiness of the number three to the ancient mystery religions. A pyramid was a structure used explicitly to call up the demons or occult, a point of psychic activity. This eye reflects a demonic eye in the group. The dollar reads, *"Novus Ordo Seclorum,"* which means "bringing in the new order." It is the agenda that has been going on since the early 1800s. Our forefathers already were looking forward to ushering in the new order back then.

The regional councils embody the different areas of interest that they pursue. Participation changes over time as members are endorsed or relegated. The National Council consists of a national committee each from the United States, Mexico, Canada, Russia, and China. Nations in Europe also have national committees as well. The national council will look much like the one above with this one difference—these are influential bankers. It reports to the Supreme World Council. The Supreme World Council is already set up as a prototype of the one that will rule when the new world order comes into being. It meets to discuss finances, direction, and policy and to problem-solve difficulties that come up. The Rothschild's family in England and France has governing seats from both countries. An offspring of the Hapsburg dynasty has a generational seat. Descendants of the dominant families of England and France have generational seats. From the United States, the Rockefeller family holds a seat. It is one reason that the entities of the dark side have been pretty untouchable over the years. The ruling members are wealthy and powerful.

* * * * *

DOUG: Media continues to play its role in withholding the truth from the public. Since we have entered the Photon Belt, some people have transformed in their hearts but not the media. One Presidential candidate represents the Global Elite, and the other does not. We are approaching 1000 years of peace starting in 2026. Should the Power Elite lose the election unexpectedly for Donald Trump?

JOHN: Well, and you see, the energy - it's all about energy, and all these things that are in chaos and crass in the media need to be exposed, and it needs to happen. And the energy is going to go where it needs to go for the next indicated growth of the population. However, we are at the end of the - this is the End Times. And it's - the energy at this point is growing and growing for a person elected that would be more conducive to the population needs rather than the elites. So, even though it looks like it's in great turmoil and even though it seems very chaotic and the words being spoken are very - you might say the mudslinging politicians of their day, what's going on behind the scenes is what the news does not tell you.

And that's, of course, the invisible Spirit is moving to remove all that dark energy of the elite. So, at this point, the energy people are awakening, as you said, out of the religious dogma and coming to grips and seeing a bigger of how life is meant to be and what's going on. And so, the media is still in control by the elite. And so, what's going on behind the scenes is not evident. But, it is happening. And this will come to a point where there'll be a tipping point.

And so, who's ever taking the poll is going to promote their viewpoint. So, the - you should use your common sense with the polls and then say, "Well, where did this poll come from? Who's sponsoring it?"

Because they're going to present their point of view, they are not neutral. Let's put it that way.

DOUG: My book is still being edited by the publisher and would not go out until after the election. Should I mention the Dark Side pushing their agenda through Hillary Clinton to preserve their control?

JOHN: Right. Mm. I think in - from my understanding that would be substantial, this view might call history, and even though it won't be current history, it will be truthful history. And so many of the books out there have not brought forth the actual truth of what's going on. And to have another book that presents it from the more accurate presentation would be advantageous. I would not take it out. Leave it in what you just said about Hillary. Leave it in there. No, if you have space where it seems to segue as just kind of part of the natural flow of what you're conversing and telling about in the book, it will fit in just kind of smoothly in the chapter you have in mind. Yes, I wouldn't make it a focal point, but I would include it.

They are working on a spiritual sign to make it as smooth as an adjustment as possible. So, it will be an as minimal a timeframe and as smooth as possible because of the technical aspects of the computer system, et cetera. But, they are trying to make it go as smoothly as they can.

And so, when we trust the spirit is involved, God is involved. God has all the power. So, when the Dark Side falls, God's power will be in charge, and it will come together in as smooth as possible away because God's grace is efficient. We will not have to suffer devastation. It will just go as smoothly as the best possible way that they can handle it.

* * * * *

One of the strongest lines for the occult in Europe is the Hanoverian/Hapsburg descendants' rule from Germany. The British line with the royal family is just under them. In the occult realm, they rule

Door to Glory

the UK branch under the Rothschilds, even though the parliament rules the country. The French Rothschilds hold the reigns over all the occult realms in Europe. The United States is considered lower than the European branches. The children of US leaders are being sent to Europe for training where education is seen as better.

* * * * *

DOUG: Now I am going to ask about the former US president, John F. Kennedy.

JOHN: What do you want to know?

DOUG: Was he assassinated because he refused a nuclear war that the dark side had wanted?

JOHN: He was murdered for several reasons but primarily because he had signed a bill to take the Federal Reserve out of private banking hands and put it into the public back where it belonged so that the money was under the auspices of the real federal government and not the elite or the wealthy or those who ran the banking system, which was headed by the Rothschilds. So the mob was just the façade of killing him so that the banking system would stay economically under the control of the Illuminati.

* * * * *

We have witnessed an extraordinary growth of monetary stimulus by US and European governments to combat disinflationary pressure on their economies during the past decade. It remains to be seen whether this policy is effective or whether it could contribute to a financial collapse that would lead to the new world order.

The United Nations was formed in the twentieth century as a precursor to establishing a one-world government. The United Nations is helping to overcome one of the biggest barriers if the dark side decides to impose a military rule and dictatorship—nationalism or pride in one's country. It is set up as a forerunner of the Supreme World Council that will represent every nation. They rewarded every ambassador to the United Nations who made the organization look good. The United Nations has a stated goal of world peace and wants to incorporate into its fold military and peacekeeping functions. It reduces the individual military strength of nations. The United Nations revealed that the new world order will be openly divulged by the year 2020.

The dark side hates Israel and hopes one day to see it destroyed. They are covertly supplying guns and funds to both sides to keep the conflict fueled. They are deceitful people. They used to funnel guns through the Soviet Union to Palestine, for example, in the name of promoting *friendliness* between the Soviet Union and this state and other Arab nations. Then the dark side from the United States would help funnel guns to Israel for the same reason. These people love the game of chess and see warfare between nations as creating an order out of chaos. It confirms the role of Russia in the Bible as the term Gog or Magog. If God the Father had not stepped in to foster the fifth dimension of love and light on December 21, 2012, then more than likely World War III would have occurred with the destruction of Israel toward the year 2020.

* * * * *

DOUG: The dark side had planned to kill between two and four hundred million Christians, those who resisted the planetary initiation 666? Well, it doesn't matter because that's not going to happen, so I'm going to ignore this question.

JOHN: Yeah, it's really at this point a question of what history, and at this point in time, the energy has shifted out of that result. It's going to be a different result.

* * * * *

However, it is all about to change by the planetary realignment to the fifth dimension on December 21, 2012, as the positive entities will rule for a period until the cycle turns again in twenty-five thousand years.

If the plan of the dark side had gone accordingly, the world would have been unified by the human incarnate demonic masters into a new world order. They would have been able to fight the return of positives and defeat them. Normal people would have been wiped out by disease or systematic mass murder and the planet repopulated by hybrid aliens produced through the alien abduction program.

* * * * *

DOUG: Is it true a country on Earth right now is producing human clones for its army? Is this the green race?

JOHN: This is not the green race. There are clones on earth. They are not necessarily for military reasons. Some political figures have been cloned, so the public is not aware of this process going on. It is happening at this point, and they will be revealed at a point down the road when more people will become aware that some of their leaders are not whom they think they are.

DOUG: What is the life span of the reptilian souls? How long do they live?

JOHN: Well, that is an interesting question. They have varying life spans depending on how they use their energy. If they use the loving energy, they will have a longer life span than if they are of the destructive mind-set that is not conducive and supplying the energy of spirit that would sustain them. So it is a choice. It is a personal decision. You might see individual decisions of how long they choose to live because of the lifestyle or their thinking, whether their mind-set has moved into the light or the dark.

DOUG: Now they do not go through to Nirvana, is that correct?

JOHN: That is correct.

DOUG: Because they do not have guardian angels in their energies or their DNA?

JOHN: Nirvana is primary. Well, there are other spiritual beings that have gone to Nirvana, but primarily, it is for the human beings.

* * * * *

If it was not for the change of energy, there could have been more chaos with more loss of lives. The world would have been deeper into the third dimension with a possibility of a nuclear annihilation during the Cold War. This nuclear disaster would have forever separated the world from God. The Bible has talked about Jesus saving the world. It was his spirit of truth from Pentecost that did it.

Mankind had misused higher technology toward the destruction of the human race similar to what had happened to the fifth planet, Maldek, more than fifty thousand years ago. As mentioned earlier about the fate of the Japanese World War II victims, the nuclear bomb would have disintegrated our souls, and we would have been forever lost.

The controversy over Syria in 2015 has renewed attention in end-times Bible prophecies, especially since both Russia and Iran have supported the Syrian government. Many Christians believe that Russia and Iran will play key roles in the fulfillment of end-times Bible prophecy that ultimately leads to Armageddon. It is a common thread of the third-dimensional thinking. The spirit of truth had this dark energy shifted away. Many end-times enthusiasts believe Russia is Gog/Magog, the leader and the evil empire that Ezekiel 38–39 says will lead to a multinational invasion of Israel. However, the end times have nothing to do with world affairs. It just has to do with the placements of the souls for relocation to another world that fits their vibrational level of the third dimension.

* * * * *

DOUG: Now could the spirit of truth alert God to evil thoughts of destruction? If someone tried to destroy the world, could the spirit of truth alert God?

JOHN: Well, that is what's going on now.

DOUG: That is what's going on now, okay.

JOHN: We are not going to be destroyed because love is real, and love is going to the light of God, which will dispel the darkness so it cannot be destroyed.

* * * * *

Hitler was beguiled by the dark side in his campaign of cleansing the Jews. In my opinion, the Christians would have been next on the plate if he had succeeded in his war campaign.

* * * * *

DOUG: Now, I'm going to ask you about World War II?

JOHN: Yes.

DOUG: Now, did the Illuminati wanted the Jewish people exterminated because of their lineage to Adam and Eve?

JOHN: It's a complicated explanation. The Illuminati used Hitler for genocide. They were trying to create a pure race of which of course they would be the sole leader of the world, by eliminating the population and eliminating those that they felt were inferior to them. So, it was part of the Jewish karma, but it was also part of the selfishness of the Illuminati and wanting to be in control. So, it was a multifaceted experience.

DOUG: Okay. Now, going back to AD 70, when the Romans overran Jerusalem?

JOHN: Yes.

DOUG: Now, did God see trouble as evidenced by the destruction of Jerusalem in AD 70 where as many as 1.1 million Jews died, so God sent Jesus to teach people kingdom of God? An avatar seems to have come whenever there was trouble on earth?

JOHN: Jesus came down because the people of the planet needed to have a new understanding of love. And every avatar that came before him was not accepted because the people's consciousness was not open to hearing that message. And so, it then - to take. But when - after the many different people before Jesus, the different masters that came to share the message of love.

You see, the Old Testament was about bringing all the people into the understanding of one God. And the New Testament is all about bringing the message of love. And Jesus, for whatever message that was that he brought of love, people did not understand it, and that's why it was written in parables. But he brought it to plant the seed, and it did take root, and we still have that seed today flowering and making fruit from the message of love. And that's the ultimate fruit, as we're in the process of moving into the fifth dimension of ascension.

So, his message on earth was to bring everybody to find love in all of us, and we come back into the spirit of God as one. And it's been, as you can tell, 2,000 years of very slow growth for people to be able to say, "God is love, and that's - the kingdom is within." For people to find that has been very slow. And that's why things do not move fast. People are not ready for that quick little change of mind. It's a slow process.

DOUG: So, that's why this book will be helpful to educate people that Jesus' intention was to teach people kingdom of God.

JOHN: Exactly. Exactly. And the churches re-contrived it into their dogma so that they got half-truth. They didn't get the whole truth.

And so, what you hear from the pulpit is not what you read in the Bible necessarily.

* * * * *

The abduction program then was an elaborate plan conducted by the dark aliens in collaboration with these dark side and politicians of the new world order. The plan was to engineer genetically a hybrid race whose bodies would allow only demonic souls to reincarnate on earth while the rest of humanity would be eradicated or kept for slave labor.

It has all been sanctioned to occur since the Earth's electromagnetic field has been in the negative half of its oscillation for the past two thousand years. It allows evil entities to infiltrate our reality and distort our history. All is lost for the resurrectionists if they fail to root themselves physically in our world. They require several of their demonic masters to be born as humans to take the reins of antichrists. Since their reincarnations are premature, it takes much effort to fit a wicked soul into a human body. It is like squeezing a blubbery ass into fitted jeans. The infusion of a human body with a demonic soul requires an essentially difficult position, timing, and location on earth. Thus, there is a definite target for the resurrectionists and new world order to complete their goals.

* * * * *

DOUG: And maybe a part of this new world order includes the destruction of the Judeo-Christian religion and all who follow it based on Revelation 13. Is this true?

JOHN: That originally was the ultimate goal, yes. However, with the coming of Jesus, the Christ consciousness becoming aware in people, the energies changing with new and higher energies being focused on earth through the last several years, especially the last twenty years, that will not occur, but that was the goal.

DOUG: Now the crux and heart of the Illuminati is mass planetary initiation 666. Where they will force the world to invoke Satan as God and receive a digital scan able tattoo on your right hand and forehead and without this mark would not be able to buy or sell and those without the mark would quickly be identified, arrested, and put to death.

JOHN: Well, that was the original plan was to rule the Earth and subdue the people into slavery, and yes, they were planning to have some way to identify the people. It's not necessarily specifically as detailed as what you're saying. They had various options in their plan, and at this point, it is to inoculate everybody with vaccinations, so their plans have changed over the years into options that are more viable for the current civilization.

* * * * *

Since the beginning of time, the dark side has had its roots in the ancient practices. The Babylonians created ziggurats to their deities, whom they worshipped. They were honored that it was supposedly an unbroken occult line from then until now. The names changed; the primary group was the same. The ancient mystery religions of Egypt, the heart of dark magic, were another forerunner. The dark side believes their bloodlines have come down from the ancient kings of Egypt. However, the Scriptures have condemned this *religion*. "And there followed another Angel, saying, 'Babylon that great city is fallen, it is fallen: for she made all nations to drink of the wine of the wrath of her fornication'" (Revelation 14:8).

Practicing black magic is similar to worshipping the Devil or even golden calves. However, according to John, neither Lucifer nor Satan is real. The churches created them as a campaign to instill fear in people as part of their campaign of controlling people. They are just a negative energy force coming from our ego, which does not does not have any magic or creates any miracle. Practicing black magic just emboldens our desire to get what we (ego) want.

* * * * *

DOUG: Is practicing black magic like worshipping the Devil?

JOHN: Yes.

DOUG: Moses warned people not to worship golden calves. Could black magic be similar to that?

JOHN: Exactly. Black magic is the wrong use of energy. Moreover, if you are worshipping something that isn't God, you've made a false god of it. To put your attention on something that is not God is taking your focus off the only God there is. And you give away your power, and you will have all kinds of consequences because you are coming from a selfish point of view when that happens.

DOUG: I read in the book of Atlantis (Ref. 3) that black magic was practiced and it was exported to India.

JOHN: Primarily, it was from the African continent. However, other sources picked it up as time moved on, so the black magic was adopted into religions. Some of them are operating at that level, even though they do not tell the public that. The Catholic church has much black magic going on in the depths of it. So you see, where it starts is not necessarily as important as to just say, "I choose to focus on God's love." Focusing on God's love will not have to interfere with my life because the only power is God. If the focus is on something that isn't God, then I am making it a god, and that is not what you want to do in your life.

* * * * *

Section 2.3: Harmful Effects on Health

The inoculation is happening here today. Recently, the California legislators passed SB277, a bill to force vaccines on children. Now they are working on SB792, which would force the same on adults. It is an alarming trend that needs to be stopped. We need to empower ourselves as voters to demand the politicians stop forcing harmful inoculations on the people. Please refer to references 22 through 32 for details.

Douglas Grady

* * * * *

DOUG: Can we talk about vaccines, vaccinations? You mentioned a previous conversation about vaccinations that would harmful to person's health. What do you mean that vaccinations can prevent us from going to nirvana?

JOHN: Well, vaccinations are just another form of a drug, and they're putting the drugs into what you might call a soup, which has not gone through any kind of research to show the consequences of those particular drugs acting on the body, and drugs are poison. And so therefore, you are poisoning your body, which would lower your consciousness, and if that occurs, if you were to transfer into Nirvana at that state of your situation, you would probably go to a lower station of Nirvana than if you did not have the drugs in your system. You see, people who are using drugs have a low consciousness and those who have toxic-free bodies are going to have a higher consciousness. The drug literally stops the energy of the live God..

DOUG: So you're talking about this is while the person is alive.

JOHN: Yes.

DOUG: Would it prevent heaven on earth?

JOHN: Well, if you're using the vaccinations and that drug is in your system, you probably will not experience heaven on earth because your consciousness isn't open enough to allow that to happen.

DOUG: I see. Now how could we stop that?

JOHN: Well, that's a very good question because Marilyn's been working on that too.

DOUG: Okay.

JOHN: To write all the congress people, all your state legislators and start informing as many organizations and politically adept people.

Door to Glory

One of the people who is helping this and has a great name is John Kennedy. Or pardon me, Robert Kennedy, Jr. He has been on the Internet with an interview with Bill Maher that is expressing not very strongly that vaccinations are very poor for people to be involved with, but we have to have more people who have a view to the public. The media is stopping any newscasts about this particular topic. They don't want people to hear correct information. So sending out all kinds of news releases, writing articles, doing anything to bring it into the public view is going to be necessary, and the more you do that, the more energy you're putting into making people aware that this is such a difficult spot, you don't want to be involved with it. It's really not much different than when the people of Johnstown took the Kool-Aid several years ago in Africa, and they all died. The vaccinations are basically taking poison, and you're going to die eventually if not right away from it. So in fact, there was a situation in Canada recently where a hundred children were given vaccinations and seventy-five of them died or were immediately sick, so you see, people need to know this information.

* * * * *

Actually, it was in Mexico where 75 percent of the children who received the vaccines either died or were hospitalized (Ref. 32 and 33).

* * * * *

DOUG: Yes, I talked to Marilyn about the movie, and I can mention it in my book as a reference so people can learn more about it.

JOHN: That is a superb way to do it.

* * * * *

The movie is called *Bought: The Truth behind Vaccines, Big Pharma, and Your Food* (https://www.facebook.com/BoughtMovie/). The text is also available upon request.

* * * * *

DOUG: Doctors are not going to like this book.

JOHN: No. And if you get into the GMO problems and the fish farms and they ruined all the food and contaminated the food. They've poisoned the air through chemtrails, and they've contaminated the water through chloride. We are being poisoned. Marilyn has an article about this.

DOUG: I juice my fruits and vegetables, and they must be organic.

JOHN: Yes, yes. If you want the nutritional value, they should be having the nutrients of the soil part of the plant so that you are getting the spiritual, nutritional energy that is there for your body.

DOUG: Interesting.

JOHN: If you're eating GMO's, then you are eating toxic substances.

DOUG: So, you have to receive the energy of God to stay healthy.

JOHN: That's what medicine does not understand. The more your heart is open, the less medical problems you will have because the spirit is flowing through your system through what you people call meridians. That's that acupuncture could release the blockages. Chinese herbs help to change the energy so that the spirit is moving freely through your body. You do not want any obstructions and medicine does not understand it's the spirit that keeps you alive and healthy. And medicines primarily are drugs, and they are poison, toxic in your body and do stop the spirit. And so medicine is not a substantial support. It's a detrimental death wish. The alternative energy, your levels of a higher consciousness are the only real ways of having a healthy life. Anything else that's toxic is going to be poisonous

Section 2.4: Nuclear Bomb

Since the world shifted to the fifth dimension and to the new age of love and light, there is a need to resolve some of the old third-dimensional issues that had the world on the brink of a disaster of a second death, which is the death of our souls. Angels in the spiritual realms to this day are still trying to piece together the spiritual remains of the World War II victims of the bombings of Nagasaki and Hiroshima. There were major bombings back at the time of Atlantis and Lemuria, but they were crystal bombs that caused large casualties but did not cause any harm to the souls of the victims.

There have been attempts of a nuclear detonation that would have started World War III in the recent past, but the bombs were disabled by our space friends according to John (see March 31, 2015, dialogue). God had ordered an edict that no nuclear explosion would be permissible. It would have inflicted terrible harm for the entire human race, especially the souls beyond the physical existence. For the sake of humanity, as citizens of the planet, we need to make this issue known to governments and world political organizations so they will ban nuclear weapons in their entirety.

Table 5 – World Stockpiles Report (Ref. 15)

Country	Total Nuclear Weapons
Russia	8,000
United States	7,300
France	300
China	250
United Kingdom	225
Pakistan	120
India	110
Israel	80
North Korea	< 10
Total Nuclear Weapons	16,300

According to the report, the world's combined stockpile of nuclear warheads remains at unacceptably high levels after the end of the Cold War more than a decade and a half ago. The United States and

Russia have a total of 15,300 warheads, which represents 94 percent of the total world capacity. Despite talks of nuclear warhead reductions, both Russia and the United States are still modernizing their nuclear forces.

As of early 2015, the authors estimate that the US Defense Department maintains about 4,760 nuclear warheads. Of this number, they estimate that approximately 2,080 warheads are deployed, while 2,680 warheads are in storage. In addition to the warheads in the Defense Department stockpile, approximately 2,340 retired but still intact warheads are in storage under the custody of the Energy Department and awaiting dismantlement for a total US inventory of roughly 7,100 warheads. Since New START entered into force in February 2011, the United States has reported cutting a total of 158 strategic warheads and eighty-eight launchers under the treaty. It has plans to make some further reductions by 2018. Over the next decade, it also plans to spend as much as $350 billion on modernizing and maintaining its nuclear forces (Ref. 17).

* * * * *

DOUG: If there was going to be a nuclear war, could an angel or an alien prevent a nuclear attack since this world is arriving in the fifth dimension?

JOHN: There will be no Third World War, and there will be no nuclear attack. If you are not aware, there have been many chances at this point to start another world war and to launch nuclear weapons. However, they never went off. Somehow the spirits have been notified, and they have messages and handle detaching all the necessary connections for those particular weapons not to detonate. So you see, the Creator has deemed there will be no more nuclear explosions. The severity of damage to the soul from that type of explosion is almost irreparable, and they are still helping certain souls heal from the damages of the Second World War. It was not a spiritually wise solution, and it caused more damage to the spirit than was predicted. Of course, people just went for it because of their egos, pushing through for a victory. However, it was not a victory spiritually because it caused a great deal of difficulties in the spiritual world. Therefore, there has been a decree that even though the dark forces are desperately trying to keep control of the planet, they cannot do it from those sources.

DOUG: In World War II, nuclear explosions in Japan caused not only death to the bodies but also disconfiguration of their souls. Because of the nuclear blast affecting the energies (souls), I was wondering. Could God prevent another nuclear attack on the planet Earth?

JOHN: I am so pleased you asked that question because that is exactly what happened. God has never taken away free will, but after the Second World War, he declared there would be no more nuclear attacks or bombs. It is devastating to people's souls. Aliens and angels in the spirit world are trying to restore their health and put their pieces back together, you might say, of who they are. It was so devastating that some souls were lost and not repairable. It was one of the greatest sadnesses of God. So even though this happened, it was irreparable, and that was not to ever happen so that his pieces would not be able to heal. So he declared that there would be no more nuclear war.

DOUG: Now I understood that Russia had deployed a bomb, but it did not go off. You do not have to respond to that. I am going to the next question if that is okay.

JOHN: Okay.

DOUG: But the answer is God will prevent another nuclear attack. That's all I need to know.

JOHN: Yes, he already has by disarming many, many warheads.

DOUG: Could a negative alien group pass a nuclear weapon design to scientists?

JOHN: Yes, that happened. The negative alien group called the Grays gave it to the US government. Aliens gave the technology for many, many technological items that we have today as far as your civilization, elements of the computer, the nuclear bomb, all kinds of technology that have created new, higher, and more advanced abilities through the scientific realm. So you see, actually much of what your scientists are working with today, especially if they're government secret-type sciences, they're working with what's been given to them from aliens, but instead of using it for good, they've used it in ways that are destructive.

* * * * *

UFOs have been seen hovering over nuclear missile sites, particularly White Sands. An Apollo astronaut, Edgar Mitchell, claimed this (Ref. 41).

Section 2.5: New World Order

The dark side believes the new world order will be marshaled when an economic collapse devastates the world economy, particularly in the United States and Europe, in a similar fashion as the Great Depression. One reason that our economy continues limping along is the artificial supports that the Federal Reserve has given it by manipulating interest rates. However, one day the next great depression will occur when the government calls in its bonds, loans, and credit cards. As a result, there will be massive bankruptcies worldwide. Europe will stabilize first, and Germany, France, and England will have the strongest economies. Through the United Nations, an international currency will be instituted. Japan will pull out. The United Nations will send out peacekeeping forces to thwart riots. The leaders will divulge themselves, and people will be requested to make a vow of loyalty during a time of turmoil and financial devastation. A Russian economist had developed an economic theory that there would be a devastating depression in the year of 2020. That is when a new world order would be revealed.

* * * * *

DOUG: I wonder if the light of God (photon energy) is coming, would that plan change?

JOHN: Yes. There will be a time when the economic structure is going to be readjusted, and there will be some adjustments necessary for a few days while this occurs. But it will not be as drastic and severe as predicted because that was a prophecy that no longer is sustainable.

DOUG: Now could it be that God is providing photon energy to help people cope with the most difficult economic times of 2015 to 2020?

JOHN: Yes.

DOUG: Really?

JOHN: You see, when people raise their consciousness, inside they're feeling healthier. They're feeling abundance. They're feeling joy, and that comes from the grace of God. Whatever you need will manifest. God's grace is sufficient, so whatever you need will come to you.

DOUG: So it was not a coincidence. It was all part of the planning.

JOHN: Yes.

* * * * *

How did the dark side envision a new world order by the year 2020? It most likely came from an economic cycle theory developed by Russian economist Nikolai Kondratiev, who was later executed by the Soviet government in 1938. It predicted a significant economic contraction for the period from 2015 to 2020, culminating in a depression by the year 2020 (Ref. 13).

However, the economic forecast was based on third-dimensional thinking that had governed the world for thousands of years. When the effect of the fifth dimension of love and light takes hold, we will see a significant transformation taking place in the world.

It is important to acknowledge that we are eternal souls. Whatever calamities take place on earth for the coming years, stay close to your heart as the remnants of the third dimension are fading away. Heaven on earth is coming to light when last of the remaining dark energies are removed from the world.

Section 2.6: End Times

We are living in the end times today. The planet Earth already shifted from the third dimension to the fifth dimension on December 21, 2012. The effect of this change is gradual, however. Each dimensional change replaces the previous one that held the prevailing energy. From the third, the current energy is anxiety. As the dimension comes to an end, the individual results will be seen in the flow of the new prevailing energy. Any fear-based manifestation will begin to break down as the connections to it are removed. Every thought or belief that is released or healed removes a connection and collapses its third-dimensional aspect, replacing it with a higher vibration. This higher vibration has to come from an external source. The earth and solar system are fully entering a two-thousand-year band of photon energy coming straight from the galactic center. The photon energy is a form of the Holy Spirit and serves as a cleansing agent to root out all the dirt and negativity here. It happens twice during a twenty-six-thousand-year cycle, usually in the ages of Leo and Aquarius.

Negative beings and aliens cannot survive the vibrational pure photon light. They become extremely petulant in its manifestation. It creates deep polarization among the third- and fifth-dimensional people, those who are evil and those who are good.

* * * * *

DOUG: Now let me talk about Arcturus, are they one of the most advanced civilizations?

JOHN: Well, they're highly, highly evolved, and they have been instrumental for thousands of years in seeing planet Earth come into the place we are today. So yes, you might say they're the good guys.

DOUG: So they're waiting for us to ascend to the fifth dimension. Then they will come to help us?

JOHN: Well, they're actually around us all the time, but they can't be noticeable and visible until the actual shift of energy occurs, but yes, they're evident in our experience in making sure things go if they need to.

* * * * *

The end times are only for the shifting of the evolutionary state. For instance, the time of the third dimension is moving over to the fifth dimension. Planetary ages are time periods with ages, which are time periods each with certain commonalities. One period comes to a close, and a new age or world to come where different realities are present begins. The world to come as depicted in the Bible is the fifth dimension.

When one stage to another is the subject of eschatological discussion, the phrase "end of the world" should be replaced by "end of the age." Typically, when an age comes to an end, you will find a crisis brewing such as a war, a change in the environment, or reaching a new level of consciousness. Concerning the final events of history, eschatology is a part of theology. It believes the final events of history or the ultimate destiny of humanity is the "end of the world."

Most modern eschatology and apocalypticism perceive the end time as a violent disruption or destruction of the world. It is not the case of what is going on today. The rulers of the dark side have already left the planet or were forced out. What remains are the human elements of the group that is likely not of reptilian nature. The Christian and Jewish eschatologists view the end time as the consummation or perfection of God's creation of the world. For example, according to ancient Hebrew beliefs, the world began with God and ends with God's final goal for creation, which is the fifth dimension of love and light.

* * * * *

DOUG: Is the coming end time for the third dimension or the fourth dimension?

JOHN: The end times are about the third dimension. That means that the third dimension is being dissolved through the light of God and no longer will be sustainable. So the third dimension is leaving the planet, and its influence is reducing consistently.

DOUG: So basically, the dark side is facing the end time? Is that correct?

JOHN: Exactly. That is why the crisis and turmoil are so pandemic. They are struggling for the last breath of air, you might say.

DOUG: I see. Now I'm going to talk about the end time in the book of Revelation.

JOHN: Yes.

DOUG: Is it true that the process of the end time began on December 21, 2012?

JOHN: Yes, that is a crucial date in the exchange of, you might say, turning the world upside down. At that point in time, the energies did rearrange themselves to allow more love to come to the world. Therefore, there has been a tipping of the scales in that the most loving energy that is now available to planet Earth is sustaining more loving light into that energy instead of more fear and more dark energy coming from the planet, which is the third dimension. So yes, it was a definitive time.

DOUG: So it was the dark side? The church is part of that Dark Side?

JOHN: Yes, they created churches to continue to have followers and mislead them.

Chapter 3

Civilizations

Section 3.1: Super Universes

Universes in other star systems have already progressed to a higher state. We are residing in the seventh super universe, Orvonton, which is the youngest super universe in all of God's creation. It is now traveling north around the peripheral of the central isle of paradise (Havona). Orvonton is experiencing the adventure of one long, uncharted plunge into new space while remaining in harmony with an orderly, well-understood, and perfectly controlled movement, swaying in the majestic state around the first great source and center and his residential universe.

"The seven super universes traverse a vast ellipse. Our solar system and other worlds of time are not plunging headlong without chart and compass into unmapped space. The local universe to which the system belongs is following a counterclockwise course around the central universe. This planetary path is well-charted and is just as thoroughly known to the star onlookers across the super universes as the orbits of the planets constituting our solar system are known to the astronomers." (The Urantia Book 2015, Paper 15:1.2)

> "The first super universe swings relatively due north in an easterly direction to the paradise residence of the great sources and centers. This position, comparable to the west, represents the nearest physical access to the

spheres of time to the eternal Isle. The second super universe canvassing the north sets for the westward swing, while the third controls the northernmost segment of the vast space path, having already turned into the bend headmost to the southerly plunge. The fourth is likewise on a straight, southerly flight, the leading regions now drawing near opposition to the great centers. The fifth super universe has left its position opposite the center of centers and is in a direct, southerly course just past the eastward swing. The sixth occupies most of the southern curve, the segment from which our super universe has nearly passed." (The Urantia Book 2015, Paper 15:1.4)

"Our local universe is Nebadon, which belongs to Orvonton, the seventh and swings between the first and sixth super universes, having turned the southeastern bend of the super universe space level recently. Today the solar system to which Earth belongs is past the turn around the southern curvature. We are just now advancing beyond the southeastern bend and are moving rapidly through the long and comparatively straight northern path. For untold ages, Orvonton will pursue this direct northerly course" (The Urantia Book 2015, Paper 15:1.5). These realms contain operations seeking intelligent control for both physical and spiritual forces. The universal gravity functions in majestic power and perfect harmony.

The universal Father is the Father of personalities. Every super universe has its own eternal Son, and the infinite Spirit are creator partners. The universes are localized under combined rule of the creator Sons and the creative Spirit. Outside of paradise, there are seven inhabited universes that hold jurisdiction over the circle of the first postHavona space level. The seven master spirits emanate their influence to the outer region of the grand universe from the central isle. This constitutes the vast creation of one gigantic wheel, the hub being the eternal isle of paradise.

"Early in the materialization of the universal creation, the sevenfold scheme of the super universe organization and a government was formulated. The first post-Havana creation was divided into seven extraordinary segments, and the headquarters worlds of these super universe governments were designed and constructed. The present arrangement of administration had existed from near eternity, and the rulers of these seven super universes are rightly called Ancients of Days" (The Urantia Book 2015, Paper 15:0.2). There is a reference to an Ancient of Days in the book of Daniel, "I beheld till the thrones were set up, and the Ancient of Days did sit, whose garment was white as snow, and the hair of his head like the pure wool: his throne was like the fiery flame, and his wheels, as burning fire" (Daniel 7:9).

Every super universe is under the jurisdiction of the government of God. This government monitors the spiritual progress of its people and helps them attain the status of love and light. It is a beautiful arrangement of helping hands in promoting the love of God to every soul. Jesus is in charge of our universe. While he was on Earth promoting the kingdom of God, Archangel Gabriel took reign of the government. "And it is turned about by his government, that they may do whatsoever he commandeth them upon the whole world" (Job 37:12). "For the Father judgeth no man, but hath committed all judgment unto the Son" (John 5:22). "For judgment shall return to justice, and all the upright in heart shall follow after it" (Psalm 94:15).

Our super universe, Orvonton, was created by the forces of God millions of years ago. Orvonton is the youngest super universe among the seven super universes that revolves around the paradise center of the Creator God. "Practically all of the starry realms visible to the naked eye on Urantia belong to the seventh section of the grand universe, the super universe of Orvonton. The vast Milky Way star system represents the central nucleus of Orvonton, being largely beyond the borders of the local universe. This significant aggregation of suns, dark islands of space, double stars, globular clusters, star clouds, spirals, and other nebulae together with myriads of individual planets, forms a watch-like, elongated, circular grouping of about one-seventh of the inhabited evolutionary universes" (The Urantia Book 2015, Paper 15:3.1).

> "From the astronomical position of Urantia (Earth), as we look at the cross section of nearby systems to the great Milky Way, the spheres of Orvonton are traveling in a vast, elongated plane, the breadth being much larger than the thickness and the length far greater than the breadth.
>
> Observation of the so-called Milky Way discloses the comparative increase in Orvonton stellar density when the heavens are viewed in one direction while the number of stars and other spheres decreases away from the chief plane of the super universe. When the angle of observation is favorable, gazing through the main body of this realm of maximum density, we are looking at the residential universe and the center of all things.
>
> Of the ten major divisions of Orvonton, eight have been roughly identified by the astronomers. The other two are difficult of separate recognition because these phenomena can only be viewed from the inside. If looking upon the super universe of Orvonton from a position far-distant in space, we would immediately recognize the ten major sectors of the seventh galaxy.
>
> The rotational center of the minor sector is situated away from the enormous and dense star cloud of Sagittarius, around which the local universe and its associated creations move, and from opposite sides of the vast Sagittarius sub-galactic system, we may observe two great streams of star clouds emerging

in astonishing stellar coils." (The Urantia Book 2015, Paper 15:3.2-3.5)

"The nucleus of the physical system to which the sun and its associated planets belong is the center of the former Andronover nebula. This spiral nebula was slightly distorted by the gravity disruptions associated with the events that led to the birth of the solar system, which were occasioned by the near approach of a large neighboring nebula. This near-collision changed Andronover into a somewhat globular aggregation but did not wholly destroy the two-way procession of the suns and their associated physical groups. The solar system now occupies a relatively central position in one of the arms of this distorted spiral, situated about halfway from the center out toward the edge of the star stream." (The Urantia Book 2015, Paper 15:3.7-3.14)

"The Sagittarius sector and all other sectors and divisions of Orvonton are in rotation around Uversa, and some of the confusion of Urantian star observers arises out of the illusions and relative distortions produced by the following multiple revolutionary movements:

- the revolution of Urantia around its sun.
- the circuit of the solar system about the nucleus of the former Andronover nebula.
- the rotation of the Andronover stellar family and the associated clusters about the composite rotation gravity center of the star cloud of Nebadon.
- the swing of the local star cloud of Nebadon and its associated creations around the Sagittarius center of their minor sector.

- The rotation of the one hundred minor sectors, including Sagittarius, about their major sector.
- the whirl of the ten major sectors, the so-called star drifts, about the Uversa headquarters of Orvonton. and
- the movement of Orvonton and six associated super universes around paradise, the counterclockwise flow of the super universe space level.

These multiple motions are of several orders. The space paths of the planets and solar systems are genetic, inherent in origin. The absolute counterclockwise motion of Orvonton is also genetic, inherent in the architectural plans of the master universe. However, the intervening motions are of composite origin, being derived in paring from the constitutive segmentation of matter-energy into the super universes and in part produced by the intelligent and purposeful action of the paradise force organizers." (The Urantia Book 2015, Paper 15:3.7-3.14)

"While each super universe government presides near the center of the evolutionary universes of its space segment, it occupies a world made to order and is peopled by accredited personalities. These headquarter worlds are architectural spheres, space bodies specifically constructed for their special purpose. While sharing the light of nearby suns, these spheres are independently lighted and heated. Each has a sun that gives forth light without heat like the satellites of paradise and is supplied with heat by the circulation of certain energy currents near the surface of the sphere. These headquarter worlds belong to the greater systems situated near the astronomical center of their respective super universes." (The Urantia Book 2015, Paper 15:7.1)

"The headquarter worlds of the seven super universes partake of the nature and grandeur of paradise. They are central patterns of perfection. In reality, all headquarter worlds are paradisiacal. They increase in material size, beauty, and spirit glory from Jerusalem to the central isle. Moreover, all the satellites of these headquarter worlds are architectural spheres" (The Urantia Book 2015, Paper 15:7.3).

"The various headquarter worlds have every phase of material and spiritual creation. All kinds of material, Morontial, and spiritual beings are at home on these worlds of the universes. As mortal creatures ascend the universe, passing through the material to the spiritual realms, they never lose their appreciation for and enjoyment of their former levels of existence" (The Urantia Book 2015, Paper 15:7.4).

The headquarters of the super universes are the seats of the high spiritual government (throne of God) of the time-space domains. The executive branch of the super government is directed by one of the seven master spirits of supreme supervision, beings who sit upon seats of paradise authority and administer the super universes through the seven supreme executives stationed at the seven special worlds of the infinite Spirit, the outermost satellites of paradise (Havona-see Figure 1).

Although the planetary creations have provided opportunities for spiritual growth for all kinds of mortal creatures, there have been wars and conflicts in the past between the competing participants out in space.

* * * * *

DOUG: Now that I've asked you about war in heaven, how about war in space?

JOHN: Well, there is no war in heaven because war comes from the ego, which comes from separation from God. There have been wars in space in past histories, and the planets and civilizations that were involved in those wars have come to a harmonious agreement and become councils. Where there is leadership, there is harmony and cooperation among all. They discovered how barbarous wars were, and they are evolved beyond being in that mind-set. At this point, wars in space do not exist.

DOUG: Is it true the book of Revelation is about a war in space?

JOHN: No, it's about the war inside yourself between you and your ego.

The aliens have existed for millions if not billions of years. Their technology is beyond our capabilities on earth today. We are living in one of the younger universes with limited technological capabilities. The dark lords destroyed the planet Maldek around fifty thousands of years ago, and the remains are asteroid belts floating in space in between Mars and Jupiter.

DOUG: Did God send angels, aliens, and spiritual guides to help keep Earth from suffering the same fate as the former planet Maldek?

JOHN: God did sent angels to Earth, aliens included, to help bring life to the planet because it is considered the gem of the planets in the solar system. Earth was to be the planet to help the universe rise out of lower consciousness into a higher evolution. Some in the universe needed help to do this, and extraterrestrials from outer space were brought to Earth to help provide the information and the effort to bring Earth back to the beauty that it was created in so that it can rise into that higher consciousness. Earth is rising into higher consciousness, which means the whole universe is evolving. However, the angels and aliens did not provide help with other planets in mind. They always focused on bringing Earth back to its glory.

* * * * *

The Illuminati were created by one of the dark lords as a means of controlling the masses on earth since the beginning. It goes way back to the time of our first two civilizations disappeared, Atlantis and Lemuria. There was a standoff between these two early colonies that was instigated by the dark aliens, which resulted in terrible destructions by crystal bombs. The war was so devastating that the inhabitants had to move to inside the earth for protection. As a result, underground tunnels and cities were developed that are being used today.

* * * * *

DOUG: Okay. Like, we've talked about the Global Elite or the Illuminati.

JOHN: Yes.

DOUG: The Cabal and the 300 richest families.

JOHN: Right.

DOUG: Okay. Now, who was the leader of that umbrella?

JOHN: It goes back - how far do you want to go back? In the - several hundred years ago, it was the Rothschilds, but way back in Atlantis, it was the Sons of Belial (BAAL).

Section 3.2: Time Matrix

Many implant network systems are present on Earth, set up by the two principal alien competitors, the Anunnaki and the Drakonians. Although many Illuminati think that the enslavement of the human race is the concluding agenda of the invaders, this is not the case. The Anunnaki intend to install scalar-pulse power plants on Earth to open the portals to the inner earth. It would be a foremost step toward their final goal, the complete adjustment of the time matrix, a segment of the universe, which they have been planning for hundreds of millions of years.

The inner earth portals lead to upper dimensions of our time matrix. If they did not get far through these portal systems because of their incomplete frequency patterns, they would prevent higher sources of energy from reaching the lower levels. Altering alignments would enable them to assimilate the lower dimensions. Food gives them the energy to stop their slow black hole degeneration. The planetary and stellar configurations for ascension and portal access only occur every planetary time cycle, twenty-five thousand years, appearing from 2012 until 2017, when lower and upper dimensions merge for the time being.

Back during the time of Atlantis, different factions, motivated by corresponding, controlling ETs, attained possession of various geographical territories on earth. They have installed spikes embedded in the earth's grid system. These are seed implants of crystalline metals inserted deep into the crust by means of photo-sonic pulses. The spikes act as receivers and broadcasters, and they create an implant network for enslaving society.

When the spikes activate, they establish a myriad of mini wormholes that run to the large main Phoenix wormhole in the Bermuda Triangle. It provides the Anunnaki with a connection to the twelfth planet, Nibiru. There are electromagnetic corridors, portal systems, and a principal universal star gate that were put in place by extraterrestrials in the crust of the planet.

The wormholes provide time travel that either connects two separate regions within the universe or two different universes. If a wormhole contained sufficiently exotic matter, whether naturally occurring or artificially added, it could theoretically be used as a method of sending information or travelers through space. "A wormhole is not really a means of going back in time, it is a shortcut, so that something that was far away is much closer," NASA's Eric Christian wrote (Ref. 53).

* * * * *

DOUG: I'm going to talk about aliens.

JOHN: Yes.

DOUG: The Bermuda Triangle was one of the locations for a wormhole?

JOHN: It's a vortex that is part of the energy surrounding the planet, and there are several. It's not just the Bermuda Triangle, but that's the most famous one. But it's part of the energy that's necessary for earth, and if the vortex, which does—there have been planes, people, and boats that have disappeared in that area.

* * * * *

Since around 10,000 BC, government buildings and places of worship have been built over the spikes. Society was cultivated by the ET-controlled Illuminati Leviathan family lines for thousands of years.

The Drakonians copied the Phoenix wormhole with their Falcon wormhole in the Bermuda Triangle. Frequently, the Anunnaki would block the Falcon, and then the Draks would blow it off. They were warring continuously. These wormholes formed part of the implant interface systems of these rivaling ETs and were designed to merge with other support systems, such as the grid spikes and even the government HAARP. These large implant network systems need ascension cycle Stella activations, but they need a continuous linkage system with sufficient global coverage to be activated.

The Philadelphia experiment in 1943 was set up by the Zeta-Draks to complete their interface system by activating the Falcon. In 1983, the Zetas again controlled the Illuminati for a further experiment and linked the Falcon to the Necromiton network.

In 2000, the Phantom Matrix Anunnaki, Draks, and Necromitons formed an alliance—the UIR (United Invader Resistance). The two wormholes were to be blended to augment the final network, creating sufficient power to pull the whole planet into the phantom matrix. Note that the *big* Anunnaki and Draks come from the separate

Wesa matrix (consisting of Wesedak-Anunnaki and Wesedrak-Drakonians). These dark lords created the incredible *beast* technology.

The Phoenix-Falcon experiment did not work because of a higher planetary consciousness. They thought it would work through Indigos mainly and stellar ascension activations by creating a critical mass of the twelve-code pulse—that is, a D-12 current. The guardians refer to it as a twelve-dimensional current fully aligned with the source or divine blueprint. The UIR technology and consciousness cannot work at D-12. Their DNA only goes to ten and eleven strands (dimensions), and these strands are operating on reverse coding primarily.

Many of the Anu-Melchizedeks have to be awakened into motivation by the invader ETs. Before the ascension period, spontaneous changes in their DNA occur that could cause them to turn against the invaders. There is a race against time. A further powerful tool of these ETs is the type-three programming of the Indigos. They are vulnerable, having agreed to aid the Nephilim (Anunnaki-human hybrids) by rehabilitating their sharing of their DNA. This creates the Anunnaki *magenta* race, which is recognizable by a red streak in the aura.

The Montauk-Phoenix wormhole grid-spiking network became due for activation in 2001. It is accomplished by means of scalar sonic pulses. These subsonic pulses are known to have a dangerous spread. As a result, prominent buildings, such as the twin towers and the Pentagon, which had primary spike sites under them, would be expected to collapse.

Nevertheless, to destroy the buildings was all part of the greater plan and the cover of terrorists. It was set up to serve the purpose of stirring up further conflict, mass psychological fear, and another war. It pitted countries against one another based on whether they sided with the antiterrorism coalition.

These subsonic scalar pulses are created by combining calibrated electromagnetic waves at particular angles to one another, sparking these with an individual electrical charge. This creates the 4-D particles and underlying protons, which directs the charges to the target, turning matter into ashes.

* * * * *

DOUG: The end-time struggles are the dark side's last grasps for power, right?

JOHN: That is correct. It is the last energy that needs to be brought into the light so it can be dissipated. The dark side has created great havoc in its struggle for power. However, the reality is, its energy has been buried deeply for thousands of years, and it is time for the light to eliminate it. This is the final struggle.

DOUG: Essentially, the golden age (fifth dimension) does not begin until the dark side has been removed from control, true?

JOHN: Yes, we are in the end times on Earth.

Section 3.3: Planet Nibiru

The new information on Nibiru is more mysterious than its origins. Few people know the true details of Nibiru, and why it exists in our solar system. Planet Nibiru was supposed to be the twelfth planet in our solar system. Its name means the "planet of crossing." Planet Nibiru moves in an elliptical orbit rather than a standard horizontal orbit. The planet took around 750,000 years to come between Mars and Jupiter, and when it did, it generated devastation on all the planets during its flyby. According to historians, Tiamat (Maldek), a planet that had orbited between Mars and Jupiter, was a victim of Planet X. As Tiamat collided with one of the moons of Nibiru, it crashed and broke in half. One half became the asteroid belt and Phobos, one of the moons of Mars. The other half is the planet Earth. "Out of destruction comes life," reads the ancient Hindu text Bhagavad Gita (Ref. 42)

Nibiru was twenty times larger than Jupiter, with a burning moon that acts like Nibiru personal sun. Since Nibiru orbits much farther away from our sun, the following theory makes sense: The Anunnaki, the citizens of Nibiru, came to planet Earth around twenty-five thousand years ago. They gave much knowledge and detail to the developing humanoids, who at that time did not have the brain capacity to comprehend what the Anunnaki were saying. Even the Mayans predicted the existence of Nibiru or, according to them, a dark energy in the shape of a planet that would be coming near Earth in the distant future. Every time this planet came around, entire civilizations were wiped from the earth. James McCaney, an expert on Planet Nibiru and Mayan history, explained that ten thousand years ago, major devastation destroyed many civilizations on our planet, and ruined cities in South America vanished. He also went on to say that before Nibiru passed by ten thousand years ago, the North Pole was somewhere in the state of Wisconsin while the South Pole was somewhere in Pacific Ocean (Ref. 42).

Then we should not worry about Planet Nibiru for next 74,000 years or so, right? Wrong. Remember, even if Nibiru crossed between Jupiter and Mars, it is now surging upward to make its longest route around the sun. Its elliptical orbit goes in a roundabout close to the sun on one end, while 80 percent of the orbit is away from the sun. The earthquakes that are happening in Japan and Chile could be caused by Nibiru magnetic pull increasing as it nears our planet. The pull from Nibiru will increase the gravitational force of each planet in a rubber-band effect.

It is a satanic rebellion, likely by the dark energy lords, that brought devastation and chaos to our solar system and beyond. There may have been two planetary destructions, the wreckages of which besieged the solar system by asteroid belts, comets, wayward moons, and planetary rings. It appears the planet was destroyed by planet-sized spaceships. Every planet in the solar system is a planet-sized spaceship because it moves in space around the sun. Therefore, Maldek was destroyed by a collision with one of Nibiru moons.

* * * * *

DOUG: Are the Nibiruans a part of the dark side?

JOHN: Yes, I believe they could be.

DOUG: It's interesting whether it's a planet or just a spaceship. It's big like a planet, so is it a spaceship?

JOHN: You might call it a spaceship. It's an object that is in space and is moving, and people are traveling on it as it goes around the sun, so many literary people have called it a spaceship. People on Earth define spaceship as a flying saucer, so this would be just another version of that.

* * * * *

Section 3.4: Lost Civilizations, Atlantis, and Lemuria

The continents of both Atlantis and Lemuria have been submerged under water since the since the crystal bomb explosions around eleven thousand years ago. They represent some of the earliest civilizations of man. Atlantis was located in the middle of the Atlantic Ocean. The Atlantic Ridge was a desirable location for people with its rich, fertile, volcanic soil and warm winds from the Gulf Stream caressing the land. The living conditions were ideal for the first group of fully evolved Homo sapiens, known as Cro-Magnons (Ref. 3).

However, the region of Atlantis was unstable because of several geologic situations. Two tectonic plates move at the Atlantic Ridge, which disturbs the delicate crust of the earth. This makes the area one of the most active earthquake and volcanic sites in the world. Three plates interact in the area of the Azores Plateau. Continents are composed mainly of granite and remain stable for millions of years. Granite is light enough so continents continue to float on the surface of the mantle. But the basalt structures, such as the Atlantic Ridge, are dense and will sink (Ref. 3).

Knowledge of Lemuria stems from the nineteenth century when

Door to Glory

scientists unexpectedly found small nocturnal animals called lemurs living in Madagascar and New Guinea. They believed the original home of these monkey-like mammals was 250 miles away in Africa, and there was no obvious explanation of how they had traveled so far. The missing land was named Lemuria in honor of the lemurs. Today the ancient sunken continent in the Pacific Ocean is a place with two names. Lemuria and Mu are used interchangeably. During the hundreds of centuries of its existence, the motherland of Mu, like everywhere else on the fragile surface of our planet, changed in size and shape.

Between 50,000 BC and 10,000 BC when an immense amount of water from the oceans was incorporated in the snow and ice of the glaciers, sea levels were hundreds of feet lower. Islands everywhere were much bigger, and ocean waters ceased to cover the fertile continental shelves. Col. James Churchward first learned about Mu from records on the sacred Naacal tablets in India.

Figure 7 – Map of Ancient Atlantis

After many years of searching in Asia and Central America for further information about the lost continent, Churchward believed that until 10,000 BC, the largest remaining island of the motherland of Mu lay in the southeastern Pacific on a broad area of uplifted seafloor. It extended southeast from Hawaii to Easter Island with its center somewhat south of the equator. Narrow channels of ocean divided the land into three sections. To the west, Lemuria's several thousand square miles included the Society, Cook, Austral, Tuamotu, and Marquesas islands, all of which are relatively close together, south of Hawaii and south of the equator.

Discoveries of coal and a long history of floral growth on the island of Rapa, one of the Austral Islands, suggest that this portion of the Pacific Ocean was once above the surface. The western section of the large island of Lemuria gradually sank, and as ocean waters threatened their homes and temples, people moved to the higher, safer ground of Sumatra, Java, Borneo, New Guinea, and Australia. Churchward determined that four major cataclysms in 800,000 BC, 200,000 BC, 80,000 BC, and 10,000 BC were the culprits responsible for nature tearing the beautiful land in the Pacific Ocean to pieces. Numerous volcanic islands and coral atolls, which endure where Lemuria once stood, confirm the instability of the region. The instability of the ocean floor in the southeast Pacific constantly subjected the Lemurians to the problems of unexpected earthquakes and volcanic eruptions. As an illustration of the instability, sailors traveling in that vicinity sometimes report islands that are not on maps. But before long, the greedy ocean devours them, and they are never seen again. In 1836, the island of Taranaki, south of the Cook Islands, suddenly disappeared with all but one of its inhabitants, a man who was visiting a nearby island at the time of the surprising disaster. Gently rolling hills and tumbling rivers that circled through the land characterized the countryside of early Lemuria. The vaporous steam rising from the abundant, bubbling hot springs gave a surreal, misty impression to the landscape. Gradually, the environment changed as sections of our planet's crust shifted and pushed against each other and forced mountains up from the depths of the earth. Lemuria became a hillier continent. Some of the islands in the Pacific today are the rocky summits of its mountains. The Ring of Fire, a chain of active volcanoes that surrounds a large section of the Pacific Ocean, demonstrates the presence of the hot molten lava that was never far beneath the surface in Lemuria. A theory proposes that El Niño and La Niña, weather patterns that occur every four to twelve years, originate in this troubled area. When portions of the earth's crust expand and contract, it increases or decreases the amount of volcanic activity in the Ring of Fire. As hot lava from deep inside the planet shoots out, it changes the temperature of the ocean water. When the water grows warmer, it produces El Niño. A decrease in ocean temperature induces La Niña (Ref. 6).

* * * * *

DOUG: From Genesis 15:12; "And when the sun went down, there fell a heavy sleep onto Abraham. And, lo, a very fearful darkness fell upon him." Did the darkness come from the volcanic ash from the sky? Could he be from Atlantis or Lemuria?

JOHN: Abraham is a word in the Bible that represents the God Consciousness. And, you see, there was a time when in Atlantis -- you're right. There was a lowering of consciousness that was perpetrated on the masses to bring in darkness so they wouldn't have that connection with God. And this has been going on for 13,000 years, of which you are now, in your glory, coming out of it. And this is a beautiful time to say that darkness is leaving. It's no longer going to return for over the next 2,000 years. You will be in delight. And it's a symbology of the fall of man.

* * * * *

The lush tropical vegetation of giant ferns and evergreens that covered most of Mu made it a continent of unsurpassed beauty. Sacred lotus flowers, one of the first flowers to appear on our planet, glistened like jewels along the shores of its shallow lakes. Coconut palms lined the rivers and fringed the ocean beaches. Just as plant life flourished in the warm climate, so insects grew to an enormous size. Fossilized specimens from islands in the Pacific reveal that in the tropical climate of Mu, roaches were four to five inches long, and two-inch ants with large wings were capable of flying long distances. Archaeologist Stacy-Judd reports that the natives of Easter Island (Rapa Nui) have said that they are living on the peak of a holy mountain of Mu. They believe Easter Island, which is formed from three extinct volcanoes, is the only portion of their motherland that the sea has not covered. Located 2,300 miles from the coast of Chile, the mysterious island has some of the most impressive structures in the Pacific (Ref. 6).

* * * * *

DOUG: That's like a tree of life which kept Adam and Eve alive for an extended period?

JOHN: Yes because it was living energy. Now we come into a group of a faction that was called the Son of Baal and there was the faction who wanted to stay One with God called The Law of One. And there are books written by the Law of One, and they are available to read. They became to have their disagreements of the Sons of Baal would be those without light, the Dark Side and the Law of One were the people that were following the oneness of Christ consciousness, so there was becoming a faction between the two. When the Sons of Baal wanted to be in charge of the planet they were willing to blow it up to take concur so to speak, they went from the primary power source of the crystals. So, that was the explosions that were heard in Atlantis until it did fall to its wayside because it was devastated through the blasts and the people from those planets, continents left as best they could, and not everyone did of course. Mack happened to be in the explosion of Lemuria during that time when Lemuria was damaged through explosions and volcanoes too and did not survive that lifetime because of the continent sinking, and he was caught on a boat out in the ocean and didn't survive. Throughout the many centuries since this devastation with the blow up of the continent, it was strictly out of wanting to control, the Dark Side has gradually taken over control of the planet that's what we are coming to the end times of that control.

* * * * *

Figure 8 – Map of Ancient Lemuria

* * * * *

DOUG: Now, the Great Flood, that happened before Atlantis and Lemuria got into a war?

JOHN: There was no war. There was an explosion of a huge crystal that created the enormous devastation of the different parts of Atlantis, which was several islands of thinking. There wasn't a war as such. There was sabotage, and you might say, by the people of the Dark called Sons of Belial. And they sabotaged the continuation of the spirit of love, and for - in that case, the islands of Atlantis sunk and the Lemuria sunk. And the Great Flood was the cleansing of that dark energy. That's why Noah's Ark was so important because they were still in the light of God, and the flood was to disseminate the darkness and dispel it so that it no longer could have a thriving access to continuing. So, it was a cleansing.

DOUG: I just wanted you to help me clarify some discrepancies regarding timelines. I'm not sure if you can give me a hand, but we've talked about the extinction of Maldek?

JOHN: Yes.

DOUG: And how long ago was that just approximately? Was it much sooner because the ape souls did transfer over here during the time of Atlantis. So, it could not be like 500,000 years ago but rather just 50,000 years ago?

JOHN: That is closer to the truth, yes.

DOUG: So, it would have to be during the time of Atlantis.

JOHN: If it happened - Atlantis was 13,000 years ago so that it would be before that.

DOUG: Okay, so 50,000 years ago would be more logical.

JOHN: Yes.

* * * * *

It all began with the rebels or renegades of the fallen angels that were made up of a group of the Atlanteans, Nephilim, and Annunaki. Their kind was pursuing them across the galaxy, and they ended up in our part of the solar system. They set up a decoy, a false base to lose their pursuers on the former planet Maldek, which was between Mars and Jupiter. Maldek was a large water-based planet fifteen times the diameter of our present Earth. The sun's reflection on this oceanic world caused it to shine brightly like a brilliant star from afar.

* * * * *

DOUG: I mentioned this book, Nine Freedoms and this book talks about, I don't know if it's true, but this book says people died by a hydrogen bomb that murders the whole civilization in one blinding flash of searing flame?

JOHN: What planet are we talking about?

DOUG: Maldek.

JOHN: Okay. Yes, I think for the most part that is accurate.

* * * * *

The destruction of Maldek caused incredible chaos and disruption across the entire solar system around the time of 50,000 BC. It razed and cratered some of the nearby planets and caused the orbital or axial displacements of planets as far away as Uranus. Earth and Mars were primarily affected, the former acquiring much of Maldek's water and the latter losing most of its own. Much of the debris of Maldek is asteroid belts. The other parts are meteors and comets as well as the stray moons and small planets of our solar system.

Earth had an irrelevant amount of water before the catastrophe of Maldek, but after the dissolution of the planet, Earth was covered with more water than land. The particles that bombarded the earth caused many of its depressions, craters, and current cracks or fault lines. They forced most of the Atlantean renegades and our primitive native inhabitants, to flee to caves, mountains, and the earth's interior. The native populaces of Earth at this time were the Neanderthals. Later they became the Cro-Magnons (Lemurians) and then Adamic (modern man) through Atlantean genetic manipulation.

* * * * *

DOUG: Were Homo-sapiens or Cro-Magnons third-dimension entities from Maldek?

JOHN: No, they in a way you might say they were seeded on Earth from an outer planet, yes, so I guess you could say yes. Third-dimension, plant - animals are third-dimensional. They just have - they just don't have the soul of the human. They have souls but not in the human dimension.

* * * * *

The destruction of Maldek destabilized our solar system to a significant degree. As a result, the breakup of the planet created three rings of asteroid belts. The pursuers were unable to find their targets because of time restraints, and they were forced to return to their home world(s). However, before they returned, they scanned the planets for signs of the renegades who were hiding on Earth. To avoid destroying another world, they set up an etheric barrier or gate around Earth so that their rebel brethren could not escape from it. In effect, they quarantined it from the rest of the solar system. The pursuers established a loadstone on the Moon, which was an invisible etheric gate or barrier around our planet. It is still there today.

After the turmoil of our solar system had settled many years later, the Atlantean renegades reemerged from their underground lairs of the inner earth and began regrouping and reconstructing their civilization. Their home was on the continent of Appalachia, which stretched from what is now Greenland to northernmost Europe to the Siberian peninsula. That is an approximate location of the North Pole entrance to the inner earth. Their city was named Atlantis after their king, Atlan, and the ocean below them was called the Atlantic. They were a small group of fifty to two hundred people, however, and the task of rebuilding was enormous and laborious. They relocated from Maldek to our planet by spaceships.

* * * * *

DOUG: Were the souls transferred from that planet, and did they transfer by walk-in? Or were they transferred by incarnation?

JOHN: Good question. Let me see what I can find. They came through spaceships.

DOUG: Now is it true the people on Maldek were advanced, that they had advanced technology? Is it true that they could manipulate the weather with technology and that they had an abundance of food?

JOHN: They could manipulate the weather. They had a great deal of technology, and it was applied in an inappropriate way. On Earth in the past century, the dark side controlled the weather. Hurricane Katrina was a carefully controlled weather device that was concocted and perpetuated to flood out the area on purpose. So it has happened not only on Maldek. It has happened right here on the planet. They did have high-degree technology. That's where the energy problem was on Maldek. They were using it for the wrong reasons.

* * * * *

DOUG: Is it true a nuclear bomb destroyed both Lemuria and Atlantis?

JOHN: No, it was not nuclear. It was a crystal; a very powerful crystal was exploded. You could maybe say it was a bomb like force because it was that powerful, but it was the crystal that created all of the earthquakes and the continents to be gradually sinking so that it was no longer part of the cultural – people had to flee and leave because the continents were disappearing.

* * * * *

Many of our traumas and phobias, both individually and collectively, have yet to be healed or resolved in this period of Earth history. Many of the Atlanteans and Lemurians and others foresaw the great bomb explosions and took refuge in the inner earth caves and tunnels that existed for such crisis periods. When the turmoil was over, they returned and planted the seeds for new civilizations—empires such as Egypt, Sumeria, India, and China. Regrettably, they also brought back bad science, occultism, and technology, which are again bringing us to the verge of destruction or even annihilation.

Douglas Grady

* * * * *

DOUG: Is it true that the second-dimension apes had experienced fear from its native planet Maldek, and this fear carried over to the third-dimension Earth?

JOHN: Yes.

* * * * *

The rebel Atlanteans or renegades came here fifty thousand years ago from the former planet Maldek. They got stuck here, and their mission has always been to get out again. To do so, they had to rebuild their technology. It took many thousands of years and will hopefully penetrate the barrier or star gate their pursuers erected around our planet. It is a question of whether there is any conspiracy going on today with the dark side, which has been ruling the earth for ages. Whatever the case may be, they are using us to help them achieve their goal of returning to their original home planet. They have changed primate man to modern man, and in return, they have acquired some of our characteristics. The Atlanteans are male, left-brain dominant, and a warlike and patriarchal society. In contrast, Lemurian and Eve descendants are right-brain dominant and a peaceful and nature-loving matriarchal society.

Perhaps the meeting of Atlanteans and humankind was not an accident at all. Perhaps it was a great experiment of some sort in which both parties have benefitted somewhat. We have acquired their cunning and intelligence, while they have acquired some of our emotional or even spiritual characteristics? They changed us mentally and biologically and sped up our evolution dramatically—but was this good or bad? Were we better off pursuing our evolutionary course? And did they learn anything from us? Have we been and are we still the instruments of their regeneration? The results have yet to be tabulated. Our DNA today is based on this genetic modification by the dark side that took place more than thirteen thousand years ago. It only created two strands in our DNA for the purposes of their control. For the upcoming new age, we will receive the missing ten strands back when we attain Christ consciousness. It will return us to our original birthright before we arrived the planet as celestial beings.

* * * * *

DOUG: I read somewhere that is it true that our DNA could increase from seven to twelve?

JOHN: Yes, in fact, it can go higher. So this is because you are becoming interdimensional personalities, and it has been limited to two strands to keep you in that limited framework. But as you grow spiritually, you will have the next stages to go into the twelve strands of DNA.

* * * * *

The Atlanteans, Anunnaki, or fallen angels who are trapped here or "reserved unto judgment" had until AD 2012 to change their evil ways or escape the planet. Otherwise, they were doomed. In the year 2012, the Earth and solar system fully entered a two-thousand-year band of photon energy coming straight from the galactic center and serving as a cleansing of all the dirt and negativity here. It has happened twice before during a twenty-six-thousand-year cycle in the ages of Leo and Aquarius. Negative beings and aliens cannot stand this clean, pure photon (light) vibration and become extremely irritable or restless in its presence. That is why there is currently such a high polarization between those who are evil and those who are good and why technology is speeding up at an incredible rate.

Our pathological leaders seem to have chosen not to change and are desperately seeking a way out of here, and they cannot seem do it. HARRP (Ref. 19) was used to try to burn a hole through the barrier, the etheric ring, around this planet, but instead it backfired and caused the ozone situation over the poles. They are trying all sorts of technologies to break out, and they are having negative consequences on the planet. If they do not succeed, they will try to bring us down with them. We are in a cage with an angry beast and must be ready to defend ourselves. However, according to John, they've run out of time and have been captured;

* * * * *

DOUG: Could the United States and Russia have tried to develop a space technology to find an escape route for the ruler of the Illuminati?

JOHN: Well, the Illuminati have tried many different escape routes of—actually, the public paid for them through their taxes. Right now one of their escape routes is to Mars, and there is a base up there where they have started a community. And at one point, they had bases under earth that they were planning to use in case of needing to because of explosions and whatever needing to be saved. And so it was like a bomb shelter. They had a whole series of half a dozen or so of these areas underground that were blown up at one point, so they couldn't use that as an escape. So most of their escapes have been blocked.

DOUG: Now suppose the dark side has tried to escape Earth. They will most likely maybe go to Mars or another third dimensional planet. Is that true?

JOHN: They already have gone to Mars and have bases on Mars. People just have not been told about it.

DOUG: Now you have mentioned that leaders of the dark side have already left for Mars?

JOHN: Well, some of them have. But the ones who are here and have caused so much difficulty with the planets are in the process of being—they're being put in jail. They're being taken to court. They're being held responsible for their crimes, and so they need to stay on earth so that they can face their consequences. And this is important for the changes that are coming along with the earth's elections and the earth's moving into this new consciousness. And so the people need to be held responsible, or they cannot in their own soul growth move out of where they are. They have to, so to speak, step up to the plate and acknowledge what they have devastated for other people in their social life and be accountable. So they have not. The ones who are meaning to do this are still here and are in the processes of being held accountable.

DOUG: Now I understand that the lizard people are still in control of earth.

JOHN: Not currently. They have lost their control and have come into human form from that dimension, and they are being imprisoned and put in jails and rounded up. Their money is dwindling, and they are losing ground every day. The energy of the earth does not support them any longer.

* * * * *

When the ancient pursuers return, they will chain and sequester the beast and undo the barrier, and humanity will finally be at peace and in unity with the rest of the solar system.

Section 3.5 Myth of Great Flood

The photon energy of love and light makes the entities of the dark side disappear or dissipate because they can't handle it. Some pockets of them remain on the planet, but in time they will be gone. A new home or planet will be found for them somewhere else, most likely in another constellation to get away from the influence of the Photon Belt. The negative forces have plagued and polluted our planet for so long. Finally, this planet will come into its own and enjoy a much-needed golden age or millennium of rest, peace, and abundance from the fifth dimension.

Our entire galaxy has reentered the Photon Belt. The previous encounter was thirteen thousand years ago back in the time of Atlantis. As mentioned in section 1.2, the universe is completing a trip of a twenty-five-thousand-year cycle around the center isle of paradise. The twenty-five-thousand-year cycle is a universal measurement of putting together a plan of energy changes. Our universe is a part of the seventh super universe that revolves around God's paradise. The photon energy is a divine energy that connects the planet and individuals to our divine source. The inhabitants of inside earth will come out and integrate with our society. They have already ascended to the fifth dimension while we are still in the third dimension.

* * * * *

DOUG: What is the highest dimension of people inside the earth? Is it fifth or sixth or seventh?

JOHN: Very good question. Let me think. It takes me a minute. Some of the people inside earth have moved into the eighth dimension. They are ready to go into the spirit. So, they have been evolving, even though they were inside the earth, so to speak. That didn't stop their consciousness growing, so they have continued to move into a couple of higher levels. But remember that the levels are from a third-dimensional point of view, and the higher you go, there are no levels. It's one consciousness that's multidimensional.

* * * * *

They have remained on earth for over 11,000 years, ever since the explosion of the crystal bombs that have damaged the planet's canopy around 9000 BC. The melting of the polar caps elevated the sea levels that eventually buried our earliest civilizations, Atlantis and Lemuria, in the Atlantic and Pacific oceans, respectively. The polar openings to inside earth were opened during the first Golden Age while the "firmament" covered the planet, bringing a warm tropical climate throughout the world. There were palm trees buried near the North Pole, according to John.

* * * * *

JOHN: The climate—that's what the big controversy about climate is actually about. The planet is changing in a Mediterranean climate like at the time of Jesus. So there will not be the extreme environments that we have, like where you are right now. You will find yourself in a beautiful, warm, comfortable Mediterranean afternoon or morning when the sun is out, and it will be pleasant and a nice atmosphere to enjoy. The whole planet is moving into that kind of environment, and the scientists, of course, do not have the prophecy to understand that the earth is changing into a new, higher consciousness. There still will be mountains to go skiing, and there still will be areas that will be similar to what you have today, but primarily it's moving into a very warm and moderate tropical climate.

DOUG: Interesting. That might explain why the polar caps will melt, so the weather up there will be nice?

JOHN: Exactly. In fact, in some of the excavations in the frozen areas, they have discovered palm trees that were buried under ice. So this is not anything new, but it will be returning to that climate.

* * * * *

"Again God said, let there be a firmament in the midst of the waters, and let it separate the waters from the waters. Then God made the firmament, and separated the waters, which were under the firmament, from the waters which were above the firmament: and it was so" (Genesis 1:6-7).

The sea level rose and eventually blanketed Atlantis and Lemuria more than thirteen thousand years ago (previous golden age). The flood's waters receded to the polar areas where they are to this day and will someday evaporate from to form a canopy around our planet once again. It may happen when our orbit changes and exposes us to our binary sun system. All the other planets appear to have canopies or thick cloud covers with the exception of our earth and moon.

Earth may have been purposely positioned not to receive the strong radiation from another sun or star behind our visible sun, or it may be that earth's inner central sun is being somehow hindered from emanating its full power, which would melt the ice caps and produce a cloud cover over the planet.

The planet has entered the Photon Belt again. During the new golden age, the firmament will be restored, bringing Mediterranean weather for the entire world. The polar regions will melt, bringing the two civilizations, inner earth and outer earth, together.

Scientists have theorized that global warming is due to the emission of greenhouse gases (Ref. 43). Scientific understanding of global warming is increasing. The Intergovernmental Panel on Climate Change reported in 2014 that scientists were more than 95 percent certain that global warming is mostly being caused by increasing concentrations of greenhouse gases and other human (anthropogenic) activities. Climate model projections summarized in the report indicated that during the twenty-first century the global surface temperature is likely to rise a further 0.3 to 1.7 degrees C (0.5 to 3.1 degrees F) for their lowest emissions scenario using stringent mitigation and 2.6 to 4.8 degrees C (4.7 to 8.6 degrees F) for their highest. The national science academies of the major industrialized nations have recognized these findings, and no scientific body of national or international standing disputes them.

Could the actual warming be coming from the photon energy from space that began in 1996?

* * * * *

DOUG: The poles shifting on Earth had caused the ice age to occur. Was there anything behind it?

JOHN: No. Part of the evolution of Earth is everything is in motion, as I mentioned once before. Everything is changing. Even your climate today is changing, and so these things happen. And the news says, "Well, it's all because of pollution that the climate is changing."

DOUG: Was the evolution process hampered by the ice age on Earth?

JOHN: These things are natural occurrences as the planet is evolving. Good question. No, I would say it was all part of God's plan, that these things needed to occur, so every time there has been growth beyond, this was all part of a plan, and it has been a long plan. It has gone on forever, and it will continue. So this is not the end of the planetary changes. They will continue.

DOUG: Was fear created to help force body/mind/spirit complexes to focus on the inner power of God?

JOHN: To focus on the outside power or no God. If you read *The Real Meaning of 2012*, it explains that the ego was part of man's ability to come to planet Earth and be able to observe what was necessary for their survival. The ego used the five senses—smell, touch, sight, hearing, and taste—to give information to the person. However, when the ego got threatened, then fear stepped in and became an emotional scare to human beings, and that has been perpetuated over the last thirteen thousand years from Atlantis on. Fear was an overreaction to the information human beings needed to survive on planet Earth.

* * * * *

The flood during the time of Noah was likely around 5000 BC which was 4,000 years after the solar system had left the Photon Belt. It was not a worldwide flood event that many people were led to believe. Some religious teachers today are claiming that Noah's flood did not cover the entire earth nor all the mountains of the day. Further, they claim that Noah and the animals floated on a shallow, temporary inland sea caused by the flood, somehow covering only the Mesopotamian region.

"For thousands of years after the submergence of the first Eden the mountains about the eastern coast of the Mediterranean and those to the northwest and northeast of Mesopotamia continued to rise. This elevation of the highlands was greatly accelerated about 5000 B.C., and this, together with greatly increased snowfall on the northern mountains, caused unprecedented floods each spring throughout the Euphrates valley. These spring floods grew increasingly worse so that eventually the inhabitants of the river regions were driven to the eastern highlands. For almost a thousand years, scores of cities were practically deserted because of these extensive deluges." (Ref.2, The Urantia Book 2015, paper 78:7.2)

"Almost five thousand years later, as the Hebrew priests in Babylonian captivity sought to trace the Jewish people back to Adam, they found great difficulty in piecing the story together; and it occurred to one of them to abandon the effort, to let the whole world drown in its wickedness at the time of Noah's flood, and thus to be in a better position to trace Abraham right back to one of the three surviving sons of Noah. The traditions of a time when water covered the whole of the earth's surface are universal. Many races harbor the story of a world-wide flood sometime during past ages. The Biblical story of Noah, the ark, and the flood is an invention of the Hebrew priesthood during the Babylonian captivity. There has never been a universal flood since life was established on Urantia. The only time the surface of the earth was completely covered by water was during those Archeozoic ages before the land had begun to appear." (The Urantia Book 2015, Paper 78:7.3-7.4)

"But Noah really lived; he was a wine maker of Aram, a river settlement near Erech. He kept a written record of the days of the river's rise from year to year. He brought much ridicule upon himself by going up and down the river valley advocating that all houses be built of wood, boat fashion, and that the family animals be put on board each night as the flood season approached. He would go to the neighboring river settlements every year and warn them that in so many days the floods would come. Finally, a year came in which the annual floods were greatly augmented by unusually heavy rainfall so that the sudden rise of the waters wiped out the entire village; only Noah and his immediate family were saved in their houseboat." (The Urantia Book 2015, Paper 78:7.5)

* * * * *

DOUG: Was the flood a myth perpetuated by the church? Could the flood be coming from the warming of Ice Age?

JOHN: Yes. Very good question. It's a combination that what happens is people's consciousness determine what's around us and we do create our reality. And at that time the consciousness on planet Earth was very low and negative fear-based energy. Therefore, it needed to be cleansed, and water is a cleansing agent. So, they produced their demise through the flood so that it could be cleaned out. And it was brought on by their consciousness. And the universe cooperated with the water needing to be available.

* * * * *

"These floods completed the disruption of Andite civilization. With the ending of this period of deluge, the second garden was no more. Only in the south and among the Sumerians did any trace of the former glory remain. The remnants of this, one of the oldest civilizations, are to be found in these regions of Mesopotamia and to the northeast and northwest. But still older vestiges of the days of Dalamatia exist under the waters of the Persian Gulf, and the first Eden lies submerged under the eastern end of the Mediterranean Sea" (The Urantia Book 2015, Paper 78:7.6-7.7).

* * * * *

DOUG: Did Noah emigrate from Atlantis?

JOHN: Well, if you understand you're talking about thousands of years in between situations, and therefore, it would be in the broadest sense he would have. You could say he migrated from Atlantis, which was thirteen thousand years ago. Because when he was working on his experience with the ark was less than thirteen thousand years, there were many generations between leaving Atlantis and the experience of the ark. If you followed it in a long linear path, you would see that he was a descendent of that.

DOUG: Did he share his enlightenment experience with the people?

JOHN: Yes.

DOUG: Did Noah share his enlightenment experience from the ark during the time of the flood?

JOHN: I believe so.

DOUG: Was the Book of Jubilees one of the Dead Sea Scrolls? Is it true this book was passed down from Jacob to his son Levi?

JOHN: Yes.

DOUG: Also, was the knowledge given to King Solomon the Book of Jubilees?

JOHN: King Solomon was open to the spirit of God's message from his heart. He was in direct connection to the higher spirit and listened to that, and that's where it came from.

Section 3.6 Violet Race: Forefront of Present Civilization

Thirty-seven thousand years ago, the planet Earth was spiritually isolated from the universe because of the rebellion taking place by the previous god of this world, Caligastia. The throne of God had considered improving the race from a purely biologic standpoint and dispatched Adam and Eve to help improve humanity on the planet.

"Jesus said, "This voice was for your benefit, not mine. Now is the time for judgment on this world; now the prince of this world will be driven out. And I, when I am lifted up from the earth, will draw all people to myself'" (John 12:30-32)

"Adam and Eve were the founders of the violet race of men, the ninth human race to appear on Urantia. Adam and his offspring had blue eyes, and the violet peoples were characterized by fair complexions and light hair color — yellow, red, and brown.

Eve did not suffer pain in childbirth; neither did the early evolutionary races. Only the mixed races produced by the union of evolutionary man with the Nodites and later with the Adamites suffered the severe pangs of childbirth.

Adam and Eve, like their brethren in Jerusem (spiritual side of Jerusalem), they were energized by dual nutrition, subsisting on both food and light, supplemented by certain super physical energies not revealed to Earth. However, their offspring did not inherit the parental endowment of energy intake and light circulation. They had a single circulation, the human type of blood sustenance. They were designedly mortal though long-lived, albeit longevity gravitated toward the human norm with each succeeding generation.

Adam and Eve and their first generation of children did not use the flesh of animals for food. They subsisted wholly upon "the fruits of the trees." After the first generation, all of the descendants of Adam began to partake of dairy products, but many of them continued to follow a nonflesh diet. Many of the southern tribes with whom they later united were also nonflesh eaters. Later on, most of these vegetarian tribes migrated to the east and survived as now admixed in the peoples of India.

Both the physical and spiritual visions of Adam and Eve were far superior to those of the present-day peoples. Their special senses were much more acute, and they were able to see the midwayers and the angelic hosts, the Melchizedeks, and the fallen Prince Caligastia, who several times came to confer with his noble successor. They retained the ability to see these celestial beings for over one hundred years after the default. These special senses were not so acutely present in their children and tended to diminish with each succeeding generation."

The Adamic children were usually Adjuster indwelt since they all possessed undoubted survival capacity. These superior offspring were not so subject to fear as the children of evolution. So much of fear persists in the present-day races of Urantia because your ancestors received so little of Adam's life plasm, owing to the early miscarriage of the plans for racial physical uplift.

The body cells of the Material Sons and their progeny are far more resistant to disease than are those of the evolutionary beings indigenous to the planet. The body cells of the native races are akin to the living disease-producing microscopic and ultramicroscopic organisms of the realm. These facts explain why the Urantia (Earth) peoples must do so much by way of scientific effort to withstand so many physical disorders. You would be far more disease resistant if your races carried more of the Adamic life." (The Urantia Book 2015, Paper 76:4.1-4.7)

"On a normal planet, the arrival of the Material Son (Adam) would ordinarily herald the approach of a great age of invention, material progress, and intellectual enlightenment. The post-Adamic era is the great scientific age of most worlds, but not so on Urantia. Though the planet was peopled by races physically fit, the tribes languished in the depths of savagery and moral stagnation" (The Urantia Book 2015, Paper 73:1.1).

"Ten thousand years after the rebellion practically all the gains of the Prince's administration had been effaced; the races of the world were little better off than if this misguided Son had never come to Urantia. Only among the Nodites and the Amadonites was there persistence of the traditions of Dalamatia and the culture of the Planetary Prince (Calagastia)" (The Urantia Book 2015, Paper 73:1.2).

Dalamatia was the city of the former Prince of this world Caligastia. "The city of Dalamatia was located in the Persian Gulf region, corresponding today somewhere within the region of Mesopotamia. Five hundred thousand years ago when the city was established the Persian Gulf extended farther inland since the delta area hadn't yet built up as large as it is today. It is speculated that remnants of the city exist deep below the soil of the region." (Ref. 33)

"The Nodites were the descendants of the rebel members of the Prince's staff, their name deriving from their first leader, Nod, onetime chairman of the Dalamatia commission on industry and trade. The Amadonites were the descendants of those Andonites who chose to remain loyal with Van and Amadon. "Amadonite" is more of a cultural and religious designation than a racial term; racially considered the Amadonites were essentially Andonites. "Nodite" is both a cultural and racial term, for the Nodites themselves constituted the eighth race of Urantia (Earth).

There existed a traditional enmity between the Nodites and the Amadonites. This feud was constantly coming to the surface whenever the offspring of these two groups would try to engage in some common enterprise. Even later, in the affairs of Eden, it was exceedingly difficult for them to work together in peace.

Shortly after the destruction of Dalamatia the followers of Nod became divided into three major groups. The central group remained in the immediate vicinity of their original home near the headwaters of the Persian Gulf. The eastern group migrated to the highland regions of Elam just east of the Euphrates valley. The western group was situated on the northeastern Syrian shores of the Mediterranean and in adjacent territory.

These Nodites had freely mated with the Sangik races and had left behind an able progeny. And some of the descendants of the rebellious Dalamatians subsequently joined Van and his loyal followers in the lands north of Mesopotamia. Here, in the vicinity of Lake Van and the southern Caspian Sea region, the Nodites mingled and mixed with the Amadonites, and they were numbered among the "mighty men of old.

Prior to the arrival of Adam and Eve these groups — Nodites and Amadonites — were the most advanced and cultured races on earth." (The Urantia Book 2015, Paper 73:1.3-1.7)

The Nodite race that had existed for over 120,000 years and they were the last link to the planet's evolutionary race. They have eventually perished under the waters of the Persian Gulf.

"Then Cain went out from the presence of the Lord, and dwelt in the *land of Nod* toward the East side of Eden." (Genesis 4:16)

The creation of the ninth race by Adam and Eve was the cradle of civilization that exists today. It further is the offspring of the following races that spread around the world.

"This paper depicts the planetary history of the violet race, beginning soon after the default of Adam, about 35,000 B.C., and extending down through its amalgamation with the Nodite and Sangik races, about 15,000 B.C., to form the Andite peoples and on to its final disappearance from the Mesopotamian homelands, about 2000 B.C." (The Urantia Book 2015, Paper 78:0.2)

> The Jewish and Palestinian races were likely originated from the Ancient Canaan and Phoenicia races dating 13,000 to 9,800 years ago, "Canaan is often referred to as the "Natufian" culture, which was an Epipaleolithic culture of Africans who migrated into the area thousands of years earlier. The Natufian existed from 13,000 to 9,800 years ago, it was unusual in that it was sedentary, or semi-sedentary, before the introduction of agriculture. The Natufian communities are possibly the ancestors of the builders of the first Neolithic settlements of the region, which may have been the earliest in the world. There is some evidence for the deliberate cultivation of cereals, specifically rye, by the Natufian culture. Generally, though, Natufians

made use of wild cereals, hunted animals like gazelles, and fished" (Ref. 34).

"Although the minds and morals of the races were at a low level at the time of Adam's arrival, physical evolution had gone on quite unaffected by the exigencies of the Caligastia rebellion. Adam's contribution to the biologic status of the races, notwithstanding the partial failure of the undertaking, enormously upstepped the people of Urantia (Earth).

Adam and Eve also contributed much that was of value to the social, moral, and intellectual progress of mankind; civilization was immensely quickened by the presence of their offspring. But thirty-five thousand years ago, the world at large possessed little culture. Certain centers of civilization existed here and there, but most of Urantia (Earth) languished in savagery." (The Urantia Book 2015, Paper 78:1.1-1.2)

"And this is the story of the violet race after the days of Adam and of the fate of their homeland between the Tigris and Euphrates. Their ancient civilization finally fell due to the emigration of superior peoples and the immigration of their inferior neighbors. But long before the barbarian cavalrymen conquered the valley, much of the Garden culture had spread to Asia, Africa, and Europe, there to produce the ferments which have resulted in the twentieth-century civilization of Urantia (Earth)." (The Urantia Book 2015, Paper 78:8.12)

The red strains of the Native Americans did not receive any of the genetic imprints of Adam and Eve unlike any of the other races. Their ancestors fled Asia to settle in North America around fifty thousand years before the arrival of Adam and Eve. The American population was large of European descents of the predominantly blue race which had Adamic strains. From the voyage of Christopher Columbus back in 1492, the people of the Americas went from 10 million to 100 million by the end of the 20th century. It was all part of God's plan to allow the expansion of descendants of Adam and Eve to Americas.

"The North American Indians never came in contact with even the Andite offspring of Adam and Eve, having been dispossessed of their Asiatic homelands some fifty thousand years before the coming of Adam. During the age of Andite migrations the pure red strains were spreading out over North America as nomadic tribes, hunters who practiced agriculture to a small extent. These races and cultural groups remained almost completely isolated from the remainder of the world from their arrival in the Americas down to the end of the first millennium of the Christian era, when they were discovered by the white races of Europe. Up to that time the Eskimos were the nearest to white men the northern tribes of red men had ever seen.

The red and the yellow races are the only human stocks that ever achieved a high degree of civilization apart from the influences of the Andites. The oldest Amerindian culture was the Onamonalonton center in California, but this had long since vanished by 35,000 B.C. In Mexico, Central America, and in the mountains of South America the later and more enduring civilizations were founded by a race predominantly red but containing a considerable admixture of the yellow, orange, and blue.

These civilizations were evolutionary products of the Sangiks, notwithstanding that traces of Andite blood reached Peru. Excepting the Eskimos in North America and a few Polynesian Andites in South America, the peoples of the Western Hemisphere had no contact with the rest of the world until the end of the first millennium after Christ. In the original Melchizedek plan for the improvement of the Urantia races it had been stipulated that one million of the pure-line descendants of Adam should go to upstep the red men of the Americas." (The Urantia Book 2015, Paper 79:5.7-5.9)

How did the red race of the Native Americans blend with the blue race of European descents? It might have helped America embrace immigrants of different nationalities as we are all the descendants of Adam and Eve. 'In the earliest days of New World settlement, relations between the natives (red race) and the newcomers (blue race) were friendly. Native American culture valued trade as a means of binding two tribes and increasing extensive cooperation, so the tribes provided food, clothing, and shelter for the dependent settlers in exchange for metal tools like knives and hatchets. The Native Americans also traded knowledge; they taught the settlers to be self-sufficient.

"The population figure for indigenous peoples in the Americas before the 1492 voyage of Christopher Columbus has proven difficult to establish. Scholars rely on archaeological data and written records from settlers from the Old World. Most scholars writing at the end of the 19th century estimated that the pre-Columbian population was as low as 10 million; by the end of the 20th century most scholars gravitated to a middle estimate of around 50 million, with some historians arguing for an estimate of 100 million or more. Contact with the New World led to the European colonization of the Americas, in which millions of immigrants from the Old World eventually settled in the New World." (Ref. 43)

'As the European settlements began to grow and encroach on more and more Indian lands, relations became more strained. Cultural differences became more insurmountable as British dependence decreased. Large numbers of Native Americans died from European diseases such as small pox and influenza against which they had no immunity. Not known for their appreciation of indigenous cultures in developing British lands, the English followed the lead of the Spanish and French settlers before them and began to demonize the natives in an attempt to excuse their own behaviors (enslaving tribes, stealing land, taking their women as concubines, and over-hunting game).

The British ignored their role in the diseases that were decimating entire tribes and instead chose to view the deaths of the Native

Americans as a sign of divine disfavor. According to John Winthrop, God was killing Indians and their supporters to ensure "our title to this place." And as the "instruments of Providence, divinely appointed to claim the New World from its 'godless' peoples," the colonists felt it was their duty to destroy the "godless savage." In the words of Captain John Underhill, "We had sufficient light from the word of God for our proceedings" -- he refers to the massacre of 500 Pequot men, women, and children at a village along the Mystic River.' (Ref. 47)

Section 3.7: Disappearance of the Lost Fifth Planet Maldek

There was once a planet that orbited between Mars and Jupiter. Today it makes up the asteroid belts. It was a watery planet similar to the size of Earth—a green, flourishing world inhabited by people who were reasonably satisfied with their advancement. Planet Maldek is also known as Lucifer and Tiamat. This civilization had not achieved the fifth dimension culture that we are approaching today. Nevertheless, they attained a stage of life comfortable for all. The Maldekians appeared to be a combination of human and reptilian.

The people of Maldek had a Third-Dimensional civilization that made many of the same technological advancements as Atlantis did. They used this technology to preserve their personal sphere of thoughts, ideas, and actions. The devastation that wracked their biosphere and caused its disintegration resulted from the war.

The Maldek people exceeded terrestrials in intellectual and scientific advancement. Robots managed all essential tasks. The inhabitants had discovered a basic form of space travel but soon found that their fuel was too heavy to allow deep exploration. Their technology permitted them to control their weather, so drought and famine became forgotten. With an abundance of food and no menial tasks, most of the Maldek people wiled away their hours in the sun. They became a selfish, joy-seeking people similar to the majority of terrestrials. These people had likes and dislikes as well as hopes and ambitions. Male and female procreated just as the people of Earth do.

All that remains of this planet that once teemed with life is the asteroid belt—thousands of pieces of cold rock, burned, broken, and dead, spinning lifelessly through space.

* * * * *

DOUG: Planet Maldek was located between Mars and Jupiter before it exploded. Could the remains be the asteroid belt?

JOHN: Yes.

* * * * *

Earth has formally recognized as a planet of human habitation in the angelic realm 993,000 years ago. Biologic evolution had once again accomplished human levels of will and dignity. The Life Carrier group planted life plasma, including that of dinosaurs, into earth waters approximately 550 million years ago (The Urantia Book 2015, paper 62:7.7).

Approximately 120 million years ago, the dinosaurs starved to death, as they required an enormous amount of food. They lacked the intelligence to cope with this situation and became extinct (The Urantia Book 2015, paper 60:2.1-3).

* * * * *

DOUG: Was Maldek exploded by nuclear blasts?

JOHN: No, it exploded because of friction. What I'm receiving is that the planetary movements went askew in the geometry did not allow for the change to happen in a harmonious way and therefore there was a collision.

* * * * *

Maldek was once populated by third-dimensional beings. These entities, after destroying their planetary sphere, were forced to find room to grow their souls in the third dimension. Around sixty thousand years ago, Earth was the only planet in the solar system at the time that fostered spiritual growth on the third dimension.

The movie *Planet of the Apes* is in part a metaphor for fears of nuclear destruction. In reality, the *Planet of the Apes* was Maldek. The population was destroyed by an atomic bomb more than sixty thousand years ago, and the planet later dissolved because of a collision in space.

In the last twenty-five thousand years, the Earth's population has increased from a few hundred thousand people to more than seven billion people. Primarily, the Pleiadeans and several other star systems provided the soul seeds. Two billion souls were transported either by the aliens through spaceships or through the Maldek spiritual realm. Then they filtered through the incarnation processes to take physical form on the earth's surface. Similarly, the 1.9 billion souls of other third-dimension neophytes are from Mars and other planets whose vibratory patterns match Earth's dimensional pattern.

* * * * *

DOUG: What appearance did the people of Maldek have? I asked a psychic this question. However, her vision was blocked, and she could not answer.

JOHN: They were not of human form. I suppose an artist could sketch them. They are difficult to describe because they are not in your frame of reference, and that could be why the psychic had trouble explaining it.

* * * * *

The debris and impact of the explosion created the modified planets' orbits. According to John, this resulted in a collision with one of the

Nibiru moons that caused the explosion of the planet because of the friction. Mars's surface was particularly damaged, leaving it a scarred and barren wasteland. Our moon is heavily cratered because it was originally Maldek's moon and received the brunt of the explosion. It had served as a kind of Noah's ark for Maldek's survivors before it was blasted away and captured by Earth. Another theory circulating is that what was left of Maldek became Earth. Maldek's other moons were also sent hurtling in all directions. Mini planets like Chiron, Quaoar, or Pluto may have once been Maldek moons (Ref. 18).

Billions of lives were lost, and the Maldekians reincarnated on other planets, mostly Earth, where they are replaying the same nuclear scenario of their former home (Ref. 18). There have been deployment of nuclear weapons on Earth that would have started WWIII, but they were thwarted by our space friends;

* * * * *

DOUG: It is true that the teaching of Jesus that man needs to subdue his ego to avoid using nuclear weapons?

JOHN: That is true, but there is also an edict from the Creator God, the highest God. After World War II and the bombs were dropped in Japan, Creator God, because of the dissemination that had an effect on the souls of the people involved and made them irreparable and because God does not destroy, matter cannot be destroyed. And therefore, to stop anything like that ever happening again, there is an edict out that that cannot happen. It's from a higher source than Jesus.

DOUG: Could the second death from the book of Revelation be applied to victims of nuclear explosion where souls were forever lost like from World War II? Could that make the second death?

JOHN: Oh, that is something that is very puzzling. The first deaths are of your ego and the next—yes, I am sure that you must be on the right track. That would follow the logic, yes.

Section 3.8: Red Planet

Mars is a small rocky body once thought to be very earthlike. Like the other terrestrial planets—Mercury, Venus, and Earth—its surface has been changed by volcanism, impacts from other bodies, movements of its crust, and atmospheric effects, such as dust storms. It has polar ice caps that grow and recede with the change of seasons. Areas of layered soils near the Martian poles suggest that the planet's climate has changed more than once, perhaps caused by a regular shift in the planet's orbit (Ref. 44).

Martian tectonism, the formation and change of a planet's crust, differs from Earth's. Where earth tectonics involve sliding plates that grind against one another or spread apart on the seafloors, Martian tectonics seem to be vertical with hot lava pushing upward through the crust to the surface. Periodically, great dust storms engulf the entire planet. The effects of these storms are dramatic, including giant dunes, wind streaks, and wind-carved features (Ref. 44).

Scientists believe that 3.5 billion years ago, Mars experienced the largest known flood in the solar system. This water may even have pooled into lakes or shallow oceans. However, where did the ancient floodwater come from? How long did it last, and where did it go?

At present Mars is too cold and its atmosphere is too thin to allow liquid water to exist on the surface for long. There's water ice close to the surface and more water frozen in the polar ice caps, but the quantity of water required to carve Mars's great channels and flood plains is not evident on—or near—the surface today. Images from NASA's Mars Global Surveyor spacecraft suggest that underground reserves of water may break through the surface as springs. The answers may lie deep beneath Mars's red soil (Ref. 44). Unraveling the story of water on Mars is vital to unlocking its past climate history, which will help us understand the evolution of all planets, including our own. Water is also believed to be a central ingredient for the initiation of life. The evidence of past or present water on Mars is expected to hold clues about past or present life on Mars as well as the potential for life elsewhere in the universe (Ref. 44). John mentioned people there having to go underground for their water supply.

Mars has some geologically remarkable aspects, including the largest volcanic mountain in our solar system, Olympus Mons, and volcanoes in the northern Tharsis region that are so enormous they deform the planet's roundness. There's also a vast equatorial rift valley, the Valles Marineris. This canyon system reaches a distance equivalent to the distance from New York to Los Angeles. Arizona's Grand Canyon could comfortably fit into one of the side canyons of this great chasm.

Like Earth, Mars has seasons due to the planet's tilt on its axis, but it also has a secondary seasonal effect because of its highly elliptical orbit. The southern hemisphere is pointed away from the sun when the planet is farthest from it, resulting in far colder winters (and far hotter summers) than those in the northern hemisphere (Ref. 38).

If we were to live in the northern hemisphere, we'd enjoy about seven months of spring, six months of summer, more than five months of fall, and only about four months of winter. (One year on Mars is about 1.88 earth years, and a day lasts a little more than twenty-four hours.)

The average temperature on Mars is -80 degrees Fahrenheit (-60 degrees Celsius), but temps can range from -195 F (-126 C) in winter near the poles to sixty-eight degrees F (twenty degrees C) during summer near the equator. The temperatures can also change greatly within a single week.

Mars's temperature variations often result in powerful dust storms, which can sometimes shroud the entire planet after just a few days. Though these storms probably wouldn't physically harm us, the dirt could clog electronics and interfere with solar-powered instruments, Vasavada said.

At just 1 percent the density of Earth's atmosphere, the Martian atmosphere is thick enough to burn up meteors smaller than marbles.

Meteorites larger than that are relatively rare, so we'd be unlikely to get hit by them, Vasavada said. We also wouldn't have to worry much about volcanic and tectonic activity while living on Mars (Ref. 39).

"The No. 1 thing an astronaut would be concerned about is the radiation from space," Vasavada said. Unlike Earth, Mars does not have a global magnetic field and thick atmosphere to protect its surface from radiation (Ref. 39).

If we were to experience some unfortunate incident, a message sent home to Earth would take an average of fifteen minutes to get there. While not terribly long, "it is annoying enough that it'd be hard to Skype with anybody," Vasavada said (Ref. 39).

Regarding weather, we might see an occasional wispy cloud or cold morning frost because Martian air contains low levels of moisture from the polar ice caps. However, we would not find any storm clouds in the sky or raindrops hitting the ground. With these clear skies, the Martian night is full of stars. Amateur astronomers would want to look out for Mars' moons, Deimos and Phobos, which can come out at the same time. These satellites, both of which are far smaller than Earth's moon, can also partially eclipse the sun during the day. The daytime sky has an orange tint to it because of all the dust, Vasavada said. Sunrise and sunsets look similar to those on Earth during a very hazy day, except that the area around the sun is blue (Ref.38).

The surface of Mars offers up a few great opportunities for sightseeing. "If we were to colonize Mars, ultimately, there are certainly places that would become national parks," Vasavada said. For example, Olympus Mons is the tallest volcano in the solar system, reaching sixteen miles (twenty-five kilometers) above its surrounding plains. Valles Marineris, on the other hand, is a huge system of valleys, about the distance from Los Angeles to New York. We'd also probably want to visit the Viking landers and Mars's large polar ice caps, which sometimes get dry ice snowfall, Vasavada said.

However, with a gravity that's only 38 percent of Earth's, getting around on Mars would be challenging at first. "Running and fast movements would probably take quite a bit of relearning," Vasavada said. "But it'd be better than moving around on the moon."

The solar wind is not the kind of kite-friendly breeze found on Earth. It is made up of hot, ionized plasma that peels away from the sun's outer atmosphere, hurtling fast-moving charged particles to every corner of the solar system. Those particles with their speed and charge can pull parts of an environment away from a planet like a static balloon lifting the hair from your head as it whizzes past. Earth is lucky. The magnetosphere—the magnetic field covering the world that keeps our poles polar and our compasses pointing north—prevents most of the solar wind from affecting our planet. It is like Earth's anti-frizz helmet, shielding the atmosphere from the solar wind.

Earth is protected by a firmament created by God.

> Again God said, let there be a firmament in the midst of the waters, and let it separate the waters from the waters. Then God made the firmament and divided the waters, which were under the firmament, from the waters which were above the firmament: and it was so. And God called the firmament, Heaven. So the evening and the morning were the second days. God said again, let the waters under the heaven be gathered into one place, and let the dry land appear: and it was so. And God called the dry land, Earth, and he called the gathering together of the waters, Seas: and God saw that it was good. (Genesis 1:6–10)

This firmament protects our atmosphere from any damage caused by incoming solar winds from the sun. Even John had mentioned there are some "grids" in the sky to protect the planet's atmosphere.

* * * * *

DOUG: Okay. Is it true that Earth was dry before, and God created the firmament that helps to water the planet and brings tropical weather around the world?

JOHN: Yes, it was a very slow process of bringing together all the elements to create the beautiful planet of Earth, and it was not just like a magic wand. It did evolve, yes.

DOUG: Okay. So could—I mean, could Mars be going through another garden of Eden like what happened here on Earth according to the book of Genesis? Could that same thing happen to Mars?

JOHN: It could happen, yes.

DOUG: Now I had a conversation with another engineer at work, and I thought it could. It must be too hot to be livable in the future though.

JOHN: No, this planet will not have that problem. It's protected with all kinds of ways to do that, or the Earth would be in a problem right now. So no, there are grids in the sky that only allow the right amount of energy.

* * * * *

Metaphorically hatless, Mars is much less fortunate. Without a strong magnetic field, some scientists believe the solar wind blew away water stored as condensation in the ancient Martian atmosphere. Over time as water continually evaporated from the ground into Mars's atmosphere, the solar wind may have pulled more and more away from the planet until it was dried out.

To do that, the researchers look at stars in other galaxies with similar solar winds and infer how the sun may have acted a long time ago. Scientists believe that the sun was much more intense in its younger years and could have been much more damaging to the Martian atmosphere than it is today.

Liquid water appears to flow from some steep, relatively warm slopes on the Martian surface. First identified in 2011, features known as recurring slope lineae (RSL) were confirmed to be signs of salty water running on the surface of the planet today. The dark streaks that appear seasonally on Martian slopes were found in images taken by the High-Resolution Imaging Science Experiment (HiRISE) camera aboard the Mars Reconnaissance Orbiter (MRO). Spectral analysis of RSL led scientists to conclude salty liquid water causes them (Ref. 46).

The Mars Atmosphere and Volatile Evolution mission (MAVEN) launched on November 18, 2013, and entered orbit around Mars on September 21, 2014. The mission's goal was to explore the planet's upper atmosphere, ionosphere, and interactions with the sun and solar wind. Scientists used MAVEN data to examine the loss of volatile compounds—such as CO_2, N_2, and H_2O—from the Martian atmosphere to space. The understanding of atmospheric loss will give scientists insight into the history of Mars's atmosphere and climate, liquid water, and planetary habitability (Ref. 45).

* * * * *

DOUG: Okay. So Earth and Maldek are the only planets that people lived on the outside of the planet?

JOHN: Well, at this period of time, in the last, I would say, many years, there have been people living on Mars in that past. And there are some people living there today. The government just hasn't released that information. They have bases. They have—

DOUG: On Mars? It seems like it is difficult to live on the surface with extreme cold temperatures.

JOHN: Well, they aren't necessarily on the surface, but there are bases on Mars. And people are living up there. And there are people who have lived on the Moon at times. So you see, it is possible in a spiritual way to handle these kinds of environments that the scientists on earth are not aware of.

DOUG: Will Mars be watery like us in the future?

JOHN: Oh, interesting question. They have had water on Mars in the past. And the people living on top of Mars did go underground because they needed to for their water supply, which was a major part. There are great changes coming in the universe as planets are going to be moving orbits. And it is possible that Mars will go back into being a planet of water, yes.

DOUG: Okay. Now is the consciousness of Mars in the third dimension?

JOHN: Yes.

DOUG: Would Mars go into the fifth dimension eventually?

JOHN: Eventually, all planets are going to move into higher dimensions, yes.

* * * * *

Today the entire universe of the seventh super universe is approaching the Photon Belt. The dark energies are being sucked up by the belt. It occurs every thirteen thousand years (see figure 2). The planet Earth has already been ascending to the fifth dimension, starting in 2012. We will see significant changes in people's consciousness in the years ahead. For those who are resisting the change, they will find themselves living their next lives on another third-dimensional planet while planet Earth experiences the state of higher consciousness of love and light for almost two thousand years. Mars is considered one of those destinations as well as some other third-dimensional planets. The rulers of the dark side (renegades) plan to relocate to Mars, and they will play out their karma of bringing evil to the world, similar to the time of Atlantis during the period after the planet had left the Photon Belt.

* * * * *

DOUG: So there is such a thing as other planets? I thought there was only one planet that we live on, Earth.

JOHN: Well, the planets go around the sun. You've heard of Pluto and Mars and Uranus.

DOUG: Oh.

JOHN: We all have lives on the other planets in the solar system. It's a multiverse—multiple universes. So our horizons will continue to expand as we move beyond the planet Earth.

DOUG: Is it true the inhabitants of Atlantis and Lemuria came from there? Well, you mentioned that souls come from space.

JOHN: Well, they come from a piece of God. Souls are parts of God's Spirit as it manifests on this, in our case, planet Earth, so that could be some of them. You see, the souls in Lemuria were very spiritual. There was no human form. They were spirits. They didn't have bodies that walked around on the planet as you and I do. As they stayed on the planet and became more dense in their spirits, then Atlantis had physical bodies, and there was a fraction of the white light of God within, of what they came to Earth with. So then there were those who turned from the light and wanted to be in control, and those are those people today who are still trying to control the planet, those you people call the Illuminati. They have continued through all these centuries and thousands of years and separated away from the light because that's where witchcraft started.

DOUG: I got in my writing that most of the population here on earth was seeded from Maldek and Mars.

JOHN: No, that is not true. It was seeded by the Pleiadeans.

DOUG: But it came to Earth from Mars?

JOHN: There were civilizations on Mars, and people are living there now. However, they did not seed the earth. The people of the Pleiadeans and several other star systems brought the seeding to the planet.

Chapter 4

Reincarnation

Section 4.1: Reincarnation

Most people are returnees. They've lived earlier, and they'll revisit again. The tenure for this recycling of lifetimes is called the wheel of rebirth. Its engine is karma, which plays a major role in people's action and reaction in life. The cycle goes on, lifetime after lifetime. Love and forgiveness play a fundamental role in transforming the hearts of individuals. People of the Christian faith believe in one life, and a judgment awaits them in heaven or hell when they die. They do not acknowledge the unchanging law of karma that inevitably plucks them back to Earth. They have chosen to ignore many references to the spiritual meaning of life in the Scripture as they remain in the lower worlds of matter, energy, space, and time, which are embodiments of the third dimension. The law of cause and effect governs the universe. Each act and each event are a cause leading to a consequence, and each act and each event is itself the effect of a cause. So cause and effect are indistinguishably linked, but a human life is too brief for us to observe this immense sequence of cause and effect at play. Today we witness consequences of actions that took place prior to our existence. We cannot anticipate the consequences of our actions that take place now. So today we find ourselves confronted with situations that are either causes or effects. The meaning of fate is often not understood. If your friend is going through a difficult time, then it could very well be that he or she is trying to overcome past tendencies and is ready to embrace a new change in life.

People's lives do not terminate when they leave the planet. The consequences of their actions stay with them when they move into the world beyond. They are also with them when they reincarnate. "As I have seen, they that plow iniquity, and sow wickedness reap the same" (Job 4:8). We cannot claim that this person does not deserve the good conditions he or she enjoys in this life and that someone else does not justify being the victim of injustice. We do not know anything about the lesson he or she needs to learn. As long as people do not accept reincarnation, they will not understand divine justice. People have not had enough reincarnations to advance to that state of ascension that is the fifth dimension. These souls will continue their third-dimensional journey. Since we are infinite spirit, there is no time table or deadline to move out of the third dimension. The end-time scenario, as we know it, is all theology based. It does not take into account the planetary realignment of love and light. It is a photon-based energy source emanating from the Creator. Those who are ready to ascend into higher consciousness will still be on planet Earth, but they will see it from a different perspective—through eyes of love in God. Therefore, they will not buy into the trauma and drama that is going on around them. So we will still have a mixture of people on Earth who have different levels of consciousness.

This is an evolution, but there's also free will, so some people have chosen to stay in their ignorance. Now many of those people are dying on the planet right now. They will remain in their current consciousness.

Our mind stays with us throughout our soul journeys. If there were any karma created from our previous life existence, then would need to relive that circumstance by being on the other side of the coin. Our Ascended Masters want to raise our spiritual awareness to be loving people.

"Mind is your ship, and the Adjustor is your pilot, the human will is captain." (The Urantia Book 2015, paper 111:1.9)

We originally came here on earth as light-beings with a pure mind. We would need to return to that state of mind before we revert to the universe. As my father explained from heaven (see chapter 5), "guidance and love and understanding of those on this side that can give me that help necessary to finish healing my soul." Even though he had taken off his physical body from his passing, his mind still had some recollections of his prior life. He stated that his soul (mind) was in healing. He is recuperating in astral heaven to get himself ready for his new life.

We continue to reincarnate until our mind enters the state of love; "ye shall, therefore, be perfect, as your Father which is in heaven, is perfect." (Matt. 5:48). This state of love is the fifth dimension, and when we get there, we have returned to our birthrights.

Some people put off dealing with consequences until after reincarnation, and this is their right. The doors to heaven are never closed, as the church tells us. We do not go to heaven … and *presto*, we are home free. It is through our service work of changing our consciousness through helping others. While helping others, we raise our energy into a giving power of helpful service and unconditional love. We can help and contribute to all those around us. We make better experiences for everyone so they, too, can avoid the trauma and drama. We are becoming more giving, less selfish. The lack of selfishness becomes unconditional love, so everyone is in his or her own perfect space for that evolution. It is not wise to put a number on it because everyone is at his or her positioning whether a new or older soul. Older souls are nearing the end of their last lifetimes. It is up to the person to decide when they feel safe enough to move on. It all happens at the right time. The more love and forgiveness we exhibit, the less fear we will have about our future. It would be helpful to understand that there is always love in heaven. Heaven is on Earth and always has been, but with the fear blocking our vision, heaven could not be something these spirits participated in. People release their fear, and as they do so, they can move up the scale of consciousness and see a little bit more of what heaven would be like. Things begin to fall into place for these people, but it's a gradual progression.

Why is one born to a particular family or a particular country? Why is one healthy, wealthy, illustrious, and powerful or on the contrary, sick, handicapped and wretched? Those who think they are exclusively free must put up with their fate because of their ignorance of the laws that govern the invisible world. The reply to these questions not only helps people unravel the tangled threads of their lives but also gives them the means by which to become masters of their destinies. When considering destiny, we may be inclined to say that such lifetimes are illogical. These people had the opportunity to learn, to understand, and to do something useful, but they seem to have learned nothing, known nothing, and done nothing … except make mistakes! Was there any point in their being alive? It is important to understand people are here for a particular lesson regardless of whether they are aware of it. To rectify this, being kind and loving toward others puts us in a right place to deal with our lives. It is a win-win approach for everyone. We have already lived our past lives over the centuries and millennia. It is good to know that our soul is eternal and that this lifetime will endure into the future. "There are ranges of operations, but God is the same which worketh all in all" (1 Corinthians 12:6). Love is perfect in paradise.

Most likely we will be drawn to those regions we have desired to live. If we use our energies to ask for intelligence, love, and beauty, then we can be sure there is no force that can prevent us from getting there. Living each day in observance of the divine laws helps us contact and unite with spirits of light. When these people leave the Earth and their physical bodies disintegrate into the four elements, they will find themselves in the next world. They will be in the company of spirits they have attracted. We are working to create a society that we will be a part of in the world beyond. The terms heaven and earth have been determined by religion. When we are completely free with no more karmic debts to pay, then we are no longer subject to the law of reincarnation. Love and forgiveness conquer fear and remove the karma from our past third-dimensional lives. From then on, they have gone to the other side of the heavenly regions that become their new dwelling place. They live in bliss and light there. However, among those beings who have realized freedom, a few choose to come back to Earth to support their human brothers and sisters who are suffering. Even after thousands of years, these spirits still remember in the fullness of their heart. They come back down from Nirvana to share in their hardships and help them.

It is common in today's media to come across some direct or indirect references to reincarnation. Some of the stories give a clear understanding of it. How easy it is to lay off a past-life story with "just another dreamer's tall tale." Moreover, it is a real temptation to doubt young children who give in-depth accounts of past lifetimes, even if it means overlooking the candid descriptions of settings, situations, and possible family ties of old. Children relay these stories up until the age of five or six. It is hard for a handful of people in a Christian society to understand this evidence about reincarnation as a foundation for the wonder of birth. So they make up other explanations, perhaps that past-life claims are maybe some fascination to avoid the reality of their dissatisfaction. However, wouldn't it be less of a problem to accept the mere fact of rebirth? Then we would find sense behind the bounds of reincarnation. The Bible has clearly stated the case of it. "My little children, of whom I travail in birth again until Christ be formed in you" (Galatians 4:19). Reincarnation allows people to develop divine love. This opportunity comes from the hardships and insecurities of life as well as in the joys and happiness of living. So we expand the quality of divine love. Love is the only human attribute that can overcome the fear of the unknown. As we move forward with time, our intuition is telling us to go in a particular direction. However, we feel more comfortable going in another direction because we have been there before, even though we might not feel right about it. Fear plays a huge role in that process.

The soul begins each life span with a clean slate. The lords of karma erase the memory of an individual's old mistakes, which allows for a fresh start. This helpfulness sidesteps a dead end. It keeps away the error of someone taking up a new life and squandering it on past-life setbacks like revenge for a lost love, property, or social position. Such memory loss is thus helpful to the soul's progress. Then someplace along the line, the divine Spirit sends a spiritual wake-up call typically during sleep or meditation. Of course, the memory of one's spiritual mission is seldom transmitted in such clear speech. Many go through years of suspicion and ambiguity. They sample one religion or another, trying out different aspects of them. They look in all disciplines for answers. Sometimes a seeker makes few occasional gains. Some inner push leaves him or her unhappy with the knowledge so far gained. Some hidden impulse of the heart drives him or her on in the unending pursuit of God and truth.

The divine energy sustains all life. They are the spirit of truth. It is a fragmentation form of God that resides in our souls and minds. They have long been a part of religious practices throughout the world. Examples of sound in the Christian tradition are chants and hymns. The singing of cantors plays a significant role in Judaism. Some Eastern religions recite *om* for meditation. I have applied this routine, and it had worked well for me. The light of God is embodied symbolically in most religions. Churches have stained glass, precious stones, and skylights. Native Americans use fire and drums for their celebrations—examples of light and sound. Every ceremony represents the effort of people to communicate with God through their customs. The light of God has appeared to saints and mystics, including Kings David and Solomon. Saul of Tarsus had a remarkable encounter with the light of God on the road to Damascus that opened his spiritual eye. Moses saw the light in the burning bush. Throughout history light has been depicted in images of holy people and illustrations of angels. Today many refer to this view in popular books about near-death experiences. It comes as an inner scene or vision. It can be a spark of blue or white light, or it could just be peace in silence. "For the kingdom of God is not meat nor drink, but righteousness, and peace, and joy in the Holy Ghost" (Romans 14:17). As we unfold spiritually, we learn to convey the love of God through service to others, which is how the upcoming fifth dimension raises the spiritual consciousness of the people. It is what will raise the consciousness of the society on the whole to the status of love and light.

A particle of God from space is sent into the lower worlds for us to gain spiritual experience. As we make our way through the experiences of life, the Holy Spirit is within us. Our souls are cleansed by the spiritual exercises. We come into contact from within with the Holy Spirit. Our goal is ascension into the fifth dimension, which is a spiritual freedom in this lifetime. When we have ascended, we become coworkers with God, both here and in the next world. Eventually, people will embrace the fundamental tenets of karma and reincarnation. The Holy Spirit purifies one of karma (sin), making it possible for him to accept the full love of God in this lifetime. Then he gains wisdom, charity, and freedom. As an ascended being, we will no longer reincarnate. We have saved ourselves, and there is no more rebirth. We are free to move around to assist our loved ones that are still experiencing fear and a lack of love from the third dimension.

Dr. Ian Stevenson, the director of personality studies at the University of Virginia, is at the forefront of research on reincarnation. He drew from his fifty years of education and research into the foundations of human personality. Dr. Stevenson's study (Ref. 8) focused on children ages three to five. They not only remember previous existences but can also recognize loved ones from those lives. Many Westerners are shocked by this. Perhaps this is why the world's foremost investigator of the phenomenon, Dr. Ian Stevenson, has attracted so little attention. Since the late 60s, he has documented cases in India, Africa, and the Near and Far East. He also has done work in Britain, the United States, and elsewhere in which young children have amazed their parents with precise details about the people they claim to have been. Some of these children have identified former homes and neighborhoods as well as still-living friends and relatives. They have remembered events in their purported previous lives, including their often violent deaths. Sometimes their birthmarks resemble scars that correspond to wounds that led, they claim, to their deaths.

Déjà vu is a responsive feeling when something happens and we feel like it has happened before, but we think it hasn't. What influences us? An appeal, say, to knights, medieval wars, and battles could be from a distant memory of past lives in a particular period of history. A Civil War fan, no doubt, saw military service during the chaotic 1860s. That war left such a wound on the American nation that it shows itself as a profoundly felt interest in Civil War history. A child with a craving for model airplanes may have flown as a pilot in one of the world wars or even as a spaceship commander from Atlantis. Someone with an emotion of ill will toward an individual church or country for no seeming reason may once have been a sufferer of religious or political fervor. An ailment without a known cause, such as chronic neck pain, may be a tip-off that a person was hanged or beheaded. Whenever intense loves or hates appear with no seeming cause, it means we are drawing the past into the present by a bond.

After we make it through the light, then we are in Nirvana, where our spiritual guides reside. They review our work from our previous incarnation and discuss the needs for our next lesson in life. More likely, our lessons will involve family or friends whom we have lived with before. Our spiritual guide will discuss our options with us. Imagine we are back in the ether, and we are getting ready to design our next life. To use an analogy, we are given a form with checkboxes for the kind of life we want to have. We fill out the paperwork indicating we wish to focus on learning compassion, perseverance, and kindness. We also elect to have a large impact on the planet instead of just living in our quiet little corner of the globe. We turn in our paperwork to our spiritual guide whose task it is to help us find a life circumstance we can be born into so that we will learn these things. Working his vast ethereal computer, he enters all our preferences, and the computer pops out twenty families who have the particular life situation we would need in order to learn compassion, perseverance, and kindness. Using other considerations, such as the people we'd like to marry, their locality, and the political situation surrounding these families, the computer reduces the choice down to ten. The computer reduces the search further by analyzing the families' current financial situations. Two families remain. The computer gives us the information on each family with a projection of how likely it is that we will accomplish in learning compassion, perseverance, and kindness, and we read it carefully. We are given time in between incarnations there until we have recovered from the wound of our past death. About 54 percent of the time (Ref. 1), we will choose our parents with the similar spiritual vibration as ours. Everything is contingent on our free will.

* * * * *

DOUG: Are birthdates determined by people's past lives?

JOHN: You come in with the traits you need to transform into the new energy of love. Your personality traits, which are your human qualities, are the different signs of the Zodiac. As you matched up with your masters before you reincarnated and were writing your script, and you came in at the exact time necessary to have those traits and to be able to identify those other people that have similar characteristics to you because of your sign. So, those were the characters that you came into the manifest, but also transform into more positive, loving, and projective characteristics so that you can move on to your spiritual growth. They're your guideposts of what you need to improve in your life.

Section 4.2: Origin of Souls

New souls are those souls that have not been to Earth. All souls were created at the same time, and some came to Earth at various periods of history. Some did not come to Earth at that time and waited for other opportunities. Planet Earth will be been overpopulated if they all have come at once. They are around the universe in various places serving, experiencing, learning, exploring, and adventuring.

However, the people were prioritized for birthing on Earth in order to keep the population in balance. The ones who came from other planets are interested in transposing and transmuting their energy into a higher level, and they can do that much easier here on this planet. The energy on Earth allows them to change from fear to love much easier. So this is a very desirable planet to come to, but they do not all come at once. So if we have not had our opportunity to come yet, then we would be new souls. Alternatively, if we have only had a chance to come a few times at this point, we have not gained the wisdom and the experience necessary to move on.

There were a few hundred thousand people on Earth twenty-five thousand years ago (Ref. 1). Today there are more than seven billion souls. People of Pleiades and several other star systems seeded Earth. Souls of people from the former planet Maldek and Mars have come to Earth as transfers to continue their third-dimension experience. Some entities from Maldek had come here by spaceships approximately fifty thousand years ago before a collision destroyed the planet. What the remains are asteroid belts. The souls of Martians came to Earth by the way of incarnation. The planet's environment became too inhospitable for the entities to continuing their third-dimensional experience there. They came here to grow their energies to a higher dimension. It is unlikely there will be any further new souls coming to Earth from outer space since Earth is one of the younger planets in all of God's creation. Other planets and galaxies have grown significantly further along. Instead they will come here to assist us in growing in the fifth dimension. The Creator has not set the time table for that to happen, according to John.

* * * * *

DOUG: As we are approaching last days, what happens to the people who are still in third dimension? Would their souls move to another planet after their death to continue in the third dimension?

JOHN: Exactly. That is exactly what will happen. The planet is full of souls at all levels of growth. Some are new souls, and some are old souls. The new souls still need to have their levels of learning and experience to move into higher consciousness. So they will, as you said, move to another planet that will look just like Earth, and they will continue their progress not even realizing they have been transported.

* * * * *

Reincarnation is about moving forward until we come back to the oneness of God. When that happens, then reincarnation is no longer necessary. We have advanced to a new consciousness whereby we can come back and help others. We can go to other planets that are going through a similar process of what we are doing here on Earth. We can go and help others in different planets do all kinds of things as far as proceeding with studies in music, art, or other fields. We have numerous opportunities to move on to energy. There are lives on other planets of our solar system. John would call this multiverse, which means multiple universes.

* * * * *

DOUG: But they are friendly?

JOHN: We are all made of spirit, and that is what is going to bring us all together. It does not matter how you look. Every blade of grass is made of spirit. We are one with that grass, that tree, the flowers, the birds, the animals, the snake that is peeling its skin. That is the energy, and we are changing *skins*. We are outgrowing old ideas and moving into a new understanding. We are transforming like snakes do, so it does not matter what the form is. We are all spirit.

Door to Glory

DOUG: Is our DNA our soul?

JOHN: At a soul level, you have access to all conscious levels, but now you only have access to the material world level. So you were limited to the material world level. That is why so few people have progressed into Christ consciousness and become ascended masters over the years. They broke the mold of the third dimension by leaving and going beyond the visibility or the spirituality of higher consciousness. Currently, your DNA is being reinstated, and you will be able to use all of your brain power. Scientists have often called some of it junk DNA, which is totally inaccurate. God does not make junk.

DOUG: So that's for spiritual?

JOHN: Spiritual—the scientists do not have machines to even calibrate.

DOUG: What is consciousness of level thirteen which is the great mystery (see table 2)?

JOHN: Well, that is a great mystery because the DNA has stopped you from being able to see and go beyond. There are still more levels higher beyond that you are going to be able to accomplish if you grow spiritually into the new age. So at this point, calling it a mystery is fine because it is unknown yet to mankind.

DOUG: Now according to Internet sources I got on the computer Internet, for oldest living people, you see many around 117 years old. Could this be the term limit for the DNA? One hundred and twenty years?

JOHN: Well, the DNA has been and is now being restored in peoples' physical and spiritual bodies. People can live much longer than that if they open up to the new higher consciousness that is coming on planet Earth at this point. So there is no specific time for life or death; it is totally available to you to live. In fact, that walk-in—you asked about Anna—lived to be 606 years. So you see, when it talks about Methuselah, those things are happening even today. There is a master on Earth called Babaji who has lived for thousands of years. So putting a time frame on this situation is a man-made way to limit yourself.

* * * * *

When the fifth dimension had arrived on the planet Earth, God had restored the DNA to beyond the 120-year term limit. The age limit restriction was imposed thirteen thousand years ago around the time of the flood. "Therefore the Lord said, my spirit shall not always strive with the man because he is but flesh, and his days shall be a hundred and twenty years" (Genesis 6:3). The ascended masters were the exception to the rule since they have already ascended to the fifth dimension. Let's take a look at the following table for the list of top ten oldest survivors;

Table 6 – List of Oldest Survivors (Ref. 9)

Rank	Sex	Birth date	Death Date	Age (at death) or as of 03-24-2015	Place of death or resident
1	F	02-21-1875	08-04-1997	122 years, 164 days	France
2	F	09-24-1880	12-30-1999	119 years, 97 days	United States
3	F	07-16-1875	03-21-1993	117 years, 248 days	United States
4	F	08-29-1880	04-16-1998	117 years, 230 days	Canada
5	F	03-05-1898	Living	117 years, 19 days	Japan
6	F	09-14-1889	08-27-2006	116 years, 347 days	Ecuador
7	F	07-04-1898	Living	116 years, 263 days	United States
8	F	01-18-1879	07-12-1995	116 years, 175 days	Japan
9	F	08-15-1890	12-11-2006	116 years, 118 days	United States
10	F	08-26-1896	12-4-2012	116 years, 100 days	United States

DOUG: If a person dies unexpectedly due to his smoking or drinking, could that create a new karma for his soul?

JOHN: Well, that's a very good question. You don't die before your contract. That is all scripted before you come in, and as people leave, it is on the schedule. So sometimes they leave through calamities such as earthquakes and tidal waves. Some people leave through car accidents, and some people leave through smoking, as you mentioned, or alcoholism, other addictions or medical problems. Those are all usually the best way for that person to transform into the spiritual side at that particular time, so it was, it's the vehicle for their shifting into the spiritual world. And, if they have not raised their consciousness from when they came in into a higher level of viewing spiritually, they will return and continue on the same consciousness through having another opportunity to clear that energy into a higher consciousness.

DOUG: Would love of God help a person live up to a full contract?

JOHN: Exactly, that's what we're here on earth to learn, is that all there is love and that is the answer, and when we move into that our other problems are resolved.

Douglas Grady

DOUG: Now today here on Earth, how will we know who the master is?

JOHN: Master?

DOUG: I mean, who can we go to release the negative energy so that we can receive the daily bread from God?

JOHN: Well, the twelve-step programs have twelve steps to do that. There's counseling that you can go to. That is the kind of counseling that Marilyn is involved with, helping others release those energies that are not productive and are barriers to your conscious connection to God. I think you are right on the money when you are talking about this, Doug, because so many masters talk about moving into the consciousness of God. However, they do not talk about removing what's in the way so that you can do it. You are right on the money. Because without the action of—well, it is called purifying your soul. If you just keep doing what you've always done, then you are not making spiritual growth. So something has to change. As you release all your fears, list them on paper, and know that they are barriers to God's consciousness inside your heart. Replace them with love and grace. Do this for all the negative issues in your life—people, places, bosses, relatives, institutions, whatever you are angry at, including all of the situations or people who have harmed you. So you go through a forgiveness process. However, as you are releasing people, understand that you wrote the script they played, and you need to say, "I love you because the Christ in them is the Christ in you. So if you do not have love for yourself, you cannot love others." Also, you love yourself when you love them because they are a mirror of you reflecting the Christ love of them back to you. So you love them because they are part of the Christ consciousness. So then you tell them, "I forgive you," because you want to give up those negative emotions that are holding you back from growth for a new today. So then you thank them for playing that part so well that you finally had to come to change that energy and find compassion, forgiveness, love, and gratitude that they were in your life. So you can let that energy go. So you have then transformed. That is why you came to Earth. You have transformed now that resentment or that perception of a person that damaged you in some way. You've transformed your anger into loving energy that is no longer holding you back from your spiritual growth.

DOUG: Now suppose if they come back and reincarnate and they are expected to live a better life, but that person's still showing dark energy. Could his life be shortened?

JOHN: Energy is forever. No eternal energy is ever shortened. You never lose energy. It transforms, but you never lose it.

DOUG: What I mean is if he is not following the right path or, as you call it, the script, his DNA would be programmed to live a certain number of years, right?

JOHN: No, that is not how it works. Everybody will eventually return to God. It is just a matter of when.

DOUG: But I am talking about if the person does not fulfill his or her script?

JOHN: There's no judgment. See, you are trying to judge that a person should do it by a certain time, and there is an eternity.

DOUG: Okay, yeah, life is eternal.

JOHN: People can keep coming back as often as they choose until the right lessons have been learned. It is not right or wrong. It is just when are they open to handling it and to making that transformation, and not everybody can address the fears he or she's gone through. People will judge, but we need to let them do it in their own time. It's between them and God.

DOUG: Now if they continue to live in the third dimension, I guess heaven on earth is a foolproof system, so everyone will attain it. Is that correct? We need to be more loving.

JOHN: That is what this dimension is about. We release all the dark energy and move into the light of God where it will be all harmonious and pleasant and caring.

DOUG: If priests or pastors were worshipping Satan and taught the Word of God, is there any forgiveness for their soul progression?

JOHN: Yes. Definitely. Yes, everyone—no one, no one is left out from the grace of God or from the kingdom within. It is truly a spiritual individual choice, and that is why reincarnation has been necessary for people to come back and in various ways to learn. It was a choice that the ultimate best favor of their moving on in the universe.

DOUG: Now when people reincarnate, would the chakra stay with the soul?

JOHN: Yes. Those energies that you each time come into clean a little bit more. So it is a gradual process with each. You are exactly right. With each in a reincarnation.

DOUG: Was King David Christ? I guess he was Christ.

JOHN: We are all Christ because we are all children of God, and that is the God energy.

Section 4.3: Reference of Reincarnation in Scripture

DOUG: Now could the church have manipulated the New Testament to a certain degree?

JOHN: They manipulated it to a significant degree. Some of the words they put in Jesus's mouth were not said. They left out some that were. They took out reincarnation except for about half of a dozen passages they let slip through the book. So there are a few indications in the Bible of reincarnation, which most people do not pick up on because the churches do not stress it at all. They just ignore them, and so people do not even know they are there. So yes, the New Testament was an opening for people to look at themselves and learn to love their neighbors as themselves. However, there were also many misinterpretations of or changes to dogma so that it kept them going to Jesus instead of God directly. The Catholic church's undertaking was to prohibit people from thinking they could reach God on their own.

DOUG: You have mentioned reincarnation in your gospel, the book that you wrote.

JOHN: Yes.

DOUG: Was there compelling evidence there in it before it was removed?

JOHN: There were Bible verses that specifically talked about returning and continuing spiritual growth. Also, the verses that are in the Bible that did not get removed are just—you might say—a step away from directly saying that you reincarnate. They asked Jesus who he was. Was he John? Was he Elijah? Was he one of several prophets who had died? Was he one of those who had returned? So Jesus said, "Who do you think I am?" So one of the disciples spoke up and said, "Well, you are the Christ." So you see, they saw him as if he was a returning soul, and in this case, he was one of those. But he did not say it directly. He just said, "Who do you think I am?" So there are various verses like that that refer to that but do not come right out explicitly like the ones that the church removed.

DOUG: Where in the Bible has the most evidence of reincarnation?

JOHN: I would say, well, there are several verses throughout the Bible. However, as you read the book of John, especially chapters 13 through 17, you start to understand that the spiritual aspects of your being and existence. Gradually, if people are meditating, they come to an understanding that there is more than one life and that the spirit lives on, and this is a continuation of growth in that spirit of love. So it is a combination that people are becoming through reading the information, especially in the book of John. That is the reality of that experience to say, "Oh, there is more than one life, and this person has another chance to continue their path." There is an old commercial on television that says you only go around once. When people think like that, that is a bad thing to have in their memory because it is not accurate as far as what goes on in truth. So if you remove those old understandings and realize you keep returning until you have come back into the oneness of God, then the truth is there for part of who you are. So it is learning and knowing through inside.

* * * * *

DOUG: Now was New Testament supposed to be based on the Kingdom of God where there is no mediator between man and God?

JOHN: Exactly. Jesus came to say the Father and I are one, and the Father, the Kingdom of Heaven is within. And those were his significant changes from what people were taught in the churches, and that's why churches do not preach that from the pulpit.

DOUG: Heart disease is the leading cause of death in America? Could this be due to lack of love or could this be resulting from the busyness of life?

JOHN: I think you hit the nail on the head. It's a lack of love. You see, if you are closed off to love, you cannot be alive. And so, therefore, what you people call pass over happens because you are without that loving energy which needs to flow through you. And if your chakras are closed, it cannot flow through your heart and nurture the rest of your body with that spiritual energy that is necessary for life. So many people will have heartbreaking situations, and the heart attack will come on. In a short time following their heart has been broken they have heartbreaking situations where children die, or spouses leave, or various things, financial disasters, and it breaks their heart. And so, heart attacks are most often from an emotional cause, which is the lack of love, you are right.

DOUG: There's much evidence for clues of reincarnation in the gospel of John you wrote, especially chapter 3, I think it was. Okay, now do souls pick a family to come back to?

JOHN: Well, you reincarnate primarily in soul groups. So you have probably. This is mostly likely the same people who have been your mothers, fathers, brothers, uncles, aunts, friends, and relations. So they come down and play different parts for you.

So Marilyn had a friend that she dated for a while, and he was safe to date. She knew at one point because she knew from her psychic abilities that at one point she had been married to him in a past life. At another time he had been her wife. So she was the husband. They had many lifetimes together, playing different parts that were necessary for their spiritual growth. Also, her parents in this life were her parents in several other past lives.

Section 4.4 Jesus The Miracle Worker

The soul of Jesus had taken him a soul journey from the life of Adam to the life of Jesus where the populace of Earth was perilously in danger of losing contact with the Heavenly Father of creation similarly to what had happened to the former planet Maldek that had crumbled into asteroid belts over 50,000 years ago.

"Now there are also many other things which Jesus did, the which if they should be written every one, I suppose the world could not contain the books that should be written, Amen" (John 21:25).

DOUG: I've got a few questions, but maybe one or two that I would like to ask you. You mentioned in your Gospel of John that all of what Jesus has done could not be written in one book. So I want to ask you about Jesus reincarnating as a baby as some of the major religious leaders. Is this the proof that Jesus was serving for all humanity?

JOHN: Jesus was serving for the whole of mankind to learn about love, which not all the religious leaders of the world have done. He did not reincarnate as leaders, but he often would come to those who prayed and asked for his assistance, and he gave guidance to many leaders at various times. Some people do not know how spiritually connected Lincoln was, but there was a séance for him in the White House, and Lincoln was very much in tune with getting guidance from Jesus. So you see, Jesus appears in different ways to different people in different situations, but he did not reincarnate as a person as being a leader of a country.

The spirit of Jesus has taken on prominent roles such as Amilius, Adam, Enoch, Hermes, Melchizedek, Joseph, Joshua, Asaph, Jeshua, Zend, Buddha, and Krishna in aligning man to the realization of his divine birthright. Jesus' soul name is Sananda. That represents the wholeness of God. The soul name is reserved only for those who have attained it.

* * * * *

DOUG: Do the names of ascended masters like David, Elijah, Moses, and so on, stay the same after they have ascended to the fifth dimension?

JOHN: No. They don't. They go back to their spiritual names. They were just a projection of a larger soul of who they really, truly are. Just as Jesus has the soul name of Sananda, Moses and Elijah and the others go back to their original souls, which is their wholeness. On earth, people are not whole; that's why they're looking and searching for God. So, when they pass back into their wholeness, they have their spiritual name.

* * * * *

AMILIUS

> Amilius was the first expression of Divine Mind (the Logos); the Christ-soul before his incarnation into

a physical body (corresponding to Genesis 1). He was the entity Cayce identified as living in the lost civilization of Atlantis who redirected the process of human evolution by creating a more appropriate physical form for the influx of souls to incarnate into rather than incarnating into the ape-like human form which souls had entangled themselves in. The first wave of souls (known as "the sons of men") became entrapped in the physical plane accidentally through their misuse of free will. These events gave rise to the legend of the "fall of the angels." The second wave ("the sons of God") consisted of those souls led by Amilius (the Christ-soul) who voluntarily became entrapped in the flesh as Adam to assist the first wave. (Ref. 35, Cayce 2016)

* * * * *

DOUG: Let me ask you about Atlantis—fascinating story. Who was behind that thinking, that disappearance of civilization?

JOHN: Marilyn explained this once in one of her channelings several years ago. When planet Earth was first brought into being, it was created in the Glory of God as an accentuate being. Earth is living. It's a living form, just like people have form. A planet is a spiritual form. And the people who came to earth, it was eons and eons of evolution for plants and so forth to come about. It did not happen in seven days. That's just a condensation of how it came together. So as people began to arrive on planet Earth from space (because you are all seeded from space family), they came in their Christendom and their Christ consciousness.

The first continent was Lemuria. It was completely spiritual. People did not have bodies like humans do. They had spiritual bodies, but they were not physically real bodies. Jesus first came in a spiritual, nonphysical body to that continent as some people call it the first

Adam. Then another continent, Atlantis, appeared, and those who inhabited it were also spiritually oriented; however, as their civilization of Atlantis progressed, they became highly technically evolved. The Lemurians were peaceful, farm-type people who were happy with living on the land and sea and having non-sophisticated lives. The Atlanteans were much more aggressive and technologically oriented. Their technology progressed even beyond what you have on planet Earth right now. They cultivated crystals for their energy, energy so strong that the crystals that were operating in Atlantis were the power supply. Some of them were enormous and created numerous technical advances and abilities beyond what you see today.

* * * * *

ADAM

> The Adamic mission on experimental, rebellion-seared, and isolated Urantia (Earth) was a formidable undertaking. And the Material Son and Daughter early became aware of the difficulty and complexity of their planetary assignment. Nevertheless, they courageously set about the task of solving their various problems. But when they addressed themselves to the all-important work of eliminating the defectives and degenerates from among the human strains, they were quite dismayed. They could see no way out of the dilemma, and they could not take counsel with their superiors on either Jerusem or Edentia. Here they were, isolated and day by day confronted with some new and complicated tangle, some problem that seemed to be unsolvable. (The Urantia Book 2015, paper 75:1.1)

"Under normal conditions the first work of a Planetary Adam and Eve would be the coordination and blending of the races. But on Urantia (Earth), such a project seemed just about hopeless, for the races, while biologically fit, had never been purged of their retarded and defective strains" (The Urantia Book 2015, paper 75:1.2).

> Adam and Eve found themselves on a sphere wholly unprepared for the proclamation of the brotherhood of man, the world groping about in abject spiritual darkness and cursed with confusion worse confounded by the miscarriage of the mission of the preceding administration. Mind and morals were at a low level, and instead of beginning the task of effecting religious unity, they must start all anew the work of converting the inhabitants to the simplest forms of worship. Instead of finding one language ready for adoption, they were confronted by the common confusion of hundreds upon hundreds of local dialects. No Adam of the planetary service was ever set down in a more difficult world; the obstacles seemed insuperable and the problems beyond creature solution. (The Urantia Book 2015, paper 75:1.3)

* * * * *

DOUG: Now did God create a new human race through Adam and Eve by creating consciousness?

JOHN: Exactly, that's what it's about. Jesus came to this planet several times, just like everybody evolves spiritually, and his earliest incarnation was Adam. He brought in this new energy so that the planet Earth could change from the old, you might call it barbaric, way of addressing life.

DOUG: OK. If Jesus was Adam, who was Eve?

JOHN: Mary Magdalene.

DOUG: Really?

JOHN: She was also his equal in spiritual development. The Bible disclaimed her because they didn't want women in the days of the early church to have the value and authority that a man would have. It was their way of discrediting women to make her less than Jesus.

DOUG: Were Jesus and Mary Magdalene considered twin souls?

JOHN: Yes.

DOUG: Now, we talked about Jesus and Mary Magdalene. What were Mary Magdalene's other incarnations? We have spoken about Jesus', but how about Mary Magdalene?

JOHN: That's an interesting question. Give me a moment. She has appeared as several nuns in the Catholic Church. Teresa was one, and the most recent lifetime, Mother Teresa. So, she has kept her energy in ways that are helpful and loving to those around her, and she has provided spiritual answers for people, especially within the Catholic Church, to find more mystical people within the Church.

So, she has tried to perpetuate that energy and those lessons, but not all her incarnations have become famous. But she was a Teresa in a past life as a nun, and she was another Teresa in this life.

* * * * *

"Adam and Eve were the founders of the violet race of men, the ninth human race to appear on Urantia. Adam and his offspring had blue eyes, and the violet peoples were characterized by fair complexions and light hair color—yellow, red, and brown" (The Urantia Book 2015, paper 76:4.1).

"And the man called his wife's name Eve, because she was the mother of all living. Unto Adam also and to his wife did the Lord God make coats of skins, and clothed them." (Genesis 3:20-21).

"Both the physical and spiritual visions of Adam and Eve were far superior to those of the present-day peoples. Their special senses were much acuter, and they were able to see the midwayers and the angelic hosts, the Melchizedeks, and the fallen Prince Caligastia, who several times came to confer with his worthy successor. They retained the ability to see these celestial beings for over one hundred years after the default. These particular senses were not so acutely present in their children and tended to diminish with each succeeding generation" (The Urantia Book, paper 76:4.5).

* * * * *

DOUG: Are we sons and daughters of God because we are descendants of Adam and Eve?

JOHN: We're sons and daughters of God because we have the same light within us that God has created. We are created in the image of God, which is light. Marilyn just wrote a chapter describing the light within. It is not a hereditary physical childhood. It is your spiritual childhood that you are a child of God.

* * * * *

HERMES

> "Hermes" of the Cayce readings is the one who designed and build the Great Pyramid under the direction of Ra-Ta. There is another historical connection between a "Hermes" and Egypt which is found in the Hellenistic writings attributed to Hermes Trismegistus—the sage who began the Hermetic tradition. Hermes is also referred to in the Poimandres, as the "shepherd of men" who teaches that "the Word which came forth from the Light is the Son of God." Accordingly, Hermes also taught that human nature consists of such divine elements as Nature, Light, Mind, and Life; and that by recognizing them we may return to the invisible, immaterial world of Truth. (Ref. 35, Cayce 2016, Edgar Cayce on the Reincarnation Past Lives of Jesus Christ)

MELCHIZEDEK

> Melchizedek was the "king of Salem" and "priest of the most high God" who shares bread and wine with Abraham in Genesis 14:18-20. He is also mentioned both in the Dead Sea Scrolls (11QMelch) and the Melchizedek Nag Hammadi codex where he appears as a cosmic angelic figure, the risen Christ. Hebrews 5:8-10 calls Jesus "a high priest after the order of Melchizedek," which explains how Jesus was a priestly Messiah without being a Levite. Per Cayce, Melchizedek wrote the Book of Job, which contains many mysterious passages that Cayce liked. Cayce once said, "For, as the sons of God came together to reason, as recorded by Job, "WHO recorded same? The Son of Man! Melchizedek wrote Job!." (Ref. 35, Cayce 2016, Edgar Cayce on the Reincarnation Past Lives of Jesus Christ)

* * * * *

DOUG: The way I wrote it in my book, I quoted your statement about, you know, Jesus not dying on the cross. So, I wrote down—I took a verse from your book, 3:16, "For God so loved the world that he gave his one and only Son, that whoever believes in him shall not perish but have eternal life." I mentioned that if we ascended this dimension, we would have eternal life through Christ consciousness, not Jesus Christ.

JOHN: All right. That's a good way to put it because at the end of his life Jesus represented Christ consciousness. He went into unconditional love when he said on the cross, "God, forgive them for they know not what they do." That's unconditional love. And he was exemplifying that. So, that Christ consciousness, he was our example that we too could forgive those who are around us and love them. Those are our lessons on earth spiritually to love our neighbors as ourselves. He was exemplifying what Christ consciousness represented, and it wasn't that he was the only Christ. We've had several Christed beings, several masters who've mastered this spiritual trip of entry into ascension, who have come back to earth. We have many who have come to restore and help bring truth to all of this understanding today, and he was an example. He was Jesus, the Christ, but he wasn't the only Christ. So, instead of saying "Christ Jesus," say "Jesus, the Christ," and then you can also have other masters. They were Christed also. So you're correct that he represented that.

DOUG: Now, Paul wrote many New Testament books?

JOHN: Right.

DOUG: I wonder if Jesus was there to help him.

JOHN: Yes. There's a lot of truth in that because Jesus has been there to support many different people throughout time. That spiritual soul came through in the Old Testament, had lives before Jesus—Enoch, Joseph, he was Melchizedek—and he has had many lives after his life as Jesus in more current times. So, he has come through often to help people. And yes, his guidance is always, always beneficial.

* * * * *

JOSEPH

"Joseph was the son of Jacob who became the Prince of Egypt. The story of Joseph appealed to Cayce, not only for its Egyptian location but its endorsement of dream guidance and also for Joseph's escape from the pit (anticipating Jesus' resurrection). In fact, there are many parallels between the lives of Joseph and Jesus" (Ref. 35, Cayce 2016, Edgar Cayce on the Reincarnation Past Lives of Jesus Christ).

ENOCH

Enoch is mentioned in several pseudepigraphical works (The Book of Enoch, 2 Enoch, and 3 Enoch) as well as some Kabbalistic writings, in addition to his brief mention in Genesis 5:18-24 which concludes, "And Enoch walked with God: and he was not, for God took him." The Book of Enoch describes the fall of the "Watchers" into materiality and Enoch's heavenly sojourns as well as his transfiguration into the angel Metatron. It is revealed to him the future up to the time of the Messiah as well. Enoch also learns about the hierarchy of the angelic realm and the divine "throne-chariot" of Ezekiel. The Book of Enoch introduces a messianic figure referred to as "the Son of Man." In the canonical New Testament, Enoch is mentioned in Hebrews 11:5 and Jude 14-15. The passage in Jude quotes directly from the pseudepigraphical Book of Enoch which shows the author of Jude, the brother of Jesus, considered the Book of Enoch to be sacred scripture. (Ref. 35, Cayce 2016, Edgar Cayce on the Reincarnation Past Lives of Jesus Christ)

* * * * *

DOUG: There is another passage from the book of Hebrews, 11:5, Was Enoch transmuted?

JOHN: Enoch. He raised his energy to be more Godlike.

DOUG: Enoch. He was translated because he found God within. "By faith was Enoch translated, that he should not see death: neither were he found: for God had translated him. For before he was translated, he was reported of that he had pleased God." So, who translated Enoch? Was it the angels, or where was he translated?

JOHN: I think they're talking about his consciousness moved into Christ consciousness. Enoch was one of Jesus' reincarnations. Jesus has had many reincarnations. He did not become the Christ through one lifetime, just as the people on earth right now are not becoming Christ conscious through one lifetime. Everyone needs to leave the old energies from the other existences and clean that out, so it becomes a pure soul. Enoch, and Jesus in that lifetime, was able to clean out enough of his older consciousness to move into that higher realm. He continued the path until we knew him as Jesus as the wholeness of God in the Bible But it was his prior life where he was trying and working on this and accomplished a great deal

DOUG: At that time, I guess the writer of the Old Testament wrote that he was no longer seen in society anymore because he was gone, he was taken away, "And Enoch walked with God, and he was no more seen: for God took him away. (Genesis 5:24) So, could he physically disappear? Or he moved to a different realm? How did that work?

JOHN: There have been certain people, such as Elijah, who went to heaven in bodily transition. Enoch was spiritually ascended enough that when he transformed into, we call it—most people call it—heaven, but it is nirvana, so that he could transform into a spiritual essence without all the dying problems that many humans have. So, he was elevated enough to be able to make a smooth transition (His spirit left his body like an "out of body experience," but he never returned to his body). So, it was not that he did it without his body, but it was a very comfortable one compared to some people having great ills.

* * * * *

JOSHUA

Joshua was the warrior who led the Israelites into the Promised Land. However, this incarnation of the Christ-soul is more difficult to account for given his military campaigns described in the Bible. Jesus' suffering on the cross would certainly have paid his karmic debt for this transgression as well. But Cayce also saw Joshua as a member of a family which had produced many highly-skilled [sic] spiritual counselors. One of Joshua's roles was as a scribe for Moses who psychically dictated much of the material from the books traditionally attributed to him. It explains how Joshua could have remembered to include such details as the creation of the universe and his death. Hebrews 4:8-10 identifies Jesus as a better Joshua, as Joshua led Israel into the rest of Canaan, but Jesus leads the people of God into "God's rest," salvation. Among the early Church Fathers, Joshua is considered a type of Jesus Christ (Ref. 35, Cayce 2016, Edgar Cayce on the Reincarnation Past Lives of Jesus Christ).

* * * * *

DOUG: I'm going to read this statement coming from Joshua: "For lo, the stone that I have laid before Joshua: upon one stone shall be seven eyes: behold, I will cut out the graving thereof, saith the Lord of hosts, and I will take away the iniquity of this land in one day." (Zechariah 3:9). Now I know one day to the Lord is one thousand years for humankind. So, could that be the millennium, the second coming of Jesus?

JOHN: There's a fallacy that God doesn't do anything. It's not a person. God is a spirit of loving energy. So, when it says, "I will cut out the graving," the spirit doesn't do that kind of thing. Spirit just is. And it flows through people for people to be loving toward themselves and others and to be of service. So, to me, that would be from the church again.

* * * * *

ASAPH

"Asaph was the music director and seer who served under David and Solomon (Ref. 35, Cayce 2016, Edgar Cayce on the Reincarnation Past Lives of Jesus Christ)."

JESHUA

"Jeshua (Joshua) was the high priest who helped organize the return from exile and the rebuilding of the temple (as recounted in the books of Ezra and Nehemiah) and who is claimed by Cayce to have compiled and translated the books of the Bible "Asaph was the music director and seer who served under David and Solomon (Ref. 35, Cayce 2016, Edgar Cayce on the Reincarnation Past Lives of Jesus Christ)."

ZEND

Cayce identified "Zend" (also spelled "Zen," "Zan," "Sen" or "San") as the father of Zoroaster, the founder of the Zoroastrian religion (of Magi fame), and the source of inspiration for the Avesta, the sacred Zoroastrian scriptures. However, the word "Zend" in Zend-Avesta means "commentary" and Zoroaster's father was named Pourushaspa. It appears the sleeping Cayce was inspired by the Book of Esther and Matthew's story of the Magi to base this "Zend" personality upon. Of interest is the fact that it was during the Israelites' exile in Babylon when Judaism (and then Gnosticism, Christianity, and Islam) incorporated the Zoroastrian theological system of monotheism, the Messiah, the dualistic struggle between good and evil, light and darkness, angels and demons, heaven and hell, God and Satan, the Last Judgment and the Resurrection of the Dead. ("Asaph was the music director and seer who served under David and Solomon (Ref. 35, Cayce 2016, Edgar Cayce on the Reincarnation Past Lives of Jesus Christ)"

JESUS

"Gabriel had reminded Jesus that there were two ways in which he might manifest himself to the world in case he should choose to tarry on Urantia for a time. And it was made clear to Jesus that his choice in this matter would have nothing to do with either his universe sovereignty or the termination of the Lucifer rebellion. These two ways of world ministry were:

His own way—the way that might seem most pleasant and profitable from the standpoint of the immediate needs of this world and the present edification of his universe.

The Father's way—the exemplification of a farseeing ideal of creature life visualized by the great personalities of the Paradise administration of the universe of universes.

It was thus made clear to Jesus that there were two ways in which he could order the remainder of his earth life. Each of these ways had something to be said in its favor as it might be regarded in the light of the immediate situation. The Son of Man clearly saw that his choice between these two modes of conduct would have nothing to do with his reception of universe sovereignty; that was a matter already settled and sealed on the records of the universe of universes and only awaited his demand in person. But it was indicated to Jesus that it would afford his Paradise brother, Immanuel, great satisfaction if he, Jesus, should see fit to finish up his earth career of incarnation as he had so nobly begun it, always subject to the Father's will. On the third day of this isolation Jesus promised himself, he would go back to the world to finish his earth career, and that in a situation involving any two ways he would always choose the Father's will. And he lived out the remainder of his earth life always faithful to that resolve. Even to the bitter end he invariably subordinated his sovereign will to that of his heavenly Father.

The forty days in the mountain wilderness were not a period of great temptation but rather the term of the Master's great decisions. During these days of lone communion with himself and his Father's immediate presence—the Personalized Adjuster (he no longer had a personal seraphic guardian)—he arrived, one by one, at the significant decisions which were to control his policies and conduct for the remainder of his earth career. Subsequently, the tradition of a great temptation became attached to this period of isolation through confusion with the fragmentary narratives of the Mount Hermon struggles, and further because it was the custom to have all great prophets and human leaders begin their public careers by undergoing these supposed seasons of fasting and prayer. It had always been Jesus' practice, when facing any new or serious decisions, to withdraw for communion with his spirit that he might seek to know the will of God.

In all this planning for the remainder of his earth life, Jesus was always torn in his human heart by two opposing courses of conduct:

He entertained a strong desire to win his people—and the whole world—to believe in him and to accept his new spiritual kingdom. And he well knew their ideas concerning the coming Messiah.

To live and work as he was aware that his Father would approve, to conduct his work on behalf of other worlds in need, and to continue, in the establishment of the kingdom, to reveal the Father and show forth his divine character of love.

Throughout these eventful days, Jesus lived in an ancient rock cavern, a shelter on the side of the hills near a village sometimes called Beit Adis. He drank from the small spring which came from the side of the hill near this rock shelter." (The Book of Urantia 2015, paper 136:4.6-4.13)

"Even prior to Pentecost no rebel spirit could dominate a normal human mind, and since that day even the weak minds of inferior mortals are free from such possibilities. The supposed casting out of devils since the arrival of the Spirit of Truth has been a matter of confounding a belief in demoniacal possession with hysteria, insanity, and feeble-mindedness. But just because Michael's bestowal has forever liberated all human minds on Urantia from the possibility of demoniacal possession, do not imagine that such was not a reality in former ages (The Book of Urantia 2015, paper 77:7.7)."

* * * * *

DOUG: Could the Spirit of Truth block the demon?

JOHN: Definitely. Demons have no power unless you allow them to have power, so the more you have God in your life, then you have the power you always need, and there is no lack of power. It's always God's power. Darkness and the demons can't hurt you unless you allow them to hurt you.

DOUG: Oh, because that's the oneness of God.

JOHN: The oneness of God is moving back into your real, original soul in which you are a part of God. Your soul energy is part of God, and I've shared this in some channelings that when you are totally one with God, there is no darkness. There is no energy to stop having all your dreams come true, so to speak. God gives you his kingdom. He gives you all the gifts of the kingdom, which is to manifest in your life, your prosperity, your abundance. The more you focus on God and stop focusing on anything that is not God, and you will have the truth. When you concentrate on the darkness, then that's a false God, and it creates fears.

* * * * *

BUDDHA

"About 560 BC, the founder of Buddhism was born in India. We are told that he was good-looking, energetic young Prince and up to the age of twenty-nine he lived a life of ease, comfort, and luxury. He had a beautiful wife and everything that he could desire. Amidst plenty and beauty he passed from gratification to gratification and yet he was not satisfied. He was the first to declare the universal brotherhood of man. Buddha also taught that all men and women should enjoy equal rights. He denounced the priests of his day and fortunately, escaped their wrath.

He inculcated a pure system of morality and advocated kindness and love towards all. He taught no cruel doctrine of sacrifice, he believed in no angry God, nor in that, a savior took the punishment for the transgressions of believers. He was looked upon as having been a god-man and was credited with a virgin birth and numerous miracles.

Those who were known in Palestine as Essenes were supposed to be the western offshoot of the Buddhist community and known in Egypt as Therapeutae." (Ref. 14, Psychic Stream 1992, Findlay)

KRISHNA

"He succeeded the god Indra in the affections of the people. Just as Indra declined, so Krishna rose in their esteem.

Indra, it was believed, suffered death as a victim by crucifixion, more than 1500 years B.C., and his death on the cross is still celebrated in Tibet and Nepal. There, it is the custom in the month of August to raise to his honor crosses wreathed with abrotonus and to represent him as crucified, with his hands and feet pierced and the forehead bearing a mark. This crucified figure is still carried about certain towns and villages in those parts. We must therefore assume that this god, who lived several thousand years ago as a man, died the death of a sacrificial victim. He reappeared after death and ascended to heaven."

"At least 1000 years B.C., a child was born at Mathura between Delhi and Agra. He came to be known as Krishna and it was believed that he was a prince invincible in love and war. He died and reappeared. In consequence he became, in the eyes of his followers, a god who fought against evil, and the representative of all that was good.

In outline the legend about this god is as follows. A couple named Vasudeva and Devaki were his parents. They lived at Mathura, referred to in one of the early non-canonical gospels as the place where Joseph and Mary took Jesus to escape from the massacre of the infants by Herod. On the night of his birth they had to remove Krishna beyond the reach of his uncle, King Kamsa, who sought his life, because the king had been warned by a voice from heaven that the son of Devaki would put him to death. Krishna escaped, but many other children of a tender age were killed by the king in his cruel attempt to safeguard his throne." (Ref. 14, Psychic Stream 1992, Findlay)

Section 4.5: Rite of Sepulcher

The rite of sepulcher is an initiation into resurrection and ascension. It directs us to a more expansive awareness of our inherent potential.

The ego is naturally vigilant about what it permits into awareness, leading to an off-balanced state of mind. The primary reason for this state is the ego's lack of discrimination between the body and the thoughts of God. Thoughts of God are unacceptable to the ego because they clearly point to its nonexistence, and it compensates for this by either distorting or refusing to accept them. However, the ego cannot make the thoughts of God cease to be. Therefore, it tries to conceal not only unacceptable body impulses but also the thoughts of God. However, Christ consciousness allows us to elevate our consciousness above the ego.

* * * * *

DOUG: This one is coming from the Book of Revelations, Chapter 2 Verse 7, "Let him, He that hath an ear, let him hear what the Spirit saith unto the churches; to him that overcometh will I give to eat of the tree of life, which is in the midst of the paradise of God." My question here is overcometh what?

JOHN: You're overcoming the ego stopping the spiritual energy from going through your chakras.

DOUG: Okay.

JOHN: The churches are the chakras. If they are not functioning and moving in with the energy of God coming through them and manifesting in your life, you can't come alive and into the light of God. So it's opening up all your chakras so that they function and the light of God can emanate into your being.

* * * * *

There is no fear, only love in that realm of Christ consciousness. God's free-flowing energy provides us with the abundance that we have never before experienced. Christ consciousness brings the oneness of God to us.

An initiation is an inner-directed experience that carries you over the threshold of irreversible change. Initiation is the testing of the soul. It is God's way of determining how we will use the gift of free will. Temptation comes before us. We have to make a decision to walk the path of honor or to walk the path that compromises the truth. As soon as we demonstrate that we are just stewards of the law and the abundance of God, God gives us more. He makes us caretakers of others and larger fields of energy, more abundance, more supplies, and more responsibility on earth. We receive initiations and send messages to our "I Am" presence every day, signaling whether we are worthy to be counted as joint heirs of Christ consciousness.

In the initiations of resurrection and ascension, our former limited identities transform us. Jesus brought in an energy of seven levels of spiritual initiation to awaken the soul—birth, baptism, transfiguration, renunciation, crucifixion, resurrection, and ascension. The crucifixion of Jesus has been widely misunderstood. The foundation of Jesus's teaching was a demonstration of how we can align our wills with divine will, release all attachments to limited identities, and open the way to being the radiant one. We all are a Christ already.

* * * * *

DOUG: Does my candlestick need to be lighted so that I can become a Christ?

JOHN: Well, you are a Christ. It is again something that churches do not want you to understand—your power. Church leaders speak about opening your heart more so that more light shines. Yesterday, Marilyn explained when you move the atom from being less dense to having more space for the neutrons to move around, the light within can finally shine. Also, that is lighting your candle. You are allowing energy to expand.

DOUG: I guess if I practice meditation, I will light my candle.

JOHN: It will shine more.

* * * * *

We can shift our focus by resurrecting our consciousness through enlightened states of happiness, joy, and bliss instead of justifying feelings of betrayal, abandonment, entrapment, helplessness, and hopelessness. We are ready to take back our power instead of blindly forfeiting it to mediating priesthoods, saints, and teachers who limit our beliefs. It is time to allow growth and expansion of our inner authority and divinity, to fly free of self-imposed prisons.

Once we understand how Jesus learned from his youth to pass through crucifixion (dying to the limitation set forth by the ego) and resurrection (aligning with eternal life and original innocence), we can begin to allow for the possibility that he did not suffer to pay any form of debt. By recalling the meaning of the rite of sepulcher, we can begin to understand that he did not die, even though all his vital signs ceased to support his physical body for a time.

Having mastered the physical and subtle realms throughout his life, Jesus did not suffer in the gruesome way we may have been taught or that we subconsciously insisted. He did not die for our sins! He lived to model love and forgiveness so that we could choose to live by the same qualities he demonstrated.

However, I had never envisioned Jesus not dying on the cross until I heard this revelation from John:

* * * * *

DOUG: Is rite of sepulcher a practice used by people (living up to eight hundred years) to have a near death immediately and come back in a new body as a walk-in? Methuselah lived 969 years, and Noah lived 595 years. Could they have learned Christ consciousness from the previous Photon Belt and this kept them alive for a long time? Bodies don't last beyond 120 years, but they lived longer than that. Could that be true?

JOHN: Well, bodies can live longer. It's a mind-set that the society has perpetrated on people to get rid of the population. Yes, they were practicing this. This is what Jesus would practice. It was called initiation, and when he was in Egypt and at the sarcophagus of the Great Pyramid, this is exactly what was going on. People in those days who were learning and growing spiritually and being going through their initiations, they would practice going into a state of consciousness where it was almost death. Where they could look and appear like they were dead. It is what Jesus did during the time. We're coming into Easter. He did not die. Jesus did not die. He went into this state of consciousness you're describing where it looked like death, but he could come out of it by resurging the energy the people would come around, the person in, practicing this ritual and restoring their energy to them. And they would come back, and you could live. His mother, Mary's mother, lived, I believe, to be seven hundred years. So what happens is you can restore your energy to live longer. It's a matter of mind-set and knowing how to do it. Jesus went through years and years of practicing this before the Easter occasion occurred. He practiced it in a way that was necessary for all of us to realize. We can go into a state and come back out alive. It's not that we died, but it just extends our life into spiritual living in a way that we hadn't been living before. So it's the body will maybe pass away whenever the person needs to for the script that they wrote, but the spirit lives forever. But the body can live longer than what we've been told. That is a man-made piece of information to control the masses.

DOUG: The body can last longer only if a person ascends to the fifth dimension, right?

JOHN: That is true. You have to cooperate. As with the chakras, your whole system has to connect to a higher consciousness, which would be the fifth dimension. Moreover, you can live longer. That is what the masters have accomplished, and that is why they are still helping people to do what they did: They learned how to transcend the ego. It extended their consciousness into an eternal life, and they have come back to Earth to help others find that path.

* * * * *

"For God so loveth the world, that he hath given his only begotten Son, that whosoever believeth in him, should not perish, but have everlasting life" (John 3:16).

When we ascend to the fifth dimension, we will have eternal life through Christ consciousness, not Jesus Christ. A misinterpretation of the Scripture has been spread. The energy of God free-flowing through the seven chakras raises our spiritual vibration to the fifth dimension that provides us eternal life.

- "O Lord, the hope of Israel that forsake thee shall be confounded: they that depart from thee shall be written in the earth because they have forsaken the Lord, the fountain of living waters. Heal me, O Lord, and I shall be whole: save me, and I shall be saved: for thou art my praise" (Jeremiah 17:13–14).
- "Go up unto Gilead, and take balm, O virgin, the daughter of Egypt: in vain shalt thou use many medicines: for thou shalt have no health" (Jeremiah 46:11).

Prophet Jeremiah made it clear that Christ consciousness is what restores our health. To accomplish this, we need to ascend to the fifth dimension. Now is the time to do this with the Holy Spirit due to arrive from the Photon Belt.

While Jesus was on the cross, he was in a trancelike state. He had learned Christ consciousness, and he did not feel pain. Jesus was unconscious, and the energy of God sustained him. Through years of practice with the Essenes, he reached a high state of spiritual development during the thirty years in which he used his body.

The Essenes were a sect that existed in Palestine along with the two mentioned in the New Testament—the Pharisees and the Sadducees. The Essenes were an exceedingly devout order, different from the materialistic Sadducees and the hypocritical, publicity-seeking Pharisees. They shunned all mention of these sects and their methods of study and worship. The Essenes are peculiar because almost nothing is known about them, and they are not referred to in the New Testament.

Jesus came down to show the people the right use of energy. If people could learn this, there would be no need for churches. He did not come to start a religion, only to show people that kingdom is within, that we and God the Father are one.

It was a remarkable discovery to learn that Jesus had never died on the cross. However, there were some clues in the Scripture that might have indicated this. For instance, after Jesus escaped from the sepulcher, he went to meet his disciples. Disciple Thomas wanted proof that Jesus was crucified. Jesus showed him the nail marks in his hands.

> But Thomas one of the twelve, called Didymus, was not with them when Jesus came. The other disciples, therefore, said unto him, we have seen the Lord: but he said unto them, except I see in his hands the print of the nails, and put my finger into the print of the nails, and put my hand into his side, I will not believe it. So eight days after, again his disciples were within, and Thomas with them. Then came Jesus, when the doors were shut, and stood in the midst, and said, Peace be unto you. After said he to Thomas, put thy finger here, and see mine hands, and put forth thine hand, and put it on my side, and be not faithless, but faithful. Then Thomas answered, and said unto him, Thou art my Lord, and my God. Jesus said unto him, Thomas because thou hast seen me, thou believest:

blessed are they that have not seen, and have believed. (John 20:24–29)

During one of the earlier channelings, John made it clear that once the spirit leaves the body, we lose our physical skin.

* * * * *

DOUG: So when we die, the spirit leaves the body, but it remains with God.

JOHN: Right. Also, we never die because the spirit is eternal. It is just a passing of one consciousness to another. You lose your physical skin, a shell, but the spirit moves into the higher consciousness of God. In Nirvana, there is no pain and suffering, just unconditional love and unity.

* * * * *

The process of initiation is not a well-understood topic. Some of the biblical characters have lived beyond a normal life expectancy, such as Methuselah and Noah, mentioned earlier. Jesus' grandmother Anna had lived for 700 years. It is a process that involves resurging energies. Once the spirit leaves the body, the body decomposes within three days. A physical body cannot exist without its companion etheric body, or soul spirit. So, what happened was that Jesus went into a trance, and his etheric body (spirit) detached from his natural body during the crucifixion. It is a process we know today when a medium temporarily casts aside her spirit to allow another spirit to enter her body and speak through the vocal cords.

It is akin to my medium Marilyn for this book when Apostle John came in a spirit to speak through her vocal cords. Marilyn's gatekeeper, Martha, escorted her spirit outside her body to allow the mind of John to inhabit her body. Once the conversation was through, then John left, and Marilyn's spirit, with the help of her gatekeeper, resumed functioning of her body.

In the case of Jesus, his mind had returned to his body before any decomposition set in by the third day. It is a mystery part of the Bible where the disciples did not record how they revived Jesus via this rite. Jesus was in a trance-like state during the whole crucifixion. He did not feel the pain. It is possible that he would have awoken if the soldier had broken his legs, but fortunately, it didn't happen. After he was pronounced "dead," Jesus was transported to the tomb.

Paul was completely unaware of it. He had always assumed Jesus rose from the dead. He was a big follower of the pagan religion belief of a savior-god that sacrifices his body to take away the sin of the world. In the centuries before the opening of the Christian era, when Krishna was worshiped in India, Mithra in Persia, Osiris in Egypt, and Dionysus in Greece, Bel alone among the savior-gods had lost his worshippers. The beliefs surrounding him were taken over by his successor Murdock. The Jews were the only people who didn't have a Savior.

Nevertheless, when Paul saw Jesus after the crucifixion, he thought Jesus had resurrected from the dead, which was the basis of the Christianity belief.

- "By man came death, by man came also the resurrection of the dead." (1 Corinthians 15:21)
- "Christ our Passover is sacrificed for us." (1 Corinthians 5:7)

* * * * *

DOUG: Did Paul know that the disciples had revived him from his sleep?

JOHN: No, he did not understand the energy shifting that occurred, but he was a trusting person. He was a good friend of Jesus and that he trusted what Jesus said as being truthful and accepted. The fact that there had been a change, but the scientific part he did not understand.

DOUG: Is it true that Paul had always thought Jesus had risen from the dead and ascended to heaven and came back with a heavenly body?

JOHN: His spirit has ascended into a higher consciousness. So, with that ascension, that's the ascension that everybody can do and that's the glory of Easter. Jesus was the symbol and the representation that our souls can rise back into the unconditional love of God, and when we rise above the old ego into the higher consciousness, is which Jesus had demonstrated, and we are a new creature according to the Bible in Corinthians II. So it's the old creatures based on the ego and the new creatures in the unconditional love of God. And so you do change into a new physical body because of the spiritual inside the change, and therefore it reproduces a new physical body of change.

* * * * *

One strong argument against the story of the physical resurrection of Jesus is that neither Matthew nor John tells us what became of him after he had come out of the tomb. Their accounts close with him represented as still living on earth, so they either never heard the story of the ascension or did not believe it. Mark states that "he was received up into heaven" and Luke that "he was parted from them and carried up into heaven." If Jesus had appeared in his flesh body, we would have much more information than this. Matthew's and John's silence, and Mark's and Luke's casual references to the parting are sufficient in themselves to prove that there was no accepted tradition of his return in his old body.

DOUG: Now, since Jesus knew he wasn't going to die on the cross, what was the meaning of the Last Supper?

JOHN: It was his way of saying good-bye to the old situations that had occurred and his, and his celebrating companionship and fellowship and their loyalty to be with him and follow his ways and be disciples and the message of love. They didn't understand they were disciples of love. But they were loyal, and they stayed with him and shared the message if they knew it, at the time of where they were in their spiritual development. And it was the last supper of the ego you might say. The ego is going to die when Jesus was on the cross, and he rose above the ego in that new beginning of what he showed that everyone could do. So, it was kind of a celebration of that transition coming. The old leaving the ego and the new moving into the oneness of God. It was just a gathering of neutral people that support each other and there for each other. So it was the combination of, of bringing together their energies and of course when more people gather, the energy is stronger. And that was one way of giving Jesus more support from the spiritual world through the people's energy, helping him to go through the next things that were going to come into his life.

DOUG: It was as he went into a trance before he was put on the cross?

JOHN: He was in a séance, and he learned through the séance, and in particular through his grandmother Anna, the spiritual lesson is necessary, and she made sure that he did have those lessons for initiation, took him around the Mediterranean to other Essene communities, even into England. So, Jesus was well trained in how to handle his energy of ascension, and he prepared himself before he came on this earth to do this particular example to all on, on the planet that it was possible. So, he, he had a lot of training throughout his childhood and growing up to be able to be to where he was at that point, that his energy was high enough to pull it off.

* * * * *

DOUG: The book of Revelation calls the church the "Synagogue of Satan" (Revelation 2:9). "I know thy works and tribulation, and poverty (but thou art rich) and I know the blasphemy of them, which say they are Jews, and are not, but are the Synagogue of Satan."

JOHN: Everybody is a son of God. We all have a divine spark. It's how much of that divine spark is awake and functioning. The more light you have in your life, the more God you have in your life. The more love you have in your life, the more people will be attracted to your care and generosity. You have fruits of the spirit, and people will know you by your fruit, as stated in the Bible. (Galatians 5:22 says, "But the fruit of the Spirit is love, joy, peace, longsuffering, gentleness, goodness, faith.") However, if you have little light activating your life, you will become dark, devious, selfish, cheating, and dishonest—what people call Satan. It is your lower nature. It does not have much of God in it, so when Jesus said, "Satan gets you behind me," he was talking about those parts of his being that did not have the light of God.

DOUG: Do the other worlds and universes have churches?

JOHN: No, the church is a man-made institution.

DOUG: Just for this world.

JOHN: In this world the church is one of the learning devices that have been set up in the third dimension. It was primarily developed to control people and limit their thinking to prevent them from going beyond what they preach and finding the God within. When people find the God within, they do not need a church. Churches are limiting thoughts and consciousness with fear so that people do not think for themselves and instead become followers.

DOUG: What makes a church exist here? Like in other worlds, the Book of Urantia called the other worlds normal worlds, but here is not normal?

JOHN: Normal would—I'm assuming what they mean by normal—is to have returned to the oneness of God.

DOUG: Through evolution?

JOHN: Have reached the highest evolution. There are other civilizations, you understand, that are much more advanced than Earth, and they are working from harmony and unity and cooperation. They don't need jails and punishment like we have on the planet Earth. This is a barbaric planet, you might say.

* * * * *

Even though Jesus was the Son of God, he had a human body that dispersed upon death. However, according to John 20:24–29, he has remained in his body. When we ascend to the fifth dimension, we have the ability to change from physical to spiritual forms by focusing our thoughts on becoming whatever we chose to be.

The author of the article (Ref. 36) presented sixty-five reasons to believe that Jesus did not die on the cross. I selected several of these for this book.

1. Jesus was not buried in the grave.

The Jewish custom for the last thousands of years was to bury the deceased in the ground. Because the disciples knew the predictions, which were made earlier by Jesus Christ, they kept Jesus's body in a sepulcher. If they had buried him in a grave, he would have died. However, his disciples placed him in a roomy sepulcher rather them burying him in the ground, according to the Jewish custom and traditions.

2. Why crucifixion?

Jews wanted Jesus to be killed through crucifixion so they could prove that Jesus was not beloved by God and that a curse of God was upon him. Jews could have killed Jesus easily, as they were hundreds of thousands in number and unyielding. If killing had been their desire, they could have done so easily. They paid thirty pieces of silver to one of his disciples. If they had paid him more, he might have done this service too. However, they wanted Jesus to be crucified so they could prove that he was not from God but an imposter and fabricator.

If he were from God, then God would save him. Maybe that was the reason that Jesus was so reluctant to suffer on the cross.

3. Crucifixion was demanded by the Jews.

"Then when the high Priests and officers saw him, they cried, saying, Crucify, crucify him. Pilate said unto them, Take ye him, and crucify him: for I find no fault in him" (John 19:6).

"The Jews answered him (Pilate), we have a law, and by our law, he ought to die, because he made himself the Son of God" (John 19:7).

4. Jesus's prayers and supplications to be saved from crucifixion.

"Then went Jesus with them into a place which is called Gethsemane, and said unto his disciples, Sit ye here, while I go, and pray yonder" (Matthew 26:36).

"So he went a little further, and fell on his face, and prayed, saying, O my Father, if it is possible, let this cup pass from me: nevertheless, not as I will, but as thou wilt" (Matthew 26:39).

"So he left them, and went away again, and prayed the Third time, saying the same words" (Matthew 26:44).

Actually, he did not pray not to be crucified. He prayed that he had human concerns about what he had committed to. We pray before the tests and challenges in our lives for help from God too. He came to fulfill predictions of the Old Testament that a Savior would come. Only he came to save their souls and not their physical bodies as such, to show that we could ascend in spirit above the body because the kingdom is within.

5. Why was Jesus hiding?

The Jews paid thirty pieces of silver to Judas to gain necessary information about Jesus.

"Neither go into the town nor tell it to any in the town" (Mark 8:26).

"And he sharply charged them, that concerning him they should tell no man" (Mark 8: 30).

6. God always hears Jesus's prayers, and his prayers were heard.

"And Jesus lifted up his eyes, and said, Father, I thank thee, because thou hast heard me. I know that thou hearest me always, but because of the people that stand by, I said it, that they may believe, that thou hast sent me" (John 11:41–42).

"Who in the days of his flesh did offer up prayers and supplications, with strong crying and tears unto him, that was able to save him from death, and was also heard in that which he feared" (Hebrews 5:7).

7. Pilate delayed judgment.

Pilate intentionally delayed giving his verdict and did not deliver his judgment until he was sure that because of the Sabbath, Jesus would be on the cross for only a few hours. Young at thirty-three years old, Jesus was on the cross for three to six hours only.

8. Pilate gave favor to Jesus.

Pilate was in full favor of Jesus, considering him innocent, and because of his wife's dream, he was trying to save his life. That is why Pilate wanted to use his special right to free Jesus, but the Jews did not let him do it.

> When they were then gathered together, Pilate said unto them, whether will ye that I let loose unto you Barabbas or Jesus which is called Christ? (For he knew well, that for envy they had delivered him. Also, when he was set down on the judgment-seat, his wife sent to him, saying, Have thou nothing to do with that just man: for I have

suffered many things this day in a dream because of him.) But the Chief Priests and the elders had persuaded the people that they should ask Barabbas, and should destroy Jesus. Then the governor answered, and said unto them, whether of the twain will ye that I let loose unto you? And they said, Barabbas. (Matthew 27:17–21)

9. Pilate's wife sees a dream to save Jesus.

"Also, when he was set down on the judgment-seat, his wife sent to him, saying, Have thou nothing to do with that just man: for I have suffered many things this day in a dream because of him" (Matthew 27:19).

Why was this dream against the purpose of the advent of Jesus, which was to give his life on the cross? Her dream should have been to crucify him immediately and let him finish his work. But her dream was against it, and this was mentioned in the Bible.

10. Pilate finds him "not guilty."

"When Pilate saw that he availed nothing, but that more tumult was made, he took water and washed his hands before the multitude, saying, I am innocent of the blood of this just man: look you to it" (Matthew 27:24).

11. Pilate marveled.

"And Pilate marveled, if he were already dead, and called unto him the Centurion, and asked of him whether he had been any while dead" (Mark 15:44).

When Pilate was informed about the death of Jesus on the cross, he marveled at hearing it. We know that Pilate was the most experienced person in this field. He may have experienced hundreds of crucifixions in his time. He knew well that a young, unmarried person of thirty-three years should not die in a few hours while the other two thieves (older than him) were still alive after the crucifixion.

12. The other two (thieves) next to Jesus were still alive, so the soldiers broke their legs.

"Then came the soldiers and brake the legs of the first, and of the other, which was crucified with Jesus. However, when they came to Jesus and saw that he was dead already, they brake not his legs" (John 19:32–33).

13. Blood and water was a great sign of Jesus's life.

When a soldier pierced a spear in Jesus's side, blood and water gushed out from his body with full pressure, a sign that Jesus's heart was still pumping and he was alive.

"But one of the soldiers with a spear pierced his side, and forthwith came there out blood and water" (John 19:34).

The importance of blood and water is described by the narrator. "And he that saw it, bare record, and his record is true: and he knoweth that he saith true, that ye might believe it" (John 19:35).

This narrator has stressed the truth of this incident because of its vast importance.

14. Why did soldiers checking if Jesus was alive or dead pierce him with a spear? What were the criteria for recognition?

The concept that one of the soldiers pierced Jesus with a spear to check whether he was alive does not make sense until and unless this was a way of checking. Did they pierce Jesus with a spear or something else? What was that? How did they do it? One of the soldiers pierced a spear in Jesus's body. It was not to check his life or death. Otherwise, they would have done the same to the thieves.

15. Neither Jews nor Christians are sure about Jesus's death on the cross.

There was a strong earthquake, a storm, and a solar eclipse just after the crucifixion of Jesus that made all the Jews and Romans run away from the crucifixion site. That is why neither Jews nor Christians are sure about the death of Jesus on the cross.

16. Jesus said he had not ascended yet. What did he mean?

"Jesus saith unto her, Touch me not: for I am not yet ascended to my Father: but go to my brethren, and say unto them, I ascend unto my Father, and to your Father, and to my God, and your God" (John 20:17).

What is the real meaning of ascension here when Jesus said to Mary, "I am not yet ascended to my Father"?

Indeed, it was understood and very clear without any doubt that Jesus had not ascended, as he was standing just in front of Mary. Then why did Jesus say that he had not yet ascended? (He had not ascended in spirit at that point.)

17. Jesus ate food in the presence of his disciples.

"He said unto them, have ye here any meat? So they gave him a piece of a broiled fish and a honeycomb. And he took it and did eat before them" (Luke 24:41–42).

"Jesus said unto them, Come, and dine. And none of the disciples durst ask him, who art thou? The disciples knew that he was the Lord. Jesus then came and took bread and gave them, and fish likewise" (John 21:12–13).

A spirit does not need food, but the physical body becomes weak without it. Why did Jesus need food if he had gone back to his original body of God? Note that people in a higher consciousness eat food to be social and not for substance.

"Appearance of an Angel, saying, why, you looking for a living person into the dead. So it came to pass, that as they were amazed thereat, behold, two men suddenly stood by them in shining vestures. And as they were afraid, and bowed down their faces to the earth, they said to them, why seek ye him that liveth, among the dead?" (Luke 24:4–5).

"And when they found not his body, they came, saying, that they had also seen a vision of Angels, which said, that he was alive" (Luke 24:23).

18. Jesus was in flesh and bones after he had risen.

Jesus displayed his hands and feet to his disciples, proving that he was alive bodily.

"But they were abashed and afraid, supposing that they had seen a spirit. Then he said unto them, why are ye troubled? And wherefore do doubts arise in your hearts? Behold mine hands and my feet: for it is I myself: handle me, and see: for a spirit hath not flesh and bones, as ye see me have. And when he had thus spoken, he showed them his hands and feet" (Luke 24:37–40).

19. Jesus awakened his disciples, requesting special prayers for his safety.

> "Then went Jesus with them into a place which is called Gethsemane, and said unto his disciples, Sit ye here, while I go, and pray yonder. So he took unto him Peter, and the two sons of Zebedee, and began to wax sorrowful, and grievously troubled. Then said Jesus unto them, my soul is very heavy, even unto the death: tarry ye here, and watch with me. So he went a little further, and fell on his face, and prayed, saying,

O my Father, if it be possible, let this cup pass from me: nevertheless, not as I will, but as thou wilt. After, he came unto the disciples, and found them asleep, and said to Peter, What? Could ye not watch with me one hour? Watch, and pray, that ye enter not into temptation: the spirit indeed is ready, but the flesh is weak. (Matthew 26:36–41)

20. Jesus' wounds were a great sign of his survival.

Jesus, through showing his injuries to his disciples, was proving that he was alive bodily:

> The other disciples, therefore, said unto him, we have seen the Lord: but he said unto them, except I see in his hands the print of the nails, and put my finger into the print of the nails, and put mine hand into his side, I will not believe it. And eight days after, again his disciples were within, and Thomas with them. Then came Jesus, when the doors were shut, and stood in the midst, and said, Peace be unto you. After said he to Thomas, Put thy finger here, and see mine hands, and put forth thine hand, and put it into my side, and be not faithless, but faithful. (John 20:25-27)

A spirit cannot have wounds. This means Jesus was alive bodily.

Why did Jesus tell Thomas "not to be faithless but believing?" Jesus advised Thomas to have faith, but in what? Belief in the fulfillment of the promise of God saving Jesus from the accursed death on the cross that the Jews had designed for him?

Why did Jesus have a physical body after rising from the dead? Why did this physical body have wounds? Shouldn't there have been nothing but his soul and spirit? Did he want to take these wounds along with him to the heavens to show them to God? If that was the case, we know well that these wounds alone did not kill him, but many other things did, including the cross. If Jesus needed to present proof of his service to God, then he should have taken all his wounds, including the signs of flogging, beating, hitting, kicking, spitting, and hanging on cross on which he was crucified.

21. Jesus's shroud, the shroud of Turin, is a sign that Jesus was alive.

"So Joseph took the body, and wrapped it in a clean linen cloth" (Matthew 27:59).

22. Jewish practice included using one hundred pounds of aloe, myrrh, and other spices at the burial.

Alternatively, special arrangements were made for Jesus's safety. Nicodemus, who was a physician and a disciple of Jesus, made this particular agreement before the crucifixion of Jesus: "And there also came Nicodemus (which first came to Jesus by night) and brought of myrrh and aloes mingled together about a hundred pounds. Then they took the body of Jesus, and wrapped it in linen clothes with the odors, as the manner of the Jews is to bury" (John 19:39–40).

23. Jesus never mentioned that the purpose of his coming was to give his life on the cross.

24. Salvation doesn't come through keeping the commandments of God.

Jesus never said that people's salvation is in believing Jesus's death on the cross. Salvation is not through keeping the commandments of the Old Testament but keeping New Testament of loving God with all thy heart, mind, and soul and loving your neighbor as yourself. The Old Testament was meant to bring a moral code and values. This was to be replaced by the New Testament. Rather he promised that heaven's eternal life is in following and obeying the commandments of God. As it is in the book of Matthew, "And behold, one came and said unto him, Good Master, what good thing shall I do, that I may have eternal life? And he said unto him, Why called thou me good? There is none good but one, even God: but if thou wilt enter into life, keep the Commandments" (Matthew 19:16–17).

(The first two commandments relate to ascension to the fifth dimension. Christ consciousness opens up our seven chakras, which enable us to receive the "fountain of the living waters."

25. A soldier saw Jesus walking and informed the chief priest.

"Now when they were gone, behold, some of the watch came into the city and showed unto the high Priests all the things that were done" (Matthew 28:11).

John made another revelation in one of our earlier channelings (May 18, 2014) about Jesus not dying on the cross. However, Jesus was beaten on the ground. He did not experience any pain because he was in an unconscious state, communing with God. Jesus was of God's grace. The energy of love from God was in Jesus's heart and soul. Jesus had the ability to transform his conscious at will.

* * * * *

DOUG: Elijah was taken up, but Jesus died on the cross.

JOHN: Jesus died emotionally to demonstrate that the spirit can rise. When he was crucified—that's another church idea—he was not on a cross. But he was beaten. This was his way of acknowledging that no matter what happened to him, he was in the grace of God. The beating was not painful. Jesus was in a state of grace when it happened. Movies that depict Jesus's crucifixion as horrendously violent, scaring viewers to death, do not reflect Jesus's message. The message was that if you are in the grace of God, you cannot feel external pain. Jesus's death demonstrated that we can rise above persecution and live in the loving, unconditional kingdom of prosperity that is our birthright. We do not have to be indebted slaves or tyrannized by the government or oppressive institutions. We can rise above.

DOUG: Yeah. I am glad to be talking with you again. It is kind of interesting what you said in our last call.

JOHN: And what was that?

DOUG: That Jesus never died on the cross.

JOHN: Yes. That was—he went into a trance, you might say, of a very low vibration, which he had practiced over the years in what they call initiations, and his grandmother taught him how to do that, Anna. And it was—the whole scenario worked out like it was meant to for people to see that we don't die. We come back in spirit. However, the church has distorted that to a degree in that so many people have been misled because that way you could be guilty. The church wanted to make people guilty so that they would have followers. *How am I going to get out of condemning and killing Jesus? You know that it's my fault he's dead, and he just came to fulfill the prophecy.* It wasn't anybody's reason for killing him. It was the necessity of showing people that if you go from one state of consciousness to another, you do not die, and that's Easter. And the churches do not represent that in the way that it's spiritual.

DOUG: Interesting. I wonder if when Jesus said to have faith that was meant to be as in faith in God, that God keeps his promises.

JOHN: Exactly. The faith is your connection. When you consciously talk with God, you are connected with the God source inside. That is your connection, and your faith is that you are using that connection in your life for guidance and direction. So then everything is in spirituality. It is all scripted. It is all working out. The end is going to be glorious, and it is all within. So when you trust God within—and that is another part of where the church has misled people—you look to Jesus, and Jesus said the kingdom of heaven is within. He said it.

He said, "The Father and I are one," but the churches tend to gloss over that and say, "Well, Jesus saves you," but the reality is you save yourself by focusing and having that faith and trusting God.

* * * * *

An important distinction can be drawn from John's statement regarding justification by faith. Before Jesus was to be put to death, he prayed hard to God the Father. Jesus was facing death. Although he had proclaimed, "Father and I are one," he was facing the inevitability of dying on the cross. He was confronted with a situation where he placed his life in the hands of God the Father. He recited his prayers to God three times for reassurance. It was a test of his faith by trusting God's words.

> Then said Jesus unto them, my soul is very heavy, even unto the death: tarry ye here, and watch with me. So he went a little further, and fell on his face, and prayed, saying, O my Father, if it be possible, let this cup pass from me: nevertheless, not as I will, but as thou wilt. After, he came unto the disciples, and found them asleep, and said to Peter, What? Could ye not watch with me one hour? Watch, and pray, that ye enter not into temptation: the spirit indeed is ready, but the flesh is weak. Again he went away the second time, and prayed, saying, O my Father, if this cup cannot pass away from me, but that I must drink it, thy will be done. And he came and found them asleep again, for their eyes were heavy. So he left them, and went away again, and prayed the third time, saying the same words. (Matthew 26:38–44)

John had confirmed the meaning of justification by faith. It is saving ourselves by focusing and having faith and trusting God. We need to go inside of ourselves to receive his guidance.

Having learned that Jesus had never died on the cross, what does that do to the doctrine of the church? Was Jesus's teaching corrupted?

* * * * *

DOUG: Okay. Now I got this from the Internet. I am not sure if it is true, but I want to ask you a question. There's this quote coming from Pope Leo X.

JOHN: Right.

DOUG: It was back in 1513 through 1521, and he was quoted, "How well we know what a profitable superstition the fable of Christ has been for us." He was quoted. I am not sure if that was true or if that was made up by someone who was against the church.

JOHN: Well, you are saying they were superstitions?

DOUG: Yes, superstitions.

JOHN: Well, there's an element of truth to that because the church has predicted—they predominantly preached there is a hell, and that's a superstition. And they predominantly teach that we go to heaven. Well, we can be in heaven on earth if we remove all the obstacles of our fear and emotional obstructions to being receptive of the heavenly energy that's already around us. So you might say there is a lot of superstition in the churches.

DOUG: Okay. Now there's another quote I think it was coming from Bishop Eusebius, and he's a bishop from the Catholic church.

JOHN: Okay.

DOUG: From AD 260 to 339, so obviously, he was there at the Council of Nicaea.

JOHN: Okay.

DOUG: There was a quote from him saying that, "It is an act of virtue to deceive and lie when by such means the interest of the church might be promoted."

JOHN: Exactly. It was at that particular meeting that all the references to reincarnation were removed from the Bible. However, there's still a half a dozen verses that were overlooked because they were not as obvious about reincarnation. However, there are—Marilyn has written about this. There are verses in the Bible that if you understand the significance and deeper meaning of them, you see Jesus is referring to reincarnation. Yes, that was a major shift in the Bible, to take out the idea that we are eternal and live forever. However, it's mentioned in there, but it is always applied to how Jesus could be God. It was not ever offered that the general public or the people and individuals had that the energy of God was already there within their souls. It was always focused that it was without, and other people like God were in Jesus, but they wanted you not to look within. They didn't want you to find and to open your heart to see that the spirit of Christ is in all of us. And that's what Christmas is truly about. It's for everyone to see that they are Christ. And it says in the twenty-third psalm that you are Christ. "Thou anointest my head with oil." That's being Christ. So you see, they distorted the focus to the outside rather than within, where the kingdom of God is

* * * * *

DOUG: Yeah. I prayed the other day, and I was asking God if I should include it in the book, asked for his guidance. And sure enough on the next day, I got ahold of one of my spiritual informants, Tracy Williams, and she said, "Yes, God wants you to include it in the book." So He answered my prayer.

JOHN: Right. That's exactly right.

DOUG: So I spent a whole week—oh, fortunately, my work was closed for the weekend because they put in a new computer system. So I had the luxury of time to research, and I found some useful information on the Internet about the topic. And there was one author of an article where he says he found sixty-five different reasons to believe that Jesus never died on the cross.

JOHN: Oh, so I am not the only one saying that. That's marvelous that people are finding that out.

DOUG: But I found evidence from your gospel that Jesus had never died because he still had nail marks in his hands.

JOHN: Well, you see, the church has construed things to make it believable. And another thing the church has changed was doubting. Thomas was never doubting. He was just curious in trying to understand what had happened to Jesus, and in looking at his hands, there were nail marks because, you know, there were crucifixions. There was damage, and very much so. Jesus was beaten and whipped, and he was crucified in a way where it was harmful to his body. So there were marks, not necessarily the way we would think of them. But there were marks on his body, and he was curious. But he wasn't doubting. And see, the Bible wants you to question things because then you don't have 10 percent faith, and it takes 100 percent faith to move into Christ's consciousness because that's the true consciousness. And if you have any elements that are not totally in line, in alignment with the God consciousness, then you don't have the connection you need. So anything that could distort the story of the Bible has been distorted. And so you have to take it with a grain of salt, and anything that isn't entirely truthful, like you're doing, question it because there are a lot of things to question in the Bible. Anything negative is questionable. One Catholic priest took the Bible and tried to take out all the dogma from the Catholic church in the Bible and printed his own New Testament, and even that came through with a few pieces of dogma in it that he had missed and misunderstood himself. So it's very hard to have 100 percent truth, but the more you search, the more you will find.

DOUG: Where did Jesus live after Easter?

JOHN: Well, he stayed around for a short time in his regular location and community where different people did—he met with different people. They didn't always recognize him, and you know, for the Sermon on the Mount, he was still there. So he was still in his community for some time, and that's another thing that, you know, they limited his connection with people after the Easter particular time of season. And actually, in the Bible, it seems like a very short time, but it was longer than it was expressed in the Bible. And then he did move on.

DOUG: When did he die? Or he was always alive?

JOHN: Well, his physical body passed as he was living out of … he had moved into India and was living there with his family, his wife, and children.

DOUG: What time frame was that?

JOHN: Well, that is not some in my immediate knowledge. So I can get back with you on some of that if you're interested, but right now I—he lived to a fairly old age. I'm not picking up the actual time right now, but I can get that for you on another visit if you want.

DOUG: Okay. No problem. You mentioned that Mary Magdalene, his wife, had died and was buried in India. So obviously, that's where Jesus went.

JOHN: Well, he went to India and lived there, and there was a time before he lived there I believe he was in France. So that's—she was in France at one point, too. So there is some concern about how all that came together. The biblical history did not follow that accurately, and no one has put the times together exactly at this point. So let me do a little work in finding answers for you, and we can hopefully have more answers next time.

DOUG: Okay. Where was Jesus during the Pentecost? That's where the 120 disciples were initiated. Was Jesus there?

JOHN: At Pentecost? Yes.

DOUG: I have read from some source that the disciples went into hiding after Easter. Was it because there were some suspicions that Jesus went into hiding, and the authorities were going after him?

JOHN: They were concerned about their welfare and fled to different countries to spread the word. So they were for a period incognito, you might say. And of course, the letters to the Romans by Paul, those were written during their travels. And so when they were away from the Roman Empire, they were at a safer place.

DOUG: Were you ever inside a mountain?

JOHN: Yes. He often went into caves for rituals around the Mediterranean that had Essene communities. This was part of the Essene initiation, to move out of being visible to those around them and move into caves where it was safer to take part in their ritual of cleansing their souls.

DOUG: Now could the Dead Sea Scrolls contain the teachings of Jesus that the Catholic church wanted to burn or bury?

JOHN: Oh, yes. They were not happy with the Dead Sea Scrolls because you see a lot of information before Jesus within those scrolls. He was not the first one to proclaim many of the messages. They actually—many of the messages were taken from the Essene literature, and therefore, it was not originated, you know— The church would like to think everything started with Jesus, but it started thousands of years before Jesus. And so to have information surface that showed that the Bible wasn't the first and original document was threatening to them.

DOUG: Okay. Did the Catholic church know that Jesus was still alive?

JOHN: That's a good question. Give me a moment. Well, they were not quite into seeing a spiritual understanding of life. And so they discounted his ascension, and that's why it has never really been celebrated in the churches on Easter. They said he rose from the dead, but they didn't want to acknowledge anything beyond that because that would validate that we do have a spiritual life that continues. There is life after physical death that is never ending. It's eternal. And that's not what they were there to preach. They wanted you to believe there was only one life to live. And you'd better live it right now the way they want you to, or you'll go to hell. So they did not look forward or want to encourage anything about eternal life.

DOUG: The way I wrote it in my book, I quoted your statement about, you know, Jesus not dying on the cross. So I wrote down—I took a verse from your book, John 3:16, "For God so loveth the world that he hath given his only begotten Son that whoever believeth in him, he should not perish but have everlasting life." So I mentioned that that if we ascended this dimension, we would have eternal life through Christ consciousness, not Jesus Christ.

JOHN: All right. That's a good way to put it because, see, Jesus represented at the end of his life Christ consciousness. He went into unconditional love when he said on the cross, "God, forgive them, for they know not what they do." That's unconditional love. And he was exemplifying that. So through Christ consciousness, he was our example that we too can forgive those that are around us and causing us to love them spiritually because that is our lesson on earth, to love our neighbors as ourselves. Then he was exemplifying what Christ consciousness represented, and it wasn't that he was the only Christ. We've had several christed beings, several masters who've mastered this spiritual trip of entry into ascension and who have come back to Earth. We have many who have come to restore and help bring truth to all of this understanding today, and he was an example. He was Jesus, the Christ, but he wasn't the only Christ. So instead of saying Christ Jesus, say Jesus, the Christ, and then you can also have other masters. They were Christs also. So you're correct that he represented that.

DOUG: Now Paul wrote many New Testament books.

JOHN: Right.

DOUG: I wonder if Jesus was there to help them.

JOHN: Yes. There's a lot of truth in that. Jesus has been there to support many of the different people throughout time. That particular spiritual soul has come through in the Old Testament and has had lives before Jesus, Enoch, and Joseph. He was Melchizedek. He had many lives after his life as Jesus in more current times. So he has come through often to help people. And yes, his guidance is always, always beneficial.

DOUG: That's interesting. Now did Jesus choose the seventy disciples, not Paul?

JOHN: Paul was an apostle, not a disciple. Paul was a friend of Jesus, but he was not one of the original disciples. He knew Jesus as a good friend. They got together and had discussions. And as he changed his mind and turned to understanding the message, then he became an apostle and carried the message, but he was not one of the original.

DOUG: Okay. But he had meetings with Jesus in real life?

JOHN: Oh, yes. Uh-huh.

DOUG: Because the Bible only shows that he met Jesus in the spirit, but not through real life.

JOHN: There's a book that was channeled—not channeled. A person went into regression, past-life regression, and wrote a book about his experiences as Paul when he was alive at the time of Jesus. And he gives quite a lot of detail about his relationship with Jesus, not as a disciple but as a friend, and it was very enlightening. He did not always agree with Jesus in the beginning. As things progressed, he became more and more in tune with what Jesus was saying, but it was a gradual growing into the understandings of what Jesus was saying.

DOUG: Oh, so really, Jesus helped convince Paul more about his teaching?

JOHN: Yeah. He brought spiritual understanding through his conversations with Paul.

DOUG: Okay.

JOHN: They were what you would consider friends.

* * * * *

Now that the dark side has lost control, the truth can no longer be withheld from us. We will find the truth and learn to ascend to the fifth dimension by increasing our level of consciousness to Christ consciousness. There is no substitute for the truth we must meet. We must be led to it through gentle understanding. Where God is, we are. Nothing can change the knowledge God gave us into unknowingness. Everything God created knows its Creator. The Father, his creations, and the creations of his Son join in the holy meeting place. There is one link that joins them all together, which is Christ consciousness.

The connection with which the Father joins himself to those he gives the power to create can never be dissolved. Heaven itself is a union with all of the creation and its Creator. And heaven remains the will of God. Lay no gifts other than this upon altars, for nothing can coexist with it. Here, small offerings are brought together with the gift of God, and only what is worthy of the Father will be accepted by the Son, for who it is intended. To whom God gives himself, he is given. Small gifts will vanish on the altar, where he has placed his own.

Jesus had shown us the way to get to this state. We were never given a chance to expound on it while the dark side was in control. They have created churches to keep us from the truth. However, now we are reentering the Photon Belt. The Christians will get stuck behind in the spinning wheel of reincarnation if they cling to the old church dogma. It keeps them inside the shells of their egos.

* * * * *

DOUG: So those Christians would just simply be reincarnated many times over?

JOHN: Until they come to an awakening, yes.

* * * * *

"I am the God of Abraham, and the God of Isaac, and the God of Jacob? God is not the God of the dead, but of the living." (Matt. 22:32)

Christ Consciousness opens our door to have a living God within our hearts. It is what raises our spiritual growth and elevates our consciousness. The future flow of the photon energy of love and light will enlighten all of us. As we move into the golden age, love will conquer the remaining dark energies that have held us hostage for thousands of years since the previous golden age during the time of Atlantis.

Section 4.6: Life of Jesus after Crucifixion according to John

JOHN: Well I'm so glad to talk with you again, and you did have some questions last time. And I do want to fill in the best I can with answers to those questions and have some information that I think that you might find helpful. I have come to understand more of what you were asking about, so you might be interested to know that Mary, the mother of Jesus, died in Turkey officious in AD 66, and that was, I think, one of your concerns. Through the portals of crucifixion and resurrection, Jesus did ascend, and that was much later. He lived a fair amount of time after his resurrection. His resurrection and crucifixion are metaphors for everybody losing their negative, ego-driven, fearful lives, which I call—and Jesus called—Satan in the Bible. The negativity that produces bad results in our lives did not come from love. So, we crucify to remove the negative energies and move out of them into a resurrection into the love of God. The presence of God, so he had practiced, Jesus had practiced going through this from childhood, from about the age of eleven or twelve. His grandmother, Anna, taught him how to go through the rituals of going into a state of being that looked like death. It was a practicing ceremony for a later date that people could extend their lives by doing this. It was a way to regenerate the body and the mind and the soul. It was something they had seen on a continual basis if they were part of the initiative, and he had practiced this for many years. So this was not a new or first time for him to go through a crucifixion as most people would call it. In fact, when he was traveling in Egypt, this is part of what the open sarcophagus in the great pyramid is really about. Having that ceremony where you move into the sarcophagus, those around you are attending you so that there is no harm done while you are in this very gentle state of being removed from the current energy and giving yourself a regeneration. In fact, his grandmother did this quite often and lived to be seven hundred years old through being able to regenerate her life through this process. So he was well indoctrinated in that this was possible, and that is what he did on the cross. So he looked like he had died, and so they took him down. But he actually moved into a space where he was regenerating even before he was taken off the cross, so he was then able to complete the process in the cave and, of course, resurrect into a new life of love where he was filled with the grace of God and his consciousness within the highest consciousness of God's presence that you could have in a bodily form and in this form he did travel around, helping others until AD 72.

He recognized the frequency of consciousness could be adapted in any way when he was in this higher state after the resurrection, and did come back and reappear many times for people and situations too, so he would appear not always as Jesus. In fact, not as Jesus, he would appear in a form that he was just another individual helping somebody or could appear as an animal. He could appear as the wind, both a dimension state, and humankind is now ascending into being multidimensional being. He could adjust his energy to be whatever was necessary to help the situation at the time, and so with this higher interdimensional state that he moved into, he has returned often and not always recognized, generally not recognized. In fact, most people today would not find him recognizable because he is not the same Jesus who was perpetrated in the Bible, and that was not him originally. But people have a prerequisite of what they thought he was and what he was like, and of course, that wasn't his real journey. It was distorted in the Bible, and when he came back in this higher state of conscious, people could not recognize him because his energy was definitely different from how people had been taught to think of Jesus. But he has come back and helped in many cases. I think I did mention once he even walked with Luther Burbank for a period, so when we get in the multidimensional state, we can come in and out of the third dimension and help those who are still looking and growing and needing assistance. And this was his job. He traveled to Britain, France, and Eastern Europe, doing these deeds, assisting through others that were there and met in various forms, and it wasn't always a human form.

He lived with his family for a while after the ascension while he was traveling in these countries and ended up in India at the last part of his travels while he was still alive. He decided at that point to go to the Himalayas—sometimes people call it the Himalaya—and to continue his spiritual growth. Now his father, Joseph, had done this. His father went to the Himalayas and continued his spiritual growth in a cave up with the masters in the Himalayas, and many, many masters have a community up there. In fact, the spring equinox will occur again because the masters join yearly to come together in celebration, and so this was a regular natural place for him to travel to in order to continue his work as far as his spiritual growth. He watched his father go through this initiation into becoming one of spirit with God. His father died in a cave in the Himalayas with the masters up there. He was ascending from his spiritual, earthly life and leaving that human life through the chakra. He ascended into the oneness of whole spirit, and Jesus followed his path. At the time he decided it was time for him to finally join his father, not just in the physical form but with spirit. He sat in a cave in the Himalayas and did his ritual that was necessary for raising his consciousness even further into the Spirit of God. There he is now still. His remains are in a cave in the Himalayas, and he did this in AD 72. That is when he physically left the earth, and he is still returning to earth in various forms and still connecting with those like me and those who channel. I'm John, and those who channel his spirit are still very strong and present. His spirit is very strong on the earth for those people who are genuinely wanting to follow the path of ascension, raising their souls and healing them so that they return to the father. It is the trip that everyone accomplishes at some time. It is only in their own time frame. It is not necessarily when their friends want them to or (inaudible) wants him to improve their lives. But they have their script they have written, and at the right time and in the right places, people will gradually all come back to the Father in spirit. The separation will be no longer present. As you turn on the light of God, the darkness is distilled, and all there will be will be light in the peace that is coming upon earth. So the darkness—that is what it means by Satan—will be bound, and the darkness will have dissipated. The light will shine it out of existence. That was what Jesus was doing with his life. Many masters have done that with their lives. He was not the only one, and because of this light-changing effort of so many people, the balance of light and dark has occurred. The planet has gone into the Photon Belt, which is the Christ consciousness and makes this possible and supports this change. Before that, the change was much, much harder. The masters of old had a much more difficult time adjusting to a new higher consciousness because the energy did not support it, but now people are in a fortunate position where if they choose to move into a higher consciousness. I hear you are going through some states of this yourself. As you do this, it is going to be more supported than ever in history. People tried this at the time of Atlantis to move into this higher consciousness, and the dark side, of course, brought about the demise of Atlantis and the Lemuria. You know about that. It was thirteen thousand years for the population to move gradually into a place where the planet again supported it and made it possible, and this time it is guaranteed to be successful. But the dark side will not be able to stop it again.

As you probably know, 9/11 was purposely planned to happen when it did because when the new law of NESARA, this would have been the opening about ten years ago for people to start ascending higher and more frequently and more quickly at that point and time without announcement, but of course, the dark side had a plan to stop it. That was 9/11. They put a focus in a different place, and the announcement of that new law, which was going to allow a high consciousness for people in their lives, was never made. So the wheels have turned around at this point to allow this change and this ascension, which was stopped through the time of Atlantis. It is now your time to continue to make that effort to move into the higher consciousness without the barriers and impediments that were produced thirteen thousand years ago to stop it, but to allow the doors to open, the portals have been adjusted through the various astrological cycles. The different portals have gradually opened! People's chakras are being adapted to handle the crystal forces inside rather than carbon-based lives. Part of the ascension is changing the inner structure of your being so it is not so dense and it is not as heavy. Most people will notice they feel lighter, and that is because the light is shining in them as obliterated to heavier darkness because the carbon composites in their bodies have been spiritualized. So in this ascension it is a complicated ascension, but the body has to go through many rigors of adjustments and change. You have been so forced into a denser, deeper energy to keep you out of your consciousness of a higher power, a loving force that is in the universe, it has been obliterated through the fear, and with that fear dispelled, people are awakening. People are getting wiser that things aren't really right. And the government things aren't right in the world. Things are not going the way people want them. Freedoms have been taken away. They don't have the rights they normally would have had, such as the constitutional rights, and all those things will be restored gradually. All the rights and freedoms will come back into place over time, and in the next ten to fifteen years we will have gradually moved into a place where we normally would have been if 9/11 hadn't happened. It just happened to be a deterrent along the way that was not necessarily planned, but it did occur. The dark was stronger in some ways than had been predicted, so the barriers were more to handle than heaven had been prepared for. But the new plans were put in place, and things are coming together. It is not in the media yet that these changes are occurring. Bits and pieces of this news—the light coming to earth in a way that we will actually manifest in our lives and have the peace and harmony and the prosperity—are gradually coming to the surface in various ways and manifesting in people's life. Marilyn is an example. Many things are demonstrated today that she didn't think were possible. So you see, they are very pleasant and good things, and they have always been there for everybody, the abundance and prosperity. And as the light obliterates those barriers, when people accept the fact that they are one with the father, the father is within. As Jesus said, "I and the Father, are one." That is the basis of her class coming up, and her book is about how can people actually come into that acceptance and live that life of knowing they are children of God, not just saying it but experiencing it, sharing that loving, unconditional energy with one another. As that occurs—this new age of love, unconditional love for yourself and your brothers, you know—we will have our hearts focused on only God, and that will be our first commandment. *Love thy God with all my heart, mind, and soul.* And our focus will no longer have to be distracted by those things around us, those things that the dark has put in place to keep our minds off of God's love, which has always been there. The athletic situations will be adjusted rather than be competitive. They will be focused more on maybe improving your skill instead of who wins. This is not a game of who wins. As you have come to understand, it is about how can you be part of it. So as you improve your own experience and are part of the situation, that is what the new life will be like. No one will really be a leader. Nobody will really be the underdog that you vote for or support or cheer for because we'll all be one. We will come back into the oneness of us all being part of that energy in all of us who are good, have been beneficial, prosperous, and abundance. Now the unity and cooperation of humanity can come together. There is a song about the brotherhood of man, and that will become not just a song but an experience for everybody to come into harmony with all those around and to find the grace of God. He will supply everything you need. Your working situations will change because God will bring to you those things you need. And you will have more time and freedom to express your talents and your experiences with others so you can enjoy life and find your passions and pursue that just as you have been seeking this book—if you are to continue writing and if you are continuing any way that brings you joy. Life is about joy and enjoying life, and so there will be more time for that, more availability of funds for that so that you don't have to work as hard. And you will have time to express those incredible abilities that are God-given.

I am so pleased that you have been putting this book together and helping people understand what they were not told or could not come into that information before. It has been a great privilege to work with you. It has been an immense understanding that you're providing for your readers, and hopefully, many books will be in the hands of people who will understand and be open to your message. I know that you worked so hard, and there is a path that is for you that will open up and allow you to get the book wherever it needs to be, into the hands of people who are open and receptive, those people who are willing to hear through ears that they did not hear through before and see through eyes they did not see before that the invisible is the power. It is not those things around us that can take and give away our salaries, or they can give away our homes. There are so many people who have had these difficulties. However, it is the power within that is the power we need to focus on, to know that it loves us and supports us in all things. The universe was set up as a helpful experience to move into the grace of God in his presence and have the ability to have a higher consciousness of joy, ecstasy, and bliss. As you move into higher consciousness, you will have an expansive vision of what Spirit is about as you move forward into that new adventure, not just being a human being but being a spiritual being, releasing the healing in obstacles and the human faults that have stopped that spiritual experience from occurring. You will more and more become that spiritual being, that child of God, knowing that you are good and have worth and value and all those things or people who brought you into a place of feeling worthless or not real. That was not reality because only God's love is reality, and those items will obliterate in the past. They will no longer be motivations for your life because as you move into heart and open your heart completely, you will be totally safe in God's love. Nothing can hurt or harm love. It is only when you stop it by closing your heart, you create the problems. So opening your heart and being totally vulnerable, entirely in the spirit of God, is the safest place to be, where you truly have been yearning to be and learning your lessons to change the energy. Jesus came with one purpose, and that purpose was to tell people the right use of energy. And the right use of energy is to be loving to yourself and others, so therefore, his commandments were very, very truthful to love God and let that energy flow through you, which then flows to those around you. And you are all one in the love of God, oneness returning to the one spirit, and as you mentioned earlier with Marilyn not being the leader but just being one, you are part of that energy equally, and you are as important part as any of the other parts. The whole has to have every part together. It is like a puzzle. It can't be missing any soul to be whole and complete. Everyone is part of the whole, and everyone is essential to bring it into wholeness, and that will be a skill, an ongoing process over many, many years. There will be many thousands of years before this actually takes place in a complete way but people are now on the path and now on the journey for that to happen in a way that will be productive and real. The reality is that the presence of God will never leave them, and anything that is not loving is not of God. Just release it, forget it, and turn your focus immediately back to the reality that you are in joy and gratitude and the presence of God, and that is reality and the truth of who you are.

Section 4.7: Walk-in

When the individuated, embodied part of Spirit, the soul, has fulfilled what is set out to accomplish in a lifetime, it has three options—take on a new life goal (reincarnation in same body), die, or walk out. If the soul desires to walk out, an agreement is made with another soul to walk in and maintain the embodiment. It is not possession, and it is not an obligation that a person be a walk-in to ascend. It is simply an individual agreement and another way of appearing on the planet.

Prior to an actual walk-in taking place, the new soul would try out the body for a few days or weeks or even months. The personality may or may not be aware, as it often comes about while sleeping, meditating, or channeling. There may be a sense of someone hanging around or feeling the loss of time. The new soul is getting the feel of the body. Some beings coming in have never been in physical bodies and may need to get the experience of being so densified. In addition, the new soul is also encoding the DNA and the existing energy patterns stored in all of the bodies and choosing what to keep or release.

Sometimes right before a walk-in, the personality may feel a sense of completion with the lifetime. It may reveal as extreme fatigue, severe depression, or suicidal feelings.

For example, Abraham Lincoln had a fourth-dimensional entity taking over his body through a walk-in during the time of his distress. He was weary of life but without thoughts of self-destruction. The one known as Abraham Lincoln had an extreme difficulty in many ways because of physical, mental, and spiritual pain. In 1853, this entity was contacted in sleep by a fourthdensity being. This being was concerned with the battles between the forces of light and the forces of darkness, which have been waged in fourth-density for many years. This fourth-dimensional entity accepted the honor/duty of completing Abraham's karmic patterns. Abraham realized that this entity would attempt those things that he felt he could not. Thus, the exchange was made (Ref. 1).

* * * * *

DOUG: That is what happened to Abraham Lincoln. At some point he was praying, and I guess, I got these from the book *A Law of One*. So a higher density entities came in and took over his life, and he went to heaven.

JOHN: Abraham Lincoln had an immense spiritual connection. There was a room in the White House for spiritual séances. So he was very connected, and yes, this can easily happen.

* * * * *

A sense of completion is the personality's way of deciphering that a transfer is about to occur. The personality may not be aware of it. The transfers often occur during a deep trance or sleep state. On occasion, the soul may choose to manifest trauma to the body, such as accident, illness, coma, concussion, or emotional shock. It allows the new soul to integrate immediately to a deeper level. Because all of the body's system disruptions are from the habitual patterns of trauma, they are more receptive to the new soul. In the case of walk-in, this was the most commonplace route the two souls would agree to for the transfer of energy.

Now the walk-in progression is somewhat easier for several reasons. Today people have a potential of activating his or her light body. For a walk-in, this suggests that the physical body is better able to admit a new energy at the cellular level and the personality can acclimate to a new identity. Also, now there are support systems and integration services for walk-ins, so the rationale for changing through trauma is unwarranted. At the time of the walk-in, the old spiritual, mental, and emotional bodies go away with the departing soul, and the new spiritual, mental, and emotional bodies are attached to the physical body. The etheric and physical bodies provide some continuity of the new soul for the new patterns and emotions. Most walk-ins recollect life facts without any emotional attachment. To them, memories of the previous soul's experiences are like watching a movie without any emotion. This neutrality means a feeling of emotional detachment from people such as the spouse, children, and friends. The old issues, unresolved circumstances, and personal difficulties of the former incarnate are often easy for the new walk-in to handle. They are more likely to leave the unsettled marriage or unsatisfactory employment that the former occupant could not resolve.

A new walk-in often goes through personality changes. The personality is completely malleable at this time, and the new soul tries on new character traits until a right combination to achieve the new life goal. Also, changes in personal preferences are common as well, such as different foods, clothes, and lifestyles than the former occupant. A new walk-in is like a newborn baby because the emotional and mental bodies are new and a sponge for the emotions, traits, and beliefs of the people around them. They may not realize or believe that a transfer of souls has occurred.

If the body firmly believes that it is dying, then it may shut down the body entirely. Also, the body may refuse the new soul, much like it can reject a new heart or liver. A common manifestation of body rejection is severe allergic reactions to food, soaps, clothes, and plants. Sometimes in the very beginning, a new walk-in may have epilepsies like seizures as a result of the brain change.

Typically, a walk-in experiences psychic or multidimensional openings, as the seventh chakra is still open from the transfer. The sudden opening may make a person feel crazy or disoriented. When people channel constantly, they may have some difficulty knowing their energy as a result. Most physical and personality signs of rejection and confusion pass very quickly with a little integration. However, the process of releasing the dysfunctionality and obsolete pictures of the experience of the previous occupant could take years.

Strong grief states are common as the body discharges these old energies. The trick is not to resist and express the grief fully as it comes up. Then it seems to pass quickly. Walk-ins have new life goals and bring with them new abilities to assist them in accomplishing it. Also, usually an embodiment is chosen that has skills the new souls can use their missions.

Some walk-ins never know what happened—just that they went through a dramatic life change. Some souls may just have a major karma that they wish to complete. Others, perhaps coming in from other dimensions or universes, may be here to raise consciousness during this planet transitioning to the fifth dimension. There are many reasons for a soul to walk-in, but the main one is that it is usually quicker to integrate a new soul into a new body than it is to grow a body from scratch.

* * * * *

DOUG: Could an angel block negative energy from possessing me? For instance, some individuals with multi-personality disorder might have been possessed. Could an angel protect that person or really an angel can't do anything?

JOHN: Oh, they can protect you. There are two parts of that. The angels are always there, and as you just identified a minute ago, you need to ask for help. The other part is if you are going to be killed and overly harmed in a way that would spoil your script so that you would possibly die and not complete your script, then they can intercede. Mack found himself on a railroad track, stuck in a pickup truck in Italy, and he was going to be— The train was coming down the track, and it was just a matter of a moment. He would be hit by the train, and the next thing that he knew, he was literally lifted to a small hillside. And he was standing beside the truck as the train went by in front of him. So Marilyn has had similar experiences where her husband was going to beat her up intensely and angels held him from beating her up. And she was told to pray for him, to say, "God, forgive him, for he knows not what he does," and in saying that twice, she sent love to him. That love heals. Love melted the anger he had, and she was never touched again. So angels stopped him from harming her, and God came in and told her to send love through this prayer of God forgiving him, for he knows not what he does. And it broke the interaction between the two of them—his anger and her trying to protect herself. It turns out when you are trying to keep yourself safe, you are sending out anger to the other person. So he was retaliating, so yes, angels can intercede when it's drastic. And in her first book, there were several times she went off cliffs, and angels put her back on the cliffs on the road. So yes, angels usually do not intercede without request, but in immediate emergency, if you're not supposed to leave the planet yet, you won't.

* * * * *

DOUG: Was Melchizedek a walk-in?

JOHN: Yes.

DOUG: And would there be other walk-ins? Are they biblical characters?

OHN: Yes.

DOUG: Who are they?

JOHN: Well, one is the mother of Mary. Her name was Anna. So she was a walk-in, and she came in through another lady who was in desperate straits. They made an agreement that Anna would come in and complete that life. There have been other walk-ins, but you named two of the most well-known. The most famous and most important one is from the Bible.

DOUG: And could—I know you can't name names, so I'll keep the question in general—some of the world's leaders, such as the US president or president of the Soviet Union or the prime minister of Japan, could any of them be a walk-in?

JOHN: They could be, yes. However, in many cases people have been through many reincarnations, growing into the abilities to be in the leaderships they have today, or if they have had leadership in the past, they don't have that particular leadership today because they have experienced it already and don't need to continue in that part of their spiritual growth. And walk-ins are not very common, but they do exist.

DOUG: If the person was doing evil, could a walk-in will replace that person and keep the evil from, you know?

JOHN: Interesting topic. Oftentimes illnesses can be from an attached entity that controls the person, so the person's own individual physical behavior and thinking is not his or her own, Instead dark energy that is attached controls the person. So walk-ins are not the only way that our energy could enter into a person. In fact, I know of one situation where a person went to the hospital, and because of all the drugs and anesthesiology that are used for operations and surgery that open up your aura and your soul, a dark energy did enter that person upon being exposed. It is why alcohol, prescriptions, and drugs are death. They are not very practical because they open up your aura, and those dark energies can enter, yes.

Chapter 5

Spiritual Realm

Section 5.1: Earthbound Souls

An earthbound spirit is a human spirit that has not properly passed over. They have not gone to the next level into the light. Some spirits may remain at or near the site of their death, especially if death was sudden and unexpected as in a hospital or site of their passing. They remain confused and do not understand or accept their death. They are able to observe the event around them and realize the rescue team is working on them. They can hear all the communication of the people there. These spirits may stay in the area and try to make a contact or not with anyone who is near and who is sensitive to spirits.

Some of the earthbound entities think they are assisting their loved ones by bringing guidance. Almost anything that a spirit feels obliged to do may add time to its earthbound stay. The living can also hold a spirit earthbound by not letting go of the person who passed over. The spirits need for the person to release them for their advancement. There are no feelings but love in the spirits. However, they are concerned about the welfare of their loved ones and their own availability to be free of their attachment.

Grieving survivors usually are not ready to communicate with their loved ones yet. Ghosts usually are harmless. Some disembodied spirits remain earthbound to watch over loved ones and their possessions. They may also attempt to convey a message to those who are living.

Usually, there is not a reason for spirits to remain earthbound—unless they are obsessively bound to the person or the person refuses to accept their passing and release them.

The only time they adversely affect a living human is if a dark soul attaches to make a person sick and addictive or become a home for that dark soul. A few earthbound entities continue to hang around cemeteries, drinking establishments, and mental wards to attach to innocent victims. Disembodied spirits are able to coexist with souls passing over, producing health issues when a person is not careful. This affects the behavior, medical conditions, and attitude of the person still living. They can be released through psychic counseling.

DOUG: Why are earthbound souls still earthbound after they die? Is it true that only 5 percent, roughly just a number, make it through the window of heaven?

JOHN: Well, it depends on how you are looking at the picture. There's a bigger picture than 5 percent. At this point through history, 5 percent has been considered a valid figure because the ego kept people from looking at who they truly were inside and people were afraid to open their hearts to the love. It was too scary. It was actually the biggest fear on Earth. While some may think public speaking or death causes the most fear, it's actually the fear of opening up to the love of God that dominates those on Earth. So when people were able to bypass that fear, yes, there was less than 5 percent who were able to find the courage to move beyond their old paradigm. Which is what Marilyn's book is about—moving beyond that paradigm. This is a time in history of awakening. This is Christ consciousness, now in the consciousness of planet Earth. Christ consciousness is feeling the love of God within, and it is allowing people to open up to more and more love, so that figure will change. This is a time of great renown. This is not affecting just planet Earth but the whole universe. The new higher consciousness on Earth matches those of other universes that already have a higher consciousness. We are growing up, you might say. We are coming of age on planet Earth, so more and more people are coming into that space of growing into loving beings that they would be as God is inside them. Now there is another thing to remember is that different souls come to Earth at different times of their spiritual development, but not all souls are ready for that transition into higher consciousness. They have been working through their releasing of ego and karma. It is a condition of shameful experiences such as hate, anger, tragedy, and trauma. Also, some people have an early soul with fewer life journeys than have the old souls. The old souls are awakening because they have gone through the processes of reducing the influence of the ego. However, not everybody on planet Earth has gotten to this point because they are young souls. They have not gone through enough reincarnations to advance to that state, so those souls will continue their third-dimensional journey. Those who are ready to ascend into higher consciousness will still be on planet Earth, but they will see the planet Earth from a different perspective—through the eyes of love in God. They will not buy into the drama that is going on around them. So there is a mixture of people on Earth who have different levels of consciousness. Furthermore, because of evolution and free will, some people will grow out of ignorance. Now many of those people are dying off the planet. They are leaving to continue in that consciousness. Some people have decided to deal with it later on in another reincarnation. They have the right to do this. However, these people are not included in the 5 percent. The doors to heaven are never closed though. That's another church thing. You do not go to heaven. You work to help others and change your consciousness. Work with people around you to make things better for everyone. Avoid the drama and trauma. In this, you become less selfish, and this is what your learning is about. The lack of selfishness becomes unconditional love so everyone is in his or her own and perfect space in that evolution. It's really not wise to put a number on it. Everyone is in his or her own position. Marilyn has been told this is her last reincarnation, but she also works with people who have been newly put here on planet Earth. Ultimately, it's the person's decisions whether he or she is ready. He or she must feel secure enough and safe enough to move on. It all happens at the right time.

DOUG: I can see that love conquers everything, and it conquers fear.

JOHN: Amen.

DOUG: And also, would it be helpful for people to understand that there is love in heaven and to know what heaven is all about?

JOHN: Yes, they have definitely been deceived about heaven. Heaven is actually on Earth. Fear blocks their vision. Heaven on earth is not a place they've gone to or participated in because fear blocked their energy. This is the kind of counseling Marilyn has done quite successfully. She helps people release the fear, and each time they can move up the scale of consciousness and see a little bit more of heaven on earth. Their lives go on a smoother path. They are slightly more comfortable in their being, and things fall into place a little better than before. This is all a gradual process.

DOUG: Do earthbound souls lack understanding of the cosmic value or eternal value?

JOHN: That is a good question because there are a variety of reasons they remain earthbound. Six reasons come to mind. Some earthbound spirits are here for unfinished business. Did you see the movie *The Sixth Sense*?

DOUG: No, I have not seen this film.

JOHN: Well, you should see this movie. I am trying to think of the fellow who played the part so well. There was a little boy in the film who saw a spirit. This man died, and he saw him, so it is an interesting story. It is about a person who had unfinished business to take care of, so he did not leave the planet until that happened. Sometimes people are drawn to stay on Earth because they are so emotionally attracted to another person. They love the person so much that they cannot bear to leave that person behind. So they stay on Earth as ghosts, you might call them. So there are a variety of reasons. Some people have such dense energy they do not know how to go to the other side, so they wander around, unsure of how to leave.

DOUG: So how do they get out of it?

JOHN: Well, as time goes, they learn. An interesting thing happened to Marilyn. This one particular energy that was earthbound was living in a hotel called the Tokeland Hotel on the Washington coast, which is the oldest hotel in Washington state. It is still functioning, and there were several ghosts living in that particular establishment. Marilyn and Mack went there to spend a couple of nights. Mack was bicycling on the coast with his friends, and they ended up in the room with a ghost. Mack asked Marilyn if she would mind having this room because of the ghost. Marilyn, not afraid of ghosts, took the room. So she slept fine that night. In the middle of the night, though, she got up to use the restroom, which was down the hall. As she walked into the hallway, she saw the ghost sitting in a rocking chair in the corridor. As she spoke with him, she learned that he had vacated the room the previous night so that she could sleep well. Marilyn thanked him. They conversed several time that weekend, any time she was in the hallway. She came home that Sunday afternoon and told Mack about this ghost. So she went to her program the next night. When she returned home, she realized the ghost, named Henry, was still with her. He explained that he followed her because he knew she could help him go to the other side. It was right after September 11. He explained how he had attached himself to her and asked for her help. He explained that they needed help on the other side. Things there were in disarray because of the terrorist attacks. So many people were moving over at once, and they needed more hands, so to speak. So Marilyn had Henry stay, and she called Mack and said Henry was with her. They visited for a while, and then it was time to send him over, so she sent him to the light. So this is an example of an earthbound entity asking for help to move out of his earthbound state. Now when Marilyn and Mack do free healings on Thursday afternoon, we have had a few entities show up because we invite them. Marilyn and Mack would say if any of you are needing help to get to the other side, we'll be glad to assist you. So if they are aware enough that they can change that positioning into moving out of being earthbound, then it is possible.

DOUG: Earthbound souls remain on Earth because they have not gone through the tunnel?

JOHN: That is right.

DOUG: So what happens then? I mean, would they still be earthbound for another five hundred years, or they will eventually move out?

JOHN: Free will comes into play, and they can make a choice about staying in their consciousness. They need to be ready to change.

DOUG: Okay, so can they see what's going on while they are earthbound? Can they see what is going on with their families and friends?

JOHN: Oh, yes.

DOUG: Oh, so that will help them to want to change?

JOHN: Well, people are earthbound for several different reasons, one of which may be unfinished business. Did you ever see the movie *The Sixth Sense*?

DOUG: Yeah.

JOHN: Bruce Willis. He stayed around on Earth to complete some unfinished business, and then he could move on. Some people stick around because they are emotionally tied to another person. They are not able to release that connection and free themselves. The bond could be positive love or negative abuse. There are a variety of reasons why they stay. There isn't one answer.

* * * * *

The condition of the individual before passing will be the remaining state of the disembodied spirit. Emotional traumas are still felt, even though the spirit is no longer within a body. If the addiction to drugs, sex, or alcohol remains, then those same addictions are present in the spirit. In fact, these addictions and traumas will drive the disembodied spirit into trying to find some relief. The ghost looks to the past and becomes a prisoner. The spirit cannot see the future or a way out of their earthbound state. The light and loved ones become invisible to the disincarnate.

* * * * *

DOUG: Now does the dark side make spirit entities a living hell while they are earthbound?

JOHN: Oh, definitely. That is very true. Marilyn has had people come to her who were going through terrible difficulties, and it was because of the attachments with those entities. It was directly the dark side. The dark side is a loosely knit organization, so smaller sections of the network project dark energy onto people through various sources. It's not the work of the Illuminati directly, but they have their hand in it.

* * * * *

Shadow ghosts are earthbound people who have not moved beyond this earth, having chosen to remain behind with humanity. A ghost needs to undergo a cleansing review. If the ghost does not do this, then he or she will continue to carry around emotional baggage from Earth. This does not imply that these ghosts have ill intentions. They are no different from those spirits that have accepted their past deeds and went toward the light. Beyond the light, they meet with their spiritual guides in Nirvana, and they work out a plan for their next lives (reincarnation). The shadow ghosts happened to fear God because they felt they needed to live perfect, sin-free lives. No one can accomplish this in the third-dimensional world.

Our spirit carries a spark of infinity within our soul. The spirit is eternal. It is a gift from the Creator. It takes a number of lives to remove the darkness of our energy and to acknowledge our imperfection as part of our learning experience. It is the only way to achieve a higher dimensional state for our soul. The angels are there to help guide us.

* * * * *

DOUG: Who assigns my next life?

JOHN: Oh, you do. What happens in Nirvana is that you stay there. This is something not often talked about. You get yourself healthy from your death transition. You develop a musical or artistic talent, and you have the ability to learn how to change energy from that space and time. For instance, you can learn how to enter the dream of a loved one. You learn how to do those things in Nirvana. There, you have all kinds of opportunities and colleges you can attend. You come back and head to Earth with your feelings again. In Nirvana, there are no feelings. It is all love, and it is smooth. However, you cannot change your feelings in Nirvana, so you come back to Earth to purge your soul.

DOUG: So an angel will guide me?

JOHN: Oh, okay, you were talking about the script that you write. Yes, when you are in Nirvana and you've gone through, you feel you've been there long enough to learn the skills to bring back with you. Then you call for a meeting and say you are ready to reincarnate. At that point, your masters and guides meet with you. They sit you down, and they give you an important lesson of how the process works and about your soul's history. These are the things that you are learning in your life. They let you know what you've already accomplished, so you don't reinvent the wheel once reincarnated. You must change other things in your life instead. Your guides and masters have written a script for you or a contract. The script outlines the best choices for you, and you agree to them. These are the traumas and the dramas necessary for you to change your fear into love, compassion, and forgiveness. You will work to change all of your energies into unconditional love, gratitude, and compassion. You want to have that loving energy reunite with the energy of God. So you go through this, and it takes a fair amount of time to sort the right path for the next reincarnation. May I suggest a movie that is not perfect but gives you the idea of how this works? The movie is called *Defend Your Life* with Meryl Streep. In this film Albert Brooks (Daniel Miller) goes to this place where his guides talk to him about what he needs to do to move on spiritually. He must agree to the terms before he can move on. It is a very involved process, and it is critical because when you come to Earth—and if you deviate from that script—you will be coming back for another reincarnation to get your script right.

* * * * *

There is a misconception about demons working for the Devil. Possessing them does not make them disembodied people who look menacing and work for a devil. There is no Devil. It is only a term used for a lack of light. We can find many scary people here on Earth who are actually very nice, good-hearted souls. In other words, appearances can be deceiving.

A spirit possession would be better termed as *ghost possession* as well as *attachment*. No matter what we label this phenomenon, it is not *demon possession* as some might have us believe. Consider them *unseen influences* from others who are with us. Ghosts have been found to possess people for many reasons, such as the following:

- continuing to experience physical life;
- experiencing former physical addictions;
- having a strong attachment to earthly wealth or loved ones;
- not knowing they have died because they still have consciousness; or
- seeking revenge on another person through harm.

Bindings between people and ghosts might be strong and exorcised spirits do not come back and possess these people again. Hell exists only in their minds. There is no such place in the immaterial world, but the mind makes it right for them. There is a phrase in the Scripture that talked about this. "When an impure spirit comes out of a person, it goes through arid places seeking rest and does not find it. Then it says, 'I will return to the house I left.' When it arrives, it finds the house unoccupied, swept clean and put in order. Then it goes and takes with it seven other spirits more wicked than itself, and they go in and live there. So, the final condition of that person is worse than the first. That is how it will be with this wicked generation" (Matthew 12:45). The seven other spirits are considered the seven deadly sins, which do not always come from separate spirits. They can come from karma too. They include

- gluttony, an excess in eating and drinking;
- greed, an excessive or reprehensible acquisitiveness;
- sloth, an avoidance of physical or spiritual work;
- anger, which spurns love and opts instead for fury;
- envy, a painful or resentful awareness;
- pride, inordinate self-esteem; and
- lust, an inordinate craving for the pleasures of the body.

These are the common lower energy that might contaminate our souls. When we pass through the light, our spiritual guides will heal this energy. The guides then work out a plan to overcome them in your next life if the task is not completed.

Mary Magdalene was healed of the seven devils. "And when Jesus was risen again, early the first day of the week, he appeared first to Mary Magdalene, out of whom he had cast seven devils" (Mark 16:9). Even the Bible would not disclose that Mary was one of the disciples in Jesus's eyes. She found the light of God within through meditation. When we find the light of God within ourselves, then the seven deadly sins are individually healed by the love of God. It is a process.

* * * * *

DOUG: So you're saying that Mary Magdalene was healed of the seven devils?

JOHN: Well, those were emotional upsets, such as anger, fears, worry—some people call these the seven deadly sins. You've heard that term?

DOUG: Yes.

JOHN: When you release anything that is an obstacle to God—yes, those need to be released, and that is why Mother Mary was selected. And not many people know this about Marilyn, but she was one of the girls chosen to be the mother of Jesus. So they were all in training with the Essenes. Also, Jesus was a student of the Essenes. His teacher was Judy before he went to India and the Far East and learned some of the spiritual things of that religion.

* * * * *

Ghosts are people in spirit, unclean spirits who need assistance moving past the temporary prison that their minds have produced. Not everyone on earth is an unclean spirit, not just the ghosts. This type of aid would be similar to what a psychologist might do through counseling. We read in 1 Peter 3:19 that Jesus "preached to the spirits in prison." We, too, should help unclean spirits by letting them know they should

1) not be afraid to move on with their lives, for better things await them;
2) understand that their bodies have died, even though they are still alive at the present time;
3) not fear eternal punishment (in hell), for it does not exist; and
4) reunite with loved ones who await them by turning toward the light to experience freedom, real peace, joy, and most importantly, love.

Loved ones of enlightened spirits attempt to reach these lost people, and at times, they may need our help assisting the ghost. This is similar to the idea in the movie *The Matrix*. People were able to remain behind and oversee others who went into a virtual world.

These *watchers* aided and guided them back out of that world into reality. Helping ghosts is about moving the spirit, who is a person, into the present moment while leaving behind troubles from the past. Maybe it takes the assistance from both planes to help some of the departed make it home to the afterworld.

Perhaps two accounts of Jesus in the Bible would give us important keys to understanding the spirit world. Jesus stated to Nathanael, "You shall see angels ascending and descending upon the son of man." James, Peter, and John witnessed Jesus speaking with Moses and Elijah from the other side at the transfiguration. Perhaps Jesus was showing us that the angels ascending and descending represented two-way communication between spiritual and the physical worlds. So that the pulling back of the veil (so to speak) revealed Moses and Elijah or disembodied spirits in the light (spirit world) talking to us. It could be that Jesus's real mission was to free earthbound spirits and assist them in moving on with their lives. Maybe his advice was meant for earthbound entities. Jesus was one of the few who had the capability of seeing spirits with his third eye, the spiritual eye.

This thought aligns with certain sects of Judaism that understood spirit attachment. This concept focuses on aiding the attached ghosts in moving on through a ceremonial of exorcism that benefits both the ghost and the person who is suffering the attachment.

Think about Jesus in the Bible casting out unclean spirits, and imagine what happened if it were true. It is possible that witnesses had a third eye that saw the physical demonstrations of the real ministry Jesus was performing in the unseen realm. It is possible that he was freeing the hidden captives in spirit while freeing people bound by them in the physical world. He demonstrated the power when he spoke with the possessing spirits, directing them to leave the person. The rightful owner of the body would be transformed and freed from whatever physical and mental abnormalities were present prior to the exorcism.

Most ghosts are not harmful or ill-willed, though entities with not-so-good intentions do exist. Such spirits are simply human earthbound spirits manifesting as ghosts. The term *dark shadows* describes the adverse entities because they only lack the light of God. Everyone has dark shadows to release.

In dealing with negative entities, it is vital to understand that they are simply spirits of humans. They may have bad dispositions and possibly ill intentions. They are not demons or the Devil. However, the source of any negative entity's power is through instilling fear into their victims. The fear will allow a negative entity to gain control over the mind of the person whom they seek to influence. Regrettably, most people fear what they do not understand, so it is easy for a negative ghost to find fearful victims. (Like attracts like.)

If looking at human beings in general, we should understand that people who attack others do so because of low self-esteem. The attack is rooted in fear and is a way to seemingly elevate one's position of standing in their mind.

The realm of the spirit world consists of multiple planes of existence for earthbound entities. There are multiple levels of darkness. Some levels are temporary places that mirror the condition of a lost soul. These hellish planes are where the ghosts dwell and absorb self-condemnation in all forms. The Earth plane would run comparable to these lowest levels, allowing for (lower-level) ghosts to be in our world from time to time. In contrast, there are most likely infinite levels of heavens that are also equal to the state of one's perception. The heavens would hold those of a higher place of recognizing spirit world.

Therefore, the plan for all humanity will be to continue growing as spiritual beings. One day when heaven on earth takes hold, it is likely that we will comprehend that everything is connected. All of these spirits of light share in the task of conveying the whole of creation into the light of this peace, joy, love, and truth.

What purpose might spirits have on Earth? The spirits speak messages of guidance and encouragement. Also, spirits come to observe, watch over, and share experiences with us in a brotherly fashion on this earthly plane. These spirits come from a higher place of understanding and therefore live in the light that is the truth. This enlightenment is present with their countenance and presence. An enlightened spirit is light and always brings a presence of peace and joy. If we have received a message, it is likely it has come from an angel. Thus, anyone who brings a message may be considered a messenger or an angel.

In contrast, ghosts are those who have not gone through the tunnel of light experience or a life review in the present reincarnation. Their state is one of darkness or lack of understanding as they struggle with present, past, or future fears. There are other ghosts that have been witnessed to be noninteractive with the physical world. Alternatively, could they just be disembodied people who have completely lost their minds by the tragic situations of the past? Is it possible some ghosts might even be unaware that their physical bodies have passed? Many ghosts have attachments to this world, such as a negative emotional near-death experience if they don't experience the Tunnel of Light. It has no trauma usually, unfinished business, and unresolved fears. This self-created prison, regardless what the people's circumstances are, needs to be unlocked. Should we encounter them, we need to say peace and bless the ghosts. We can ask their loved ones to support them as we speak words of comfort with prayers. Many spirits seek only acknowledgment of their existence. They need to know that turning toward the light (and loved ones) will bring peace, love, and joy to them. There is no eternal damnation, and facing the future is always a positive thing. Hell or darkness can only be a place to work through lack of understanding, traumas, and negative emotions. The truth is light, and light removes darkness. Only you release yourself! Enlightened can only send love for the ghosts to love themselves into self-love to raise their consciousness. No one assists a ghost unless the ghost requests help. It is always the responsibility of the person (ghost) to release him or herself. You can never save another. Love conquers all fears.

When a ghost is one that has not gone to the light and progressed through the life review, could it be that ghosts shadow people? Could darkness, represented by shadow demons, indicate the inner condition of an individual, such as hatred, anger, lack of knowledge, being lost, or void of truth? They have sought to hide in the darkness, and fear coming forth to the light, which will open up their deeds. Light indicates enlightenment, wisdom, knowledge, and above all, truth.

* * * * *

DOUG: So the earthbound soul would be in a third dimension obviously, right?

JOHN: Yes, the third dimension is a heavy density planet where there is duality, and there is fear-based energy keeping you in its domain. So you are more of a victim, acting out what someone in authority has written for you.

DOUG: If a person is in a trance or meditating to the higher realm, is it required to have a guide, an angelic guide, to protect you? Well, I guess that is like channeling, right?

JOHN: Well, you all have a guardian angel, and it is always there to help protect you. When you move into higher consciousness, more protection is advisable. So you do not have to have it if you have a very strong connection with your God of your understanding. However, there are, as I just said a little earlier, entities out there of darkness that are earthbound and do attach to people, so keep yourself as safe as possible.

DOUG: What happens to earthbound souls or ghosts during the golden ages or the fifth dimension?

JOHN: That is a very good question. Most of those who have passed over and have discovered that they are no longer living in the real world as they knew it. They are in spirit form. So those people, those entities, often will find somebody who has the spiritual ability to help them transcend into the higher consciousness of where they need to be instead of staying earthbound. So it is a dilemma that, again, the church has created. The church has explained death, but it does not address what happens when people do pass over. They need to look at the light and move forward with their angels that are there to escort them. I use Marilyn's examples because they seem to be quite useful. When she attended the Lutheran church, she was told that people are buried in the ground, and they stay there until Gabriel blows his horn. That is not what happens. So many people do not know what happens when you die. So have the right understanding that you move into the light of God when you pass over and that you move into Nirvana, not heaven. The correct term is Nirvana. So you find yourself in other environments that match your own so that you can continue your spiritual growth. You are not buried in the ground, and your spirit continues to grow when you understand that you are just going through a passage of learning and expanding your understanding and spiritual growth. So we never just stop growing. Also, in death, you are passing into new dimensions of growing, and the church has not been very good explaining that.

DOUG: Can earthbound souls reincarnate, or do they have to go to heaven first and then come back to Earth to reincarnate?

JOHN: Earthbound souls can reincarnate, but they have to leave and cannot be connected to anything. You have to give up all your emotional attachments. Take the case of my aunt and uncle. My uncle died of cancer and came back in spirit to haunt my aunt, prompting her to join him. She created an event in which she died so she could join him. He could not move on because he was coming back to her, tied to her until they both went into the spirit. So he was free to go on. So you have to move away (pass over) from the Earth plane to be able to reincarnate. Whatever holds you back, eventually that person will come to an understanding that it is time to move on. Also, now with the planet energy so highly into love, earthbound entities are becoming fewer and fewer. They are not sustainable. You cannot have dark energy when it is only light. So you see, it would evaporate all the dark energy, so this is becoming less of an issue.

DOUG: Would there be an angel or guardian angel guiding them?

JOHN: That has to come from a self-awareness and self-awakening to realize what they are doing is not working for them. As soon as they wake up and say, "I need help because I cannot get where I want to be," then immediately, their angels will be there to assist them.

DOUG: They have to ask for help?

JOHN: They have to ask.

DOUG: So an angel will come and respond?

JOHN: Yes.

DOUG: So there is an angel watching over them?

JOHN: Always.

DOUG: What kind of angel?

JOHN: Well, we all have a history of spirits around us, and the angels we were born with are the ones that stay with us. Also, there are some that come and go with different talents as you are learning new experiences and new understandings. As your life changes, you have different places you go. You need different information, so new angels will come in and help you with that. You always have that spiritual protection around you no matter how desperate the situation.

DOUG: So earthbound souls, are they in the astral world?

JOHN: Well, they are in a physical world in the third dimension.

We are all in the world. We happen to be, in your case, on a planet of the third dimension that is leaving that and moving into heaven on earth, which is a consciousness. People or inner beings are being transformed to have unconditional loving hearts with which they will influence their lives so that the hardships of the past will no longer continue.

Section 5.2: Nirvana

When we die, our soul goes to Nirvana, which is a spiritual weigh station. Nirvana is where the people collect spiritually with like-minded consciousness. The reason churches call Nirvana heaven is there's no trauma, drama, or fear. It is a very comfortable place to be. When we realize our physical form and our spirit, we then travel to this weigh station that is off from the planet Earth. Yes, it is not on the planet—that is true. We are in a space where we can regenerate our spirit into healthiness. We can also regenerate our minds. We have to let our bodies assimilate to accommodate that higher vibration. So Nirvana is not on Earth. It is a place where we go in between reincarnations, and then when we come back to Earth. The Earth never changes, only our perception of it. We'll come back to the same consciousness, ready to move into a new higher one.

A question of predestination has concerned and divided the churches throughout the ages. Are some predestined to life and salvation and others predestined to condemnation? However, there is no condemnation. We will keep coming back to get our script right and move onto another script if necessary. This process continues until our soul is free of dark energy. Since our soul is eternal, there is no limit to the number of scripts for life experience.

I found out from the conversations with John, whom I had met in a past life, that my name was Jacob. Several times he had mentioned that name during our channeling, so I asked him if it was true that he had known me back at the time in Israel. I found out I used to work with him for his father's boating business. I was a carpenter. I must have known Jesus at the time because he was there working for John's father to help support his mother Mary financially. I eventually became one of the 120 disciples after the twelve, and seventy were ordained.

* * * * *

DOUG: Now have I met you, John, in one of my past lives? I noticed that you have called me Jacob twice. I was wondering if you knew me as Jacob before.

JOHN: I think you are right in perceiving that, yes.

DOUG: Yeah, and I have worked with you and your father in his boating business.

JOHN: Yes.

DOUG: Also, was I among the 120 disciples after the seventy disciples were ordained?

JOHN: Yes.

* * * * *

It is a dimension transcending time and space. Nirvana is beyond time. There is no movement and so no aging or dying. Thus, Nirvana is eternal because it is beyond space. There is no causation, no boundary, no concept of self. Heaven on earth is a state of consciousness within your being. It is not a place. "Neither shall men say, Lo here or lo there: for behold, the kingdom of God is within you" (Luke 17:21).

After you have completed a life journey, you will be greeted by a spiritual guide at the tunnel. It is imperative that we proceed to the tunnel and allow an angel to escort us through it to get to the other side, or else you will become a prisoner on Earth.

* * * * *

DOUG: When you see the light at the end of the tunnel, is this when you see flashbacks of your past life?

JOHN: Well, everyone has a different version of that because we're all individuals, but that's often true. It's more of a review of how well you did, and that is the church's version of judgment.

DOUG: Now is that the light Jesus or God the Father?

JOHN: God the Father's light.

DOUG: And many people wonder why when they approached the light, they said they want to go back.

JOHN: When you are in perfect peace and harmony, why would you go back to turmoil and crises?

DOUG: Is that the only thought that makes it through?

JOHN: There is not a percentage that makes it through. It has more to do with whether you put yourself totally into the love of God. And release all that that isn't God.

* * * * *

One of the nine elements that occur during NDEs (Ref. 7) is the tunnel experience. It involves being drawn into darkness through a tunnel at an extremely high speed until reaching a realm of radiant golden white light. Also, although they sometimes report feeling scared, most do not sense that they are on the way to hell or that they fell into it, which is their spirit. There have been people who stayed with tormenting creatures until they asked for help. The tunnel is really levels of dark consciousness around the person. As you rise into more light the darkness is no more. Instead of a tunnel, some people report rising suddenly into the heavens and seeing the Earth and the celestial sphere as seen by astronauts in space. Once on the other side of the tunnel or after they have risen into the heavens, those who have passed over meet people who glow with an inner light. Often they find that friends and relatives who have already passed are there to greet them.

By analyzing a large number of NDE accounts on this website (Ref. 7), a map of the various paths to heaven were demonstrated as shown in table 7. Please note that Dr. Raymond Moody developed the paths, and the table was created by the author for the book. It is more likely it is #4 where only 5 percent of the souls have gone through the light because of their fears of the unknown beyond it.

Table 7: Various Paths to Heaven (Nirvana)

Path	Designation based on NDE accounts by Dr. Raymond Moody (Ref. 7)
1	Journey from earth to earthbound realm
2	Journey from earth to the void
3	Journey from earth to the void then to heaven (nirvana) by tunnel
4	Journey from earth to heaven (nirvana) by tunnel
5	Journey from earth to earthbound realm to void to heaven (nirvana)
6	Journey from earth to void, through tunnel to spirit receiving station in heaven (nirvana)

DOUG: Okay, so let's suppose I die in this life and I was baptized by the Spirit. Do I reincarnate to another body or go to heaven?

JOHN: You go to nirvana. Nirvana is a spiritual weigh station and Nirvana is where the people collect spiritually with like-minded consciousness. The reason churches call nirvana heaven is there's no trauma, drama, and fear. So, it's a very comfortable place to be so when you realize your physical form and your spirit then travels to this weigh station which is off from the Earth. Yes, it is not on the planet that is true. You are in a space where you can, and if you've died, and there's a terrible trauma, you regenerate your spirit into healthiness. And you can also renew your spirit into a simulating the higher consciousness of nirvana where there is no fear and where there is no pain and disease. You have to assimilate your body to accommodate that higher vibration, so nirvana is not on earth that is true. It is a place where you go in-between reincarnations. Then when you come back to earth, the earth has never really changed it's just your perception. You'll go back with the same consciousness ready to move into a new higher one and then it will say oh this looks different to me this time, it's because your perception changed, the earth didn't change.

DOUG: If was told that I reincarnated eight to nine hundred times, would that be correct?

JOHN: Give me a moment.

DOUG: Yeah, someone told me this.

JOHN: The number I get is 866.

* * * * *

It's a gradual progression. No one can handle one reincarnation and be in the total light of God. Your systems as a human being could not handle it. That's like having a circuit of electricity that has too much energy in it. It's going to go poof. So a human body can only handle energy in small increment, called precept upon precepts in the Bible. So as you go by increments into more lighting, yes, the person is going to become more enlightened. That's a major change in growing into the light, of course, and doing that, it takes many, many reincarnations for your human system, your energy system. If all that change happened at once, you'd likely end up in an insane asylum. It just would be too much to handle. So even Jesus had thirty-two reincarnations, and that's very minimal. Most people have had hundreds and thousands. Getting on track to enlighten ourselves is not what we are focusing on. Reincarnation always involves bringing people to new places so they can experience new living to help them work out their karmas. So our reincarnations are just gradual stages into the light and doing it at a pace that our system can handle.

While Nirvana is a place outside of Earth, heaven on earth is a state of consciousness while we are living on the planet.

* * * * *

DOUG: Now I have the illustration of Nirvana being above space, but I wondered if only people with a spiritual eye can see it.

JOHN: Well, that's true. It's this place you go to when you pass over from Earth until you come back and return in the process of reincarnation. It's a spiritual place that is not a planet. It does not have any physical ground to it. It's strictly invisible, but it's an energy that's off the planet Earth.

DOUG: Does the tunnel lead to nirvana only, or does it also go inside earth?

JOHN: The tunnel does not go inside Earth. It's a spiritual experience to rise into higher consciousness. So you leave the fears behind when you go through the tunnel (dark levels of consciousness) and move into the unconditional love of the universe.

* * * * *

When we come back to reincarnate during the fifth dimension, which is happening today, our spiritual growth will accelerate more gradually through a loving environment of the love and light energy forthcoming. There are still some remaining pockets of dark energies existing today that needed to get dispersed. Eventually, they will go away as people are moving move out of the third dimension.

* * * * *

DOUG: Okay, so we will still be here on the same planet?

JOHN: Exactly, you will not go anywhere. If you have moved your consciousness into a God consciousness, you will stay, but with a new reality.

DOUG: Okay. Now again, I just want to double check. nirvana—I know heaven is a state of consciousness.

JOHN: Nirvana is where the spirit goes when you pass to the other side.

DOUG: Oh, that is what passing to the other side.

JOHN: It is.

DOUG: I am now going to talk about Nirvana. Now from the Internet, [I found material] prepared by Dr. Raymond Moody.

JOHN: Yes.

DOUG: And he had identified six different paths from his studies. The first path we're on a journey from Earth to earthbound realm. Second path, journey from Earth to the void. Third path, journey from Earth to the void and then to heaven (Nirvana) by tunnel. Fourth path, journey from Earth to heaven (Nirvana) by tunnel. Fifth path, journey from Earth to earthbound realm to void to heaven (Nirvana), and then sixth path is journey from Earth to void and then through tunnel to spirit receiving station in Nirvana. So those are the six paths. Do they make sense to you?

JOHN: Well, yes. There has to be a variety of paths because there're so many different people who have so many different journeys to take and everyone is different, so to lump them into six is probably a practical way to look at them.

DOUG: Okay, thank you. I'll make a note that there are other paths that have not been defined. It depends on the individuals.

JOHN: It is very much individual. Society tries to label everything, and it is not always accurate because everybody has a different path and purpose. And all you can do is find as many similarities as possible. So some people will fit the path, and some won't.

DOUG: Okay, good. Now let me ask you this: Where is the void?

JOHN: Well, the void is where nothing is. It is the creative source without an emotion. When people call God the Father, that is basically the void. That is where all things are produced from manifestation. It's the energy that has not been defined or projected in a particular way to manifest, so when that void's energy moves, that's what people call Mother God. And so the movement of that void is what creates what you see in your reality.

DOUG: So would that be like a ghost?

JOHN: Well, no. That's kind of a different topic. Ghosts are energy that has not left the planet Earth. You just don't see them visually.

DOUG: Okay, now suppose after the death of the body, before approaching the tunnel, could the dark side try to keep that person from going to the tunnel?

JOHN: No. That is a path that is not accessible to that particular group. The only way they could prohibit something like that is if they have people so well drugged. That would prevent people from realizing higher places for their soul's healing. Nirvana is about healing the soul into a higher consciousness, but if you're drugged by the vaccinations, you won't get there. You would go to a lower consciousness and continue the hell you were experiencing.

DOUG: Now, if the void is of the astral world and physical world, would earthbound entities find themselves trapped?

JOHN: Not everybody goes through the tunnel, and that tunnel is just - is moving through the darkness is what it is. It's your light moving through the darkness. There isn't a tunnel, but most people in human form don't know how to explain it. So -

DOUG: The void, it's like nothing, and is that between the other side and the physical side?

JOHN: You're looking at it from a third-dimensional point of view, and all of this is within you, so you're not going anywhere. It's just becoming aware and allowing that reality can manifest into your life in a bigger, truer way than what you've had in the past. It's all about perception.

DOUG: Is the nirvana - we talked about nirvana, is that on the astral plane?

JOHN: Yes.

* * * * *

The astral plane consists of seven different spiritual vibrations, "In my Father's house are many dwelling places: if it were not so, I would have told you: I go to prepare a place for you." (John 14:2)

* * * * *

DOUG: Where are the seven mansions of the worlds?

JOHN: Okay, you're using terms, if you're talking about the mansions in the Bible where God says I will go before you and make a place, a mansion, mini mansion?

DOUG: Yes, that's correct.

JOHN: What he is talking about is again levels of consciousness. So, what you're saying is different people are at various stages of growth, some have moved out of their denial and are in a state of accepting love into their lives. And that would be one mansion. Some people have grown into learning if they release their desires and wants they can leave that space open. And the happiness of love comes in that's another mansion or dimension. So as Marilyn explained yesterday you might think of it as a parking garage with different levels of consciousness, and those are the, there are many mansions, there's one for every consciousness of every person. However, they are grouped together, and that's what you are referring to is the seven mansions is the groupings of that consciousness. Where within a range of that consciousness you will find different levels within that range, and they are all similar enough that they can continue in that mansion until they are ready to move to another higher mansion.

* * * * *

We go to the astral heaven after we die. It is invisible in the "air" of the planet. Each level corresponds for each of seven levels of consciousness. We all have a varying degree of spiritual vibration that destines us to a certain astral level where we spend some time preparing ourselves for our next life. We continue with our soul journey on the physical plane for more life lessons and sojourn on the astral plane for a rest after each incarnation. We pursue this cycle until we have attained perfection on the physical plane at the fifth dimension: "Ye shall, therefore, be perfect, as your Father which is in heaven, is perfect." (Matthew 5:48) After attaining the fifth dimension, we no longer have to reincarnate any further.

The astral world or astral heaven has seven astral spheres. They serve the purpose of readying us for our next soul journey on Earth. Our spiritual level determines our astral sphere destination. The first sphere has an appearance of the physical world, where the residents live a life similar to what they did when they were residing in the physical world. The thoughts of the residents produce the second sphere, but they have a similar lifestyle as in the first sphere. In the third sphere, they take classes in many arts, crafts, and so on. In the fourth sphere, we find artists who work independently by themselves, medical people who do research, and students who exchange ideas for further learning. There are also mental hospitals for those who still have mental problems resulting from their previous soul journey. In the fifth and sixth spheres, specialists such as psychoanalysts, philosophers, mystics who meditate, and religious people exist. In the seventh sphere, the inhabitants live in mediation, in seclusion, in silence. Usually, they used to be monks and the like in their previous life on earth. If we have not attained the fifth dimension

These seven astral spheres correspond with the terms *Morning Land* and *Summer Land*. Morning Land is those astral spheres of lovely landscapes, with trees and a brilliant sun, and where residents live in love. Summer Land is where the colors are much more intense and beautiful. The residents are formed into groups with the sign of their stature on their robe. Each order exhibits a particular mental perception.

The lower astral spheres are reserved for newly deceased entities who need time to adjust to their new environment and also for those who are in their negative emotions and thoughts inhabit the lowest astral spheres. They just cannot let go of it and thus create their hell. They are void of heavenly light that might liberate them from their vicious circle.

These spheres of existence are all temporal in nature. So, there is no eternal damnation of hell or eternal delight in the heavens that particular religions preach. There is no stagnation in the universe, as everything evolves, and every living being will eventually reach the Light. When we have attained perfection, we have returned to our birthright as celestial beings before coming to planet Earth. The story of Adam and Eve was an example of how we grow and overcome our ego of the third dimension and work our way up to the grace of love. God is love, and His plan is perfect.

When people pass, they maintain the level of consciousness of their previous lives on earth. It takes another reincarnation to raise their consciousness into a higher one. They do no regress lower as some believe.

Those who pass over can become spiritual guides to give direction and guidance to their loved ones still on the earth plane. Their love and support is most helpful if the relative is aware of their presence or not. The spirit passed over retains their level of consciousness as if they were still alive. This is demonstrated in the movie *The Sixth Sense*. The passed-over Bruce Willis remains to complete unfinished business. These spirits are never destructive or harmful if they were not destructive before their passing.

The person who passed over becomes aware of the truth about life—that life endures into infinity. The tunnel is symbolic of the darkness of the consciousness of the planet. Each soul travels through these levels of dark consciousness, which feels like a tunnel, into the light of higher consciousness beyond the darkness.

It was described by my father who passed away on July 4, 2015. I asked him through a channel what his experience was like passing to the other side.

Here is the text of the channeling with my father on October 15, 2015. It was channeled by Marilyn Redmond:

> DAD: Okay, good morning, Doug. This is your father.
>
> DOUG: Hey, Dad, how you doing?
>
> DAD: Well, I am so pleased to be able to talk with you. This is such a treat. I have been wanting to talk with you, and I've been watching all of your progress. And I'm so pleased with how you're proceeding. And I just want you to know I love you and I'm so proud of you, and I'm so please that you are my child and that you are this wonderful boy who is growing into learning so many wonderful spiritual new ideas and helping others. This is just why you came, and I was there to help you keep that. And I am so pleased you are following your path. So I am very proud of you.

DOUG: Thank you, Dad. So I'm ready to go. Now after you have died, did you stay around before you went through the tunnel?

DAD: I did stay around for a short time because I wanted to see what would happen in my passing, and I wanted to be aware of people being in the places they needed to be and things were in order. So I was around until after the funeral. And I know they're still in grief, and I know that they're dealing with it in their own way as they will move on. I felt comfortable that they would get in touch with their inner part and know that all was okay and the right timing when they were through with their grieving. When I did, it was like it was an easy passage to move to the other side. It was like there was no encumbrances. Sometimes people, when they move over from passing over and people hanging onto their spirit, they fear for survival, or they feel they just can't let go of that person. And that person can't move over. But I didn't feel anyone tug on me to stay, which was actually a gift. It was a lot. It was like I was allowed to move on spiritually, even though physically in their human form, they're still having their days, which are sometimes difficult for them. That's the human condition, when you go through this kind of losing of a lost—loved one and you were very close to them—there's an emotional adjustment that they're going through, but it wasn't to the extent that they couldn't handle it on their own devices and just draining me and holding on to me, so I couldn't move on. And that part was a blessing.

DOUG: Did you feel like you have never died because you were still seeing things like before?

DAD: Well, everybody is always alive. It's just our perceptions, and so yes, it was like I didn't die. It was more like my physical body was an overcoat, and I took it off. And just my spiritual part of my essence was able to move out of the skin, which was confining me, and my essences could be more of the truth of the size of who I am. And the space that I occupy wasn't being stuffed into a body. I was more free to be myself and my spiritual essence. So, it's a—you lose that confining feeling.

DOUG: After you have died, who greeted you? Grandma or Grandpa or Uncle Allan or even Aunt Dot?

DAD: Well, it was all—they all were there to greet me,. It was not really. As I was passing, my mother came and helped me to understand that she would be there for me, and my angel through helping me to understand that there was nothing to fear. And they would be escorting me, but if I actually moved into the new consciousness, it was like they were all standing at the edge of the beach and waving me on and sharing me and wanting me to come into land so to speak. It was kind of like a big celebration. There were even some of the family animals there. So it was like a big banner, "Welcome home," and they were all joyous and happy. And yes, I spent time with my mother and father and our other relatives that were there also waiting for me. It was like a family reunion, and it was just a joyous, joyous. Oh, our hearts were just singing. It was marvelous.

DOUG: Oh, I'm so happy to hear that. Did you meet Jesus?

DAD: Well, yes, as you're moving into—as you're moving into this new consciousness of being out of any fear, criticism, the light of God comes in, and it's like you're absorbed into that light and you— It's not like Jesus appeared in physical form. It's his energy filled me and engulfed me so much that I felt like that I was just there with him in this beautiful embrace, that he was welcoming me home. And there I belonged at this wonderful place that I had actually grown into and that he was there for me always and would always be there for me and that I was to not be without any doubts any longer and just enjoy.

DOUG: What is it like on the other side? Was it beautiful?

DAD: Well, I did go through the tunnel. Tunnel is the—a way of describing leaving the old consciousness, I discovered. The darkness is that what we really did on earth. The darkness is the fears and the resentments and all of the negative energies, and as you move out of that, you move from consciousness into a little higher consciousness, and continuing into a higher consciousness. You go through many layers of different awareness into—from fear into the love of God, and as you ascend you're going to see the light, because that's what you're coming into, is this perfect health of perfect peace, perfect love of energy and you're leaving the total darkness of what you have been experiencing on earth, that lower dimension where most people are in depression and anger and just mainly survival in many cases. So, as you leave that it's the darkness, and the tunnel is really a metaphysical term or a symbolic term to describe the transition out of that older energy and moving into the pure love of God.

DOUG: Did you loved by God right after you died, like feeling the love of God right away?

DAD: Well, that's good question, there was a huge relief in this transition of the tunnel. I can't say I was immediately overwhelmed by God's love, but I grew going through this change of energy from the dark to the light, I became more and more embraced by God's love until it was all encompassing. So, it was what I would call a transitional, if you do it too fast, your system, your physical body system can't handle all of that energy at once. So it's a transitional evolutional thing and then in this case, it goes fairly quickly. You know, people are learning to do this on earth. But so it's a much slower process moving the earth's energy and most—and now you know that the planet is moving into the fourth and Fifth dimension so it's actually a little quicker process on earth than it has been in the past, but it still takes time, not a lot of time, in this case, because most people that have passed over with more physical and health problems than I had, do take a longer time to make this passage. I was actually quite fortunate that I didn't have a lot of, you might say left over baggage that needed to be dealt with, and when you first—after you have your bit rejoining of your relatives and ancestors coming all together, you're taking to - like two people on earth would maybe call a sanitarium or a nursing home. Some place where you can - your spirit can be brought back into that connection of love, which is what you would call the other side. So the loving experience and presence of God. And that is a transition, again, where you're in a setting and angels and attendants are there helping you to make this transition, because you're physical consciousness has to also be adjusted a

Door to Glory

lot with your mental, mental, emotional, and spiritual change. It's not an overnight snap of your fingers like I have a magic wand experience. One is the longer transitions of coming into that healing that you go through when you come to the other side, so that you can actually assimilate that loving energy of God. Some people are not aware but when Lincoln was shot and it was such a terrifying trauma to the body as his emotional energy, his whole system, it actually took him a couple of years of being in this assisted health environment to come physically back into, we call it physical, but it's the spirit energy of the physical, to restore that energy back to health and it's mental, emotional, and spiritual aspects balanced again. So I have been fortunate in my time, I'm still in that resting situation, where I am still adjusting to God's total grace and I am not out and about you might say, available to me and coming to me in this other dimension as of yet. I hope to have the progress happens fairly quickly in my case. It turns out that I had so many last past lives, working on my spiritual growth that in this particular lifetime I had healed a great majority of my karma. And so therefore you call that an old soul. So, I was an old soul and the last of my healings are being taking care of at this point, with the help and guidance and love and understanding of those on this side that can give me that help necessary to finish healing my soul. So you see I'm not really what you might say out of the woods yet, but I know some [inaud.] had for me, and I have some inclining about what that's about. I haven't had an opportunity to experience that yet. And I'm looking forward to it, so my healing is going fairly quickly, and I don't have resistance to it, and I am looking forward to moving beyond this hospital type setting where I am in recuperation you might say, you might call it a recovery room. The surgery has been done, and I'm in the healing stages at this point.

DOUG: I saw you one month before you died, and you were in intense pain.

DAD: Well, the pain, I would like to explain that for people that might be able to benefit from this information. The pain they experience in the physical needs to be felt on an emotional energy level, and not drugged by depressants or pain pills, by anti-depressants I meant. Because that pain is of the ego and it has to be expressed in a release from your system, and yes it was very difficult to go through some of that pain of my past, but it was part of my ego's experience in needing to express it rather than [inaud.] it. When people use alcohol or other addictions, gambling, shopping, eating, those stuff your feelings and eventually feel that pain, if you can understand it at a human level, it's actually a gift, because without feeling it, you never lose it. You can't release it. It's stuffed inside of you. It has to be felt from an emotional point of view and it leaves its course and time. So as you do pass over that pain, resolves immediately you are not in pain when you pass over, it's actually the release from pain, because you have experienced and it no longer is part of your soul, messages that need to be healed. So, when I went through that pain it was very agonizing time and it was not comfortable, but I am glad that I did experience it, that I allowed it to happen, because without that I would have needed to come back and reincarnate on earth to experience it again until I had enough courage and self-love to actually walk through those experiences that I never actually dealt with. I just ignored and stayed in denial about. So, pain is actually the touchstone for growing and most people don't want to grow up and so they hid from the pain and whatever manner will cover it up, such as being compulsive, obsessive behaviors, there's a million ways to hide from pain in the third dimension. So, people get so addicted to video games, or distractions that keep them occupied so they don't feel the pain, workaholic is another one. And all kinds of ways. So, it's really important to understand that pain is not something to run from, if you actually can embrace it and ask God to help you with it, release it and know that you experience the pain of the past that you did not choose to do at that point in time, but it's still always going to be there until you make the choice to let it go after you've actually gone through the experience of feeling the pain. The pain is the separation from God. And when we are separated from God, there is no love connecting with us, and there—it's very painful. I've had many past lives where I was not in the presence of God, I was very much in denial, very much into my ego, which is some people call it "edging God out," so without God in my life, it's painful. And I had to experience that God was not in my life at that time, and at that particular point in presence it was now time to understand, that how painful it is to be without God's love. And I'm so glad that I went through that pain. It's something not comfortable to do, but everybody lives through it. Fortunately, there is enough energy in our systems to allow that, it's usually a very low energy, and so the pain is not totally over coming us, but so we have some of God's help and angels around us when we go through it. So we know that - I know today that if I don't [inaud.] sooner, especially when it first—I realized that I was not connected to God, I would have had less pain when I died. So pain can be a blessing if you understand it when you connect to God, the pain will leave, and every time you have an energy string, you might call it, that has not been connected to God, to love that part of you and say, I haven't been connected to God and now I choose to release that disconnection so that all my consciousness is in God's consciousness. And the more you handle and do it by accepting God's love into your life, the more pain will disappear and dissipate because love heals.

DOUG: I remember one week before you died, you mentioned to Mom that it was your ego that you thought you could go to the bathroom without falling down.

DAD: Exactly.

DOUG: This question is for Mom, what is something that only she knows about you that the family does not know?

DAD: Well, you know, you're asking a test, and the real test is in her heart, she knows that I came into her life to help her through her situations and be there for her that we made an agreement spiritually before we met, before we even came to this planet that we would be there for each other through this particular part of our growing and lifetimes and in her heart she knows I was there for her and I came to her to be with her and support her and be there, in her presence that she would have that support and energy on planet earth while we were going through these experiences and if she really gives into her heart she will know that we made this agreement and I followed through and I am there for her even in spirit today. Just because I am in another dimension doesn't mean I am not still her heart. She can talk to me through her heart, I have not left her, only physically, and I have not left her spiritually and never will. So, if she is honest with herself, she knows I am still with her and I always will be. We have a connection we have gone through many lifetimes together. And as she starts to grow and learn more about her spiritual experiences, she'll realize that I agreed to play the part I did and that we came together and she asked me to do this for her. And I was willing because I loved her so much, to be there through her ups and downs of life and help her in every way I could. It was best, in her best interest to learn what she needed to do, I was there for her unconditionally, and I hope that in her heart she can come to feel and become attached and connected to that experience that we have been together the spirit before this lifetime, and we will be together in spirit forever.

DOUG: I told Mom that she would feel your presence when she opens her heart.

DAD: That's what I'm saying. Exactly.

DOUG: What message do you have for Mom?

DAD: She was a wonderful woman, and whatever ups and downs we had were necessary. I hold no grudges, no resentments, and no angers toward her. That I always loved her and understood but I did not have to look at her behavior, it was not the behavior that was the situation, but the love that was really in heart that I really loved. And no matter what her experience was, it was a painful, harsh, difficult time, it wasn't about her actions, and I was there to be with her in her loving and understanding that no matter what happened she would be okay. And I want her to know not to have any regrets or beat herself up for things that she might have done differently that she might have not understood or could have handled in a more of appropriately, that those were all necessary for her learn from. And I understood that, and I want her to learn life is but a lesson, it's a school to learn how to change our energy. So everything has misgivings about, to forgive herself. I have forgiven her and she is to forgive herself.

DOUG: This concludes the interview. Thanks for sharing this remarkable conversation!

DAD: Well, I would like to have you talk with me anytime, Douglas. You are my son with whom I am well pleased.

DOUG: Thank you. Take care. Bye.

DAD: Good-bye. I love you dearly.

A comment from my father validated the fact that your soul possesses the light of God. It was his body, which he had termed it as his "overcoat," that kept him from realizing it. He was raised a Catholic and was a devoted Catholic right up to the day of his death. However, as I was writing this book at the time several months before he died, he didn't quite comprehend my spiritual messages of this book. The book was in a draft stage at the time. There is a passage in the Scripture from God the Father at the transfiguration, "While he yet spake, behold, a bright cloud shadowed them: and behold, there came a voice out of the cloud, saying, this is that my beloved Son, in whom I am well pleased: hear him" (Matthew 17:5) Although the "oneness of God" pervades throughout his creation, you do not lose your identity or your personality. There is a common misperception that you lose it as you merge your spirit with God's. In the spiritual realm, every soul has its own unique feature. It belongs to you and you only.

Your soul journey continues beyond the planet Earth into eternity of space. It never dies. You continue your loving presence and sharing it with other human or spiritual entities that are spiritually growing. There is always a room for growth forever. It starts here. When you have found God within despite that fact you are still in control by your overcoat, human body, you will realize the loving God like the departed souls are finding out after crossing over to the other side of the tunnel. You will feel the abundance. When you have found God, you have it all. His love transcends you. No financial gains or any career success could trump that. It is all you would need to be totally happy with your life.

Getting back to the tunnel. The spiritual location is termed Nirvana. It has many levels of consciousness also called mansions. There is no fear in the light of God. Those who pass over return to earth for another opportunity to release their fears again. Most spirits do not stay earthbound and want to be released from human dependence to move into new lessons in energy. Life is about evolving.

Most spirits move to Nirvana with entities of the same consciousness. Together, they have a community of like-minded souls. There is only a harmonious and loving experience when you pass over. That is why many people call it heaven.

This is where the planning to return to earth occurs. Their masters help those passed over judge the past karma that still needs resolving and make appropriate decisions about who can manifest in their lives to reflect that energy that still needs to shift for their advancement in consciousness.

The earthly emotions of guilt, shame, and fears are again revisited when they return for another opportunity to transform any negative energy still in their essence. This includes karma and harms from the prior life just completed. Suicide victims have the opportunity to return and complete their personal transformation in another life. It slows down their evolution into a higher consciousness, but there is no punishment or retribution. They stay in their consciousness at the time of their departing. This is depicted in the 1998 movie *What Dreams May Come* with Robin Williams.

A ghost is not a lost soul. No soul is lost. We have always been with God in eternity. It is an illusion to think we have been lost. Our culture, religions, and society have misinformed us for their benefit. However, in the transition into spirit, awareness opens to the full understanding of life, and it starts the process of returning to this oneness, which feels so wonderful and warm.

Most souls that pass over go through a life review. There is no judgment, except by the people themselves seeing where they still need to transform part of their lives to align more with the love of the universe. You do experience the feelings of those you hurt. This is part of coming into balance. You reap what you sow. The cleansing of your soul can only happen during your earth life. When you have the help of your masters and guides to reveal where changes are still needed for love to replace the negativity still in the consciousness, you return at an appropriate time to again move more energy from darkness into the light of your being.

Section 5.3: Spirit Guides

Our life path is something that we and our spirit guides create together before we are born so that we have someone guiding us from the other side. They know all the things that we hope to accomplish throughout our lifetime. Our life path is like our chart. It is the curriculum for when we come down to Earth. It will include all of the things that we would like to experience while we are on our journey here on Earth. When we are young children, we do a splendid job of starting our journey off on the right foot usually. Our spiritual body and our physical body are very much in harmony and balance, so we are in tune with our spirit guides as well as universal laws. These allow us to work very well with the ebb and flow of the universe. The rules are basic and very simple: we are to follow the happiness in our heart. The heart center is where we can feel ourselves being guided by our spirit guides. It is here that we can also feel when we are accessing our soul DNA information. As babies, since we still have a strong spiritual connection and memory of the other side, it is natural for us to plug into our soul DNA and access its information. Naturally, we are guided by happiness if we had a pleasant womb experience. If we take a moment and think back to when we were children, we can usually remember that when we were growing up, we only did the things that we loved to do. It was usually something simple that brought us joy, such as making mud pies, singing, or playing dress up. It is the time in our lives when we were blissful doing the things that we liked to do, and when we no longer enjoyed what we were doing, we just stopped and did something else. As children, we often base all of our decisions on what makes us happy and safe in the heart center. If we watch little children, we can see how happy and carefree they usually are. It is not just because they do not have anything to worry about. On the contrary, some children have many things on their minds, but they are coming from a different place. They plug into their soul DNA, so they naturally make decisions from their heart center. They have a natural trust in the universe that everything will always work out. Children do things that make them happy. If these children were to follow their heart center throughout their entire life, they would continue to develop the gifts and talents that have given as part of their soul DNA. Ironically, most of the time the things that we loved to do when we were children have something to do with what our gifts and talents are when we become adults. When we follow our hearts and what we enjoy doing, we are very much in harmony with our soul DNA and our life path. In other words, one of the reasons that we enjoy doing certain things is because they are already a part of our soul DNA. They are a part of who we are. Otherwise, we would not enjoy doing them (Ref. 5).

* * * * *

DOUG: I am going to read this passage from the book of Hebrews 11:13-16.

> All these died in faith and received not the promises, but saw them afar off and believed them and received them thankfully and confessed that they were strangers and pilgrims on the Earth. For they that they say such things declare plainly that they seek a country. And if they had been mindful of that country from whence they came out, they had leisure to have returned. But now they desire a better that is heavenly. Therefore, God is not sent to them to be called their God for he hath prepared for them a city.

Now that means that a soul can pick where he or she wants to go to when it comes back to reincarnate another body?

JOHN: Well, yes, that does happen. You sit with a conference committee, you might say, with your guides and angels. So they help you to direct where and when and how the necessary experiences you need to transform your energy and how those best will suit your needs of where you need to be for those experiences to happen. So you do select what nationality. Many of you do not understand how you've had thousands of lives. We have been in different countries. You've all played different roles in professions or lack of occupations, talents, and abilities or ways of handling your affairs in godly ways or less than that. So you go through every vibration to change your energy back into the higher consciousness of love. The higher loving energy is a high vibration. So as you raise that consciousness, you are going to be in whatever place that's necessary for that experience to give you the best opportunity for that.

DOUG: So do we have spiritual helpers like guardian angels because we are in the dark?

JOHN: As Marilyn said, we were born in the manger. That is the lowest form of consciousness, and you are coming into the light. You are putting your plant out into sunshine. You are coming into awareness, and you are moving into that higher consciousness.

DOUG: So that is why we have a guardian angel. It's because guardian angel can hear spiritual messages. So they help us grow until we can hear those messages ourselves.

JOHN: Yes, that is a wonderful way to put it. Are you familiar with Psalm 23? "Though I walk through the valley of the shadow of death I will fear no evil; for thou art with me, thy rod and thy staff they comfort me." So when you are walking through the valley of the shadow of death is Earth. So if you know that spirit, that rod is within, and God is your heavenly Father the staff. He is the Shepherd. Then you will not have to fear walking through that predominately difficult time. You have God's Spirit with you through the whole thing. There is nothing to fear because he is there.

DOUG: What is the dimension of a guardian angel?

DOUG: God's Spirit through the guardian angels.

JOHN: Right.

DOUG: What is the spiritual dimension of a guardian angel?

JOHN: Well, that is a very good question because everyone has what you call a guardian angel. Angels are energy, and you are energy. When you came to planet Earth, you have lowered your energy dimensionally. You are an angel and were originally one with God. So as your energy broke off a piece of God to be able to descend into this realm of earthly experience, you were losing a lot of your spirit. Also, you lost a major part of your spiritual awareness, knowledge, and understanding and ability to have the spiritual aspects of your existence. It's only a part of your soul. You don't have all of the dimensional spiritual Christendom about yourself, and you need help to make it through the various lessons on the planet that take a great deal of wisdom and understanding and support ... and energy as well to maintain and sustain you in this darker, denser energy. So everyone is provided with spiritual help, invisible help so that you can accomplish the lessons in front of you. If you are aware, Mack was on a railroad train track in Italy. He was in a pickup truck. There was a train heading toward him, and he would have been killed. So the next thing he knew, his guardian angel had picked him up off the tracks and laid his truck and him beside it on a little knoll, raised area with a tree. And he was standing up there, watching the train go by. He knew at that moment—before that he had been on that track and knew that he was going to be killed. So your energy that comes with you, you call it a guardian angel. It is there to protect you. It is there to keep you safe, and you can succeed in the lessons that are in front of you. Marilyn herself has had at least a dozen experiences where angels or that invisible energy has kept her alive so that she could continue her work here on planet Earth. There were times when she knew at one point would not be going home alive one night. Other times when things happened in similar ways, and so she is still here because the spiritual energy was protecting her. If any unfortunate event took place that was not written in your script to die unexpectedly, then your guardian angel is there to help you, to make sure that you continue your path. Usually, they cannot assist you until you ask for their assistance. So you have to say God consciously, please help me, and they show up. However, there are instances as Marilyn had, where it was so instantaneous that the support was immediately provided.

* * * * *

Are real children of God without fault? Yes. We lowered our energy coming to earth, where souls become lessons to overcome. They still are the being of the first birth, that which the Bible calls the flesh, the carnal or earthly man. They still have the faults, infirmities, weaknesses, hang-ups, problems, and yes, sins with which they must struggle and overcome. When they reincarnate, they learn several

Door to Glory

lessons of life one at a time to get to overcome sins. It is their choosing on how to progress their spiritual vibration to a higher level through life's experiences. The fact of the matter is that we find perfection through reincarnation. Even Jesus was reincarnated thirty-two times. The author has reincarnated 866 times. Every child is a real child of God because he or she is already a Christ. It may take some longer to achieve perfection.

* * * * *

DOUG: Now was Jesus born as an infant for Krishna, Buddha, and Muhammed?

JOHN: They were all born as infants, yes. Now there were some who were not. Walk-ins are not born as babies, and there was a group of prophets called Melchizedek. They wrote the psalms, and so some have not been born as infants. But yes, the ones you named were.

* * * * *

Before we are born, we choose someone from the other side to help guide us through the experiences that we will have here on Earth during our lifetime. These spirits are what we refer to as our spirit guides. Our spirit guides are spirits that have incarnated before. When they enter into an agreement with us, however, they will stay on the other side for the entire time while we remain in the physical realm. Everyone has at least one main spirit guide who works closely with him or her on a day-to-day basis. If our spirit guide were someone we knew while we were here on Earth, that would mean that we would have been here without any guidance from the other side. That is just not the case. They are with us from the day of our conception, and they stay with us until we release our physical bodies. Sometime your guide can change in your lifetime depending on your life situation.

Our spirit guides are always around us. We might not feel their presence. They are there always to guide us throughout our life. If something were going to put us in harm's way, they would pull us out of it. They are very cognizant of our script. "For he shall give his Angels charge over thee to keep thee in all thy ways."

There is a way to *communicate* with them. We can learn to meditate. Their energy is within our soul, so they are very accessible. The author has two personal angels for two specific tasks. One takes care of my finance and travel, and the other coordinates of my communication with the ascended masters. Every day I sit quietly for ten to thirty minutes. The kingdom of God is within you. It is peace and joy in the Holy Spirit. If you read about visualizing the glory of light, it does not happen that way all the time. I have not experienced it. When I meditate, for the most part I experience peacefulness. I usually get answers to my questions from my angels on the next day. I focus on the question, and an answer comes to me in a form of knowingness. It enables me to have more convictions with my decision making. I sleep over it until the next day, and my answer comes either in a form of joy or sickness. Of course, I would go with the feeling of joy!

* * * * *

DOUG: I am attuned with my finance angel, and his name is Greg. So it seems like this whole thing was planned out by the angels for me to do this book work.

JOHN: I am sure of that. There's much information that you might want to review in your meditations. These are some good questions you might bring just one at a time into your meditation each day and just see what kind of information comes to your heart. Also, start paying attention to those answers within because you will find your answers there.

DOUG: That is why there's an angel for every human being.

JOHN: Yes, Marilyn had many past lives where she had some very drastic situations occur. So Archangel Michael has appeared several times, telling her that he was always with her during those situations, even though the physical harm was traumatic. She was always safe spiritually.

DOUG: I almost drowned one time in a river, and I felt a pull from somebody. And he pulled me out of the water, so obviously, it was part of the script to live this life.

JOHN: Exactly.

* * * * *

Sometimes we have just blocked our ability to receive guidance from them, or we think that it is just our imagination. Communicating with our spirit guides or receiving information is built into our soul's DNA, allowing us to have a natural ability to be able to receive guidance from them. So we do not have to learn or train ourselves how to do this; however, we do need to be more aware of how we receive this information. It is also important to have an understanding of how this communication system works. We have something similar to an internal transmitter to the other side. They are always there, and our connection can always be available. We may be under the impression that when our spirit guide talks to us, we should be able to hear them as we do when we are having a conversation with someone in the physical realm. So if we do not hear them, we think that there is no communication with our guides. Some of us also believe that it is something that we must work very hard at with meditation or by sitting quietly in a room by ourselves. In some instances, that can help further our level of communication, but for the most part, this is not necessary. Most psychics and mediums do not hear their spirit guides with the outer ear, as we would hear a friend talking to us. They hear with their inner ear, and we can do this too. When we hear with our inner ear, it is like remembering a conversation that we had with someone yesterday or replaying a song in our head that we just heard on the radio. Our spirit guides can contact us and say things aloud or audibly so that we can hear them with our outer ear; however, this is rarely the way in which they will communicate. Our spirit guide will most likely communicate with us through pictures and telepathy. It is usually through pictures or a feeling that you get in your stomach or somewhere in the body or an image that you will get in your head. The problem with picture communication is that sometimes there are symbols, and we need to figure out what the images or symbols mean to us. For instance, they may show us a certain color of the flower, and that flower will mean something. Also when they communicate with us clairvoyantly, we tend to question whether they are our spirit guides or if we are just making something up in our head. One easy way that we can usually tell the difference is that if we are hearing or receiving information from our spirit guide, we will feel it in our bodies, not just our minds. It is because we are raising our vibration and connecting with our spiritual bodies or our soul DNA. It is our internal connection. We will usually feel it in our heart center, the same place that we can feel our intuition. Sometimes we can feel it in our stomach like a *gut feeling* or in the back of our neck. Whatever works for us, there will be a perceptible feeling in our bodies.

When we realize that we are getting messages from our spirit guide, we need to pay attention to the pictures and symbols that are being sent to us. We need to figure out what they mean to us, and this will help us understand what they are trying to say. We need to pay attention to the telepathic messages that we are hearing or seeing and notice the feeling that we have in the body. It will heighten our awareness. When we start to notice the connection between our spiritual being and the physical body, it will become even stronger. With practice, our communication can benefit our sense of well-being with the spirit guides, and the universe work well together because they are in absolute harmony. And our spirit guide is completely in sync with the universal laws. They are guiding us with an array of knowledge from the other side and with universal laws in mind. The universe will support you when you are on the path. Just trust the universe will bring what you need. God's grace is sufficient. It will provide what you need.

We have probably experienced such a situation or heard a story of this one. For example, we have been driving the same way home from work or school day after day. However, one day we have an unexpected feeling not to go the same way that we always go, so we take a different route. Later we hear that there was an accident on the street that we normally take home. That would be our spirit guides giving us a *feeling* to take another route. It is their way of helping to dissuade us from a dangerous situation. Also, this can happen with small things, such as if we are driving down a road slightly over the speed limit and a car gets in front of us. This car is driving exactly the speed limit, and we proceed to cut them out because we are in a hurry. Then about a mile down the road, we pass a police officer and realize that we just avoided a speeding ticket, and we did not need to be driving over the speed limit.

Imagine that we are in this maze called life, blindfolded, and we have to find our way to the end. This maze does not only have corners, but it has humps in the road and several obstacles along the way. Our spirit guides are like the people above in the lookout tower. They can see the whole maze. They can see where we need to go to get to the end and the best route we can take to get there. They are a part of our team. If we listen closely and pay attention to the signs they give us, they can help us maneuver corners and steer clear of the obstacles. They can warn us when a hill is coming and help us to avoid bumping into walls. They come when we ask, and they stay as long as they are needed. However, when we are not listening and we think that we can make it through this maze all on our own, if we start veering too far off the path or too far from our destination, sometimes they must take extreme measures. They can box us in or put up a wall in order to make us turn around. It will get us back on the right track, going in a direction that is right for us. However, at this point we may be too angry or focused on that wrong direction to notice that we are being helped. It may not be until we are farther down the road that we can look back and see why we got rerouted.

Spirit guides are also different from our guardian angels. Our guardian angels have a very particular task to protect us. They can also intervene if we get ourselves into a potentially harmful situation.

* * * * *

DOUG: Do guardian angels respond to spiritual messages on behalf of their mortals? Every mortal has a guardian angel, but we can't hear spiritual messages.

JOHN: You can if you meditate.

DOUG: So, when I meditate will I be talking to my guardian angel?

JOHN: When you first start meditating, first of all, it's practice to clear your mind so that all the outer raucous and ruckus and confusion, the outside world doesn't enter in. You want to remove your thoughts, so that takes a little practice of sitting silently in the stillness, be still and know that I am God so when you're in the stillness that's the voice that comes through God, God's voice. When you start meditating and start hearing that quiet voice, sometimes it talks in words, at times, it was deafening one time in Marilyn's ear. It can also be a knowing, and it can come, and suddenly you have an indication this is what the answer is. One of the things that are an easy way to get answers is to go to sleep at night and in your prayers, say this is my question, and when I wake up in the morning I would like to have the answer before I get up that's when you are still connected spiritually. And the answer can appear so early in the morning, and you will naturally be open to that solution, that is God speaking to you. God can talk to people, and sometimes people will make a comment, and Marilyn will say oh I was supposed to hear that. It happened just this week when a person made a comment, and she said oh that's what I needed to hear so people can also provide messages from God and I think you're finding messages from God in the Urantia Book if I'm not mistaken. Marilyn was reading a book from an Ascended Master on the oceanfront one day, and this message appeared in the book, and it was just absolutely an important answer that she needed. So, she decided to read the book again to get that; she wanted to make sure it was in that book, and she could never find that again. So, God put those words at that time in that book for her and that space so God can work wonders to get attention to you. Sometimes it can be other voices also such as your masters as you grow in mediation, the more concentration you have to that still voice, then you can access your masters and angels and your spirit guides and more for the help that comes through spirit for you.

*****

Our spirit guides also can be protectors, but they are mostly around for guidance; our guardian angel is here specifically to protect us. Either way, it is wonderful to have a team help guide and protect us. It is even more wonderful when we are an active participant on the team. It makes our team that much more efficient.

Section 5.4: Soul Journey

Earth is the place for the third-dimensional people from other planets to cleanse their energies (souls). Our universe is among the younger universe in all of God's creation. Earth was created in the fifth dimension as a playground garden of Eden. However, during the course of time, things went awry, and the darkness of the energy was being exploited in inappropriate ways. And the darkness fell on the Earth, and the Earth was having difficulties. According to John, Mother Earth is a sentient being that is connected to Spirit, is manifested from Spirit just like people are. Earth has called for help after the Second World War about seventy years ago;

Earth is a young planet in one of the younger universes in God's creation. As a sentient being, it is going through growing pains. It has called for help, and that is when sunlight more energy was starting to project onto Earth from around the rest of the universe. Also, the rest of the cosmos is to bring energy to the planet so it can reverberate itself into a functioning sentient being again. It is a planet that is progressing and finally ready to grow up into a mature understanding of love.

* * * * *

DOUG: King Solomon described dark energy like thick mud (Ref. 4).

JOHN: Well, dark energy is the lack of light, so you cannot see in the darkness, right?

DOUG: Right.

JOHN: So that is exactly right, and it prohibits vision.

DOUG: So, oh, it is a tough place to be.

JOHN: It is the toughest lesson in the universe, yes, because people come here to change the energy from that darkness to the light.

* * * * *

The planet Earth is one of the last planets to turn into a fifth dimension. We all have had many, many lifetimes with most people having more than a thousand lives. We have to go through every energy change necessary to move into perfect love as Jesus did. So even Jesus had thirty-two lives. So if necessary, everybody was a murderer at one time. Everybody was a thief. Everybody was a beggar. Everybody was some professional—engineer, doctor, philanthropist, or destitute. We have all experienced all of this, and we have come to change those old energies that still needs to change from our old past lives. So we do not condemn anyone. It is possible when someone is a murderer, he or she was murdered, and he or she needed to complete the balance of energy that was what part of his or her role was. Alternatively, if somebody murdered somebody, then the person came back and got killed. So we see, there is a balance of energy. It is not right or wrong, and there's no judgment. All we are doing is transposing the energies into balance. So when people think of people being bad, that is a judgment. Jails and prisons are punishing, and the law of God is love. The angels and ascended masters do not punish and judge anyone. People are just going through their experiences necessary for ascension.

* * * * *

DOUG: So that completes the earthly sojourn, and that is when we stop coming back to Earth?

JOHN: Yes, reincarnation is about moving forward until we come back to the oneness of God. So then the reincarnation is no longer necessary, and you have advanced to a new consciousness whereby you can come back and help others. You can go onto other planets that are going through a similar process of what we are doing here on Earth. You can go and help others in different planets, do all kinds of things as far as pursuing your studies in music, art, or whatever fields of endeavor that you fancy. You have numerous and numberless opportunities to move on in energy.

DOUG: So would planet Earth be the last planet before we go back to God?

JOHN: No, not necessarily. It depends on the person's spiritual journey.

DOUG: I see.

JOHN: Everybody is right in the place they are supposed to be and not everybody will go into ascension. Not everybody has completed purging or clarifying their chakras and their energy that is negative and dense, which has been keeping them in victim and darkness.

* * * * *

New souls have not been to Earth. All souls were created at the same time, and some came to Earth at various periods of history. Some did not come to Earth at that time but waited for other opportunities. Planet Earth would be overpopulated if all souls came at once. There are approximately sixty-seven million planets inhabiting in our galaxy. Twenty-seven percent of those are in third dimension (Ref. 1).

* * * * *

DOUG: Would the third dimension end in approximately thirty years for the body/mind/spirit complexes?

JOHN: The people at the planetary point at this point are not sustainable if they are still in dark energy, fear-based energy, and they are dying and leaving the planet or accepting the light. Also, the fourth dimension is the transition like an escalator. You can accept the light and move up into fifth dimension, or you can pace to another planet and continue your third-dimensional experience. So the fourth dimension is where and when is the person going to make these choices. There are other planets that are suitable like Earth with the similar solar system that we have right here in this universe. However, they are not identifiable through science at this point, but they are there and available. They are around the universe in various places, serving and experiencing, learning, exploring, adventuring. So not everyone came to Earth at once because it was not physically possible to substantiate that. However, the people who wanted to come to Earth, there's a list and priorities of those who are allowed to be birthed on the planet. It keeps the population in balance. So the ones who want to come are kind because they are interested in transposing and transmuting their energy into a higher level, and they can do that much easier. The energy on Earth allows them to change from the fear of the love much easier than in other places of the universe. So this is a very desirable planet to come to, but they do not all come at once. If you have not had your opportunity to come yet, then you would be a new soul. Alternatively, if you had only had a chance to come a few times at this point, you have not gained the wisdom and the experience necessary to move on.

* * * * *

Door to Glory

DOUG: Is it true that very few ever get to heaven?

JOHN: That is another myth. Eventually, everyone arrives into the oneness of God. It just takes some people longer because they are younger souls.

DOUG: Okay.

JOHN: God has patience. God is with patience and will wait for all. No one is barred from the doors of heaven.

DOUG: So we will all eventually find heaven?

JOHN: Like I said, if you deviate from your script, it will take you longer than if you accept what is coming down into your life. And say, "Well, now how can I handle this in a loving way instead of denying it and running from it and finding ways to not deal with it and procrastinating and putting it off?" One of the lessons Marilyn learned early was that when her aunt committed suicide, she was desperately worried about her aunt. She was one of the only loving forces in her life at the time, and of course, the churches really have a long story about suicide. They don't understand, so she was so devastated about her aunt. So this is how Marilyn came to channel. Her aunt came back to her to explain. She said she is very sorry that she did it. She said that her husband had died and he was trying to get her to join him in the spirit. She says now she has to reincarnate and go through all those lessons again before she can move on.

DOUG: I see.

JOHN: So you see it is not just a path where you walk forward, and you arrive. You have to do your side of the work to make sure you are ready to move on.

DOUG: If the human personality does not survive, where does its soul go?

JOHN: That is a very interesting question. Not many people ask that. If the individual is so beyond redemption for spiritual growth and a few people have that is a matter of starting over you might say from scratch, then their energy goes back into the God soup we call it, the essence of God, the energy and spirit of the oneness. It just goes back to the oneness of God, and a new soul will come to Earth and start from the beginning.

DOUG: Oh, I see. Very interesting answer.

JOHN: That does not happen very often. God waits for all people to turn to the light as often as necessary. The wait might be a very long, but generally, most people do just continue to grow spiritually until they finally do become God conscious. That's when you do move back into the oneness of the whole God within you, the God that created you.

DOUG: Was Judas Iscariot given a new soul because he betrayed Jesus? This action would have brought tremendous guilt for him?

JOHN: Yes. Well, first of all, that story was distorted in the Bible. It was a different Judas who betrayed Christ, Jesus the Christ, and so when that happened, people denied the Christ in them all the time. So he is not the only one who denied Jesus. Even Peter denied Jesus three times if you remember. So people do come back and have reincarnations to change that energy. It was a different person. It was another Judas. They were confused in the Bible, and one was misrepresented as the individual who did the betraying.

DOUG: Now I have been reading much information. My friend, she was abducted by an alien, and the alien was green. Now are aliens spiritual?

JOHN: We are all spiritual. We are all created by God to play different parts in our lives. The lessons that we go through are those that we scripted, and for whatever reason, her lesson was to be part of that scenario. So it was a part that she needed to experience to continue trusting and having faith in God.

DOUG: Is it true that for people in the third dimension to grow to the fourth dimension only love needs to be learned?

JOHN: Yes.

DOUG: The only lesson needed to be learned is to show love?

JOHN: Exactly. It is all about raising from the depth—deeper, denser, dark energies back to the total light of the God within. And when you talk about third dimension and the fourth dimension, be aware that the fourth dimension does not have a clear definition like a particular step, ladder, or stairs where you move from on immediately to the next higher. There are many levels that gradually evolve into the next plane. They are not in a permanent position where you say, "I'm now in third, and I'm now in fourth." It's a gradual progression into that, and it is not a definitive place. It is more of an evolution.

DOUG: Okay.

JOHN: It's a blending of a higher energy. So it's hard to describe in third dimensional terms. But it's going up through different levels of energy, and sometimes you have energies greater than other energy, so no one is truly in one's space.

DOUG: I see. I want to ask you. People have asked me this, and I told people that I was reincarnated 866 times. And their eyes are all open—wow. They are wondering who kept records.

JOHN: The Akashic records.

DOUG: Maybe explain a little bit.

JOHN: There is a cave of crystals in the inner Earth that has a record of all of your lifetimes on planet Earth. Every time you come to this planet, it is scribed in the cosmic records on your crystal. As your experiences, thoughts, words, and actions are all, it's like a journal, you might say. It's all recorded on the record—your book of life, some people call it. So as you are going through your experiences, this is all recorded. It can all be checked out through various spiritual ways. When you leave the planet, you come back in, and then there is a new entry for your cosmic record of that lifetime.

DOUG: Okay. Boy, it must be big record keeping.

JOHN: It is very profound.

DOUG: Okay. Now this term *interplanetary man*—is that the same as ascendant master?

JOHN: Yes, that is a good term, and I had not heard it phrased that way. When you lose your connections and energy to the third dimension, you become interdimensional, and that is exactly what man is becoming in a physical form for the first time in history.

* * * * *

Other worlds have returned to the oneness of God. They are much more advanced than Earth because they are working for harmony, unity, and cooperation. They do not have the need for jails and punishment like we do on our planet. I asked John if high-minded people from the other civilizations would come here on Earth to help us transition to the fifth dimension since we are just coming out of the third dimension. Someone with a fifth-dimensional experience could influence our growth through leadership. Angelic helpers and ascended masters are here as well, but they have to remain some transparency in order to avoid invoking the law of free will.

It is not an actual planet being changed. People who are not moving into ascension will move to a different planet of the third dimension. However, what's happening on planet Earth is their consciousness. Their hearts are totally open to becoming that whole Spirit.

* * * *

Door to Glory

DOUG: This should be my last question. Okay. Have I asked you about the difference between the Holy Spirit and the Holy Ghost? Could the Holy Ghost be Thought Adjuster?

JOHN: The Holy Spirit and the Holy Ghost and the Thought Adjuster are all the same. There are different terms for the same thing. Some people are more inclined to call it one thing than another, because of how they see things or how they understand it. But the words or synonyms are synonymous. So, whichever term you use is the same meaning.

DOUG: Okay. So, which people receive Thought Adjuster? Because the first Adam and Eve did not have it, but the second Adam and Eve did. So, when do people, the average population, receive a Thought Adjuster?

JOHN: The Thought Adjuster as a Holy Spirit comes within when you find your wholeness within. You are a whole spirit. You've always been a whole spirit, but when you're open your heart to receive the whole spirit of God, then you return to the oneness of God. And that's what our whole journey is about, is to open your heart completely to reaccept the Holy Spirit and that you are that whole spirit with no broken heart. There are no fragments. You've not wounded anymore. You have been - the love of God has been the glue, has glued all the separate parts that separated you from God back into oneness.

* * * * *

So the new Earth is an unconditional, loving consciousness of unity, cooperation, consideration, abundance, prosperity. That is the new Earth of the fifth dimension that the book of Revelation has talked about. The new Earth is also called the world to come. The book of Revelation says that the old heaven and old Earth are being replaced by a new heaven and new Earth. The new heaven and the new Earth is your change of consciousness. It is not an actual planet being changed. People who are not moving into ascension will move to a different planet of the third dimension. So the new Earth is an unconditional, loving consciousness of unity, cooperation, consideration, abundance, and prosperity. That is the new Earth.

If a man debases his energy by engaging in war, particularly an old soul, he will continue to reincarnate on Earth until he overcomes that particular energy to create war, so you move into the light. The old souls are here finishing out their agenda to complete ascension, and the masters that have come back to help people with that are old souls. So there are a lot of people on planet Earth right now who have mastered their ego-driven lives of the past. They are moving into becoming masters of their lives and their emotions and helping others to do that also.

So that is precisely what planet Earth is about—everybody keeps coming back. Until they change their dark energy of fear into the light of God, that is what the planet is all about. You are not exiled, and you do not move off the planet until you ascend into the higher consciousness. At that point, then you are free to go about the universe with other activities

New souls have not been to Earth. They have been created. All souls were created at the same time, and some came to Earth at various periods of history. Some did not come to Earth at that time and waited for other opportunities. They are around the universe in various places, serving and experiencing, learning, exploring, adventuring. So not everyone came to Earth at once because it was not physically possible to substantiate that. However, the people who wanted to come to Earth, there's a list and priorities of those who want to experience living on planet Earth. It keeps the population in balance. So the ones who want to come are kind or playing adversarial roles. They are interested in transposing and transmuting their energy into a higher level, and they can do that much easier. The energy on Earth allows them to change from the fear of the love much easier than in other places of the universe.

So this is a very desirable planet to come to, but they do not all come at once. And so if you haven't had your opportunity to come yet, then you would be a new soul or if you had only had a chance to come a few times at this point, you haven't gained the wisdom and the experience necessary to move on. If new souls cannot achieve the lesson of love during their incarnation here, then they will continue their third dimensional experience of changing their energy on another planet. The new souls still need to have their levels of learning and experience to move into higher consciousness. So they will move to another planet that will look just like Earth, and they will continue their progress. They would not even realize how they have been transported. If they are old souls, it is very likely forward into fifth dimension, as this lifetime was actually completing their struggles and their challenges that needed to be addressed. So you cannot just make a blanket statement where everybody is going. If someone has ascended, they then have new choices to come back and help others or to move onto other planets and universes and go into the universe and do what is the right thing for them at that point. So there will be a disbursement of souls in the right directions that are appropriate.

* * * * *

DOUG: What is a typical amount of time in between incarnations for the soul?

JOHN: Well, that's a difficult question. It varies highly for individuals. Some individuals will immediately return out of necessity. However, generally, there is several hundred years—as far as Earth years—before people return, but not necessarily. Marilyn was here during the 1920s and then came back in 1939. She was killed in the '20s and returned quite quickly, but then because she had not healed from the bullet wounds that she had received from her death. Some of those painful experiences came into her humanness in this lifetime, and she had to understand that she came back so quickly that it wasn't enough time on the other side to actually finish her healing necessary to return. Most people, however, do have longer periods of time, and it's because your guides who are guiding you choose to come into the right energy matrix that is appropriate for your growth and the lessons necessary. Sometimes people have to wait even thousands of years for the energies to align up for them to return. So it is a very individual answer, and you cannot put it into just a particular amount of time.

Chapter 6

Channeling Notes with Apostle John

Section 6.1: May 18, 2014

Conversation with John the Divine via medium channeled while Marilyn Redmond was in her trance on May 18, 2014, in Edgewood, Washington. Martha is Marilyn's gatekeeper. She watches the transition of John's spirit coming to Marilyn body and guards Marilyn's body from any unsuspecting spirits possessing her body.

JOHN: And rather than preaching, you are setting an example and leading the way. And I commend you for that. I think it is marvelous that you have this ambition and eagerness and intention to share the spiritual aspects of your life or the answers that need to be shared with everyone. And just know that the ones that will hear it will always be the right ones. I am ready to hear your questions.

DOUG: This all started back in the 1990s when I was meditating through the Self-Realization Fellowship, and I was so inspired by that experience. And that's how I received spiritual enlightening. It came down on me. I knew it was coming from heaven. But I had never read the Bible so I was kind of naïve with the teaching. Then, I guess, it was just part of a spiritual growth, a journey, that I was relating to and this took me to places. And that's what brought me here to meet Marilyn. So I'm meeting people that will help me with my spiritual growth and my search for the truth.

JOHN: May I make one comment at this point?

DOUG: Sure, yes.

JOHN: When you said that your spiritual enlightenment came from above and came from heaven, please be aware that heaven is within. The kingdom of heaven is within. And what was happening—it didn't come from without you. It came from within. It was the beginning of opening up your heart to the consciousness of the love of who you are. And it does feel wonderful, doesn't it?

DOUG: Oh, definitely.

JOHN: It feels wonderful to get in touch with that love.

DOUG: So much love.

JOHN: Right. So and it came from within because the kingdom of heaven is within. All your answers come from within.

DOUG: Really?

JOHN: And whenever you look outside of yourself, you are denying the God within.

DOUG: That's why the Bible did not include his spiritual progression since he was a child?

JOHN: Exactly.

DOUG: The time of Jesus's life from his age of twelve to thirty because all of that was left out.

JOHN: Exactly.

DOUG: Oh, interesting!

JOHN: And it's filled in "Urantia." So the Book of Urantia explains that very well. So what happened is the girls were purging all that churches would call sins, but it's your emotional barriers to God that are stopping the love from manifesting. When Jesus said,

"Satan, get thee behind me," he was talking about his anger and fears and resentments and worries and those kinds of things that were troubling him. Because if you are one in Spirit and one in God, there's only love and those things cannot exist. So you are releasing everything that is not of love so that when you get them released and are detached from all those things of the material world outside of you, then you are in the presence of only God's love, unconditional love. And you have ascended, and you are on the trip of learning how to release any perceptions of people, places, or situations, harms and trauma, calamity in your lives. Releasing those because those were the energies that you came to earth to release. And this is the planet you do that on. This is the planet you can transform trauma into a loving, healthy resolution without it still harming you forever in the future. It's not going to replay as a cycling over and over like a hamster in a hamster cage on the wheel. And you're breaking that wheel, that cycle, by giving up your guilt and by giving up your revenge and by giving up your resentments and anger. You then release those to the love of God to be dispelled by his perfect love, and you move out of that emotional attachment.

DOUG: Oh, that's what the Ten Commandments were for—to keep people from falling into the traps of guilt.

JOHN: You got it.

DOUG: Okay!

JOHN: And the first commandment is the only one as far as the Old Testament that was of the most valuable because it says that there is to be only one God. Every time you focus on a book, a person, a situation that you feel has harmed you or done wrong, you are making it a God, a false God. The only focus is to be within your heart where God resides. And anything else is a false God. So when your focus is on a situation and you just can't get your mind off of it, you have made it a God.

DOUG: I'm going to read another passage that's from the book of Revelation.

JOHN: Okay.

DOUG: Nevertheless, I have somewhat against thee because thou hast left thy first love. Remember, therefore, from hence thou art falling and repent and do the first works. Or thus, I will come against thee shortly and remove thy candlestick out of his place, except thou amend.

JOHN: Okay. You see, do you see that as a loving verse?

DOUG: No.

JOHN: Well, then it's not of God.

DOUG: But it's in the book of Revelation though.

JOHN: It was adjusted to—you see, they put in enough to keep people interested, but it's like throwing a dog a bone. They threw you enough to keep you interested and then inserted things to keep you in their control.

DOUG: Okay.

JOHN: And if it's a statement not of love, then just say, "Satan, get thee behind me."

DOUG: Interesting, okay. So I have a question.

JOHN: Yes.

DOUG: Are we fallen angels because we left God?

JOHN: Well, we are returning to the angelic realm of fifth dimension. And I would not want to call you a fallen angel because that would mean you left God, and God has always been in your heart. You see, there hasn't ever been no separation. In the Lord's Prayer, it says, "And lead me not into temptation." You never left God. But to think you left God, that's what the prodigal son was about, and that's another made up story because you never left God. So the point is you came as a spirit to this earth to transform your energy into the love of God, which through years and years and centuries of being on this planet, as you got more—Marilyn explained this in several channelings. As you came to the planet Earth, you were having such fun with your power that you could create anything you wanted to. Some of you created animal forms and decided to join with animal forms. So you didn't come as fallen angels that were sinful, you came to enjoy planet Earth. Only it got out of hand.

DOUG: Oh, I see.

JOHN: It kind of went to the extreme as humans will do. The pendulum swings extremely one way, and then it will swing the other way extremely. So things got amiss and because of the darkness of the energy being exploited in inappropriate ways. The darkness fell on the earth, and the earth was having difficulties trying to—the Earth was created in fifth dimension as a playground garden of Eden. And we are now at the point we are bringing planet Earth back into what it was initially created as. And you will be returning to your more divine status. You are a creator with God. I wouldn't say—in the church terms, a fallen angel would be like a sinner. And sin is impossible.

DOUG: Really?

JOHN: Well, sin means to miss the mark, and you never miss the mark. You have always been a child of God. You just have not been informed of such, and so they tried to convince you otherwise. So there is no such thing—the only sin, if there is a sin, is to separate yourself from God.

DOUG: Right.

JOHN: And so actually, the churches are the ones that are causing people not to understand their true source.

DOUG: I agree.

JOHN: And so they're practicing the opposite of what they're telling you.

DOUG: Interesting. The book of Revelation, it mentioned that the Jewish people are being saved. God would subject them to a spiritual bath before they entered a new world or the world to come. Now let me ask you—this is a new question. The book of Revelation says that the old heaven and old earth are being replaced by a new heaven and new earth.

JOHN: That part is true.

DOUG: So does that mean that the new heaven and new earth is something else?

JOHN: The new heaven and the new earth is your change of consciousness.

DOUG: Okay.

JOHN: It's not an actual planet being changed. People who are not moving into ascension will move to a different planet of the third dimension. But what's happening on planet Earth is their consciousness, their hearts are being totally open to becoming that whole Spirit that they were created in. So the new earth is an unconditional, loving consciousness of unity, cooperation, consideration, abundance, prosperity. That's the new earth.

DOUG: I see. It mentioned that the new earth has no sea. So does that mean there's no water? I wonder—that's what I'm trying to understand.

JOHN: Well, you see, I can't tell you for sure that there wouldn't be water. However, your bodies will change, and you're eating habits are going to be changing, and your health is going to be changing. Because as you become more spiritual, you will have less form, and you will not have the medical problems. You will not have the same physiology. You will have a different experience. Little by little, humanity as you see it today is gradually going to shift. So it could be referring to that.

DOUG: Yes. I'll get to that in a minute. Here you have another passage from the book of Genesis. It says, "In the sweat of thy face, shalt thou eat bread, shalt thou return to the earth."

JOHN: Well, that is from the church because—it was Moses went through the desert with the people leading, and manna fell from heaven. God will supply the food you need. You don't have to go out and work hours and hours and hours to buy that loaf of bread. This is something that keeps you indebted to those who hold the purse strings and the economy. If they have you out there working, they can collect taxes from you. They can charge you fees. They can have income taxes from the sweat of your brow. And that's not spiritual.

DOUG: Now I understand it's the Word of God, or it's the fountain of living waters.

JOHN: Those are the spiritual words of truth, that you are a child of God, and you have everything you need right now. And you do not need to look outward for anything.

DOUG: Oh, that's why. Because I stopped meditating because of job relocations.

JOHN: Well, I would suggest every morning to take at least ten minutes to connect with your inner consciousness of God's love for you, asking say that only God and you together can handle whatever it ever needs to be that day. And walk forward, knowing that you are loved, and you have every ability that you need to handle whatever happens that day. You see, we are taken care of by our angels and guides around us, and you can accomplish anything necessary to take on. So you just need to reinforce that with yourself.

DOUG: Do I need to obtain a key to the kingdom from a master?

JOHN: Well, the key is—Marilyn had described the keys to the kingdom in one of her channelings. But as you forgive others, as you detach from all the things of the third dimension and as you accept the love that's the only power there is, those are the keys to the kingdom.

DOUG: I know Elijah was here. Elijah was in John the Baptist. Now Elijah was, I guess—John the Baptist was Jesus's master. I guess for the book, the Bible.

JOHN: Well, Elijah, I believe, ascended to heaven as a live person. Wasn't he one of those who rose in a chariot?

DOUG: Yes.

JOHN: Okay. He had attained ascension in his physical form. And that's what you're all doing right now. You're moving into the keys of the kingdom. You're moving into the kingdom of God, which is within, and we're doing it in physical form. And he was an example that people weren't able to do that.

DOUG: That's like body prisoner. We feel like a prisoner. I mean, we're inside a body that was not made by God. The soul was made by God, and we don't know God is there.

JOHN: Well, the body is made as a manifestation of your spirit. So it is God's vehicle, and the Spirit of God dwells in it. But it is your soul that is the consciousness that lives within it.

DOUG: There is a passage in the Bible, and I'm going to use the example of Adam and Eve did. They hid from God. They hid from God because they stopped meditating with God.

JOHN: Well, that's another dogma thing, another church thing. Adam and Eve are just symbolic of the human race coming to earth as masculine and feminine energy.

DOUG: Really?

JOHN: People in those days did not understand that energy is not even masculine and feminine, but there is a positive and a negative or a yin or a yang. And so they were examples of energy coming to earth, merging, and creating a son, so you are just a child of God. And when you combine your energies together, you create sons, so to speak. And it was just showing people that their energies are creative, and with those energies combined, you can create. The two parts of God, what we would call God's Spirit, come together and create a third entity. You are the Trinity. It was trying to say that those energies are within you.

DOUG: I see.

JOHN: So when they talk about Adam and Eve hiding, you know, in God's light you don't have to hide. There's no shame. In fact, yesterday when Marilyn helped people release their shame, there's no shame in God's loving kingdom. You don't have ever to hide from God. The big lie that they perpetuate is it's not safe to be in reality. What they do is they promote lies about it being unsafe to have love in your life. So the biggest fear people have today on Earth is to open their hearts to love. They have been totally conditioned that to open their heart is they would be a bad person. They have to hide. Well, no, you want to open your heart and let God's love be the existence of who you are. Never hide from God. You only are hurting yourself by doing that. You're living outside of the kingdom of God.

DOUG: I get what you're saying. Now I'm going through my questions here.

JOHN: Well, one of your things though that you need to add is that through the energy and spirit coming as man and woman, Adam and Eve as an example of personifying spirit coming to earth. God can only experience through people. He is the Spirit, right? So if you wanted to experience what love is like, what joy is like, or how people help and share with one another, you had to multiply the earth with lots of different spirits to play out these parts. It's like being the vine in God's hands. They're all doing different parts of expressing God in their lives, and it takes many people for those many expressions of God to happen.

DOUG: Are there seven eyes of God? Do we all have seven eyes of God?

JOHN: In a way you do. They're the chakras.

DOUG: Okay.

JOHN: And so your interface between the God source and your human body is the chakras. And if the chakras are clean—Mack and Marilyn do that on Thursday afternoons with people—help them clean their chakras. So the energy of God can come through you and manifest in your life as help. If the chakras are not cleaned out, you are not accessing all of the energy. And therefore, you become unhealthy.

DOUG: So basically, God has designed our human bodies to live up to 120 years.

JOHN: Well, it could live longer than that if you've read all of the Bible.

DOUG: But the great flood happens for a reason. People were living like more than 120. They were living like nine hundred years, three hundred years. But God saw that people were continually evil. So it seems like—

JOHN: God never sees evil in anyone. His children are all his children of Christ. That's another church thing.

DOUG: So like Joshua, he only lives 110 years. Moses lived to 120 years. They received the daily word because they—

JOHN: That's exactly it. The daily Word of God was in their hearts.

DOUG: Exactly, okay. So there's a passage in there—

JOHN: And you can live longer than that depending on what your life plan is. Methuselah lived thousands of years, nine thousand years, isn't it?

DOUG: I think I wrote it down here. Okay, here. "For ye shall serve the Lord your God and he shall bless thy bread, and they water and I will take all sickness away from the midst of thee."

JOHN: Exactly.

DOUG: Do angels live by bread? I mean, do angels—okay, let me take a step back. You say God has never left us?

JOHN: Right.

DOUG: So the angels take care of that.

JOHN: Well, they have a lot to do with it. I will tell you when Marilyn had her experience last Thursday of the phone ringing, and she jumped back into her body at an angle, which was detrimental and did damage to her spleen from the spiritual connections that she had made in that room for channeling. When she went to the spirit doctor to get help the following evening, he said it could have been worse. Now what I've discovered since then for Marilyn to better know what's going on is that she needed that experience for spiritual growth, but it did not have to kill her. Some people are mediums where that experience could have been a death situation. However, because her angels knew she needed the experience, they made it an experience as minimally damaging as possible. But it was necessary.

DOUG: Wow.

JOHN: So she was fortunate that it was not her time to go, and she prays every morning for the most benevolent outcome for whatever happens that day for her. So she had to go through the experience, it just did not have to be utterly devastating.

DOUG: Wow. Well, thank you, because I would not be talking with you!

JOHN: [Laughs] If that happened.

DOUG: Wow. Now since I'm in Connecticut, I'm going to be finishing up my book probably in the fall. The title of the book could be *Door to Glory*.

JOHN: I think that's an excellent title.

DOUG: Because really, glory to God is right behind that door.

JOHN: Exactly. It's just making the decision. I believe that is an excellent title.

DOUG: I don't know where that's coming from. Maybe my guardian angel.

JOHN: That's your feedback system. It's called your guidance system, your feelings. Your emotions play a big part in your life. And if people are open to, like you are, paying attention to that, they'll never lead you astray. Trust your feelings. Trust your instincts.

DOUG: I had a dream from my master through self-realization fellowship. He said -- just for 10 minutes of doing his spiritual exercises that were in home study courses. That's how I learned. That's how I practiced. Then I stopped doing it and got away from it. And now I feel my life has settled down. I'm ready to get back to it. I know that's the right thing.

JOHN: Right. And an interesting thing is if something is not settled down, that's the fastest time to sit down and find and look for the peace inside so it can settle down. Your outside is just a signal to what's going on with you emotionally inside. So pay attention to when things are in disarray around you, realizing that inside you're in disarray too. You're not connected. And it's manifesting to show you that. So that's the time you want to connect. There's a lady who got very, very ill in the spiritual person. And she says, "Well, when I get my medical problems solved, I'll come into your healing course—your healing—let Marilyn do healing for healing on Thursdays. And I'll come to your healing group." And that's backward. When you're sick, that's when you go for the healing so that you don't have to go for medical help.

DOUG: Right.

JOHN: So you see, sometimes you want to be connected. In fact, 24-7 is—there are some wonderful things in the Bible when it says "Pray without ceasing." They're talking about constantly focusing on the love of God in your life. You might want to practice this, which is a very big help to keep you in reality. To tell yourself you are in joy, you are grateful, and you are in the presence of God. And when you do that, you will move into the peace that surpasses all understanding. So every morning, throughout the day, and even when you go to sleep at night, say, "I am in joy. I am in gratitude. And I am in the presence of God." Those are all fifth-dimensional terms that will raise you into a higher consciousness. As other things come up to lead, just realize, "Okay, if I'm in this reality with God, those things are not sustainable."

DOUG: Okay. Thank you. Now I'm going to share this passage. It came from the Old Testament. First of all, was the spirit of Jesus in Joshua?

JOHN: Jesus is in all of us because we're all one in spirit. So if you call on Jesus, he will be there for you. So he was in everybody's spirit if they're consciously aware. But most people deny that that's possible, so they just don't even think about it. And it's, of course, not going to happen if it's not part of your awareness. If you're in denial, you're excluding it from your experience.

DOUG: But like Jesus had played many roles.

JOHN: Jesus had many incarnations, yes. And he also had different times in his life when different experiences were happening, yes.

DOUG: He was—I can't pronounce this name very well—but Melchizedek.

JOHN: Oh, that is a spirit that came into the earth that did not have to born as a child or a baby.

DOUG: Right. There is no history of him being born.

JOHN: Right. And there is more about the Melchizedek—I have trouble saying it too—in the Book of Urantia. If you want to know more about that particular spiritual segment, it's a marvelous group of energies that somebody on planet Earth right now claims to be part of that spiritual group. It has come to bring spiritual answers to people. And so part of the Bible was written by that energy, yes.

DOUG: I'll talk to Marilyn about getting that book.

JOHN: Okay.

DOUG: Now where do unclean spirits go after the person dies?

JOHN: Well, unclean spirits can go anytime you release them. And they just dissipate, and they're cleansed in the ethers. So when you are releasing, you have to identify your fears and identify your anger, determine your grudges. Whatever part of your consciousness needs to be cleaned out. We'll call it the Roto-Rooter system. We're getting rid of the stuff that you don't want. And you can ask God to humbly remove that particular fear—fear of heights just as an example. And then you immediately ask God to replace that void that is left by the fear leaving with his love and grace.

DOUG: So really love will keep the unclean spirit away.

JOHN: You got it.

DOUG: That's why Jesus said you forgive seventy times seven hundred.

JOHN: Well, and that's very good advice. Sometimes it's easy to forgive somebody for a simple offense, saying, "Well, I needed to learn something from that." If someone stole something from you and they say, "Well, they must have needed it more than I, and it's not mine if they took it. My things God provides for me," such a simple thing like that is easy to forgive. Sometimes there is some very great physical, mental, emotional, spiritual abuse that happens in childhood or experiences growing up that are very difficult to forgive. It took Marilyn more than seventeen years of literally practicing forgiveness to be able to come to an understanding and a calmness about her stepfather. So sometimes it's easy and sometimes you just have to keep praying unceasingly.

DOUG: Because when you have love, it's much easier to—maybe that's why I was deaf. To learn what it was like to be in the dark.

JOHN: Exactly.

DOUG: And then all of a sudden, I see love. I can love people better.

JOHN: That's the lesson that you were supposed to learn, and you have a beautiful story to help others with.

DOUG: There is a passage. I forgot to write it down here. But it's from Revelation 3:12. It says, "Thou shall go no more out." What does mean?

JOHN: Okay. Thou shall go no more out. Let me think of that for just a moment. I'm not familiar with that passage. Okay, they're referring to reincarnation. You don't have to keep going in and out of this life.

DOUG: Let's see. Now are Buddhists, Hindus, Muslims part of Christians?

JOHN: Well, you see, Christian is a label. And just because a person calls themselves a name doesn't mean they're closer to Christ or not close to Christ. It means that they have chosen to call themselves that and their actions might speak differently.

DOUG: Okay.

JOHN: So it doesn't matter what label you have. It's what's in your heart.

DOUG: So did Jesus appear as Muhammed for Islam?

JOHN: Yes.

DOUG: Oh. And as Avatar for Hindus?

JOHN: He appeared as Buddha for the Buddhists. But you see, there was never the intention to start religions. That was the people's idea.

DOUG: Right.

JOHN: So you see, things when they become a religion get distorted from the original message because it's somebody else interpreting the experience that was religious.

DOUG: Thank you very much. I have all the questions I have asked.

JOHN: Well, I'm so thrilled that we were able to meet today. I hope I have clarified some of your questions so that they better make sense to you.

DOUG: I guess I go through self-realization fellowship for a home study course on meditation.

JOHN: Meditation, yes. Meditation opens the door to the spiritual world. And that's part of the beginning step. And as you move into higher consciousness through meditation, your world will expand, and that means you're on the right path because God is energy and expansion. Your expansion will bring you into new beautiful places.

DOUG: That's the best place to start, meditation. That's the answer.

JOHN: See, that connects you to the fifth dimension. You release the ego and the third-dimensional answers to find the truth of who you are.

DOUG: I know these church people are not going to believe it, but all I say to myself is they will get there later.

JOHN: Everybody needs to go through the lessons necessary for their growth, and you cannot do it for them. You can just be in a good example.

DOUG: Okay. Well, thank you very much. I enjoyed this time with you.

JOHN: You are so welcome. It's been lovely to have you here, and I am very honored that you came for this visit. I know that you went through a great deal of effort and expense to do this. So my hat is off to you. I think that you are challenging yourself in wonderful, spiritual ways, and I know you book will be a wonderful book.

DOUG: Thank you very much, John.

Section 6.2: December 21, 2014

The following is a dialogue with John the Divine via medium channeled while Marilyn Redmond was in her trance on December 21, 2014, in Edgewood, Washington.

DOUG: All these questions are based on the Urantia Book so probably—well, I have about forty questions—and I'm going to try to get them. I'm going to look at the time and try to do it in an hour and a half.

John: Okay.

DOUG: Now, ah, there are many worlds out there?

JOHN: Exactly.

DOUG: So really this is the evolutionary world that we are growing and trying to raise our consciousness closer to the center of the universe, the central universe?

JOHN: Yes, our planet is what you might call a young planet. And it hasn't had its growing pains, you might say, and go through the difficult growing experiences it chose to live. About seventy years ago, it called for help, and that's when sunlight more energy was starting to be projected onto Earth from around the rest of the universe and the rest of the cosmos. To bring energy to the planet so it could reverberate itself into a functioning, sentient being again, and it is a planet that is progressing and finally ready to grow up into a mature understanding of love.

DOUG: Now from the Urantia book it says this is one of the younger universes?

JOHN: Yes.

DOUG: When would the next universe be in the making beyond this universe?

JOHN: It is in the making, and it has been for some time. There will be a point when the planetary shifting occurs and a new planet—we'll call it the big bang. It will pop out like a pregnancy where the baby has arrived, and this is according to the arrangement of the planets to be in the right position for this to occur and is not at that point yet. But it is in the future visionary. It will happen. There is a book you might be interested in, and I'm not sure what volume it's in. But there's a small series of books called *Lives and Teaching of the Masters of the Far East* by Spaulding, and in there it describes the birthing of the next planet.

DOUG: Oh, really? What is that again?

JOHN: *Lives and Teachings of the Masters of the Far East*. The author is Spaulding, and the publisher is DeVorss, I believe. It is a California publisher. And the volumes are new, so there isn't a lot of reading, but one of the volumes does describe the birthing of the next planet.

DOUG: Can book writing be part of the script?

JOHN: Very much so. Marilyn's book is.

DOUG: Now at work I've been sharing these findings with a couple of gentlemen people at work. There were very Christian-oriented. They study the Bible, and I can see that these gentlemen were open with my findings. But it seems like they might have talked about it with their church, and they probably got them back to not believing in spiritual values. Now how would those people change? Can I see it is very difficult to get the spiritual message across?

JOHN: Well, this is one of the things not to proselytize. You see, Jesus didn't go around proselytizing. People followed him. He did not go out and sell tickets to a theater and say "Hear me speak Saturday night," and then worry about how much money he was going to make to cover all the bills. They gathered together in groups and homes and on mountaintops It was never about preaching for people to change. It was to share the message. There's a different motivation. So when the apostles went out to start their churches, it was to share the message. And as the message grew, people were attracted to the message, and that's your biggest concern. When you find people interested and have like minds to say, "Well, let's start a spiritual study group and share what we're learning." I would like to suggest for the two fellas—and if you want to include the other people, they could come and check it out—but you ought to look into starting a spiritual study group such as called "Search for God." Edgar Cayce wrote two wonderful books that are straight from the source. They go through all the necessary things that we are talking about as far as needed to move into that heaven on earth. How do you need to grow spiritually? Each chapter takes you into a higher consciousness of growing yourself into this space you are trying to achieve in your life. So if you go through the first volume and the second volume, and you can repeat going through these because each time you read them you're at a new place in your growth and discuss, there's a little procedure you follow on a weekly basis. As you meet you go through the little routine organized starting with a prayer and one thing you read a Bible verse and discuss it, you have an exercise. You are spiritually practicing it. You practice that week and share with your friends it went. You read in the *Search for God* book, and it explains more about changing your soul, which we are talking about and understanding that most people have not heard spiritually. It is easier to read the book than *The Urantia Book*, but it has spiritual growth in it. It is the same, but it's just worded differently. But it is from source, so it's extremely valuable study group, and you might find that this would be a way to grow with like-minded friends.

DOUG: I agree. I think the biggest challenge would be overcome the resistance of the pastors.

JOHN: You don't talk to the church of pastors about this. You meet on your own, and it wouldn't necessarily meet in a church. You could meet in a church if they wanted to meet there, but most often they meet in homes.

DOUG: They sounded interested, but they are still members of the church though. Of course, they are going to listen to the church.

JOHN: Well, Marilyn did it to the extreme because her church was such a fundamentalist church. You talk about faith and what you want to talk about at church, and you leave your mouth shut for what you don't want to say at church. So just because you're in a spiritual study group doesn't mean you have to blab about it at church. You can learn from yourself and grow in yourself until you have grown enough to be able to share intelligently with other. So just because you're learning, it doesn't mean everybody has to hear it.

DOUG: Now the other side, that's where heaven is?

JOHN: The other side of what? Heaven is consciousness. It's not a place.

DOUG: Oh, so could they reincarnate? Do they have to reincarnate, or they go straight through?

JOHN: No, they reincarnate until their spirits grow and evolve into higher consciousness just like you and me.

DOUG: That's the only way to grow spiritually?

JOHN: You only grow through step-by-step evolvement of higher, higher loving service in your heart to others and those around you by being helpful, contributing, giving, everything that is unselfish that you do your consciousness.

DOUG: What makes other inhabited worlds normal? Is it true that mortals from other worlds find God through baptism of the Spirit, through the proper course of evolution?

JOHN: Would you repeat the question? It's quite complicated.

DOUG: Well, this world is a confused world because of Lucifer's rebellion.

JOHN: Because they became a dense energy that the church has called the fall of man?

DOUG: Do they speak just one language?

JOHN: Well, you see you're looking at something out there that's complex because some planets might have human beings and some do, some planets might have a different spiritual form that you would not recognize as a human, you would probably know it possibly as an animal form. I have a friend who came from a planet on Uranus, and she was a praying mantis. I know of a person who arrived in Marilyn for help on this planet who had been a horse before becoming a human on earth. So you see, there are different forms of spiritual consciousness and different planets have various types. Some of them do not look like humans, and you are not familiar with looking at other forms of being part of the God experience. So they are trying to in various ways to introduce that there are other forms. So God decides human form.

DOUG: I'm going to ask you about the war in heaven. One gentleman from work wanted to know about that.

JOHN: There is no war in heaven because the planet Earth has gone through a very low, dense time of energy. The wars were created by people on Earth who did not have light, and so therefore, they were in conflict with one another rather than harmony. But heaven is perfection.

DOUG: Okay, would earth obtain life and light status in foreseeable future?

JOHN: Yes, maybe not your lifetime. But yes, it is compared to a blink of God's eye. It is coming that the earth is moving into that new energy because as you heard yesterday the Christ consciousness has come to earth. So therefore, that love will be dispelling the darkness, and the planet will become a planet of light again.

DOUG: Now the fifth dimension. Let's see, okay. Is November 2015 the end of the thousand-year reign? Did judgment start in December 2012?

JOHN: Well, I'm not quite sure what those questions represent, but judgment day happens. There's no judgment day. You judge yourself. So when the churches try to create panic and concern when they don't need to, that's part of what they do and put out dates and deadlines and all kinds of information, so they want to scare people. The real judgment—this is what you will find in the movie *Defend Your Life*—the real judgment comes when you see what you didn't do that you needed to do, and you judged yourself for being, ah, and lack of stepping up to the plate when you needed to.

DOUG: That's like going through the tunnel, and you see the light at the end of the tunnel. That's when you see flashbacks of the past life?

JOHN: Well, everyone has a different version of that because we're all individuals, but that's often people will have. In fact, this movie explains that we'll have some review. It's more of a review. How well did you do? And that's called in church's version the judgment.

DOUG: So these spirits being baptized by the Spirit, they can feel the love of God?

JOHN: It is the beginning of an awakening to the God within.

DOUG: Oh, okay, so now are you familiar with the seven circles of life?

JOHN: Well, do you mean the seven chakras?

DOUG: No, this is what the Urantia Book was talking about. It has the first circle and the second circle up to the seventh circle.

JOHN: Well, maybe your terminology is different. Can you explain what's in your first circle?

DOUG: The first circle where everyone starts at the seventh circle. That's when the person can choose between, the difference between right and wrong. And they gradually climb to the third circle. That's when the guardian angel and the angel comes to life. You have an additional angel with you, and then it's that level. It's the level of cosmic understanding and intellectual level.

JOHN: Oh, yes, you might say it's similar to Maslow Pyramid, self-awareness.

DOUG: Yes, I think it's similar.

JOHN: So you might say it's a different terminology for emotional growth.

DOUG: Is it true that 100 percent of the brain power is used to push soul out of the body? We all use 10 percent of our brain's actual capacity, but I wonder if 100 percent of the brain is used during the transition from material body to the new body.

JOHN: What you're talking about is you were given on planet Earth only partial access to your DNA.

Section 6.3: January 27, 2015

Conversation with John the Divine via phone medium, channeled while Marilyn Redmond was in her trance on January 27, 2015, in Edgewood, Washington.

DOUG: Okay, the first question is—is harvest all about transferring souls to the fifth dimension on the new earth, which is the blue earth? The present earth is not conductive for the fifth dimension. Is that true?

JOHN: No, the earth, the planet Earth as you know it, has been going through the same transition consciously as people have. If people's consciousness has changed, it is actually been returning back to the fifth dimension, in which it was created. So it is not a separate earth. It's the same earth, but with a new higher consciousness of love. That was its original intention and created in. So it will feel like a different earth because the atmosphere and environment around you will have a different feeling. The fear and oppression feelings will not be there anymore. They will dissipate. So it will feel different, but it's actually the same earth that has been brought back into its original state.

DOUG: Maybe originally, it was spiritual earth, but it didn't turn out to be that way. The book of Revelation, maybe a new heaven and a new earth. I wonder if the new earth is the blue earth, but that is not clear.

JOHN: Well, the new earth is the earth of love which—

DOUG: Okay.

JOHN: The old is the fearful basis that has been the emphasis and the influence on the planet for thousands of years at this point, which is now been dissipated. So we are moving out of the old focus of duality from third-dimensional awareness into a higher awareness where that duality is no longer prevalent. It's all going to be coming and based on love so that peace on earth can happen. So it's going to feel like a new world, but physically, the earth is just transformed just like people are changing their inner essence, more love, releasing the fear. One might look like a new person, but it's still the same body.

DOUG: I was reading this book, and it mentioned that this earth was only good for the second, third, or fourth dimension but not for the fifth dimension. So I thought that the fifth dimension would have a different earth, a new earth.

JOHN: Well, it's really a matter of semantics rather than physical change.

DOUG: Like it is really states of consciousness.

JOHN: Exactly. Heaven and hell both are states of consciousness.

DOUG: Now is it true someone with the eighth dimension can go from point A to point B anywhere in space in a matter of a split second?

JOHN: Really, it is done within the spiritual realm inside. They would not physically in some cases move to that location; however, there are masters who have physically moved their bodies to new locations. It depends on the consciousness of the person and how spiritually accelerated they are.

DOUG: Like the seven chakras.

JOHN: Well, the seven chakras are functioning as best they can with where the personal consciousness. And what they want and need to do is to release any darkness in those chakras so they can be more and more open to that light.

DOUG: Now I don't know if you can answer this question, but you don't have to if you can't, but I am just curious of your understanding of dimensions. Like what dimension will you and Gabriel be?

JOHN: Very good question.

DOUG: Like the eighth dimension—

JOHN: Well, we would be likely between the twelfth and thirteenth dimensions.

DOUG: Wow.

JOHN: And it does go higher than that, so you can see there is still a lot of growth for people to journey through.

DOUG: Now I read somewhere that like the elder, the twenty-four elders, are they located at Saturn at the eighth dimension?

JOHN: Well, are you talking about the masters when you say elders?

DOUG: The eighth dimension, but we can't see them.

JOHN: Well, the masters are in a variety of different dimensions depending on, again, their spiritual ascension or growth into higher consciousness. So some masters are right now on earth and have a physical form, but generally, the masters have moved on closer to eighth and ninth dimension because they have already assumed the Christ consciousness and are moving beyond that. So most masters have a very intense and practical understanding of the spiritual knowledge.

DOUG: There's a group of aliens called Orion, O-R-I-O-N?

JOHN: Yes.

DOUG: Now are they the dark side, or are they independent?

JOHN: I believe they are independent. I have not—I am not familiar with that particular group, but it doesn't ring a bell as being an energy that would be a problem.

DOUG: So basically, the dark side is facing the end time, is that correct?

JOHN: Exactly. That is why the crisis and turmoil is so pandemic. They are struggling for the last breath of air, you might say.

DOUG: I have a couple more questions. Now is it okay if I include our conversation in my book?

JOHN: Yes, you can include this information.

DOUG: Is that okay with you?

JOHN: It is fine with me. People need to know this energy, these messages that have not necessarily been easily available to them. Thank you for getting the message out there, Doug. I appreciate that.

DOUG: My goal is to be as open as I can so people can because people are very skeptical. So I am going to have information in my book and references so people can go to some other sources to double check.

JOHN: Well, I think that is admirable. The more they search, the more they will find.

DOUG: It seems like the Ten Commandments were handed down to Moses. They were given by an Orion group?

JOHN: Well, the Ten Commandments were given to Moses by God.

DOUG: They were given by God.

JOHN: That's when he went to the top of the mountain and came down and found the people worshipping a golden calf. And he got angry.

DOUG: So you are saying the Ten Commandments, they were directly from God?

JOHN: Right. If you are open, if you are meditating or open completely to the spiritual energy that is within, that is God talking to us directly.

DOUG: So God talked to him directly.

JOHN: Yes.

DOUG: So we will still be here on the same planet.

JOHN: Exactly. You will not go anywhere. If you have moved your consciousness into a God consciousness, you will stay, but with a new reality.

DOUG: Okay. Now again, I just want to double-check. Nirvana, I know heaven is a state of consciousness.

JOHN: Nirvana is where the spirit goes when you pass to the other side.

DOUG: Oh, that is what passing to the other side.

JOHN: It is.

DOUG: Where is the astral world?

JOHN: Well, it's around you. It's in spirit, and it is invisible.

DOUG: Oh, so it's invisible like actually three feet above me?

JOHN: Yes, it's in the higher realms of fourth dimension.

DOUG: That is the most important thing—to have a loving heart.

JOHN: Exactly. The more you open your heart, the more you send out for the love to fill your life.

DOUG: We here on earth appear to grow usually, but we are still in the same body. How long can the body last? I mean, even though we have like seven chakras, if the energy flows through the entire chakras and we go to God for his blessing, how long can the body last? For a hundred years, two hundred years, or what?

JOHN: Longer. The Bible does talk about people who, like Methuselah, are many, many years beyond that. And Babaji—and I believe he is in India—has lived to several thousand years. So the only thing that stops you from growing into an older age is your mind. And when you come into a mind-set that you are an eternal spiritual being, you will determine your own age of passing. It will not come on you because the medical or the insurance companies have statistics that say you live to a certain age and everybody has adopted. It fits statistics and numbers, but yet you go inside and know that you are eternal. You can live eternally in a physical form. Most people, if you read—

DOUG: It is what can shorten your life.

JOHN: Yes, only the thinking is what makes the difference.

DOUG: Interesting. It is really a blessing to be doing this book work. I love it.

JOHN: Well, I am so happy that you are.

DOUG: I will get it done. Can you see what I am doing, or how do you know how I am progressing with this?

JOHN: Well, I don't see it. I feel the energy. I feel the progress you have made, and I feel you are moving forward. I see your intent and sincerity. I feel the energy that surrounds your project.

Section 6.4: February 10, 2015

Conversation with John the Divine via phone medium, channeled while Marilyn Redmond was in her trance on February 10, 2015, in Edgewood, Washington.

DOUG: First question: Now I'm going refer to a passage from the Bible.

JOHN: Yes.

DOUG: Ephesians 6:12.

JOHN: Mm-hmm.

DOUG: From New Testament. "For we wrestle not against flesh and blood, but against principalities, against powers, against the worldly governors, the princes of the darkness of this world, against the spiritual wickedness which are in high places." Now the question is—the princes of darkness, lizard people, or aliens?

JOHN: Well, some are. Not ... evil is the lack of light, so it's just a person or situation is lacking the light of God, and you can't fight that because there's nothing to fight. It's powerless without the power of God. So what they're talking about is not to fight the sins and evils of the material planet, but to turn to a spiritual, higher ... the truth of who we are is in spirit and not the material plane. The material is just a manifestation, and if it's lacking light, there's nothing to fight in the first place. You're actually ... when you fight something, you actually increase it by your attention, so not to fight it means that you are not going to focus on that, which becomes a false god, but focus on the higher Spirit of God.

DOUG: That Earth is actually seven Earths? The first density of Earth is red. The second density is orange. The third density is yellow, and the fourth density is green. When it goes into the fifth dimension, then that is where the blue Earth comes into play?

JOHN: Well, you're describing it through the chakras, and Mother Earth is a sentient being. And the people reflect into Mother Earth, what she is, and she reflects back to her people that particular. Those chakras are the connection, interconnection to the spiritual realm, so you are talking ... Mother Earth is a sentient being that is connected to Spirit, is manifested from Spirit just like people are. It's just manifested as a planet, so yes, those are the chakra colors. And as the Earth has ascended, those chakras are opening up, and they are a part of the energy, yes.

DOUG: Is it true that blue Earth is invisible to third-density people as well as the fourth density?

JOHN: A higher range than that. When a person moves into a spiritual level of existence, moves out of the third-dimensional duality of materialism, then they are in a higher vibration, and most people on Earth would not recognize that they are in a higher vibration.

DOUG: Okay.

JOHN: Because they are still visible physically, but emotionally, inside, they are of a higher vibration. And that higher vibration attracts other higher vibrations, not the earthly vibration, so it's like the higher vibration isn't there because the earthly vibration is not attracted to it. But it is there. It's just that it's not part of their scope, you might say.

DOUG: Now is this other Earth from the Bible, from Hebrews 10:34? Actually, did Paul write the book of Hebrews?

JOHN: Um—

DOUG: Or was that by a different writer?

JOHN: That I would have to go check out for you.

DOUG: Well, I have. I'm going quote a passage from the book of Hebrews. The question is about the fifth-dimension Earth, so we'll get us more of the yes and no after. Paul mentions in the Bible about a heavenly place, "For both though ye sorrowed with me for my bonds, and suffered with joy of spoiling of your goods, knowing in yourselves how that ye have in Heaven a better, and enduring substance." That's from Hebrews 10:34. Is this heavenly place in fifth dimension Earth?

JOHN: Yes.

DOUG: Okay, good, very good. Now—

JOHN: It's also a spiritual consciousness. Heaven is inside of you. It's a state of consciousness, so as you move into this heavenly consciousness of peace inside, which is not of man but which is of the Christ consciousness, then you are in a heavenly consciousness. And you manifest that as you are experiencing the world. That's being in the world but not of it.

DOUG: What form of government takes place on Earth during the fifth dimension?

JOHN: Government is of the people, not of God. So if you are talking about the government that's going on the planet at this point, it all comes from third dimension. God's government is self-governing, and it's of spiritual integrity where the governing is not done through laws and through coercion and punishment. It's done through cooperation, being a community that is coordinating together in unity. So a government of man is not the same as the government of God.

DOUG: Another question I wanted to ask you. Frankincense, is that a scent like a candle? Candles can have different scents.

JOHN: Okay.

DOUG: Someone told me to get one of those. It would help to block the negative energy from getting into the room while I'm meditating.

I'd like to ask you. Does it? Does frankincense block the negative energy?

JOHN: Well, the choice is not to block energy. It is to focus on God's energy, and it expands. And so there is nothing to block. As it expands, it grows and pushes out anything that isn't real. So you want to look at it from what is the real thing and just focus on it and let it expand. Don't focus on the negative. Focus on the positive.

DOUG: Is that the same thing that was one of the three gifts from the three wise men given to Jesus at his birth?

JOHN: Yes, frankincense was definitely one of the fragrances, and they also represented spiritual gifts, not just the actual incense itself. So they were bringing gifts of spiritual value to the baby, not just the boxed item.

DOUG: Did the wise men come from India?

JOHN: Yes.

DOUG: Okay. Now I read in a book about Atlantis that black magic was practiced and it was exported to India?

JOHN: I didn't understand the first. What was exported to India?

DOUG: Black magic.

JOHN: Oh, black magic.

DOUG: Was that practiced by the Indians or by a small group in India?

JOHN: Primarily, it was from an African … the continent of Africa.

DOUG: Oh, okay.

JOHN: But it was picked up by other sources as time moved on, so the black magic was adopted into other … well, it was actually adopted into religions too because some of them are operating from that level, even though they don't tell the public that. So the Catholic church has a lot of black magic going on in the depths of it. So you see, where it starts is not necessarily as important as to just say, "I choose to focus on God's love," and that then will not have to interfere with my life because the only power is God. And if I focus on something that isn't God, then I'm making it a god, and that's not what you want to do in your life.

DOUG: Moses had warned people not to worship golden calves. Could black magic be similar to that?

JOHN: Exactly. Black magic is the wrong use of energy. And so if you're worshipping something that isn't God, you've made a false god of it, and so the— To put your attention on something that is not God is actually taking your focus off the only God there is. And you give away your power, and you will have all kinds of consequences because you are coming from a selfish point of view when that happens.

DOUG: Did the bad alien group teach that concept?

JOHN: No, well, it was … it's not something you teach. It is a mindset that through being—how do I put this? When people are deprived and created to be victims and followers and they listen to people rather than their hearts, then they have put their focus in the wrong place, and through that, they get darker and darker. And so they're searching for God, but they are looking in the wrong places, and so it tends to grow and grow through the focus being in the wrong direction. So it's a matter of the light within the person, and it doesn't— It's the lack of God's light. It's separation from God, and if a person feels that way, then what's happened in the earthly world today is that's been perpetuated, encouraged so that people do not focus on the God within. And there is a lot of darkness in many, many people today because they are looking outside of themselves for their answers or buy one more iPod to feel good inside when God is really the truly only good inside. So it's not necessarily coming from a particular place. It's how a person is being preached to or taught that goes against what's true and real, and they pick it up and run with it and just expand on it until it becomes very devastating in their lives. And so it's an individual choice to say, "Well, this is what I choose to focus on, and because I'm looking for answers, it's just looking in the wrong places." So a person comes to, "This is what the journey on Earth is about." A person comes into Earth with a lot of thinking and experiences from the past of old energy, dark energy, and they come to Earth to—this is the planet where it's more easily to change that energy from the darkness to the light. So it is possible to transform from that consciousness into a higher consciousness or God consciousness, Christ consciousness, but it's an individual choice of each person coming to this planet with that in mind. If they keep their focus on track, however, most people reincarnate, reincarnate, reincarnate until they finally say, "I give up. I surrender to God. Now how can I move forward in the light?" So it's an individual situation, but it is definitely supported and encouraged by outside forces.

DOUG: I've learned that a planet called Maldek had disappeared from our universe?

JOHN: Uh-huh.

DOUG: Now would aliens tried to destroy civilization before Earth attains fifth dimension?

JOHN: Would you say that one again? There's something that didn't quite click.

DOUG: Okay, sure. Well, this is kind of like what happened to Maldek when it exploded?

JOHN: Mm-hmm.

DOUG: Now this question—this is for general understanding of the vibrational level. I'd like to ask you—what is the spiritual vibration of the archangels?

JOHN: Very good question. The archangels were created in the first creation beyond God's Spirit. There are different levels of creation as shown in the book *The Real Meaning of 2012 Heaven on Earth*. It has a chart in there that explains the different creation levels. So they're very, very high in God's creation as far as having a tremendous amount of energy of that higher elevation, which is very full of wisdom and experience and knowledge that they can handle. An archangel can do about the seven times more energy help than a single angel. So you see, they are much closer to God.

DOUG: Could the alien group called Orion, O-R-I-O-N, could they apply psychic attack to try to prevent humans on Earth from receiving warnings from the angels?

JOHN: No. They can't psychically attack. There is no such thing. You can have psychic attack if the person accepts it, but if a person is strong enough in their spiritual strength, it would be like a shield and an armor. It would bounce off because if you are in the one power of God, nothing can harm you. That's your armor, so people who believe in psychic attacks believe in two powers. They believe in evil and good, but there is only good,. And that good is God, and so if your belief system doesn't include a power that's going to upset or hurt you, it just disappears. It's not real.

DOUG: Now we're in time and space, so we're part of evolution. We are striving to get closer to God, to realize love of living. Are aliens— do they understand consciousness?

JOHN: The aliens today that are in contact with planet Earth, the negative aliens, the ones that were of the dark, are no longer able to contact Earth. The light is too powerful for them. They are dark, of darkness, and the planet is becoming brighter and brighter. It's impossible for them to contact Earth. There are many aliens on Earth today. They just look like everybody else. So you can't say they're out there and we're here. We're all aliens of one sort or another come to Earth. It's just like America is the melting pot of many countries that came in through Ellis Island and other countries besides of entrance that they used, and the planet Earth has many, many foreign, you might say, entities from such as the Pleiades, such as Arcturus. There are many different aliens that have come to Earth to help, and it's not bad that someone's an alien. Actually, most are of a higher consciousness and are trying to help Mother Earth ascend and the people of Earth ascend with her. So the aliens today are actually very supportive, loving, and caring, and they're here to be of help, so there's nothing to fear about seeing or working with an alien.

DOUG: My friend said she was abducted when she was sixteen or seventeen. She saw two green aliens waking her up from her sleep. She noticed some scanning in an emergency room setting. And then she came back. Her mother said she heard a conversation in her room.

JOHN: There was a time when that kind of thing happened, but that's not happening today.

DOUG: Okay, so that doesn't happen anymore?

JOHN: No, because the energy of Earth, of the planet is too high for the green aliens to be able to come into this environment anymore. It's not … they just can't handle it. They would actually disappear, dissipate because they cannot handle the light.

DOUG: So people don't have to fear UFOs anymore.

JOHN: The UFOs are actually there to help us. They're there to support us and help with the pollution to be recovered into healthy energy so that we do not have to have a planet that is full of all kinds of toxic problems that are actually not healthy for the human form. So they're actually waiting to come in and be of assistance.

DOUG: Thank you so much, John.

JOHN: Well, I want to applaud your efforts. I want you to know that you are surrounded by your guides and masters that are helping you to write this, that you open up to their energy and—

DOUG: Thank you.

JOHN: Yes, just let it flow out, just let it ... God's will is comfortable. It just flows, and it's in harmony, and it's just very peaceful, so just let it come out, and you're doing a great job, you've got a lot of big, a lot of special help, a lot of spiritual help, and just be open and receptive, and it will be a real big success.

DOUG: Thank you so much. I feel so blessed for doing this work.

JOHN: Well, you have been chosen. You have followed through and listened to the messages, and you are to be commended. It takes a great courage to step out and speak and say and do the things that you're promoting in your book, and we all want you to know that on the spiritual side you are being applauded and cheered. And they're very, very happy with you.

DOUG: Thank you very much. I feel so honored.

JOHN: Well, you are a special person, and just know you're doing God's will.

Section 6.5: February 18, 2015

Conversation with John the Divine via medium, channeled by Marilyn Redmond in her trance on February 18, 2015, in Edgewood, Washington.

JOHN: Good morning, Doug. I am John.

DOUG: Good morning. Hi, John, how are you?

JOHN: Well, I'm doing very well. Thank you. And I do have some information for you this morning that you asked me earlier, and I do want to respond that yes, Paul wrote the book of Hebrew.

DOUG: Oh, great. Okay.

JOHN: I thought you might want that information since I had to postpone it.

DOUG: Great. Thank you.

JOHN: All right. Whatever you have to do, well, I'm ready to be of service.

DOUG: I've got a lot of questions. So I'm going to ask the question, and then you can just respond.

JOHN: That sounds fine.

DOUG: Now is it true that the Earth is moving closer to the center of creation where God is?

JOHN: No, there are changes in the planetary alignment going on constantly. Because energy moves and there is nothing stagnate or staying still in time or in space. So if it's always in motion and there is motion, not necessarily toward the sun that is occurring in small degrees, so that the planets in their circles and cycles rotating around the sun are making adjustments, yes.

DOUG: Now the people of the third and fourth densities, will they suffer hardship before things become better?

JOHN: Well, when you reincarnate each time, it is a matter of learning the lessons necessary to move the energy of darkness based on dense energy into a higher light, loving space, so through loving your neighbor as yourself, you move into a higher consciousness of doing that. So it's a matter of—in the fourth dimension, it's the brains of energy, where you bring more and more light in, replacing the darkness in third dimension, and the darkness is the prevailing energy.

DOUG: The end-time struggles are, what I would call, last gasps of power from the dark side before ending of their control. Is this true?

JOHN: That's exactly true. It is the last energy that's needing to come out and be explored by the light and brought into the light so it can be dissipated. In their struggles they are created great havoc that is looking to the news as if to be terribly destructive. But the reality is it has been buried very deeply for thousands of years, and it is time for that to come out into the light and be eliminated. So this is the last struggle. You are correct.

DOUG: Upon seeing the churches today—by the way it was set up—how would you advise them how to grow in the fourth dimension?

JOHN: Well, there would need to be a lot of cleaning of house in the churches today, of releases anything that is dogma in removing those particular concepts from the preaching because anything that is negative is not of God. Anything punishing, judgmental, that would be sins are not of God, that they need to be punished. There is, as you say, a lot of dogma that would need to be rearranged into a positive, productive understanding. Rather than—the Old Testament was very much laws and rules and then culture—it was to bring people together. And to focus that these would make you a better person. And today a better person is coming from the New Testament, which is in your heart, and you manifest it from your heart, not what a rule is. So you need to remove all of the rules and move them into loving concepts that people can experience, and true religion is an experience. It's not going and sitting in a pew, but it's in that meditative state when you connect with that higher consciousness of God's love and light in your life. That's a religious experience. Most people think of belonging to a church is a religious experience, but it's a personal thing. And churches will continue to perpetuate your need to come to church, or they would have no reason to exist. So it's very difficult for churches to move completely into the truth of what is letting energy and messages about because churches would not be necessary if you just stayed home and meditated and found your answers there. They want to provide the answers. So it's going to be a gradual growing into more loving messages from the church that are truth and reality, but it will not happen overnight because soon there would be no need for churches. It is necessary, however, to have groups that can come together and have a common interest in searching for improving your higher consciousness and healing your soul. ARE (Association for Research and Enlightenment, Inc.) has study groups called "Search for God." That kind of a group would probably be replacing the church. It is a study group of spiritual growth rather than sermons from a pulpit. Rather apply it in your life. When you implement it in your life, you're experiencing that love rather than just talking about it. And that would be a major difference.

DOUG: Paul in one of his epistle letters mentioned church is within.

JOHN: Exactly. And that's what he's talking about is experiencing the love of God in your life as it manifests in front of you and within you. By health and prosperity and by feeling excited and loving and good and sharing and gratitude—those are all experiencing the love of God, and that's the church where you want to come in harmony, and if you come in peace with yourself, you can extend that to others. And that's really what a church is about—to provide the Spirit to come and merge with other spirits—and it's not for someone to stand up there and tell you how to do it. It's for you to experience it.

DOUG: Eckankar and it's called the religion of light and sound of God. Spiritual freedom is growing into a state of more godliness, becoming more aware of the presence of God.

JOHN: Well, you can always research it on the Internet. You do not need a church because the church is within as you just quoted. And so what you're probably looking for is a community of people who are studying what you would call ultimate truth. And research if you're looking for a group. There are groups of study Abraham, *A Course in Miracles*. There are groups of Edgar Cayce. These are all valid study groups, which would be very applicable to putting this energy into your life, which I would suggest rather than a religious group. Well, I will warn you about one thing. Churches, no matter how much they claimed to be spiritually oriented, they're there for you and end up having some dogma because that's how they hold the group together. So when you lose the doctrine, then you would find a spiritual study group rather than a church.

DOUG: Basically, we choose one of the two paths in life, service to self or service to others. Would you define what service to self means?

JOHN: Well, service to self would be a selfish person, self-seeking, self-absorbing, narcissistic. People who only see themselves as the center of the universe rather than that they are just parts of a bigger experience. So people who are seeking self will do things that provide only benefit to themselves rather than helping others in charity or volunteer work. They just are not interested in that. They're just everything is about making, grandiosity, making themselves a better, looking better to others, have lots of pride and arrogance. When you are serving this flesh, then you are self-serving. When you're serving God and others, your spiritual energy flows to them rather than bottled up inside of the selfish person. It flows out to the other person. It provides sustaining help, support, compassion, any kinds of ways to help that person be a better person. Service to self-person that is serving themselves is too selfish to help others.

DOUG: Does removal of the veil, which separates unconscious mind and conscious mind, reveals more of future than past?

JOHN: Well, if you're changing from a subconscious, there is not subconscious. It's really where you're focused, and if you're not feeling that particular consciousness, it's not a subconscious. It's just not in your awareness at that time. So what you want to think of is keeping your focus on the current or the present, on the presence of God. Then those good feelings will just be that manifestations from where your focus is, and your subconscious will be no longer focused on and therefore will dissipate without energy focusing on something that will not sustain. So it's a matter of where is your focus and to keep your focus in the now, in the consciousness of now, knowing that the old, the old things will leave, they will come up to leave your consciousness because you're not focusing on them anymore. They come up and say, "Well, here I am." Just say, "What are you going to do with me?" Appropriate time to say, "Satan, get thee behind me." Usually, those old focuses are based in fear and create resistance, and those are not aligned with God then. And so anything not aligned with God that might come up into your consciousness, just rebuke it. And ask God to remove it humbly and immediately. Any fearful guilt, resentment, anger, jealousy, envy, anything that some people call sin, just possibly ask God to remove them and immediately replace them with God's love, and that's what you're trying to achieve. So keep your focus here that is. Where the now is, where the love and the presence of God are with joy and gratitude. And then the subconscious will eventually no longer be an issue as you review the things that did pop up that will be resistance to leaving. Just let them know that you're not interested in having that your focus anymore. And eventually, see they come from the subconscious. Finally, the ego will be subdued.

DOUG: What would the spiritual level be when the energy flows through all seven chakras?

JOHN: Well, there's always higher and higher consciousness and higher levels of awareness, and everybody has their own path. Everyone is on their particular blueprint, you might say, or script, so there's not one final answer to that. However, a person who has that in place would be a very high consciousness, and you can more closely to the oneness of God in this earthly experience of humanity so that they would be filled with the light of God and very much in a divine. And to put a leave of dimension is hard at this time, because it as you leave human consciousness there is many other conscious nesses in the solar system that you are not even familiar with different dimensions. You will visit and participate in and continue to grow and expand there.

DOUG: Is the fifth dimension the starting point?

JOHN: That is the starting point of releasing all the resistance and dark energy of humanity and moving into the whole light of God so that you have no strings or no attachments or tethers to the material world anymore, and you are free in spirit to then travel throughout the universe.

So this is a very historical time in history that this is happening and occurring to more than just a few masters but a mass group of people. It is a unique time, and it's never happened in history before.

DOUG: Could the chosen people be a term applied to the individuals rather than a nation of Israel to serve God?

JOHN: Yes.

DOUG: Could that apply to the spiritual workers with Israelis background? Were they the chosen people just to, you know, to deliver the message?

JOHN: This is where semantics has necessarily been mixed up. And a Jewish person who was the religion of the times and nationality at the date in that particular culture. In the Bible when they're talking about Israel in that pathway—and that is Israel—they're talking about those who have chosen the way of the correct way in the life. And so anybody who's following the God within has chosen people to be in that pathway, and that is real. And so you did not necessarily—there are many Jews today who do not follow that path. They're still waiting for a messiah and not realizing it is within. They're looking for someone outside of themselves to be their leader and save them. So it is not the Jewish religion as such. It's what is in your heart that makes you part of Israel.

DOUG: A quick question—is Moses's name in Hebrew Moishe?

JOHN: I believe so.

Section 6.6: February 24, 2015

The following is a conversation with John the Divine channeled by Marilyn Redmond in her trance on February 24, 2015, in Edgewood, Washington.

DOUG: I would like to share my findings with you regarding various dimensions from first through fourth.

- First dimension—eight hundred billion to 550 million years ago
- Second dimension—550 million to one million years ago
- Third dimension—one million years ago to AD 2012
- Fourth dimension—AD 1957 to 2012
- Fifth dimension—AD 2012 onward

JOHN: All right. Well, that would be fine. Right, well, there are various vibrations within a range. So the first dimension has a wide range, actually, seven different levels within each range. And within each of the seven levels, there are ranges also of seven levels. So you see, the vibrations can be very minute, but it goes through evolution through the different vibrations. Everyone goes through all vibrations. Well, that is probably an appropriate number of years. You see, all of this is within a variety of ranges. So to say that it's cut and dry is not necessarily appropriate. So first dimension appeared, and like you said, billions of years ago. And it gradually involved into more and more mass, so that you had to plan it. And then in the planetary realm, you have the different dimensions, the soil and the rocks and the vegetation before man. So this is all very much an evolution of just a very gradual, and some parts of the species of whatever particular plant or animal or vegetation or whatever was going on. And some progressed. Other's didn't. At various rates that happened. So it's not a fine and cut-and-dry line. There are some, especially in the nature of the human being coming to earth and growing some. And even today some people are highly evolved spiritually, and some people still don't even get it. So there's always a wide range, and to say that it's cut and dry is not necessarily accurate. You can. You can say within this period of time, these dimensions were occurring. Okay. I would keep it in a general frame of mind because there's no hard lines. Right. Well, actually, the people being born today are actually being born into more of the fourth dimension. But I can say as I am surveying the whole picture, 2012 might be a quite a good accurate point of drawing the line. And yes, this is the point in time, as I've said, and historically, we are moving beyond what has happened in the past history. And spiritually, there is great ascension and development and growth occurring. So yes, that's accurate.

DOUG: Here is a question from last week: What is the meaning of "justification by faith?" How does that affect the individual's spiritual progression?

JOHN: Justifications, I think, well, that's now that I understand the word that would probably be a fairly good term to use. They just tend to start with what the faith is about. But yes, it will bring you into the spiritual realm as you have more faith in spirit. You do grow and evolve. So that term would be fairly usable, I would say. I would just say that how it's interrupted has become the problem. Very good question in regard to the justification by faith. The churches have promoted their dogma for you to have faith in. And some of the beliefs systems of the dogma actually preclude faith. Well, faith and what is necessary for spiritual growth, and when they tend to emphasize that Jesus is the only one to look to find your answers and ascend, they're encouraging people not to look within where the God is, and Jesus was trying to tell people that the spirit, the kingdom of God was within, so they have purposefully distorted that particular part of the faith. And that way people do not connect with God themselves directly, and therefore, their faith is not as complete as it might be.

DOUG: Would "thought form" work for third density like it does for fifth density?

JOHN: Yes, definitely. The thoughts that you think in third dimension can, if you dwell on them long enough, become thought forms, and that's what manifests in your life. So you really do create your own reality. In the fifth dimension, you're thinking on loving positive thoughts and thought forms, which will manifest into harmony. In third dimension, you're more fear-based, and so those fears are becoming manifested in your life. So this is a big change, as to change the thought forms and consciously be aware when these negativity ideas come into your thinking, to say, "Oh, that isn't what I chose in my thinking today."

DOUG: Did you, Paul, and Peter write a book about your experience in a higher state of dimension while Jesus spent forty days with you after his resurrection?

JOHN: Yes, actually, in the Essene, which was a community outside of Jerusalem at Mount Carmel, and his training and growing up was all about learning how to do that.

DOUG: Did Jesus raise his consciousness to the fifth dimension after being baptized by John the Baptist? He had to figure out to how to control his thinking because he could transfer by thought?

JOHN: Yes.

DOUG: The Bible talked about Paul being blind until he was baptized on his way to see Ananias in Iraq. Was Paul baptized by the Holy Spirit from within rather than being struck by a lightning?

JOHN: Well, that was a physical manifestation of the interchange that was occurring, so it was both. His blindness was blinded from the invisible energy of Spirit. So when it says that people reciting song of "Amazing Grace," they say, "I was blind, and now I see," what they're talking and explaining is they were blind to Spirit but then their eyes are opened up to the reality of God.

DOUG: Did the ice age affect the progression of second-density entities on Earth?

JOHN: Yes, and that's true, but you see it's all part of the natural occurrence of what needed to happen, so it was not a devastation, such as losing certain animal species because of the climate changes. And they're just going to other planets where they can make it in the environment that works for them.

DOUG: Does harvest mean graduation from a dimension?

JOHN: Well, when you harvest something it's the fruit of your spirit, so one of those—what they're talking about oftentimes in a biblical or spiritual sense—is as you are open to the Spirit you will harvest wonderful fruits of the Spirit, which are listed in book of Revelations. And the fruits of the spirit are kindness and patience and forgiveness, loving, long-suffering. There's a list of fruits of the Spirit. So you move out of your fear-based depression and despair, turmoil and agony, into a joyous way of living that is in harmony with others around you, and you're sharing and caring with others who are there with you in unity. So it's a moving—a harvest is moving into your higher consciousness of the grace of God, and that was where I am. Yes, they will have to leave, and this is happening in great numbers, actually. This is an interesting question because negative energy that needed to be released from here and needed to be lightened up and cleaned up spiritually, so it could go into the higher light and move on into its next steps and it is growth. So these entities, if they choose to move on, will find someone who can help them do that. And some are still not aware, and they will move on too. If they're attached to another person, wherever the person goes, they will stay with that person because they are too fearful to do otherwise, so they will move to wherever the person moves or ask for help to be taken out of that predicament.

DOUG: Please confirm December 21, 2012, is only a date for end control of the dark side?

JOHN: Yes.

Douglas Grady

DOUG: Could my first book, *Where's Your Light?*, that was banned for publication by a Christian publisher by the dark side?

JOHN: Yes. It was—you could maybe say that. It was done by most who believed very stronger in dogma, and they didn't want a different message out there.

DOUG: I've asked you about a new universe in the making. Is it in first dimension?

JOHN: No. Well, you see, if all energy is part of God and it's verses in high consciousness of the Christ's consciousness, it's what happens to the people or situations on the planet that lowers that energy, which is what happened to Earth. So that planet will be born into the image of its Creator, and those who inhabit it will then be the ones whose consciousness will then be their indicator of the energy that the planet becomes. That was the beginning of the energy not being there to sustain them; however, it took—and it is taking—it's a gradual evolution. It does not just all of a sudden zap things and change. And as you noticed when the contrary changed from 1999 to 2000, it was like the computers did not stop. The water kept running, and so it's a very gradual shift. But yes, more and more of the light is dispersing the dark at that point.

DOUG: What was your main message in the book of Revelation that you wrote that might have been revised by the churches?

JOHN: Well, they didn't revise much of what I wrote. They just plain didn't understand it and have misinterpreted it too They took everything I wrote as an allegory, and they put it into material, three-dimensional scariness for many people because they didn't understand that the seven churches I spoke about in that particular book of Revelation were regarding the chakras, and so they were looking at it as buildings. And so they're looking at the book from a different perception, from a third dimension rather than a spiritual understanding of what's behind the words. The spiritual message what was being tried to be delivered in a day and age when people do not understand energy, did not have any understanding of what love was about. Did not know about vibrations, did not have the scientific background to go along with their understanding of Spirit. And so they were just totally misrepresenting the information.

DOUG: Would they be given new souls?

JOHN: Well, 99.9 percent of the time, it is a new. It's an old soul that has been regenerated. Not very often is somebody's soul so dark that it is put back into, you might call, soup mix spirit and then totally rebirthed with a new soul. That is not very—it has happened on a few occasions, but generally, most people will cleanse out their old soul and start anew with more light coming in.

DOUG: Are animals of second or third dimension?

JOHN: Yes. Well, animals are actually third dimension. It's just they have a different soul arrangement than human beings. You see, first dimension primarily is of the level of the soil, the minerals, the rocks, the land, and ground, and the mountains. They are basically of a very, very low dimension of energy, and then when the plants started to sprout and started to grow, both vegetation became more prevalent in the second dimension. Third dimension became life-forms that were people walking on the earth and animals are part of those life-forms that can move about and have their existence be. They just have a lower energy in their soul. They're a different soul group than human beings, but they are of third dimension.

DOUG: Did God send angels, aliens, and spiritual guides to help Earth from suffering the same fate as a former planet Maldek that disappeared?

JOHN: God did send to Earth angels and help, aliens included, to bring life to the Earth planet because this is considered the gem of the planets in the solar system. This is considered a very special jewel of other parts of the universe, and it was to be the planet to show and help the reset of the universe rise out of lower consciousness into a higher evolution. Some in the universe were needing help to do this and through extraterrestrials from outer space were brought to Earth to help provide the information and the necessary work that needed to be done for the planet to be able to come back into its beauty that it was created in and actually raised it into that higher consciousness. Planet Earth is raising now into higher consciousness. It means that the whole universe is also evolving. So it really was not about another planet. It was always the focus of Earth to come back into its glory. Oh, well, I am, I am so—wanted to let you know how pleased I am with your work and your progress and your dedication. I want you to know I support your putting out information. It is more accurate than what is out there. I appreciate that you are continuing in this and know that you are doing an excellent job. All right. Well, I will say good-bye, and have Martha come in. Thank you. Have a wonderful day. Will do.

DOUG: Thank you, John.

Section 6.7: March 3, 2015

The following is a conversation with John the Divine via phone medium, channeled while Marilyn Redmond was in her trance on March 3, 2015, in Edgewood, Washington.

DOUG: Who are the entities of a negative or the entities that remove the Spirit from the mind-body spirit complex?

JOHN: Well, there's two parts to that question. The ego of the person can easily do that because of the fear that is invented—you might say it is an illusion. So the fear comes into the person's third-dimensional scenery or influences, and people react in fear. And therefore, they are in that third-dimensional realm of darkness that removes the light. The fear blocks it out, and people walk in that particular density. Also, when entities pass over, some of them have not grown into a spiritual dimension where they have light, and they are still earthbound. And these entities are very dark and tend to be controlled by a darker energy. That's not really a person as such, but you'll just call it Satan and the Devil. And this entity on the lower form, when they're invisible, will direct certain earthbound spirits to attach to people. And in attaching to the person that they seem to be connected to doing, that person in their life, and influenced by that energy of negativity and darkness, and the people lose their own ability to move about and have their own reality. It is covered and shielded by the dark energy's influence of it. So there are two parts of that. And however, it all comes from your own energy actually in that you are creating this for whatever lessons were necessary to find the light. So it can happen at a conscious level. It can happen at an unconscious level, and some people would call it Satan and the Devil. But it's all from within. There is no external influence that can actually harm you if you don't allow it. If you are focused within the center of your heart and center of your being where the truth lies, and not listening or reacting to the ego's influences, this does not have to affect you. But you have to become aware if this is happening. Marilyn just recently realized that this dark energy from her stepfather was still attached to her, still influencing her. And even though he's been dead for about thirteen years at this point, the energy was still attracted to her energy, and she didn't realize it. So the people do need to become conscious, which she did. She sent it to the light to be cleaned and purified and onto the other side. So when people take responsibility for their lives, these other influences do not have to be a concern.

DOUG: Yes. I came up with a new subtitle for the book. The title is *Door to Glory*. But the subtitle would be *Dialogue with John*.

JOHN: Well, that would be fine. You might say John the Divine or John the Disciple, whatever, some kind of information that gives people to know who John is because there's many people with that name out there, and they need some kind of reference to the John you're talking about.

DOUG: But see, how about Saint John?

JOHN: I think that would be excellent if you want to put it that way.

DOUG: Exactly, yes.

JOHN: In those terms, that would probably reach most people you are trying to connect with, yes.

DOUG: Now is it true that fourth dimension is the salvation of the third dimension?

JOHN: The salvation?

DOUG: Yes.

JOHN: No, it is just a path toward releasing your ego and moving into higher dimensions. It's not—the salvation is actually misunderstood because of the churches again. Salvation is releasing yourself and your ego. You're saving yourself from the negative dark influences. No one can do that for you. And as you go through the different dimensions, you move more and more into the oneness of the light. So there is … it's a process that takes many eons for most people. It is not just one lifetime that people keep returning to work on this.

DOUG: So salvation is really?

JOHN: Salvation is a good term, but they use it as Jesus saves you rather than you're saving yourself from your lower energy of darkness.

DOUG: Is the Law of One based on seeking God with all thine heart and all thy soul (Deuteronomy 4:29)?

JOHN: Yes, you're resolving that life energy, and that's the law of love. And you call God that love and energy. So we have already been in that state of oneness. We have already been there, and we've retained energy on planet Earth not acquired that entire consciousness without the ability to do it. We already were in one. We separated to come and show others the way to return to the oneness.

DOUG: Now this, the term Sabbath, is not ... well, I guess, subject to interpretations of that here. So I'd like to ask you—what is the true definition of Sabbath?

JOHN: Sabbath is for resting. As it said in the Bible, Jesus rested on the seventh day. And they called that, and they gave it a name for the day of resting is Sabbath, which is an opportunity for people to relax and enjoy the planet that they are here on rather than being so overdriven with having to do their work and activities that they cannot be in balance. And so the Sabbath was an opportunity for people to have balance in their lives because you cannot just always be in action. You need rest, relaxation. You need to have fun, and you need to have a variety of activities, not just your work. So it was a way to help balance the person.

DOUG: So it could be any day of the week?

JOHN: Oh, yes, it was not designed to—the calendar as we know it in third dimension was not even established at that time, so it was not intended for a particular day of the week.

DOUG: Well, that's like an out-of-body experience.

JOHN: Yes, this is a different experience, so you need additional help if you choose to have it, which is a wise thing to do.

DOUG: Did Jesus speak parables to avoid invoking the law of free will and the law of confusion with all the requirements of the Law of One?

JOHN: Well, he spoke parables trying to reach the people in a message they could understand. And he could not speak out against the religion and the government in those days, the parables, because if he did he would be imprisoned. So if you spoke against the government, it is not much different than today in that regard. If they don't like what you're saying, you can be picked up by the police today and imprisoned also as whistleblowers or other people similar. And Jesus was, you might say, a great whistleblower. So if he very carefully worded what he said to meet the consciousness of the people of where they were at, you have to talk to people where they are. You can't say something that they don't understand. They won't catch on, so you talk at their level. And the parables were a way to do that.

DOUG: I see, okay. Now I read in the book Atlantis that Atlanteans have placed Law of One documents in Alexandria in Egypt. But I was wondering—did Jesus study Law of One sources while he was in Alexandria?

JOHN: Yes, he did.

DOUG: Who are the aliens out there such as Nibiruans and Elohim?

JOHN: All right, Elohim is a high consciousness in the Law of One. It is almost getting to the top of your growth and ascension into the oneness. And the entities that you were referring to came from outer space to disempower the people of the planet so they could control. And so this has been the major battle on the planet earth of the light and the darkness.

DOUG: I just thought of this. Could the temptation be coming from a negative alien that the Bible call tempter?

JOHN: Could what be coming from it?

DOUG: Like Jesus was tempted when he was up in the mountains.

JOHN: Exactly. That was his lower nature. That was his ego.

DOUG: So was that the negative? Was Satan a negative alien?

JOHN: No, there's no person called Satan. It is an energy that is within you. It is your lower nature, which is part of what the ego supplies and nurtures to keep you out of the love of God. So Satan is not a person outside of yourself as the churches often teach. It is a just the energy that is the darkness of who you are that you have not embraced in love to bring yourself back into wholeness.

DOUG: Could Satan be a negative alien that was mentioned in the Bible, like Genesis 3:1, Corinthians 11, Acts 16, and 1 Samuel 28?

JOHN: Satan is not an entity. It is an energy.

DOUG: Okay.

JOHN: It has always been an energy. There have been groups of people in that dark energy that have employed that energy as a group, but it is not a person. It is the lack of light.

DOUG: Now Prophet Job had mentioned names of ET, such as Arcturus, Orion, Pleiades, in chapter 9 of his book. Also Job and David have discussed meditation in the Bible. Did they channel with aliens who were doing their service for God, or did King David channel with Jesus in the Spirit?

JOHN: Well, there are many who have channeled in the past. This is not a new phenomenon. In fact, it's an old experience that has come into more light with the planet having more light and people available to do this. But when it talked in the Old Testament about the rulers going into the Holy of Holies, what they were doing was, they were going in and connecting in a channeling way, connecting with God and coming out and then presenting to the people what was the information. So it is no different than what you are doing today with me. You are searching for information from a higher spiritual level than the earthly plane and then receiving that information so that you can share it. So the priests of old were doing, they were channelers. They were mediums just like what's going on in today with the many people who channel like Marilyn does. So there have been many people through life who have done this. However, it is becoming more acceptable in the current times. For one long period of time, anyone who did this was called, back in Salem, they called you a witch. So they burned you at the stake. So you see, this channeling thing going on with many people, and it's always been in some ways. But because of the fear of the people losing control, that wanted to have control.

This was threatening. They didn't want people to hear the truth that they were free to be themselves and did not have to listen to outside authority to follow the rules, that they could have their own rules within themselves that created who they are. They didn't want that message to be shared. So you see, this is not anything that's current or reasonably new. It has been going on for ages.

DOUG: That's why I'm only going to work with you and Marilyn for the book. I'm not going to go through anyone else. If I get information from another person, I will want to check it out with you to make sure it's correct.

JOHN: Well, I think that's very wise, Doug. I think that you are very astute and discerning in that, and I want to tell you I appreciate your sincerity.

DOUG: No problem. Now my next question—this is in Peter, his second epistle letter, chapter 1. "For the prophecy came not in old time by the will of man: but holy men of God spake as they were moved by the Holy Ghost." And my question is—is the Holy Ghost mentioned by Peter a thought adjuster?

JOHN: Yes, yes. You see, that's a very important verse in the Bible that many people disregard. You see, men wrote the Bible. God did not write the Bible. The men who were channeling the Word of God wrote the Bible. And because it came through human references, that's why it was not totally accurate. And so many people who get caught up in saying, "Well, it's in the Bible," have to be discerning to say, "Is this positive? Is this a loving statement?" And then it's truth. But anything negative is not of God. So as you're going through the Bible, you have to understand that people distorted what God said according to their own understanding. It might not necessarily be from God. So because people have their frailties and their shortcomings, and they have their ego driving their lives. And therefore, they're not always reporting what is truth.

DOUG: Who are the dark angels?

JOHN: Well, the dark angels are what many people would refer to as the lower energy that comes from the messages of the ego. Dark angels mean there's no light. And angels can't—this is really an oxymoron—you can't have a dark angel. Angels are beings of light. They're messengers of God. And this is, you see, many things have been perpetuated into the public that are not really accurate information, and it's mostly to scare people. So when they talk about a dark angel, that's a way to scare people. I wouldn't put any validity in that.

DOUG: Where did they come from? Where did the dark angels come from originally?

JOHN: Well, there was a separation of those who wanted to separate from God.

DOUG: Really? Okay.

JOHN: Yes, and that's—it was the beginning of the separation.

DOUG: So they were never human before?

JOHN: No, not in that state.

DOUG: Could love ones who are in the fourth dimension transmit thoughts on astral planes?

JOHN: Yes.

DOUG: Now if one is in the third dimension, then could she be in the dark and not be aware of loving thoughts?

JOHN: That's what third dimension is about, yes.

DOUG: Okay.

JOHN: And you are moving out of that, and many, many people

are awakening out of that darkness of third dimension, finding the love within and the light within, and moving into fourth dimension through the various stages of getting closer into the one light that is the love one.

DOUG: I keep getting loving messages all the time in my sleep.

JOHN: Well, that is marvelous. You are doing a very fine job, and you are getting help from spiritual help more than just what I'm giving you. Your guardian angels, there are. Angels actually come to help people with their talents, and so you are using your talents to a very high degree. So you have many loving angels that are helping you to translate and assist all this information so others can benefit. And therefore, you are attracting help from all these angels.

DOUG: Oh, that's great. You know, I get confused whether I'm being tempted or whether it's loving. I kind of let go and whatever comes. I just, you know, go along with it.

JOHN: Well, that is the best way to handle it. Very good.

DOUG: Now I have a question. This is kind of interesting. I'm aware, like I chose to be hearing impaired before I came into life. Now suppose, you know, there are people with disabilities like blindness, deafness, mental retardation, wheelchair bound, but do they need to be born again as babies to inherit normal bodies?

JOHN: It depends on their level of consciousness. In fact, it depends on their level of spiritual growth. So the reason that they came in with those particular handicaps was part of their script, part of the blueprint that they created before they entered into this body. So there could be several reasons why those happened. One could be that they needed to transform that energy into a loving energy and move beyond that state of consciousness. Now everybody has to go through every vibration from darkness into light. There are no skips and jumps to move ahead. So you go through. You would have been a robber. You would have been a thief. You would have been a killer, maybe a serial killer. You would have been a great philanthropist or a doctor that saved millions, or you may have been very rich and helped people in so many ways with finances and institutionally giving money. You could have been a minister. You could have been a gardener. Everyone goes through every stage. So it's not good or bad that you happen to find yourself in that particular experience because what you're doing is bringing that energy into a higher energy, and it was necessary for your spiritual growth. Now oftentimes these people will find themselves in a particular family. And in their situation the family benefits by learning loving compassion and being of assistance and helpfulness. And part of their karma is to be in that situation for them to learn to be giving and to be sharing and to be there in ways that they have not been before. So it is all playing out for everyone to benefit and grow. Now what happens with this particular time in history, as people are learning and waking up into more and more of the light, they can in many cases outgrow the difficulties.

One of the—there is a video out that might be most interesting called *Grounding*. And it shows people hooking up their energy to the energy of the earth. And they're actually at the end of this production, which shows that everything needs to be connected to the energy of God. That there was a paraplegic man who was connected to the grounding for some time, and at the end of the film, it actually showed him walking. So you see, you are at a time in history when these things can transmute into healthy resolution beyond the illness of them having to die and come back and go through more stages of growing.

So this is at a transforming stage in history. Not only will the starfish be able to regrow another ray when one is cut off, but people will be able to regrow arms and legs that have been taken off surgically for whatever medical problem has occurred. You will be able to regrow new teeth, to replace those missing. So we are at a time in history when things are changing, where you don't have to pass over and return to a healthier state, but you can actually move into the truth and wholeness of your real being. So this is an exciting time to be here. It will not happen overnight, but gradually, the energy will get so strong that people will be returned to their full healthiness and capacities.

DOUG: I noticed in the world of today, there is this, this group of people are, you know, murdering, beheading people, but now the nations are working together to eliminate that group?

JOHN: Yes, there was a question at channeling last week that someone asked about that particular group and how to pray for that situation. Because, you see, those situations are coming up for love. If you are familiar with *A Course in Miracles*, it says that when people are crying out, they're crying out for love. And so in sending love to those particular people and groups, sending compassion and understanding, forgiveness, that's the last of the dark energy coming up to be healed. And the more we send love to it, the faster that will be dissipated because it will not be sustainable. So this is where free will comes in. When people find that something is disagreeable, the faster they turn to forgiveness and sending love and compassion, the quicker it dissipates. And you do not have to extend that time of suffering. So this is a good example. And the last channeling is going to be getting out by this next weekend, so if you wanted to hear the answer to that, you would get a more complete answer.

DOUG: I've got a couple of questions.

JOHN: All right.

DOUG: I know you can't reveal much of what's going on today, so I'm going to go to this question. A guy, in his story, I guess it would be like a myth. The story about two seamen. They were out in the ocean a long, long time ago. One had died. The other survived in a boating accident. Now this could be an example of opt in or opt out. One guy agreed to let the other take over his life. Could this be realistically true?

Door to Glory

JOHN: Yes, that is called a walk-in. In fact, this has happened more than you realize on the planet. There have been souls that took over others bodies, so they did not have to go through birth. And so in the Bible, in Aphasiac, that particular sect did a lot of the psalms. Those particular spiritual entities—that's how they came to planet Earth, through other bodies. It's called being a walk-in. The mother of Mary, that's how she came to planet earth. Her name was Anna, the grandmother of Jesus. She was a walk-in. She did not go through birth. So this is not familiar to most people, but it does happen.

DOUG: I'm going to ask this. Jesus wanted to confirm to the people to enjoy life. That's my question. Now there's a passage from the book of Luke, chapter 20, and I'm going to read it to you.

JOHN: All right.

DOUG: "But they which shall be counted worthy to enjoy that world, and the resurrection from the dead, neither marry wives, neither are married. For they can die no more, forasmuch as they are equal unto the Angels, and are the sons of God, since they are the children of the resurrection. And that the dead shall rise again, even Moses showed it besides the bush, when he said, the Lord is the God of Abraham and the God of Isaac and the God of Jacob. For he is not the God of the dead, but of them which live: for all live unto him." Now really, he is ... he just wants the people to enjoy life and not to be so guilty of their mistakes.

JOHN: That's exactly what—he came to planet Earth to enjoy, and what has happened is the ego has been so overpowering and promoted by dark forces that to keep you in more of a slave-like existence on the third dimension rather than see that earth is a playground, that the mountains and the oceans and the deserts are, all the areas that are beautifully arranged on the planet are there to go and enjoy and have fun and be playful and to experience. The love of the countryside— this is one of the most beautiful planets in the universe. And it was designed to be a garden of Eden, of which it will be returning to that particular space. It's only been the ego and the dark forces that have kept you from the joy that is your true birthright.

Section 6.8: March 11, 2015

The following is a conversation with John the Divine via medium, channeled by Marilyn Redmond in her trance on March 11, 2015, in Edgewood, Washington.

DOUG: I was wondering—this was back in 1999. I felt the sparks of, and I knew it was coming from God. You had mentioned that it was coming from within.

JOHN: Right.

DOUG: I felt it within, so it must be coming from within.

JOHN: Right, yes, it comes from within. But it emanates around you, and there are people who can read your auras.

DOUG: Jesus looks for a light in the soul after death based on John 5:42–44? I'll read it to you. "I know you and that you have not the love of God in you. I am come in my Father's name and ye receive me not. If another shall come in his own name, him will ye receive. How can ye believe with honor one another, of one another, and seek not to honor the cometh of God alone?" So could that be what the light, the aura that my former coworker saw?

JOHN: Well, you're talk—in that particular passage, Jesus is referring to opening your heart so that the love can come out and manifest in your life, and part of that is your aura. And when you are connected, your chakras are connected, and that reflects in your aura, so your aura is actually a combination of how connected you are to your consciousness of God.

DOUG: Now would yellow color indicate earthbound as it does not wish to go to the light?

JOHN: No, it does not indicate earthbound. Yellow chakras, do you mean? The yellow chakra?

DOUG: Yes.

JOHN: Okay, it just—the colors are, tend to associate with what chakras are, how well they're operating. Each chakra has a specific color that it vibrates and manifests in that if it's a bright and brilliant color, it means that your chakras are open and receiving that spiritual energy. If they are like a dirty yellow, that means that you're closing off to all the spiritual health and energy of God and you need to release all resistance or fear so that it can function, operating as it was intended to, so colors tend to work as far as how your chakras are operating.

DOUG: Next question—could karma keep earthbound souls stuck earthbound because the victims, other earthbound spirits have not forgiven his action? Is this why like Hitler is still stuck earthbound because of his World War II atrocities, and he is experiencing hellish experience because he's still feeling the pains of his victims in the ether?

JOHN: Well, that's an interesting and complex question. I'm not sure that Hitler is earthbound. Let me take a minute.

DOUG: I've kind of got my book of Law of One and that book Law of One and the question was asked, "What's the state of Hitler?" Probably ten or twenty years ago when the book was written, and they actually would say that he's still experiencing, you know, cleansing.

JOHN: Well, he's experiencing a difficult situation. He ... everybody plays difficult parts in our lives. You see, everybody has to go through every vibration into the prized consciousness. Everybody goes through being a robber, a thief, someone who steals, someone who murders, and everybody goes through being a philanthropist and rich and wealthy and helping others. We all go through all the different ranges of personalities so that we can each move above that into a higher place. So he's not the only evil, you might call. I don't like to use that word, but evil means a lack of light. And he's not the only person who had a lack of light from karma that he had to come and act out, and he is still going through the repercussions, yes, of the devastation of what occurred. So he was beguiled into the leadership under the Illuminati, and of course, when he didn't follow their orders, then they dispersed with him. But the point is that it's not one person to point to as the blame of society. Everybody at one point does have karma from past lives that they need to heal on planet Earth and transmute that energy of darkness, allowing the light to come in, and yes, he is still going through the experience of becoming a light being. His process is not completed for him. It will take a long time.

DOUG: I was told one of my guides is Parmahansa Yogananda and he's been working with me, and it was his self-realization lesson that got me started.

JOHN: Well, that is a very good place to go to. Yes, it is a good place.

DOUG: The whole thing started back in 1995 when I found one of his books in a bookstore. It was in the wrong place. I was working at the bookstore at the time, and so my job, closing up the store, was to organize all the misplaced books that people take out. They pick up a book, and then they move around. They didn't put the book back to the shelf. Well, I found this book in the business center, and the title was *The Law of Success*. And it was a very thin book, just maybe fifteen or maybe twenty-five pages. But that woke me up. That got me started toward this spiritual path that I'm in it now.

JOHN: That was wonderful.

DOUG: Yes, he wrote that book.

JOHN: Right that is, yes, that's a good source of information.

Door to Glory

DOUG: Yes. Next question—is practicing black magic like worshipping the Devil?

JOHN: Yes.

DOUG: Now I have a question—what are white orbs?

JOHN: Well, those.

DOUG: They cleanse energies of souls before next incarnation?

JOHN: Well, they're spiritual beings that are making themselves aware today with those people on earth, and people are sensitive to seeing them. In fact, there are people who have taking photographs of these orbs, and they're just another way of sharing with you that there's spiritual energy around you—around you all the time.

DOUG: Oh, but they're like angels?

JOHN: Well, they're lower than the angels, but they are spiritual energy. Like guides, you might say.

DOUG: Now I'm going to talk about soul splitter.

JOHN: Oh, splitter? Okay, yes, people have split souls.

DOUG: Like I was told that I'm a splitter. And there are two other splitters, and there is one head.

JOHN: Well, I'm not sure that somebody is a soul splitter. I don't know what they're referring to, what I understand about the soul splitting is—when a person has to face the challenge that is very difficult, very scary, and very frightening, traumatic, and dramatic, often their consciousness cannot necessarily handle dealing with it. So that part of your soul leaves, and it splits off. And you disown it, and many people call this denial. So what happens is people have gone through traumatic, tragic catastrophes. They are split off every time there is something they could not handle, and this is very common in children who are in violent situations. They lose part of their soul in various ways for each of these calamities, and everybody is basically trying to recapture those split parts of their soul or heal what was God's love or return it so you can become a whole person, and that's what you are aiming for. You are a holy spirit, but parts of your spirit have been split off. And it's to embrace all parts of you, even those spiritual situations, and know that God was loving you throughout them. You bring it back into your oneness.

DOUG: Now I'm going to ask a question about earthbound souls.

JOHN: Yes.

DOUG: If they—okay, they are not in the Morontia world, is that correct?

JOHN: Morontia. Well, everybody is. It's a matter of how much light is involved with that person's soul. So we're all at one in God. It's just a variation of the vibration.

DOUG: Do they have to pass through the light first?

JOHN: Well, they pass into the light more gradually as they grow. Everyone does it in a very gradual way.

DOUG: Like we've talked about this, but only 5 percent actually make it through the light, so I guess.

JOHN: Well that's—that used to be the percentage, more and more people on the planet are waking up in this new millennium, a new age where more energy is being brought to earth to allow that, so I would say that that figure was a useful figure thirty-five to fifty years ago, but that is changing today.

DOUG: Is Mother Mary a feminine energy of God?

JOHN: Yes.

DOUG: Is it true a seraphic angel can enjoy energy of any soul that

Door to Glory

has a higher rate of vibration, say fourth dimension, than at the third dimension?

JOHN: Okay, now I hear. Now I understand what you're saying. What about the angel? That's a certain level of ascension?

DOUG: Yes, now I was wondering if there was some way that if a person finds a higher rate of vibration, say the fourth dimension and receive help from a seraphic angel?

JOHN: Yes.

DOUG: Then an angel would join that soul and help that soul, guide that soul through life?

JOHN: That—that occurs to everybody. As you grow old, new angels come in, and that angels that were helping you that you no longer at that level, they leave, so as you are attaining new talents, such as if people were becoming a musician, angelic musician, and angels would come and assist them in learning that new talent and skill. And the angels that were there for other reasons would now depart, and you would have a new collection of help around you, so angels come and go as to what your interests are and what you're pursuing.

DOUG: Now I got this information from the Internet and I want to verify it with you.

JOHN: Yes.

DOUG: It's the different states of consciousness, and I'm going read each line. And if you agree, I will check it off.

JOHN: All right.

DOUG: It goes from one to thirteen. One, it says existence is nonbiological.

JOHN: Existence is nonbiological. It's spiritual.

Douglas Grady

DOUG: That's probably the first dimension.

JOHN: First dimension, everything is spiritual. First dimension just means it's a lower consciousness and a different framework to work through, such as the first-dimensional type of elements on the planet.

DOUG: Good, okay. Second dimension it has ... instinctual, emotional, animalistic.

JOHN: Well, you're saying that's second dimension?

DOUG: Yes.

JOHN: But that's more of third. You've kind of combined. The first dimension is very much thought of as dirt, soil, rocks, and then you have your vegetation is second dimension, where you have plants and grass and shrubs and trees. And then third dimension, you have animals, and man is part of the species of animals.

DOUG: I'm going read everything to you, from the first to the 13, and then you -- you can give me feedback.

JOHN: All right.

DOUG: Now the third dimension—it has intellectual, logical, rational mind, ego.

JOHN: Well, the ego is definitely there, yes.

DOUG: Fourth dimension—creative, imaginative, psychic, intuitive.

JOHN: That's correct. That ... that's correct.

DOUG: Fifth dimension—pure intelligence, insight, love.

JOHN: Correct.

DOUG: Sixth dimension—natural level, soul level. It is the last level of individuality.

JOHN: Oh, I didn't. The lack of individuality actually begins at the eighth, I believe.

DOUG: Okay. Seventh—oversoul level. It's group consciousness.

JOHN: That's a good way to put it.

DOUG: Eight—avatar level, a high level of mastery.

JOHN: Yes.

DOUG: Nine—Christ level, unconditionally loving consciousness.

JOHN: Yes.

DOUG: Good. Ten—cosmic level, cosmic consciousness.

JOHN: Yes.

DOUG: Eleven—God level, God consciousness.

JOHN: Eleven and twelve, that's often referred to as twelve and … and eleven is prior, of course, to God consciousness, where you totally emerge into Spirit. so there's a problem back down in some of that to change the numbers a little bit, but the majority of that's correct.

DOUG: Twelve—universal level, universal consciousness.

JOHN: Right.

DOUG: Okay, and then thirteen—the void, the great mystery.

JOHN: Well, that's a great mystery because the DNA has stopped you from being able to see … and go beyond further, but there are still more levels higher beyond that you are going to be able to accomplish if you grow spiritually into the new age, so at this point, calling it a mystery is fine. It's because it's unknown yet to mankind.

Section 6.9: March 31, 2015

The following is a conversation with John the Divine via phone medium, channeled while Marilyn Redmond was in her trance on March 31, 2015, in Edgewood, Washington.

DOUG: So I am going to start with the questions here.

JOHN: Okay.

DOUG: I told Marilyn that it is going to be up to her if she has got objections. There were a couple of references to her being the Mother Mary, though I am going to leave it up to her, whatever she decides.

JOHN: Well, she was not the—she was one of the twelve girls selected to be the mother of Jesus, but Mary was the one picked. But she was in preparation for that. She wasn't the Mother Mary, but she was one of the groups of girls who was practicing the practices of the Essenes, where you purify your soul to be a light-based soul and therefore pure enough to conceive Jesus. And so she was one of a group, she wasn't the actual Mother Mary.

DOUG: To be in that group was pretty unique.

JOHN: Well, she was very honored with that.

DOUG: Yes. Okay, now there's a biblical verse from Matthew 19. "And Jesus said unto them, Verily I say to you that, the Son of man shall sit in the throne of his Majesty, ye which followed me in the regeneration, shall sit also upon twelve thrones, and judge the twelve tribes of Israel." Now my question is—is the term *regeneration* similar to, say, my spirit is being manifested into the physical?

JOHN: No, it is being manifested into the true spiritual essence of which you are from the physical to the spiritual.

DOUG: Okay.

JOHN: It is being manifested from a human perception with ego, releasing the ego so that you are no longer in that bondage of the earth's density and that the spirit has been released to be free of that density where you can be one with God. So that is the regeneration.

DOUG: You know, I was with a group of people over the weekend, and I have not dealt with a social life for the past three or four months while I was off from work. I didn't want to interact with people so that I didn't have to get bogged down by their negative energies. Well, I was with a group of people, and boy, I felt so drained when I got home because I felt all kinds of negative energy. I wanted to avoid going out there until I get done with the book.

JOHN: Well, I think it is good to protect yourself from that negative energy. It keeps your energy high so that you are coming from the place that you want to come from. And you can pray for like-minded people to come into your life and opportunities where they have a higher consciousness so you can acquire new friends. It is not uncommon for people growing spiritually that they gain new friends, leave some of the old friends behind, and move into a higher happier place with people who are more in the same mind-set and heart-set as what you are trying to achieve. And yes, you don't fit in with many of the people you might have in the past.

DOUG: Here under the same question as save and salvation, there's a passage from the book of Matthew, chapter 9, "And when his disciples heard it, they were exceedingly amazed, saying, who then can be saved? And Jesus beheld them and said unto them with the men, and this is impossible, but with God all things are possible."

JOHN: Exactly. It's not possible. I am sure you are familiar with the famous scientist called Albert Einstein, and he said you cannot heal a problem at the same level of which it was created. You need a higher power. So that is what Jesus was referring to is you need a power of love instead of the power of the fear and ego that has been dominating prior.

DOUG: So the conference committee will determine that. They will lay out the options.

JOHN: Well, we have a lot of spiritual help that is with us all the time. It gives us guidance, and that's what our guide to do—help direct us in the places that will be the best and more suitable for our next steps. It is up to us to accept that joyously and move on and to understand that their wisdom is there to help us.

DOUG: You mentioned new soul. What do you mean by new soul? It is not the new souls from God, but new souls from another planet? Or what is the meaning of a new soul?

JOHN: New souls have not been to Earth. They have been created. All souls were created at the same time, and some came to Earth at various periods of history. Some did not come to Earth at that time and waited for other opportunities. You see, planet Earth would be overpopulated if all souls came at once. They are around the universe in various places serving and experiencing, learning, exploring, adventuring. So not everyone came to Earth at once because it was not physically possible to substantiate that. However, the people who wanted to come to Earth—there's actually a list and priorities of those who are allowed to be birthed on planet Earth to keep the population in balance. So the ones who want to come are kind because they are definitely interested in transposing and transmuting their energy into a higher level, and they can do that much easier. The energy on Earth allows them to change from the fear to the love much easier than in other places of the universe. So this is a very desirable planet to come to, but they don't all come at once. And so if you haven't had your opportunity to come yet, then you would be a new soul, or if you had only had an opportunity to come a few times at this point, you haven't gained the wisdom and the experience necessary to move on.

DOUG: Let me see the next question here. Would murderers in this life, would they be placed in another planet that is barbarous in nature?

JOHN: Not necessarily and probably not so because planet Earth is one of the last planets to change into fifth dimension. So what happens? We have all ... in whatever lifetime. Everybody has had many, many lifetimes. Most people have more than a thousand lifetimes. And you have to go through every energy change necessary to move into perfect love as Jesus did. So even Jesus had thirty-three lives. So if necessary, everybody was a murderer at one time. Everybody was a thief. Everybody was a beggar. Everybody was some kind of a professional—engineer, doctor, or a philanthropist or very poor. We have all experienced all of this, and we have come to change those old energies that still need to be changed from our old past lives. So we do not condemn anyone. It is possible when someone is a murderer that they were murdered and they needed to complete the balance of energy that was what part of their role was. Or if somebody murdered somebody, then they came back and got murdered. So you see, there is a balance of energy. It's not good or bad. There's no judgment. All we are doing is transposing the energies into balance. And so when people think of people being bad. That is a judgment. Jails and prisons are based on punishing. The law of God is love. We do not punish and judge anyone. They are just going through their experiences necessary for ascension.

DOUG: They are being punished by—

JOHN: There is no punishment in God's eyes. There is only punishment in man's eyes. Because at some point in time, you probably did that yourself. Those who are the most adamant about the gays were gay themselves at one time, and they don't want to face that part of their soul, that they are keeping it separate because to them they can't handle—

DOUG: They are being punished by any physical realm, the police, the government were punished, the murderers. They are punished on a physical level, but on a spiritual level, they are—

JOHN: Well, as we leave their dimension, there will not be the police and the jails because people will have love in their hearts. There will be no need for that.

DOUG: There was a book written by, I think, George King, and he mentioned the nine freedoms.

JOHN: Oh, the nine freedoms, okay. Yes? I know a little bit about it, not much.

DOUG: If there is such a thing as nine freedoms—

JOHN: Well, freedom is freedom, and you can label it with any label you choose. They happen to have, what you might say, dissected, but the big freedom is the freedom from your ego, which includes freedom from insecurity or freedom from financial worry or all kinds of freedoms would be part of releasing the ego so you are free of that.

DOUG: Is the "world to come," as described in the Bible, is that on the fifth dimension Earth?

JOHN: Yes.

DOUG: Is it true that the planet Maldek was referred to as the angel that fell out of heaven?

JOHN: Well, my response is no because angels did not really fall out of heaven. Angels are an energy, and heaven is also an energy level. So what you are trying to do is put physical semantics into a spiritual concept. And there was a fall, but it was an energy fall, not necessarily angels as such.

DOUG: Angel is energy?

JOHN: Yes, I would call it energy.

DOUG: So the old soul, they tend to remain within this planet. Is that true?

JOHN: Yes, the old souls are here finishing out their agenda to complete ascension and the masters that have come back to help people with that are old souls. So there's a lot of people on planet Earth right now who have mastered their ego-driven lives of the past and are moving into becoming masters of their lives and their emotions and helping others to do that also. That is exactly what Marilyn's work is about.

DOUG: Now I would like to share with you, I got some photos of the paintings that were done by this woman who has had out-of-body experiences, Nirvana. I got a picture here. It's a painting of space. In the painting it has Nirvana. It is like yellowish color like above the top of space. And then there's a black hole, and then there's different spirals of different galaxies. I am going to include this in the book. I thought it was interesting. Also, I have some paintings and graphics of the paintings of the tunnel and angels waiting in the tunnel.

JOHN: Very good.

DOUG: And beyond the tunnel, it is like a peeping hole. It's like paradise.

JOHN: Yes.

DOUG: I am going to include those.

JOHN: That would be wonderful. That would be very nice to include in your book. It is nice to have illustrations.

DOUG: Because this woman, she checked to see if energy was flowing through my chakras. But she said that somewhere around my hair she could see a lot of vibration, but my spiritual eye is closed. So probably that would fix the chakras, the energy flowing through, but not the seventh.

JOHN: Well, part of opening up your last chakra, the center of your eye, that particular chakra is asking for God to open. You need to request that that open, be open and receptive and in a meditative state. At some point after you have asked, there will be an experience where you will feel something energy change. For Marilyn, when her third chakra opened, it opened partially, and she had spiritual vision. But then at a later date there was a cork, that felt like a cork in a bottle for a pop bottle or a wine bottle. And it felt like this cork popped out, and it came into even a higher vision. So there are various levels of that spiritual sight, and it can happen not necessarily all at once.

DOUG: I can talk to Marilyn about that.

JOHN: She would be glad to help you.

DOUG: A question here—who baptized the 120 disciples? Was that Paul, or was that Peter?

JOHN: Well, it would be Peter. Paul was not really a disciple. He was an apostle.

DOUG: He was an apostle, okay.

JOHN: Well, a disciple in those days that was part of their mission was to baptize, but Paul was a friend of Jesus who followed him and was not what you would call a disciple. He was just an associate, you might say, and he did not, in the beginning before—well, Jesus was still his friend. He did not go around preaching the Word until after the crucifixion and resurrection.

DOUG: Now I was baptized by Peter?

JOHN: Yes.

DOUG: If I was baptized by Peter in my past life and then I was baptized by Parmahansa Yogananda in my present life from Self-Realization Fellowship?

JOHN: Right.

DOUG: Well, who would be considered the master of my soul?

JOHN: Oh, you can have masters come and go. Are you talking about now?

DOUG: I am talking about now. Who would be my master?

JOHN: Well, this is a very personal thing. Does it feel like Yogananda is your master now?

DOUG: Yes, I was just wondering. I was just curious.

JOHN: Well, he is your master now. But you have other masters working with you. It is not just one, but he would be your main one. You have other masters working with you. You don't have just one. You are working in a level where you have several masters helping and working together as a group to help you.

DOUG: Okay, very good.

JOHN: But he would be the head one, the leader.

DOUG: Now I want to ask you. Let's talk about a mind and a soul and the body. So like is the mind part of the soul?

JOHN: Well, there's the mind of God. It's the soul, and it's not a brain. It is spiritual. The brain is the physical part of your body and anatomy, and the mind is the soul that surrounds your physical being. And the mind of God is that part of God of which you are. So the mind is your essence.

DOUG: What is the difference between a fourth-dimensional positive and a fourth-dimensional negative?

JOHN: Well, you are talking about consciousness. As you proceed up the conscious scale, the emotional consciousness within, you proceed out of the negative gradually into the light of the higher degrees and levels of fourth dimension. So it's like a scale moving up into the light. So each different level has a different density until the density disappears into the light.

Douglas Grady

DOUG: I would like to ask you about the nuclear explosion in Japan in World War II. I got this from last Friday. Now there were some people in Japan that had died before the blast because the contact was up, that they were picking up, taken away from the blast. Could that be true?

JOHN: Yes. The people who participated in these calamities have made a life agreement that would be their exit plan. So oftentimes people are very, very distressed because of planes crashing and tidal waves and in this case, the bomb in Japan. But it's all part of a bigger picture and a bigger plan, and that was their way of leaving the planet. So it's not— It is a sad thing for those left behind, but it was the right time and opportunity for their energy to change back into spirit, and therefore, that was the opportunity they picked.

DOUG: Okay, and the aliens came in their spaceship, and they rescued those people?

JOHN: No, those people went into Nirvana, but they were not— They were not rescued by spacecraft at all.

DOUG: Now for those who were left behind, there are (unint.) that shows that they died in the blast. Could that be true?

JOHN: Well, everybody that was participating in it, that was their way to leave this particular lifetime. So there is not … it's all about— that was the right way for them to handle their exit.

DOUG: Okay.

JOHN: There are not levels of it. It is just the way it is.

DOUG: I am going to probably make one more call maybe in April. I just got some money. It is my last dime before I go back to work. But it looks like I am attuned with my finance angel, and his name is—he calls himself Greg just for me. And so it seems like this whole thing was planned out by the angels for me to do this book work.

JOHN: I am sure of that.

DOUG: It is amazing. I mean, I could be off work, away from work for this long. So I will have enough money until the end of May, perhaps even longer into June or July to—

JOHN: The universe will support you when you are on the path. Just trust the universe will bring what you need. God's grace is sufficient. It will provide what you need.

DOUG: It is amazing how this whole thing worked out. I mean, I started some of these financial planning three years ago. And I wasn't aware that I would be doing this three years later.

JOHN: That is how things come together. If we are just listening to directions, it will fall together.

DOUG: Wow, amazing. So I am going. I will probably make one more call and then perhaps I will come to Seattle in June. And we can go over the book for the last time, and then we will get the book out.

JOHN: That sounds like a very good plan.

DOUG: Great. Thanks so much, John.

JOHN: Have a good day, and I am going to depart. Enjoy your life while you are working on the book. Do something for fun also. You need balance.

DOUG: Yes!

JOHN: You need balance, so do something for fun also.

DOUG: Yes.

JOHN: All work and no play makes Doug a dull boy.

DOUG: The publisher wanted me to write another book. It is a love story, and I am not a romantic writer. But she said that she can have it edited by a romantic writer. So yes, this story, it relates to my personal life, and she wanted it now. I told her, "Well, I can do it later. I want to get this book finished first."

JOHN: I think that was a good choice.

DOUG: And then it seems like I will be writing another book.

JOHN: Wonderful.

DOUG: And it could be about aliens.

JOHN: Ah, that would be wonderful.

DOUG: Thank you so much.

JOHN: Have a good day, and I'll talk to you next time.

Section 6.10: April 28, 2015

The following is a conversation with John the Divine via a medium, channeled while Marilyn Redmond was in her trance on April 28, 2015.

JOHN: Good morning, Doug. How are you doing today?

DOUG: I'm great, John. It seems like I'm getting some help from the universe.

JOHN: Well, I'm sure you are. You are very much in tune with what's going on, and that's marvelous.

DOUG: So maybe we can start now. I was talking with a woman who has an opened spiritual eye. She said she was unable to draw a wolf. Was there a reason for that?

JOHN: Well, certain people are blocking certain ways, and there might have been something in her history that creates a block. That's not something comfortable for her to do because of her histories in some— There was a past-life situation that she still needs to look at so that can flow instead of being blocked.

DOUG: Now are the seven mansions in Nirvana or heaven on Earth or inside Earth? The seven mansions, or are their mini mansions? We have talked about it before.

JOHN: So there's a mansion for every individual. It's the same idea as the six paths that you mentioned. Every person has their path or their consciousness they're raising into the oneness of God, and as we move higher in consciousness, in the Bible they call that a mansion because your life becomes much better. It manifests in ways that are more prolific and prosperous for you. You're emotionally and spiritually no longer living in just a small little hut. You have expanded your ability to see a bigger picture, and so the mansion is just a word to define that your consciousness has grown, and everybody has their consciousness. If everyone had the same consciousness, there wouldn't be any need for everybody. So we're together just making a tapestry or a picture that interweaves all of our various consciousnesses into the picture you see today. So it's not just seven, but there are seven described levels of that consciousness that the theosophists look at, and so in climbing Jacob's ladder, you could say it had seven steps to that. It's just, again, humans like to define and make things definitive rather than see the overlap, but that's one way to describe it so people understand it.

DOUG: Are they in Nirvana or heaven on earth?

JOHN: Well, Nirvana is a spiritual side, and heaven on earth is a physical place, so with the consciousness of heaven, so Earth is heaven. It always has been. The fear has been like sunglasses, or if you're a blind man, the fear has been stopped from your vision to see all the beautiful manifestations on this planet. It is called the planet that's the beautiful planet in the universe. It's where people come because it has been created in a way that's much more attractive and has much more scenery and elements in it that are beautiful. It's a beautiful planet so if you are in fear, you don't see that. You see a lower density through your vision, and when you open your spiritual eyes, you can see the energy in the trees, in the plants. You can see the energy.

DOUG: Where is the paradise, is that in Nirvana?

JOHN: No. There is a place in the cosmos (Havona) where the source is centered, and that is called paradise. It's a very, very, very high consciousness, and it's not visible. It's strictly a spiritual location where the energy is perfect.

DOUG: No, okay. So basically, Nirvana is just a spiritual weigh station.

JOHN: Right. It's kind of like a parking garage before you come back to Earth and try to raise yourself to a higher level of the parking garage.

DOUG: Okay.

JOHN: But no, it's not a visible place. It's an invisible spiritual location near the planet Earth where your spirit goes to reside. As it's coming out of the passing from what you people call death, it's a passing of your energy, and you go into a place called Nirvana, which suits your particular level of awareness.

DOUG: Okay, now the tunnel leads to nirvana, right?

JOHN: Yes.

DOUG: The person goes through the tunnel, and the other side of the tunnel is nirvana, right?

JOHN: Well, they come into the location where that can be accessed, and it looks very similar to Earth. That's what people are used to, and it can be very lovely with the plants and flowers. And you're met by the people who are your loved ones and your angels to escort you into the actual realm of nirvana. There's kind of like a preliminary garden area that you ascend into, and often people will meet Jesus or their relatives and the people who are waiting for them on the other side. So it's kind of like there's a receiving area before you go into nirvana.

DOUG: Now I'm going to talk about Illuminati.

JOHN: Okay.

DOUG: Is it true Jesus knew Illuminati had too much control at the time for him to help people ascend to the fifth dimension two thousand years ago?

JOHN: Well, he was aware that it was planned long before Jesus was born. Essenes was a sect of spiritual people who presented the pathway to allow his birth to happen. There were hundreds of years of generations before him that had to occur for his mother to be that pure soul. Therefore, his grandmother, a pure soul, so that he could come, and it was time in history to restore the love that's talked about in the Bible to actually living it in your life. And he seemed to present and apply that so people could see it worked. However, it was distorted by people of different religions. It was a time in history where he not only knew that his coming was necessary. There were avatars that came before him, but they weren't as well known, and society wasn't ready for it, but his particular advent to Earth, it was a time when people would be able to hear the Word at least, even if they didn't understand it. The timing was everything. He was just the channel to bringing the message of love.

DOUG: Could the Illuminati try to infiltrate your body to possess you?

JOHN: Interesting question. Give me a moment. Nobody can manipulate your soul if you don't allow it. You have whole power over yourself. It is the big lie the Illuminati have painted for people that you have to look outside of yourself when your power is inside, so the only way they could control a person in spirit is if that person allows it. That's why Marilyn can release those energies from people that have that influence, and sometimes those people in the spirit that have that influence have come to her to have that release. So when the entity is ready to take back their responsibility for their life, then the Illuminati have no power.

DOUG: Okay.

JOHN: So the way they do it is by giving people false information and toxic food and toxic drugs and substances that stop that from even happening, from a higher consciousness occurring.

DOUG: Who is the son of Lucifer?

JOHN: I'm not familiar with that information.

DOUG: Now I'm going to read it.

JOHN: You see, part of the reason that is … I'm not sure there truly is a son because an archangel is masculine and feminine. So to have a creation of a child when a particular spirit is androgynous is not typical.

DOUG: Is it true Lucifer was the first planetary prince of this world?

JOHN: No.

DOUG: Did he create the Illuminati?

JOHN: No. The energy for that came … you're mixing theology with spirituality. When people separate from God, they create their separation from God, which makes them dark, and the darkness collected other darkness and became organized into what some people call the Illuminati, and so it's more of evolving away from God that created the Illuminati.

DOUG: Now according to the Bible, it talked about a dragon. Could that be Caligastia?

JOHN: What do you want to know?

DOUG: Was his reptilian?

JOHN: No.

DOUG: No. So who was he?

JOHN: Well, it was a … it was a force of negative energy that was developed to create difficulties for certain people and used against them. It was primarily an imaginary situation where they just used the energy and put that definition onto it so that people would have a physical manifestation or see it from a physical material point of view, but it's energy that's negative.

DOUG: Is it true that after they leave, would they go somewhere else in space and carry the same dark energy out there?

JOHN: Well, what happens is when you pass off of planet Earth, you go into the same consciousness that you had on planet Earth and act out that particular consciousness until you choose to move into a higher healthier loving energy. So you—it is acted out off of earth at a lower, lower level than most of the Nirvana.

DOUG: I just want to verify this information with you. I'll read it to you, and then you can tell me if it's true or not.

JOHN: All right.

DOUG: It's about Orion Queen Project. It was deemed necessary because Lucifer lost control over the 666 Titan, who without consulting Lucifer promised the Earth to the Grays for habitation after its ecosystem is rendered unsuitable for humans because of their fire technology activities. These human activities are promoted and directed by the Grays, employed by the 666. Could they still be the Illuminati?

JOHN: Well, the Illuminati were in contact with the Grays, and the Grays did various things and provided technical information to the Illuminati, which the government has been using against us rather than with us. And the Grays are not a positive energy, and they are no longer even allowed to come within distance of the Earth to be influential anymore. So whatever is going on or did go on with the Grays is no longer happening.

DOUG: Now according to this information I received, the Grays were asked to prepare to leave our solar system. Is that true?

JOHN: Yes. In fact—

DOUG: So about 1,500 incarnated Grays in the system and twenty billion non-incarnated included one assigned to every human. These act as sentient hacker programs controlling people's minds. Could that be true?

JOHN: Well, it's partly true. The Grays were not that infiltrated into the government or into the planet. They were there, and they were connecting with government officials. And they did provide technical assistance in various ways that was beyond what the people knew of computers at that point in time, but it was not as extensive as what you're describing.

DOUG: Okay, I thought maybe the demon could be from the Grays. You know, the same kind of demon like back in the time of Jesus.

JOHN: There really are no demons. The demons are separated from God. When you're not connected to God, it feels like it is demons, and in some cases, extreme cases, there actually are negative energies. Marilyn has detached some demons from people that had attachments, but that's very rare. It's not that populated. It's not as big an issue as you have maybe been led to believe, but yes, there were a few you might call demons attached to people, but not nearly to the extent that you're talking about.

DOUG: Is 666 … is that the mark of the beast?

JOHN: No. That's another theological distortion of what 666 means.

It's that the next number is 7, which is victory, so if they keep you from victory, then 666 could I guess be described as the mark of the beast. It wasn't intended for that. It was intended to show you that you are very close to victory. You see, so many things have been turned around to use against you in negative ways. Everything is loving and positive and all these negative things are just to take you off track, so the more you focus on things that are not real, which is negativity and the traumas and dramas that the Illuminati have perpetuated, and realize that it's like a mirage. And that mirage is fading and evaporating extremely fast at this point, so the sunlight of God is illuminating those particular kinds of situations.

DOUG: Now I'm going to move to the next topic—space.

JOHN: All right.

DOUG: I've got a space question. Is it true that there are millions of millions of planets, approximately fifty-seven million planets in our galaxy?

JOHN: There are many planets, but I don't know the exact number at this point. And yes, there are many planets in the galaxy.

DOUG: Is it true that there is another Earth that orbits on the same path as this Earth but on the other side of the sun?

JOHN: Well, there isn't another Earth that has alternate realities. It looks like this planet, and it is not … it depends on the decisions people make which reality they are on. How describe it? Actually, congruent with the Earth you're on. It has to do with the path you choose. The other Earth, it just has a different grid pattern to guide you where your new choices have taken you. It's a different grid pattern.

DOUG: Who transports souls to Nirvana?

JOHN: The guardian angels are always with you and protecting your soul, so as you leave your body, that soul energy moves with angels for protection to the destination that is appropriate for you.

DOUG: Now I go to the next topic—biblical questions.

JOHN: All right.

DOUG: Where is the lake of fire?

JOHN: Well, there really was no lake of fire. That again is from the theology of trying to scare people.

DOUG: Now are the demons mentioned in the Bible from the Illuminati?

JOHN: No. The demons in the Bible are your lower consciousness, your fear, your anger, your resentments, your guilt, your shame. Those are the demons that Jesus was in the desert and saying, "Get thee behind me, Satan." Those are the demons of your negative consciousness.

DOUG: Now if they continue to live in the third dimension, well, I guess heaven on earth is a foolproof system so everyone will attain it. Is that correct? To be more loving.

JOHN: That's what this dimension is about. We release all the dark energy and move into the light of God, where it will be all harmonious and pleasant and caring.

DOUG: Okay, now I'm going to ask this question again. Earth bound souls that are Earth bound right now because they haven't gone through the tunnel?

JOHN: That's right.

DOUG: Now is the sea of glass that was mentioned in the book of Revelation, is that in Nirvana, or that's the eighth dimension octave of the ring of Saturn? Where is the sea of glass? Where is it located?

JOHN: Well, I would say the sea of glass is a spiritual term for … I think that's a very interesting question because this is what's going on with a lot of people. They can see through the glass, but they can't actually accomplish it in their lives. They can't apply it, so they see it. They know it's there. They're coming from their heads, their egos, their intellect, and that they can't move through the glass and to be able to have it as their experience. So the glass shows them what's there, but they can't actually experience it because they haven't broken through the glass.

DOUG: Now I'm going to go to next topic, which is chakras.

JOHN: Okay.

DOUG: I found a chart from the Internet. It looks pretty good. I changed in number six and number seven. I flip-flopped those two numbers.

JOHN: Very good. You did listen. Very good.

DOUG: Thank you. Now I'm going to talk about reincarnation.

JOHN: Yes.

DOUG: Okay. What happens if they are old souls?

JOHN: Old souls are … the majority of old souls have come back to actually help others go through this process of moving into higher consciousness. The old souls are appearing as masters and spiritual teachers and those who are getting all kinds of help to individuals who are ready to progress. So the old souls can show up in various ways in people's lives, in helpful ways, and some of them have moved on into other parts of the universe to do other particular experiences that are of interest to them. So the old souls are actually guiding forces to help this transition, so most of them are definitely in that higher space where they will be part of fifth dimension and above.

DOUG: Who taught Buddhism? Who was the teacher for that?

JOHN: Well, this is pretty common knowledge that … I can't think of how his name exactly, but Mahatma, whatever it started with. Mahatma became the Buddha, and it was his spiritual journey. He was a prince in a palace, a very wealthy king. They didn't call him a king in his dominion, but he left the palace to go out and find out what life was about. And in his search for finding the answers, he became the Buddha.

DOUG: I just wanted to make sure I'm getting it right. Okay. Now I'm going to go to current event.

JOHN: Okay.

DOUG: Let's see. Okay, I found a definition of death of the soul.

JOHN: The death of the soul?

DOUG: I'm going to read it to you, and I see if you agree with it. It's not what we have talked about the nuclear thing. That might be part of it, but here is one I found on the Internet. I'll read it to you. A living soul with secured mental sustenance is virtually immortal. However, it can be destroyed by eternal intervention. This happens when it is judged by the greater system as harmful to the system or the social body of which it is a part. If any such unit within a system becomes malevolent to the system, it is treated as a cancer or a virus. The angels of the spirit of truth, which is responsible for the design, operation, and maintenance of the system, step in as antibodies, like antivirus programs and destroy the software of this soul. And hence, its mental body. Without the mental body and its basic soul maintenance program or pacemaker, the soul loses its permanence, reverts to its impermanent basic nature, and soon dissipates out of existence. This is the death of the soul. Does that make sense?

JOHN: No. There's some misinformation. First of all, everything is God, so when you said disease and cancerous, those things are not possible in the pure form of God. Everything is good and healthy, and the soul is God. There is no cancer. There is no virus, but when people in their own self will choose not to have the life of God as the force in their life and become so separated from God that it is truly, truly what most people would label evil, this has only happened very rarely in the universe that that energy is reabsorbed into the God source and starts out as a new soul. That is so unusual that it's not happened even in a percentage of time. So nothing leaves God. Nothing is destroyed. It's all energy, but it can be transmuted. Energy can become matter. It's transmuted, but it's not ever destroyed. And one of the reasons that God stopped nuclear war was because this was happening with some souls were so obliterated that it was almost impossible to restore them into their health. But that has been ... at this point there will be no nuclear wars to cause difficulties for soul retrieval and souls' best interest of being healthy, so you're coming. I don't know who wrote what you wrote, but there's a lot of misunderstanding because energy cannot be destroyed.

DOUG: I have this interesting question. Who was Apollonius of Tyana? I'll spell it to you.

JOHN: Yes, and people looked up to him as a God in the Greek culture. The Greeks had a lot of gods. And so there are statues of him, and he was considered the God of love, you might say.

DOUG: Was he Apollos in the Bible? The Bible mentioned a name Apollos.

JOHN: No, it was not the same. The Apollo of the Greeks was their imagination turned into a physical, so to speak, like in the statue. They made him into an image. No, that's not the same as in the Bible.

DOUG: I know I'm aware that the stock market is going to crash at some point because the Illuminati controls the stock market, so it's going to happen. My bet, it's going to happen six to nine months from now this year.

JOHN: Well, it is imminent.

DOUG: Really? Okay.

JOHN: Imminent means it's in God's timing.

DOUG: Okay, that's a dark energy that needs to go away.

JOHN: It is going away. It is being dispelled little by little.

DOUG: Right, so I figured that that's why there's going to be a major correction to the stock market because it's making people greedy with the money, and that's taking away the attention of God.

JOHN: Exactly.

DOUG: Is it true finding oneness with God will help enable your prayer to be heard by him and not to the evil, you know, not to the evil Illuminati.

JOHN: Okay. You keep focusing on the dark side. It doesn't have any power. When you move into the power, the light of God, when you become one with God and remove all of those negative thoughts, then your prayers are answered immediately, spontaneously. It's only the restrictions and obstructions from not being totally one with God that keeps the prayers slowed down to come only when those are— Finally, those avenues of energy are available to produce in a physical form, so the more you focus on God, the more one you become, the more your prayers will be answered more quickly and eliminate even thinking about the darkness because it isn't real. It's just an illusion for us to move out of. So when we spilt the light of God onto the darkness, where does it go? It disappears.

DOUG: Now does this make sense that photon energy is what's bringing the light to the planet?

JOHN: Exactly.

DOUG: Interesting. Thanks so much, John. Okay, this concludes the call. I'll probably be talking with you again in June.

JOHN: All right. I'll look forward to that.

Section 6.11: May 19, 2015

The following is a conversation with John the Divine via medium, channeled while Marilyn Redmond was in her trance on May 19, 2015.

DOUG: I realized that Jesus and possibly you as his disciple had an opened spiritual eye, so you could see earthbound spirits and help them.

JOHN: Well, that's what Jesus came to explain was the right use of energy. And so many people have taken what his information was and made a religion out of it, but it was basically—he came to show people the right use of energy, and of course, it's been looked at from a different, like a point of salvation rather than empowering your life to be full of love and enjoying yourself on earth. It's been used against people rather than to be beneficial to people.

DOUG: Jesus came down to free the earthbound spirits.

JOHN: Right.

DOUG: I've got thirty minutes for this call. I guess we'll move on to the most important questions to me.

JOHN: That's just fine.

DOUG: Let's see. I got this transcript for the movie *The Bought*, and it's about the hidden story behind vaccines, big Pharma, and your food.

JOHN: Yes, that's a very interesting film.

DOUG: I have an extra copy of the transcript. Now I might be able to mention it in the book. I will talk to Marilyn about it because this is important to the public.

JOHN: Well, there are definitely current issues that need to be put out the public, and I applaud you for making the major steps to put that into the mainstream. The media is reluctant to do that because they are not really at liberty yet to share all of the news.

DOUG: Besides heaven on earth for physical form, what about inside Earth? Are people in physical form?

JOHN: Definitely, yes.

DOUG: Now I'm going to move to the next topic here. I'm going to talk a little bit about aliens.

JOHN: Yes.

DOUG: Now talking about Lucifer?

JOHN: Yes.

DOUG: Actually, okay, you mentioned that he had a feminine, which is a loving energy, and a masculine energy, so it would be impossible to fall from grace if he had attained archangel level, is that true?

JOHN: Well, this is—every person has choice. Only angels are energy. Well, we're all energy, but they got energy that has not manifested into physical form, and all consciousness has choice. That's what free will is about. It's not—you see, the Bible is Lucifer's situation. They've turned that around, and they used it. Lucifer actually means light, and whenever the Illuminati want to scare people or whatever, they always seem to take the opposite. They take something good and then turn it into something that isn't good. So that's what they've done with the story of Lucifer. It's not that it's a real threat or something, but they're trying to scare people about, using that as part of their story for the fears. So I would not dwell a lot on something that is being use to scare people.

DOUG: Yeah, I would like to make a point with the table of various levels of spiritual consciousness.

JOHN: Yes.

DOUG: Like you mentioned, a tenth-level like Gabriel, the eleventh level or something like that.

JOHN: Well, remember that energy does not just stop at one spot. There is no definitive line, and it's always a little overlap of one energy going into the next. So it's nothing as cut and dry.

Section 6.12: January 13, 2016

The following is a conversation with John the Divine via medium, channeled while Marilyn Redmond was in her trance on January 13, 2016.

DOUG: Okay. Now were they in Christ consciousness?

JOHN: Yes, theirs is returning to Christ consciousness, in fact. That is what Marilyn's 2012 book is about, and her new book that is being published is about how people can return to that Christ consciousness and how we will move into this higher elevation of what people call heaven on earth.

DOUG: Okay, so like the people inside earth, they were already with Christ consciousness. Is that right?

JOHN: Yes. They fled from Atlantis and went inside the earth to protect their ability to continue their spiritual life. And yes, they have a very high consciousness.

DOUG: You mentioned the book of Revelation. Really, it's not a thousand years but two thousand years that photon energy provided golden age for the planet?

JOHN: It's actually a little more than two thousand. But the Bible even has the idea that people can move into peace was a profound announcement at that time. So the Bible is written for the people two thousand years ago to be able to understand. And that was such a large time span for them to assimilate into their consciousness that to even expand on that was pushing the edge a little bit. And so they made a conservative number of a thousand years.

DOUG: Now you had mentioned that planets are meant to be lived inside. Why are people living outside on the surface?

JOHN: Well, I never said people were meant to be living inside. The Earth is a planet where people incarnate to move their energy into the unconditional love of the Christ consciousness. That Christ consciousness is a symbolic term for unconditional love without criticism, judgment, or condemnation. You move out of your fears of judging others and criticizing them into the way Jesus condemned no one and said, "No more, I condemn thee not." So it doesn't matter if you are in the earth or on the earth. So what we are learning to do is to not live in the fears of this world but to live in the love and joy of this world, and to make that transition is why we came.

DOUG: Remember, we talked about the 5 percent of the people who go to the other side? Now is this different from inside earth. If they have attained Christ consciousness, then they do not go to nirvana, is that right? They go right straight down to inside earth?

JOHN: Well, spirit can go where it chooses. Spirit has many, many options when you become a master. You can continue your educational spiritual growth in other universes. You can help assist others on the Nirvana side. You can come back to earth and assist those on still earth and growing. Some people see these as dreams. Some people see them as visions being guided by the masters. Some people see them as their relatives coming back to give them love and comfort and answers that they are looking for or compassion or meaning. So masters can be of service in any part of the world and the planet. And those who are living under the ground are already of a very high consciousness. And so, I mean, if they went to join those, that would be appropriate too. But they don't go just one place. They have choice. They have choice to move on in their spiritual growth off of the planet Earth into other realms or to come back and help or to just stay in the spiritual realm that people call heaven or Nirvana to be of spiritual help to people who have passed over. This is one of the things that people don't understand—how much there is need of angels, I'll call them, that stay in Nirvana so that when people die, they can be there to assist them in their transition and the necessary changes that have to occur for them to adjust to that newer consciousness after their death. So there's a lot of different jobs and opportunities. It is just what seems to be the right one for that particular person or spirit at the time.

DOUG: Now there was another planet, Maldek.

JOHN: Yes.

DOUG: Were there Maldek people living inside the planet?

JOHN: Yes, there were. Just as there are people inside other planets that the telescopes of your scientists have not seen.

DOUG: Is Lord a spiritual term for love. Could Lord be just a tangible value where people do not understand energy concepts back then?

JOHN: Well, I think you are on the right track. The word *Lord*, if you substitute the word *law*, the law of God, "the Lord be with you," the law of God is love. So when you say Lord, you are talking about love, and that is the law of the universe. And that's where the planet has gone amiss. The love of the universe was dissipated through the fall of Atlantis and so forth as we just discussed earlier. So when you say the Lord is my shepherd, you are really saying that love is what your guidance is. You're being guided and directed by love, the law of love. And law is not punishing. It's supportive, nourishing and enhances your life. It expands. Love is an energy and expansion. So just talking about the Lord, you're talking about the energy of love in your life, having it to expand and take care of you.

DOUG: Okay, so, like, you know, the churches here are saying Jesus shed his blood so that there would be no more sacrificing animals. Jesus came down, and he saved from any more sacrifices, animal sacrifices.

JOHN: Right.

DOUG: Is blood a spiritual term for life? Could blood be just a tangible value because people did not understand energy terms—for instance, Christ consciousness?

JOHN: Yeah, I think that's a very good interpretation. However, blood—you see, blood, it carries the vital life force. It carries the energy of life in it. And so in biblical times and even before biblical times down in South America, the pyramids were built to—they would carve the heart out of a person and sacrifice it to the gods, trying to have a spiritual connection. So when people use blood in sacrifice, that's what the Illuminati do. That's what the Satanists do. They're using that blood to try to reconnect with God, but that's not the way you do it. You do it through your heart, and your heart has to be alive and pumping and healthy and functioning. So sacrifice is actually moving yourself away from God rather than to God.

DOUG: In one of my past lives, I was told I was thrown down from some top of a pyramid in South America. And that's kind of what had happened in one of my past lives where I was thrown down the pyramid, and they took my heart from my body.

JOHN: Well, Marilyn cured those pyramids in South America and was at some of those places where that happened. And they would purposely create wars to capture the enemy and that they could then take out their hearts to try to connect their spiritual connection that was missing. They were trying to reconnect through somebody else's heart. And that actually takes you away from God instead of nurturing those around you and helping their hearts to grow so your heart can grow into more love. So it was not really a beneficial practice.

Section 6.13: January 26, 2016

The following is a conversation with John the Divine via medium, channeled while Marilyn Redmond was in her trance on January 26, 2016.

DOUG: Did the white race originate from inside Earth?

JOHN: No. The races were all on Earth and went different directions. No, it was not from inside.

DOUG: Is it true that Earth was dry before and God created the firmament that helps to water the planet and brings tropical weather around the world?

JOHN: Yes, it was a very slow process of bringing together all the elements to create the beautiful planet of Earth, and it was not just like a magic wand. It did evolve, yes.

DOUG: Mercury is the first planet from the sun.

JOHN: Yes.

DOUG: Now it's very, very hot, obviously. Could—I'm talking about maybe thousands of years later—could the sun expand, or would the sun stay the same?

JOHN: These are not typical questions, Doug. I have to just think a minute and see where I can get my answer.

DOUG: I'm going to talk a lot about Photon Belt in my book.

JOHN: Oh, wonderful. That's good information people are not usually aware of.

DOUG: Right. So I'm going to show the seven super universe that rotate around paradise.

JOHN: Yes.

DOUG: Now I'm working on the graphic. I guess we're saying north on one side of the paradise. Now where would Photon Belt be located?

JOHN: Well, the belt is … it's in the shape of a belt on a car, going from one gear to another. And the universe rotates within both sides of this belt that's extended out and curves back, like a – you might say an oblong or oval shape. And so the different planets go through that photon belt every thirteen thousand years. And that's when Atlantis blew up. They left the Photon Belt. They had been in the Photon Belt, and that's why Atlantis was such an extended high consciousness and technologically advanced civilization. It has taken this amount of time to circle the orbit back into the Photon belt where we are now going through it again and raising our consciousness into that higher energy again.

DOUG: Now I'm trying to come up with this graphic to show people.

JOHN: Yes?

DOUG: I'm going to present a graphic to show the map of universe with paradise where God the Father is located.

JOHN: Right.

DOUG: That could be like a yellow light. And then I'm going to show seven blocks circulating around paradise. Each block represents a super universe.

JOHN: You might want to make them circular rather than blocks.

DOUG: Okay. Now the Photon Belt, how can I show that on the graphic?

JOHN: Well, you would want to place this belt could even be like a vacuum cleaner belt. It's going be an oblong lengthened—a circle that's lengthened out—and it's going to be standing vertically. And so the circles of the universes will be moving through the centers. On one side, moving out into, between the belt, coming back through the belt, open again without any contact to the belt, and moving—okay, the circles are going to be moving like a clock, counterclockwise.

DOUG: I've asked you this question before, but once every twenty-six thousand years, that's like one cycle?

JOHN: That's a complete cycle.

DOUG: Okay, so that would be a complete cycle around paradise?

JOHN: Exactly.

DOUG: Oh, okay, I can picture that. Okay. I mean, I could come up with that kind of graphic. I'm looking at the picture. Will it be ovular from the top to the bottom, or would it be ovular from left to right?

JOHN: Top to bottom.

DOUG: Top to bottom, okay. So from top to bottom, does that mean the Photon Belt will be probably, there's an east-west belt of paradise? About two times within a twenty-six-thousand-year cycle, so it would make sense it would go on both sides of paradise.

JOHN: Yes, that's true.

DOUG: So that's a good representation of the Photon Belt.

JOHN: Yeah, I think you understand it quite well, yes.

DOUG: Come up with something that people can understand.

JOHN: Well, that would be very helpful.

DOUG: Thank you. Probably the most interesting chapter is chapter 1. Well, I'm going to have to be a little careful about marriage. It might offend a lot of people. So basically, and I'm going to talk a little bit about marriage.

JOHN: The information is becoming more open to the public that marriage was actually a way for the church to control people, and it's not a spiritual sacrament. It's a cultural one. It was imposed on culture for control and manipulation. So the original marriage was a contract because the man received a dowry, and it was a contract. It was not a religious marry, as said. It was a financial contract, and then the church enlarged upon it and adopted it to—for people to feel that they needed to have a marriage as such in the eyes of church to be accepted.

It was a matter of shaming people if they didn't get married. And if you're in shame, you're better ... or at least more easily controlled. So more people are beginning to understand that this was not really part of the original plan. However you want to word it is fine. I just think ... I think people are becoming, from my seeing of what goes on in Marilyn's life, people are better understanding that marriage is really an agreement between the two people to love each other, and the piece of paper is not really what provides love. It's God that provides the love.

DOUG: Okay, that's great, yeah. I like that. I'm going to talk about that. But people will want to know this about marriage.

JOHN: Well, it's time for them to realize a piece of paper does not mean you have the marriage that people are looking for. The paper is just a piece of paper. And what does it mean? And what's behind it, and where is the heart of the person that is in the marriage? Where is the heart? That's what makes a marriage.

DOUG: I think that's all of my questions, so thanks again.

JOHN: Oh, you're so welcome, Doug. And you know, we're always here for you. We think you're doing a terrific job. You're putting out information people need to hear. You're presenting things that have not necessarily been exposed, and it's time for all the hidden secrets and the misunderstandings to be recognized. And we want you to know that we on the side of Spirit. We are supporting you and with you all the way. You seem to be very connected. We're thrilled that you are persevering, even if it's taken longer than you expected. You're working it and doing a thorough job … and doing a very good job. So it isn't always speed that gets the race won, as you know with the story of the rabbit and the turtle. It's persevering and accomplishing it in a way that's going to be really helpful to so many people. We appreciate your efforts.

DOUG: Thanks. Thanks again. It's such an honor to be doing this work. So of course, it's a blessing.

JOHN: Well, you're doing … you're going to be doing that. You're going be providing information they need to hear, and this is all going to work out very well for you. And we wish you the best, and keep in touch. We're willing and here to help you any time.

DOUG: Okay, wonderful, John. Thanks again.

Section 6.14: February 16, 2016

The following is a conversation with John the Divine via medium, channeled by Marilyn Redmond in her trance on February 16, 2016, in Edgewood, Washington.

DOUG: Okay, this call could be thirty minutes. It will be mostly about Photon Belt. I'm going to ask you questions about that.

JOHN: All right.

DOUG: Now suppose the dark side has tried to escape Earth, and they will most likely maybe go to Mars or another third-dimensional planet. Is that true?

JOHN: They already have gone to Mars and have bases on Mars. People just have not been told about it.

DOUG: Okay, so, um, now if people, you mentioned you will want this to be in a fifth dimension. But people who are not ready for it that, they will go to another third-dimensional planet, right?

JOHN: Exactly.

DOUG: Okay, now the universe is huge, so it will be somewhere, someplace—um, now hold on. Let me—okay, now I'm going to go back to Atlantis,

JOHN: Okay.

DOUG: The library in Alexandria, Egypt, about Atlantis was established in 10,300 BC. Would that be right?

JOHN: That's pretty accurate.

DOUG: So Earth is moving to the fifth dimension, Mars in the third dimension, so are those planets farther away from the Sun will still be in the third dimension.

JOHN: Actually, the whole universe is moving into the Photon Belt so not just planet Earth is moving into the fifth dimension, but the whole solar system is.

DOUG: Okay, now I have a question. I have asked you about Law of One and the Old Testaments.

JOHN: Yes.

DOUG: Thank you, John.

JOHN: All right, well, I'm always available. I'm eager and willing to help you in any way I can, Doug. I applaud what you are doing. I think you're very consciousness and persevering, and you seem to have a very good understanding of these things. Your questions are very wonderful, and people will learn a lot.

DOUG: You know, something Marilyn and I was talking about. Right now I have gout in my foot, so my right foot is all swollen. I think this happens because I was using my ego to try to get credit for the job well done. I should have just been grateful to God for helping me find a solution. As a result, my ego reacted with anger, and it disrupted my peace within myself. I allowed my ego to take over, and a health problem came up.

JOHN: Well, that's a very good indication that you're aware of how your energy and your body works, and I applaud you for being so aware and in tune with how the energy functions in your system, I think that's very applaudable.

DOUG: Thank you. This is an ego-dominating world. I just let people do their thing. I need to step away from all that and just let them do what they want to do and just allow God take care of my needs.

JOHN: Well, that's very good advice for yourself, Doug. They are going to have their lessons, and they're going to do what you're going to do. But you have your purpose, and you're staying on it. And that's what counts.

DOUG: Thanks so much, John.

JOHN: Well, we're glad to help you anytime, and we will be talking to you again.

Section 6.15: March 16, 2016

The following is a conversation with John the Divine via medium, channeled by Marilyn Redmond in her trance on March 16, 2016, in Edgewood, Washington.

DOUG: For those who have ascended to the fifth dimension, do they go to inside earth?

JOHN: Well, that is a choice. Some of them can if they choose to. Some do because that is a very high consciousness level and they are attracted to helping those people. However, those people have, for the most part, moved into a higher consciousness already because they are the remnants or the inheritance of Atlantis. The whole, real Law of One from Atlantis went inside the earth as protection through the storms and turmoil of the continent breaking up. So the majority of the masters have gone to return to earth or other elements, helping other people raise their consciousness where they feel they are called.

DOUG: Now those who have extended to the fifth dimension, they do not necessarily go to Nirvana. Is that correct?

JOHN: Well, they have a longer extended life, and yes, all spirits of the Earth go to Nirvana and the level of consciousness. It's like different elevator floors you get off on, and their level of consciousness is a high building. As in New York City, they would get off at a higher level than those people still on the third dimension. But they would go to Nirvana, and then it's like a weigh station. And then you would go onto your next reincarnation or your next project for which you are being called.

DOUG: Yes, you mentioned this too. Those who have ascended to the fifth dimension do not need to reincarnate.

JOHN: Right. They do not. However, this is a different time in the universe when the Earth is coming in the fifth dimension. And many higher masters who have gone into the fifth dimension, as we say, have returned to Earth at this time to bring the rest of the people into that consciousness along with them. Their energy is manifesting on earth and providing additional help and support for moving into ascension, into the higher consciousness of fifth dimension on Earth, which you people call heaven on earth. So there are more masters on Earth at this time than there has been for some time.

DOUG: So for those who have not ascended, could they have to go to another third-dimensional planet to work out their dark energy?

JOHN: That's likely what will happen. Those who are not ready to ascend—if people are ready to surrender their lives to the power of God working through them, they can stay and continue to grow spiritually, which will be going on for many people in the next fifteen years. If they choose to keep resisting their growth, if they want to stay in a fearful state and not be able to open up to the love of the universe, they will move to another planet that is very much like Earth but continue to live out their third-dimensional experiences. They need to be changed until they finally come into that realm where they have agreed and accepted that they will change their ways into better, healthier, loving ones.

DOUG: Now there are some human elements of the dark side that are still here. Is it possible after they die, then the one thousand years of peace has begun? So we're one generation away from that happening

JOHN: Well, the light is no longer— There isn't any light left in those dark forces. They have eliminated all their possibilities at this point, and the light of the planet has, through the Photon Belt, has become so intense. They are day by day, minute by minute losing their power. So they are becoming powerless on this planet, and they are floundering at this point.

DOUG: Yeah. Some people have taken actions against companies that produces GMOs. So there's a movement there.

JOHN: Isn't that exciting to see that the changes are coming into the public awareness? These are not acceptable, and they have never been. And they are not in anybody's real interest. And that this is finally being exposed, not just at an underlying dimension but being aware in the public area, which is just wonderful. Because what you focus on grows, and this movement can change that problem that we have been working and trying to change for thousands of years.

DOUG: So the photon energy is going to make shifts in the people's consciousness.

JOHN: Exactly. You see, the photon energy is the Christ energy. And that was the energy that was surrounding the Earth during the time of Lemuria, and that's when the energy—the spirit came to earth to enjoy the planet. And they came in Christ consciousness, and your planet is returning to that consciousness.

DOUG: And spirit of truth. It's Christ's consciousness and energy from spirit of truth.

JOHN: Yes.

DOUG: Okay. Yeah, we've talked about that before.

JOHN: Well, truth is another name. It's a synonym for God. God is the truth, so when you return to truth, you're returning to the God, force, the Creator, or the source—however you choose to term it. The terms are not relevant. It's the energy that it represents.

DOUG: Now we talked about this that Mars is in the third dimension.

JOHN: Right.

DOUG: So could that delay the solar system's entry into the isles of paradise.

JOHN: No, it cannot delay it. It doesn't have enough energy at this point to do that.

DOUG: Okay. Is it true that Mars will become green about a hundred years from now?

JOHN: Yes, they are finding water on Mars, and it will gradually grow into a healthier climate with vegetation. That is visible right now.

Most of the energy on Mars is invisible. It's there and functioning, but it isn't manifested in a physical form. And with the advent of its development, that very likely will happen.

DOUG: I have different subjects, so I'm mixing the questions. Now the Bible recorded Jesus going to the mountain. Did he meet with the ascended masters, or he meditated?

JOHN: Ascended masters or what was your other comment?

DOUG: In the Bible, it talks about Jesus going up to the mountain.

JOHN: Yes.

DOUG: So was that another meaning for meditation?

JOHN: It's another meaning for meditation, yes. When you go to the mountain, when Moses saw the burning bush, he was in a meditative state. He was in meditation. He was connecting. That's the conscious contact with God. It's going to the higher mountain. In the Bible, they did not understand the terms meditation. They did not realize that you could move your consciousness into a higher one. And they used terms that the people in those days could understand.

DOUG: Now let's talk about transfiguration.

JOHN: Yes. The trance people, when they go into meditation, transfigure because the light of God starts to take place and replaces actually the energy of the darkness inside that person. Any darkness there was, the light comes on, and you see the light of God in them. When Marilyn channels, she transfigures. Mac (Marilyn's husband) transfigures when he does the healing.

DOUG: I see.

JOHN: Any people who allow the light of God to come into them and manifest to help others is—usually has a white light about them. And that's what you see in— Sometimes people's auras are a white light. That's their soul energy that has transfigured into the white light.

DOUG: I got a question from the second book of Corinthians.

JOHN: Okay.

DOUG: Chapter 12.

JOHN: Yes.

DOUG: This is coming from Paul. He says, "I know a man in Christ about 14 years ago. Whether he was in the body, I cannot tell, or out of the body, I cannot tell. God knows which were taken up into the Third Heaven." What is the third heaven, the second heaven, and the first heaven?

JOHN: Well, those are terms for consciousness. And so again, the people in that day and age had to write the Bible in terms that people would understand. And he was trying to explain this man had gone into a higher consciousness.

DOUG: So was third heaven—what level of consciousness is the third heaven?

JOHN: Well, basically, that is a level of those people on Earth. However, what he was trying to say is that he was reaching beyond the fears of Earth and moving into a loving consciousness. It wasn't that the man had grown into sainthood as such, but that the man was growing spiritually.

DOUG: Thank you for the clarification. But the practice did teach me meditation. It taught me—it was beautiful, and so I encourage people, if they want to learn to meditate, to contact that organization.

JOHN: That is a good organization (Self-Realization fellowship), yes.

DOUG: Yes. I agree.

DOUG: I have a graphic showing the Photon Belt.

JOHN: Yes.

DOUG: Also, I have a graphic showing the seven super universes encircling the center of creation.

JOHN: Yes.

DOUG: I've got the impression that the other six universes are waiting for us to ascend, so we are moving to what's on the outer boundary, whatever you call it.

JOHN: Yes. You keep reading. Because of your engineering background, you are very linear sometimes in your thinking. When you get to the ninth dimension, it becomes like soup. The energies are not in a ladder type of arrangement. It's more like having soup, and all the ingredients are in the soup and mixed in. And so it becomes multidimensional. You can focus into each of the extended dimensions like a radio. You tune into that dimension, but it's not like a ladder where you move higher into it.

DOUG: Thank you. My time is up. Well, thanks again.

JOHN: Well, we're glad to help you with your questions, Doug. We are so thrilled you are searching and planning to give people more real information. We applaud your work and your efforts and your energy. We are all behind you. Your angels are cheering you on. They're saying that you are a very persevering person. You have a good heart. You're wanting to help people understand, and your book will be of great value. We encourage you to keep moving forward, knowing that you're on a path that is showing light to others.

DOUG: Yes, I do have a lot of feelings for people. I've gone through some struggles in my life. I see love in every single soul, but they're just blinded by their egos.

JOHN: Well, and the fear that comes from that. And if you can open any eyes and hearts with your book, you will have come and accomplished a major, major accomplishment. So be proud of yourself and know that you are doing a good job.

Section 6.16: March 24, 2016

The following is a conversation with John the Divine via medium, channeled by Marilyn Redmond in her trance on March 24, 2016, in Edgewood, Washington.

DOUG: Yes, this question is mostly about relationships and marriages for the new age.

JOHN: Ah, what a good question.

DOUG: Please explain the concept of the Tree of Life?

JOHN: There were two trees in the garden of Eden. The Tree of Life was the tree of being in consciousness with God, and then you are living in a light and the spirit of love. The Tree of the Knowledge of Good and Evil is when you departed into the third dimension of the material world because the good is— There is nothing wrong with good, but you have the ego bringing up the evil, the darkness, and the obstructions to the light. And so you go into judgment and stop God's love from flowing into your life. It's all done on an intellectual level rather than an emotionally spiritual level. So when the people in the garden of Eden partook of the Tree of the Knowledge of Good and Evil, they were lowering their density. They were lowering their consciousness into a judgmental, fearful consciousness, which was from the ego, and they left. That's why they left Eden, and they were no longer connected to the God source.

DOUG: Okay. Why did God have the Tree of Life placed in the garden of Eden?

JOHN: Well, that was representative of what they were when they first arrived in the garden of Eden. They were living spiritual energy. It was before man took on a body. They were just energy that was of God and experiencing that beautiful paradise. And so what happened to follow how a man was coming from that spiritual energy to become dense in a physical form. And so literally, it's depicted as them walking out because they now had physical bodies that were not connected to God. You know their energy had materialized and become dense, and they were no longer the same. They became more human. The trick of all this is to realize you were originally a spiritual Christ being who left the garden of Eden and became a human being with a physical body. So this is what Revelation is about—returning to the spiritual being that you were created in so that the energy inside is not of the human motivation, the ego. It is now back to the motivation of God's love.

DOUG: Um, now, in the book of Genesis, the serpent tempted Eve not to eat of the tree. Now could that be sexual energy, not to be tempted by sex or what?

JOHN: Well, when she ate of the tree, she lowered her consciousness, and of course, your motivations, including sexual desires, changed. And so the motives of people became selfish, lustful, very prideful, arrogant, and self-serving. They became selfish people by eating the apple, so it was the sexual part was just one aspect of all of their connection to a loving source that was unconditional love. They walked out of that environment by succumbing to eating of the apple.

DOUG: That's only if a person ascended to the fifth dimension. The body can last longer then, right?

JOHN: That's very true. You have to have a cooperation as we talked about a few minutes earlier between chakras. Your whole system has to be connected to a higher consciousness, which would be the fifth dimension. And then you can live longer. That's what the masters have accomplished. That is why they are still helping people do what they did. They learned how to go beyond the ego, extend their life consciousness into an eternal life, and continue in that path, and they have come back to Earth to help others do that.

Douglas Grady

DOUG: I see that's interesting. Now we are entering a new era of love and light.

JOHN: Yes.

DOUG: Okay, well, thanks so much, John. My thirty minutes are up.

DOUG: Okay, because I'm open to whatever crosses my mind, I would write it down immediately, so I don't forget in the morning.

JOHN: Well, I think you've learned very well, and your lessons in writing will help others immensely, so I wish you well.

DOUG: Thank you. Yeah, so it's coming finally. I'm looking forward to getting the book out.

JOHN: Well, I'm looking forward to seeing it too, and getting your questions to me have been of the great joy. I appreciate talking with you and answering your concerns, and anytime you are welcome to call.

DOUG: Okay, thanks so much, John. Will do.

Section 6.17: April 14, 2016

The following is a conversation with John the Divine via medium, channeled while Marilyn Redmond was in her trance on April 14, 2016.

DOUG: Yeah, I'm glad to be talking with you again. It's kind of interesting what you said in our last call.

JOHN: And what was that?

DOUG: Yeah, I prayed the other day, and I was asking Marilyn if I should include it in the book or not. So I prayed to God, and I asked for his guidance. And sure enough on the next day, I got ahold of

Door to Glory

one of my spiritual informants, Tracey Williams, and she said, "Yes, God wants me to include it in the book." So he answered my prayer.

JOHN: Right. That's exactly right.

DOUG: Interesting. Okay. I'm going to get on with the questions.

JOHN: Okay.

DOUG: Okay, because the Bible only shows that he met Jesus in the Spirit but not through real life.

JOHN Well, there's a book that was channeled—not actually channeled. A person went into regression, past-life regression and wrote a book about his experiences as Paul when he was alive at the time of Jesus. And he gives quite a lot of detail about his relationship with Jesus not as a disciple but as a friend, and it was very enlightening. He did not always agree with Jesus in the beginning. As things progressed, he became more and more in tune with what Jesus was saying, but so it was a gradual growing into the understandings of what Jesus was saying.

DOUG: Oh, so really, Jesus helped convince Paul more about his teaching?

JOHN: Yes. He brought spiritual understanding through his conversations with Paul.

DOUG: Oh, okay.

JOHN: They were what you would consider friends.

DOUG: Marilyn provided me some feedback for my book, and she mentioned that one statement that was very profound. Well, she mentioned that heaven on earth is the fifth dimension, and that's really based on your loving spirit in your heart.

JOHN: Exactly. We're already in heaven on earth when we are aware and we take action to act as if we are.

DOUG: Yes, I got this good information for the book that compares the third-dimensional relationships and the fourth-dimensional relationships. And yeah, it just talked about love, all about love.

JOHN: The only thing we have to really change is to get out of our ego. It's the ego that stops the love. So the ego is edging God out. So as you merge God in, as you merge God's love in, you have loving relationships. It's only the fear and the ego's messages that stops that. So as you move out of that, you become fearless. Marilyn has become fearless. The ego is not running her show today, and her relationship is very healthy. And so it's not the way it used to be because that was the old way to handle things. And today it's a respect for each other, and they're both equals.

DOUG: Yes. That's how we will grow spiritually.

JOHN: Exactly.

DOUG: Gotcha.

DOUG: Thanks so much again.

JOHN: Okay. Well, I'm glad that we can be of help. And we'll be in touch, and have a wonderful day.

DOUG: Thank you, John.

JOHN: And have a good time. Enjoy yourself. It sounds like you're very busy. But take a little time off, and have some fun too.

Section 6.18: April 27, 2016

The following is a conversation with John the Divine via medium, channeled while Marilyn Redmond was in her trance on April 27, 2016.

DOUG: Now was Jesus born as Muhammad?

JOHN: No, that was another. You see, different souls have different experiences on earth at various times, and some souls have come back and back and back. Now St. Germaine is one of those souls that has continued for thousands of years to return, not just in spirit but as a human form. He has probably manifested in more human form than most of the masters. Most of the masters have appeared once or maybe twice but have then stayed in spirit, but St. Germaine has become throughout the years many life-forms that were physically walking. He was here during the US Constitution being written. He was there during the French Revolution. He wrote Shakespeare's plays. He was written and has appeared quite a few times in history physically, but most of the masters have stayed in spirit. Babaji is one of the few masters that has extended his lifetime in physical form and is still here helping, but that is not the typically. Most of them do continue to help through the Spirit.

DOUG: Now by the end of a thousand years of peace—I mean, two thousand years of peace—would we be in the seventh dimension?

JOHN: When you move beyond the fifth dimension, it becomes multidimensional so that you are in the fifth dimension, but you can access higher energies of information or connection. It is like having a radio, and you can tune into the seventh dimension. You can tune into sixth dimension, and you can tune into ninth dimension. So when you move into fifth dimension as you go, there are seven stages of the fifth dimension. As you go through the stages, you become more and more in tune with higher dimensions, but you don't leave the fifth dimension. And you stay a spiritual person in a physical body, but you can tune into the other dimensions and come and go in spirit much more quickly and accessibility. So it's not that you just totally have a line that where you cross over, and now I'm in the seventh dimension. It's more like soup. The dimensions mix, and you tune into the ones that are appropriate for the time.

DOUG: Thank you so much. After I send the tape to the recorder for them to type it up, I will put it in the book and send the book it to the publisher by Monday.

JOHN: Well, that would be very, very nice. I'm glad that you have stuck with this so rigidity, that you have kept your focus and kept on the project. It is to be so admired and so respected, and I want you to know that your angels are very much supportive of you and that they are very proud of you, and they are cheering and saying, "Doug has done a great job." They are just thrilled that you have been listening to their guidance and following through, getting the direction you needed to continue. They are very happy with you.

DOUG: Thanks so much. It is such a blessing! Probably in a little while from now I'm going to say what a remarkable experience it has been working with you.

JOHN: Well, I have loved working with you, Doug, and if you have any more projects, if you have any more need to call on me, I would be most grateful and happy to be of assistance.

Section 6.19 October 11, 2016, Notes

Conversation with John the Divine via medium Marilyn Redmond on October 11, 2016.

DOUG: In Marilyn's book, she described "Father and I are one." If we conquer fear from our heart, then fear goes away, bringing just love which creates Father and I for ourselves.

JOHN: Yes, it is true, because if you walk into a dark room and turn on the light, there is no darkness. So, as you move into Christ Consciousness, the light of God, which is unconditional love, and as you move into that emotional higher consciousness, which in her book there's a picture of angels on stairs, and that's like Jacob's ladder. As you move up those stairs of consciousness, the light gets brighter and brighter.

Marilyn just had an experience where she overcame her past - most desperate and devastating wounds from her past. And what happened was it felt like she had just plugged herself into the electrical socket in the wall, and she became full of energy, moving all over, and becoming alive inside. So, this is heading into the Christ Consciousness, is that aliveness comes inside, and the light - bright light that comes from that just seems to dissipate the darkness that she felt into heaviness. And it was like there was this huge change in how she felt about herself and how she handled her life with others.

DOUG: "The poor in spirit seek for goals of spiritual wealth – for God. And such seekers after truth do not have to wait for rewards in a distant future; they are rewarded now. They find the Kingdom of Heaven within their hearts, and they experienced such happiness now." Ref. Urantia Book 140:5.7 (1573.9)

JOHN: That's - I believe that to be true because so many people have been harmed and hurt. And their lives have been lacking security and lacking - they're in poverty. The homeless today is a good example, or the wars going on. All of these things that we have just been bombarded with keeps us out of the love of God. And so, people are defending themselves to try to stay safe. When you defend yourself, you stop God from working in your life. It prevents the grace of God from happening and expanding in your life.

So, the trick is to quit defending yourself and embrace God. You have to make a choice. Are you going to try to keep yourself safe, or are you going to live in God's love, which is safe? God is your safety, your fortress, and your health. So you can choose to live in that particular space, which is a Christ Consciousness, knowing that God is all. All there is is God. And then release the fear of needing to defend yourself or protect yourself or you don't have enough.

When you move into this high consciousness of Christ Consciousness, then you discover God's grace is sufficient. The things you need will start manifesting your life without you going even to have to go to a store. Marilyn recently had a person with a - show up on our doorstep that is going to be able to help her with her new audio book. And she'd been looking for two years for somebody that was the right person for the job, and lo and behold, he showed up to help her with computer work. And it turned out he is the right person. And she didn't know he would even be the right person. But, there he was.

So, when you move to God for your sufficiency, then you don't have to worry about the third-dimensional material harms and poisons and toxins and so forth. You are home. You have become the prodigal son who has come home, and your father has run out to meet you.

DOUG: Thanks so much John.

JOHN: Okay, it's good talking with you, Doug. And I want you to call anytime. I'll have Martha come in. Have a good day, Doug, and we - we're glad that you're still in touch. Blessings to you.

Section 6.20 February 14, 2017, Notes

Conversation with John the Divine via medium Marilyn Redmond on February 14, 2017.

DOUG: Could have the disciples given Jesus some of their pranas in the tomb to revive him?

JOHN: It's a transition of moving and allow the energy within, the God energies of spirit, to go into a higher consciousness. It's a total surrender to all of God encompassing your life and being within ourselves. So, it's a complete surrender, and most people hold back and do not totally surrender. It is the lesson on planet Earth, that is no harm comes when you are totally vulnerable and open to the love of God.

DOUG: But that makes sense. If Jesus were Adam, then it wouldn't make sense if Adam had sinned. I think the story of Adam and Eve was part of the whole plan of God, is that true?

JOHN: The separation from God and so in that eating the apple and their consciousness lowered into dividing into right and wrong, now their focus was not on primarily on 100% God, their focus was not of God, and that's the sin.

DOUG: Now was Adam and Eve a symbol of ego hiding from God?

JOHN: When they took part of the Apple, exactly, their egos became prominent in their lives, and they were ashamed. So, when they were in the Garden of Eden, they were one with God, they said "they were naked," that's their innocence, they were one with God in total love and sprite. When they ate the apple, they fell to a lower consciousness of good and evil. They left the one power of God to partake in the two powers of good and evil, and that was the fall of man.

DOUG: Okay. Now many people came to earth?

JOHN: Right.

DOUG: - and they were in the spirit when they came to earth, then they became physical bodies, so that kind of like Adam and Eve being a symbol of people coming here transforming their energy to return to their birthrights.

JOHN: When they came to earth, and actual lives are described in the Garden of Eden in the Bible. And so, when they lowered their consciousness to - from partaking of the apple, which symbolized the separating into, into focusing on good and evil, that created denser energy. You see in God's spirit, and it's an invisible energy that is not necessarily visible to the naked eye, it's beyond vision. So, in lowering their energy, they became visible. Then the Bible talks about the word became flesh. That's exactly, and they became visible in the world that they were walking in because they lowered their energy into the human form.

DOUG: Now, like what we're doing now when you wrote the book of Revelation, who was "John" information to you?

JOHN: When I wrote the book of Revelation, it was all a metaphor because people did not understand energy.

DOUG: I've mentioned to Marilyn that I would like to be a medium, but would my third- eye must be open?

JOHN: Yes, that's part of what this is about to see beyond the physical world. The third-eye is where you have the vision of the energy and how it's interchanging and how it's moving. And becoming newer or different energies that give you energy messages which are translated into the physical world, and to get those messages, you need to be able to see the energies or feel them or know them or have a gnawing inside. So, this puts you out of the world of the physical earth, put into the spiritual world.

DOUG: I don't know if it is part of my calling to do it, or I'm more of a philosopher and translates things into better understanding for people?

JOHN: In your progression of curiosity, Doug, you are growing more and more spiritually and of being able to be a medium. And it's truly your choice. The only limitations are the ones you put on yourself. You want to progress into the higher consciousness of being in touch with understanding what spirit is telling you at an invisible, silent way. Sometimes you can hear it speak to you, that you'll be still and know that I am God. Spirits can talk in several ways. And the best way to prepare yourself is through meditating daily, and that will grow your energy into connecting with God and the more open you are to your heart being open to receive whatever comes, your medium shift will grow and grow, and you will evolve. And there are some ways to help yourself do that. Marilyn's last book or her last one is *Road to Success*, but her book medium, *Paradigm Busters*, that book has exact steps necessary to bring you into the state of consciousness that would help your medium shift tremendously. I - if you're wanting to pursue being a medium, I suggest that you get her Paradigm Busters book and follow the directions completely. Because that is the path she took and it does work.

DOUG: Now, I can understand better about the teaching of Self-Realization Fellowship that was by controlling my sensual urges. Based on the instruction, any call that is coming from my ego, my higher mind takes over and directs me to a higher level. That's why they teach people to abstain those feelings to control the urge better.

JOHN: Right, you know, energy is neutral, so the feelings are good indications of what's going on with you and to learn and handle your life, because you understand your feelings and how to move beyond the negative feelings into the positive. But eventually, you move, into a state of neutrality, which would be fifth-dimension where the feelings are neutral. Love is a neutral experience, and so, as you move higher and higher, you are connected with your inner being. There's a CD that you can get. Marilyn can send you the information. And she listened to it for many, many years, because her third-eye needed to work on opened and functioning so she could be a medium. And this is one way that works very well for people. There are many ways that if you were here, we would, have Marilyn work on you to open your third-eye or Marilyn could do that too in a spiritual way.

DOUG: That would be great, yes.

JOHN: But since you don't live here and I'm accessing to go to Marilyn and Matt for that kind of help, this, this recording would be most helpful.

DOUG: Sounds good. I got two more appointments with, with you, so I'll talk to you next week.

JOHN: Oh, that sounds wonderful. We're glad to have you call anytime and anytime we can be of help, just let us know. We are so pleased that you are on this path. You are doing such an excellent job of learning and experiencing and questioning things that you need to know more about your work. You are just doing wonderfully well,

Doug. Know that you are loved. Your higher power, your God, and your life are very pleased with you.

DOUG: Thank you.

JOHN: We love you all, and Martha loves you, and I'm going to have her come in and say good-bye.

Section 6.21 February 23, 2017, Notes

Conversation with John the Divine via medium Marilyn Redmond on February 23, 2017.

DOUG: My first question here is, again, mainly a repetition of a question from the last call. So, pardon me if I'm asking this question again.

JOHN: No problem.

DOUG: Is it possible that Paul didn't know the disciples had applied the rite of sepulcher at the tomb to wake Jesus up from his deathlike trance?

JOHN: The disciples were not as high consciousness as Jesus, so they were not as informed with the different dynamics of raising your energy. So, they were not informed about that ritual.

DOUG: Who were there doing that? Was it all the 12 disciples or was it some of them?

JOHN: We weren't everybody was there. Are you talking about Easter?

DOUG: Yes. Like, when Jesus was taken to the tomb?

JOHN: Okay. All the disciples were with him on the night before his crucifixion, but the crucifixion has been rewritten by the churches, and so it's not entirely accurate as what the Bible says. But the disciples were there in that evening. However, not all of them were there on the morning of his rising.

DOUG: Was Mary Magdalene there?

JOHN: Oh, yes, very much. She was the one that found that he was gone.

DOUG: Has a spiritual leader of the dark side left for Mars? Could that be Caligastia or the Dragon?

JOHN: You see, everything that people proport or predict that is evil is real of themselves. So, it doesn't matter if somebody moves to Mars or not. All they have to deal with is the enemy within, is their lower nature that is in their ego.

DOUG: Okay.

JOHN: So, this has been an onward upward struggle since Atlantis.

DOUG: Now, I have the question regarding this biblical passage from the Book of Peter that, it mentions that there were eight souls were saved by the water. Were those eight souls on Noah's Ark? Like, what brought me to that question was, did the evolutionary races that began from apes or animal kingdom survive the flood?

JOHN: Okay. These eight souls that you're talking about, I'm not familiar with what they're related to?

DOUG: Adam and Eve, as I read in Urantia book, that their race was like the ninth race on the planet and they represented the violet race. Now, my question about, in flood, of these few who survived the flood.

JOHN: Right.

DOUG: Now, the people that were in that part of the evolutionary race who were not associating with Adam and Eve, did they all perish in flood?

JOHN: The people not in the Ark did not survive because they had not - see, God is a choice. We choose that love of God, and if you don't choose that, you don't survive. That's what life's about, is to learn to - to choose to live. So, no, they did not survive.

DOUG: Is it true when we attain fifth-dimension, I understand that a human body has three companion bodies associated with it, like the astral body, the mental body, and the spiritual body?

JOHN: Exactly. They're all one and combined, but people, to understand the different aspects of how the body functions, has labeled them into different parts.

DOUG: Now, when we attain the fifth-dimension, is it possible that we would recognize all our bodies where they all merge into one?

JOHN: Exactly.

DOUG: Okay.

JOHN: You will become one with the spirits, so there will not be the separations because all of your different aspects of your body will come into unity.

DOUG: So, what is the other side?

JOHN: The other side of the veil (kingdom of God). Spiritually you have been limited with your eyesight from fear, and when the fear blanket is lifted they call it a veil, then you see completely, then you see the truth of everything, the side you cannot see because the veil is stopping you from seeing the truth is called the other side.

DOUG: How about people living inside Earth?

JOHN: What about them?

DOUG: They were aliens, right?

JOHN: Not necessarily. They were the ones that fled Atlantis when it was submerging.

DOUG: Oh?

JOHN: Yes, that's - they went underground because that was the safest place for them to escape. So, the people living underground at this point are a very high consciousness, and they were the people that fled before Atlantis blew up, and they escaped, some went to places like Easter Island and the Hawaiian Islands, and some went underground.

And some went up into the northern part of what you call the North American continent. So, that was just part of where people fled in trying to survive the explosions and desecration of Atlantis.

DOUG: So, the Great Flood took place after the explosion?

JOHN: No, it was - no, the flood had nothing to do with Atlantis. The flood was much earlier.

DOUG: The flood's much earlier. Okay.

JOHN: There were several times when the planet was supposedly purified of the consciousness. The flood was a primary purification of consciousness.

DOUG: Now, I'm going to ask you about World War 2?

JOHN: Yes.

DOUG: It's - yeah, it's about 1:30, so thanks so much. Once I get the transcript of this conversation, I'll be submitting the book to the publisher.

JOHN: Oh, well that's wonderful. And we're so glad that you have been coming for answers. There are so many people out there that have been misled and given false information and have not done the work that you have done. We want you to know we are thoroughly pleased with your perseverance.

We're thoroughly pleased with your exploring areas that most people are afraid to even open up to, so that you are presenting a piece of information, or many pieces of information, that have not been exposed and expressed and the awarenesses have been hidden.

So, we want to applaud you, Doug, knowing that you are putting out the information that is vital. And people will benefit, and you will have great rewards because you are seeking the truth.

DOUG: Thank you. Yes. I'm pleased and thrilled.

JOHN: We're so glad to help you anytime, Doug.

Section 6.22 March 9, 2017, Notes

Conversation with John the Divine via medium channeled by Marilyn Redmond on March 9, 2017.

JOHN: Oh, we're ready to fire so just start ahead with whatever your concerns are.

DOUG: I think I finally have figured out some terminologies from the Urantia Book?

JOHN: Right.

DOUG: I was confused by the terms like Jerusem and Urantia? But I realized that those were the spiritual terms?

JOHN: Exactly.

DOUG: For the other side?

JOHN: Exactly.

DOUG: You know, *The Urantia Book* talked about Lucifer's rebellion, but the rebellion disrupted God's divine plan because it tries to sidestep soul cleansing in the astral world (Kingdom of God), and that's why Jesus came to restore it?

JOHN: Right. It was the dark energy that needed to be - the light shined on it, and so Jesus came to share the message of love because love heals. Love dispel - love is light. Love and light are the same energy, and when you bring that to a situation and shed light on it, then the darkness disappears, and there is no more discord.

You know, we were all here to be in harmony with each other, and so any discord needed to be obliterated in the sunlight of God. And so that's what he came to bring that message, which it was possible to obliterate anything that doesn't line up with God's love.

DOUG: Yes, so really, the kingdom of God is the other side.

JOHN: Exactly. When you move to the other side, the negativity is not of issue, because the emotions are neutral. In the planet Earth, people can react in fear or respond in love, and you have all kinds of feelings that go along with that, but on the other side, it's neutral.

DOUG: It's not happening on the physical side.

JOHN: On the physical side, that's what people are learning to do, is to come into neutral feelings that nothing's good or bad or right or wrong. It just is. And we come into the center, which we call moderation.

DOUG: Yes. So, now I could understand better because I have asked you questions in our past channelings and I got confused. Now I understand much better. So, Jerusem is the spiritual side of Jerusalem.

JOHN: Yes, you might put it that way.

DOUG: Physically, it all started with Adam and Eve.

JOHN: It started 900,000 years ago. Adam and Eve came in to bring a new root race that was going to be moving consciously closer to God. So, there was more on earth before Adam and Eve. The Bible doesn't go into the details like you will find in other spiritual books.

DOUG: Can demons from the lowest astral level possess like-minded individual today?

JOHN: We all project what we are inside. That's what we're learning to do is project love rather than fear. So, your projection is where your consciousness and then you attract it back to you, and that's how you determine where you are.

DOUG: I just wonder, like, earthbound, and suppose for those that do not go through the transition from the dark to the light and they stay earthbound, now, are they allowed to be in the kingdom of God, which is on the other side?

JOHN: There are different levels of consciousness within a person. So, everybody has an awareness of God. It's just covered up when you're on planet Earth because of the lessons you need to learn and go through. So, everybody has a consciousness of God, but they're not always aware of it, and that's called denial.

So, nobody has left the presence of God. It's just your ego tells you have, and therefore you have difficulties in your life learning and lessons to learn to move back into the light of God.

DOUG: So, physical side, is that like close to the seventh level of astral heaven?

JOHN: In the theosophy perception of - there's a book Marilyn wrote that wrote the different levels of spiritual, where people are, and I'm not sure which level - which reference you're making. But we all go through various levels and move up. Because in the Bible they call it Jacob's Ladder. So, different people have termed it different things, and so it depends on your frame of reference.

DOUG: Is it true that in the past demons could possess humans because of Lucifer's rebellion? One thing is that before Jesus came, there were demons around in the physical realm because people that died in the past did not go through the astral heaven. Lucifer was opposed to that idea of people after they die, they go through various stages of nirvana which enable souls of people to become perfect spirits.

JOHN: Everybody is going through the evolution of lack of love and to the total level of conscious and perception of God. So, Lucifer is a metaphor for dark energy, and it means, you know, when people are called demons, it's the lack of light, which is dark energy.

So, everybody has negative energy from their karma, or if they do deeds in the earth in their current life, they have to balance that energy. So, you balance it by bringing light into it. If your person is open and available to receive the light, they can, of course, then dispel the darkness of their energy.

So, demons are just not people or entities, but that darkness can attach to people. And Marilyn has released some of those dark entities. People give them labels, and so they're not really in a physical form. It's a spiritual energy that is attached to somebody for whatever reason. Like attracts like, and so typically if someone is drawn to dark energy, it means that there's something in them that brought it to them.

And then if they choose to release it and turn themselves into more light, then the energy leaves and doesn't return because it's not connected emotionally to it, spiritually or energetically. So, we're all going through the learning to change our dark energy into light, or from the lack of God into being one with God.

It's all an evolutional trip that everybody's proceeding, and we keep coming back to continue that evolution. And that's when we go up the different levels of nirvana. We move into a - hopefully, if people have changed some of their reactions into loving responses in their life, to balance their life, they move into higher levels of nirvana.

So, that's what life's all about and those energies at times can attach to people, and they can be removed. So, it's a matter of choice by the individual, how they want to continue with that attachment, or if they're willing to move beyond it and become [unintelligible] so that the attachment is no longer available to attract and be attracted to them.

DOUG: Now are people inside the earth in physical form?

JOHN: Right. They are a kind of the spirit with physical properties, and everything is energy. When it becomes denser, it becomes form.

DOUG: Okay. Now, please help me with the timeline. Now, what timeframe was - okay, there was Adam and Eve in the first garden and then Adam and Even on the second garden. Can you help me with the timeframe? How long ago was the first garden concerning some years?

JOHN: Oh, my. I'm not used to years because I don't - in the spiritual realm, there is no time.

DOUG: Was it before Christ or –

JOHN: Oh, well definitely. Yes. Adam and Eve were thousands of years before Christ. Well, Christ is a - Christ is a label for a person who has unconditional love. Jesus happened to have unconditional love, so they called him the Christ. And everybody is born a Christ, and that's the journey, is moving into your Christ ship, and releasing everything that gets in the way that stops and is an obstacle to you returning to being the son of God. So, Adam and Eve are just part of the bigger scenario, you might say. And as the planet multiplied and there were plenty of people before Adam and Eve came. They weren't the first people, but they were the first of the newer race, root race, to bring people back into what we are doing today. So, it was - we have had many different civilizations on earth before Adam and Eve.

DOUG: It was like over 900,000 years ago?

JOHN: That would probably be closer to what you're talking about, yes.

DOUG: So, if the first humans were like 900,000 years ago, when did Adam and Eve arrive?

JOHN: It's hard to say because I'm coming from a spiritual point of view, and it's just one - it all happens at once in the spiritual realm. So, the number of years is not as significant as that it did happen so that man and human form would be able to get back on the right track.

And so for many thousands of years, there were - the people were separating themselves from God by their actions. And this was the turning point, so this was the watershed when human beings could start to return to their original birth in the Christ form.

So, the actual years isn't as important as the event itself. God doesn't give his troubles without answers. And so, the answer was for them to bring and be the starting force of people returning to God's Love and Light that is their birthright.

So, it was more of a major shift in energy, and that is the most significant part. To get hung - see, what you're doing is you're looking at light from a straight point of view, but the reality is there are no years in spirit. So, it was just a major turning point, and the years aren't as important as what it represented.

DOUG: Yeah, I just wanted to put down the timelines for the people to understand.

JOHN: If they understand this was an emotionally and spiritually new beginning in a way that was going to be their coming out of darkness, this is what it represented. The years are not as important as what it means.

DOUG: So, was that before the second Garden of Eden (the author had misquoted the question to John, it should have been read as second garden, not second Garden of Eden)?

JOHN: I have not heard of a term called the second Garden of Eden because Eden - we're coming back into Eden, which is still in our future. That's what the thousand years of peace are going to be. My understanding of the second Garden of Eden, we're still coming into it.

DOUG: Okay.

JOHN: See, the first Garden of Eden, it was like fifth-dimension. It was where everything was - had unity, harmony. Everything was viewed through the eyes of love. There was no harm and disease. Everything was perfect and perfection because it was all created by God and His image.

And the only reason that Eden was changed was through Adam and Eve eating of the apple of the Tree of Knowledge because knowledge presented a third-dimensional view of good and evil. And so, therefore, you left God's presence. So, before, the first Eden was living in the presence of God. And when they were thrown out of the Garden, that was the symbolic way of saying, "You're no longer in the presence of God."

DOUG: Now, could fall of man begin with a sexual transgression by Eve in the Garden?

JOHN: The fall of man was a choice when they took the - the apple represented - see, the snake in the Garden represented the Dark Side, which was, of course, the evil or the church's call to Satan. But so there was a choice. Life is about choice. And so, the fall of man was to choose. Instead of God, they chose not to have that connection to God.

That's - they fell away from the light, and that's the fall of man is, it's the choice that was made to leave that connection and consciousness with God. And it's just a story that represents that.

DOUG: Okay.

JOHN: It's a metaphor.

DOUG: Thank you. Now, when we arrive at the fifth-dimension, how does that affect the astral world, the other side?

JOHN: Okay. What happens is the energy and consciousness of fifth-dimension expand? God is energy and expansion, so more and more people that are returning to that God-consciousness, which is fifth-dimension, or Christ consciousness, and all these terms are interchangeable.

If you return to that, then I just grow into expanding more and more love so that it's a more beautiful place to be. The love just grows and feels so good, and it just increases. It increases that particular love.

DOUG: So, is it true that in the kingdom of God today, right now as we speak, it's just mostly the Ascended Masters and our spiritual guides?

JOHN: Technically everybody's in the kingdom of God. It's just the blinders on your eyes and the earplugs in your ears that keep you from being conscious of it. You're already born in the kingdom of God. All you need to do is remove the obstacles that are blocking it off from your emotional awareness.

DOUG: What dimension is the astral world or the other side right now?

JOHN: The other side is always a higher consciousness than what you have because you're in a lower, condensed - lower, dense vibration. Earth is a lower vibration, and the other side of the veil is always a higher consciousness. And so, when you move into that higher consciousness, you move into the higher dimension.

But it's - the dimension you move into matches your consciousness on earth. So, there's - all the dimensions are on the other side. It's just, and you will be attracted to your consciousness.

DOUG: We're going to travel after the book is out in May timeframe.

JOHN: That's marvelous. I want to congratulate you on your perseverance and that you continue to stick with it. You have been a loyal person in doing this and a responsible where your angels are thrilled with your endeavor and how well you have been sticking to the job, so to speak. And there's - all your guides are just excited that you are making such excellent progress. So, congratulations.

DOUG: It's a real pleasure working with you.

JOHN: The pleasure is all mine. I'm always glad to be here for you, and I will wish you a happy day, and I appreciate your call, and I hope that all things go well with your book. It is an exciting time for you. Enjoy it and know what you have accomplished is going to be well worth it to many, many people.

DOUG: Thanks so much. A real pleasure, and I enjoy this so much. Hope it works out and it will for the benefit of all of us.

JOHN: Oh, I know it will.

List of References

1 Law of One – Books 1&3 by James McCarty, Carla Rueckert, Don Elkins

2 The Urantia Book by Urantia Foundation, ISBN 9780911560510

3. Atlantis – Insights from a Lost Civilization by Shirley Andrews

4. Interviews with the Spiritual Entities of Abadiania by Sylvia Leifheit

5. Soul DNA by Jennifer O'Neill

6. Lemuria & Atlantis: Studying the Past to Survive the Future, Shirley Andrews

7. http://www.near-death.com/experiences/research16.html

8. Twenty Cases of Suggestive of Reincarnation by Ian Stevenson

9. http://en.wikipedia.org/wiki/List_of_the_verified_oldest_people

10. https://www.intellihub.com/admiral-byrd-tells-archived-interview-hollow-earth-real/

11. A Course in Miracles by Helen Schucman, ISBN 97818833660269

12. http://whitepowdergold.com/

13. http://www.infowars.com/if-economic-cycle-theorists-are-correct-2015-to-2020-will-be- pure-hell-for-the-united-states/

14. Psychic Stream by Arthur Findlay, ISBN - 09478231X

15. http://www.ploughshares.org/world-nuclear-stockpile-report

16. Self-Realization Fellowship, https://www.yogananda-srf.org

17. http://bos.sagepub.com/content/71/2/107.full.pdf+html

18. http://www.librarising.com/cosmology/maldek.html

19. http://www.livescience.com/45829-HAARP-shutdown.html

20. http://thegoldenlightchannel.com/council-of-angels-archangel-michael-and-archangel-metatron-via-goldenlight-the-releasing-of-all-karmic-obligation-and-debt-3-18-13/

21. http://thegoldenlightchannel.com/category/archangel-messages/archangel-michael-messages/

22. http://www.truthwiki.org/richard-pan-senator-of-california/

23. http://www.naturalnews.com/034038_vaccines_autism.html

24. http://www.naturalnews.com/vaccines.html

25. http://traceamounts.com/

26. http://www.naturalnews.com/autism.html

27. http://www.naturalnews.com/050271_SB_277_medical_refugees_autism.html

28. http://www.naturalnews.com/050272_Jim_Carrey_Jerry_Brown_corporate_fascism.html#ixzz3em9bR99j

29. http://www.naturalnews.com/050595_SB_792_vaccine_mandates_medical_police_state.html

30. http://leginfo.legislature.ca.gov/

31. http://www.naturalnews.com/SB_277.html

32. http://www.naturalnews.com/049669_vaccine_injury_depopulation_agenda_deadly_side_effects.html

33. http://truthbook.com/urantia/faq/where-is-dalamatia-located

34. http://www.realhistoryww.com/world_history/ancient/Canaan_1.htm

35. http://www.near-death.com/reincarnation/jesus/edgar-cayce-on-the-past-lives-of-jesus.html

36. https://themuslimtimes.info/2012/04/14/65-reasons-to-believe-jesus-did-not-die-on-the- cross/

37. http://www.hermes-press.com/spiritual_energy.html

38. http://www.space.com/28557-how-to-live-on-mars.html

39. http://news.yahoo.com/live-mars-192956901.html

40. http://www.space.com/52-the-expanding-universe-from-the-big-bang-to-today.html

41. www.dailymail.co.uk/sciencetech/article-3195416

42. http://www.krschannel.com/nibiru-.html

43. https://en.wikipedia.org/wiki/Population_history_of_indigenous_peoples_of_the_Americas

44. http://science.nationalgeographic.com/science/space/solar-system/mars-article/

45. http://www.space.com/17048-water-on-mars.html

46. http://www.nationalgeographic.org/encyclopedia/civilization/

47. http://www4.ncsu.edu/~wdlloyd/native_american_relations.htm

www.ingramcontent.com/pod-product-compliance
Lightning Source LLC
Chambersburg PA
CBHW030257080526
44584CB00012B/351